MASTERING THE CHANGING INFORMATION WORLD

MASTERING THE CHANGING INFORMATION WORLD

Martin L. Ernst
Anthony G. Oettinger
Anne W. Branscomb
Jerome S. Rubin
Janet Wikler

ABLEX PUBLISHING CORPORATION
NORWOOD, NEW JERSEY

We would like to thank the following authors and publishers for permission to reprint their works:

Eitan Abraham, Colin T. Seaton and S. Desmond Smith, table from "The Optical Computer," *Scientific American,* February 1983. Copyright © 1983 by Scientific American, Inc. Reprinted by permission.

Godfred Dewey, Table D2 reprinted by permission of the publishers from *Relativ Frequency of English Speech Sounds,* Harvard University Press: Copyright © 1923 Graduate School of Education, Harvard University.

Carol L. Weinhaus and Anthony G. Oettinger, Figure 15.1 from *Behind the Telephone Debates.* Copyright © 1988 by Ablex Publishing Corporation. Reprinted by permission.

Printed in the United States of America

Library of Congress Cagaloging-in-Publication Data

Mastering the changing information world / Martin L. Ernst ... [et al.].
p. cm.—(Communication and information science)
Includes bibliographical references and index.
ISBN 0-89391-876-8.—ISBN 0-89391-989-6 (pbk.)
1. Communication—Technological innovations. I. Ernst, Martin L. II. Series
P96.T42M367 1992
302.2—dc20 92-21400
CIP

Ablex Publishing
355 Chestnut Street
Norwood, New Jersey 07648

Contents

List of Figures

1

The Information Evolution

Martin L. Ernst

1.1 INFORMATION BUSINESSES AND TECHNOLOGIES

New technologies blur old boundaries, fuzzing some and obliterating others. By doing so, they can make obsolete our ways of thinking about current businesses and issues even faster than they make obsolete the products and services that these businesses provided—and over which they have competed and sometimes disputed among themselves, with consumers, or with governments. Nowhere has this process been more evident in the early nineties and the decades before than in the information industries.

This book comprises several research papers that discuss how these forces impact on the world of information industries. To make more specific the nature of the impacts, several chapters are devoted to the general activity of publishing—one of the major information industries. And within publishing, a primary but not exclusive focus is on traditional print publishing, and on the variants and alternatives that now or in the near future may supplement and, for some purposes, supplant print. The papers were published previously by the Harvard Program on Information Resources Policy (PIRP).

PIRP was established in 1972, in recognition that the possibilities opened up by a range of new electro-optical digital technologies were leading to social and economic changes of tremendous consequence. While all types of businesses (and their customers) would be impacted, the most direct effects would be felt by the information industries and users of information. Over time, these activities would be faced with a dramatic range of, not only new opportunities for growth, but also difficult requirements for survival. Of similar importance, the new technologies would drastically alter the social, economic, and political environments faced by key regulatory and other government bodies, forcing these organizations to reexamine, not only their missions and goals, but also the effectiveness of alternative mechanisms for carrying out their operations.

Thus, individuals and government or private organizations alike would be faced with a growing need for competent, impartial sources of information concerning the newly emerging options, and for impartial analysis of the implications of favoring or opposing those options that they could influence or select. The Program provides such background research through support—in the form of funding, information, and critiques—from a group of affiliates that spans the information (and the geographic) world. (A list of affiliates current to publication of this book is provided in Appendix A.) This group includes many affiliates that are highly competitive with one another, both within and across industry or government sectors.

Because the effects of the new technologies are widespread and tempered by many factors, the subjects of potential interest to the Program have been correspondingly broad. They include key raw materials, production equipment, and output information products and services (intermediate and end user). They also cover the output distribution systems and the infrastructures that support them as well as any user equipment needed to receive, display, interpret, or otherwise use the product and service materials being provided. The work also deals with existing and possible regulatory schemes, wherever these might be applicable; a variety of demographic, cultural, and economic factors; numerous international and trade-related considerations; and a host of other matters. To help bring order out of this huge variety of items, the Program developed a working tool—the Information Business Map (see Figure 1-1[1]). By the end of the 1980s, the Map had been translated into many languages and was being used worldwide.

The Map's entries comprise different information businesses—inputs, processing services and equipment, and intermediate and final outputs. Its axes are defined in terms of *products* and *services* (running south to north), and *form* and *substance* (running west to east). The product–services axis permits entries to be made in a way that parallels how business people and consumers tend to classify the

[1] From McLaughlin, John F. with Anne Louise Antonoff, *Mapping the Information Business* (Cambridge, MA: Program on Information Resources Policy, Harvard University, 1986), Figure 1. Reprinted by permission.

Figure 1-1. The Information Business Map

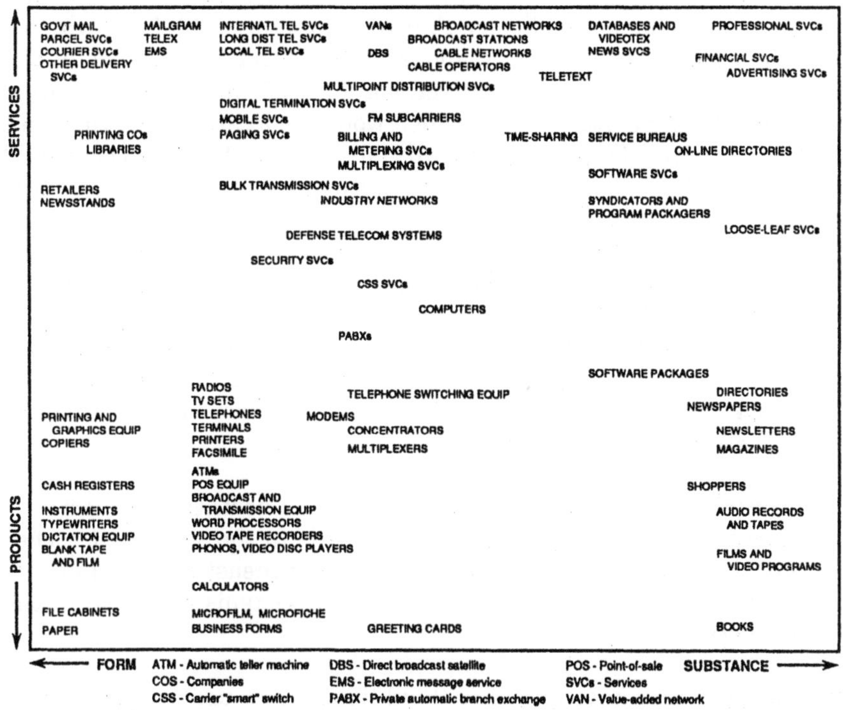

usable outputs of information businesses (and most other economic goods). Also, movement north along this axis produces entries characterized by increasingly closer and more interactive relationships between suppliers and customers.

The east–west axis offers a means to distinguish between the providers of "information" itself and the providers of information production and distribution capabilities. This distinction has long been a favorite of those seeking what appears to be (but in practice often is not) a simple basis for setting up regulatory restrictions. One example from 1990 is the limitations imposed on some telephone operating companies with regard to establishing businesses that would provide information products and services over their own networks.

Movement east along the horizontal axis implies a continuing addition of specificity—first of means to manipulate or process information in particular ways, and then of information content or substance itself. Alternatively, the movement can be associated with increasing the amount of information value-added.

One of the Map's many uses is for studying the evolution of the information industries. Over time, the items available for entry onto the Map have changed radically. Figure 1-1 applies to 1985, for which a reasonable number of entries appear in essentially all areas of the Map. In contrast, an equivalent version for 1785 would display only a small scattering of items, all of which would be located along the right and left borders. Further, practically all of these 1785 entries would have a very direct connection with traditional print publishing, while a majority of the 1985 entries do not. In effect, traditional publishing is concerned mainly with the Map's corner entries. However, most newer entries are based on electro-optical technologies, which tend to fill the Map's middle regions.

The newer technologies of the middle regions have enabled entire new industries to be established, and have forced major changes on older ones. Even as late as 1970, for example, most publishers could limit their attention to the following activities:

- Acquiring publishable content in the Map's northeast corner;
- Processing with equipment and materials in the southwest corner into the types of products shown in the southeast corner; and
- Distributing these products through the systems available in the northwest corner.

But those days have passed. All publishers now use equipment and processes from the central regions of the Map; and most of them have concerns about new forms of electronic competition as well as new possibilities for their own product lines.[2]

Figure 1-2 illustrates the dynamics faced by the information industries in general, and by the publishing industry in particular. This diagram also positions the chapters of this book (indicated by the boxed entries) and shows their relationships to one another and to the overall activity of publishing. For simplicity, only selected relationships (which operate in all directions among most of the entries) are shown explicitly.

Some factors that drive the system by creating (or stifling) opportunities for employing new approaches and/or seeking new sources of profits are shown at the top of Figure 1-2. The list is in no way complete; cultural factors, for example, including the educational systems and the business practices that particular cultures encourage,

[2] Further discussion and applications of the Map are presented in chapter 2, section 8. For a detailed description of the Map and its many uses, see: McLaughlin, *supra,* note 1.

Figure 1-2. Dynamics of the Publishing Industry Evolution

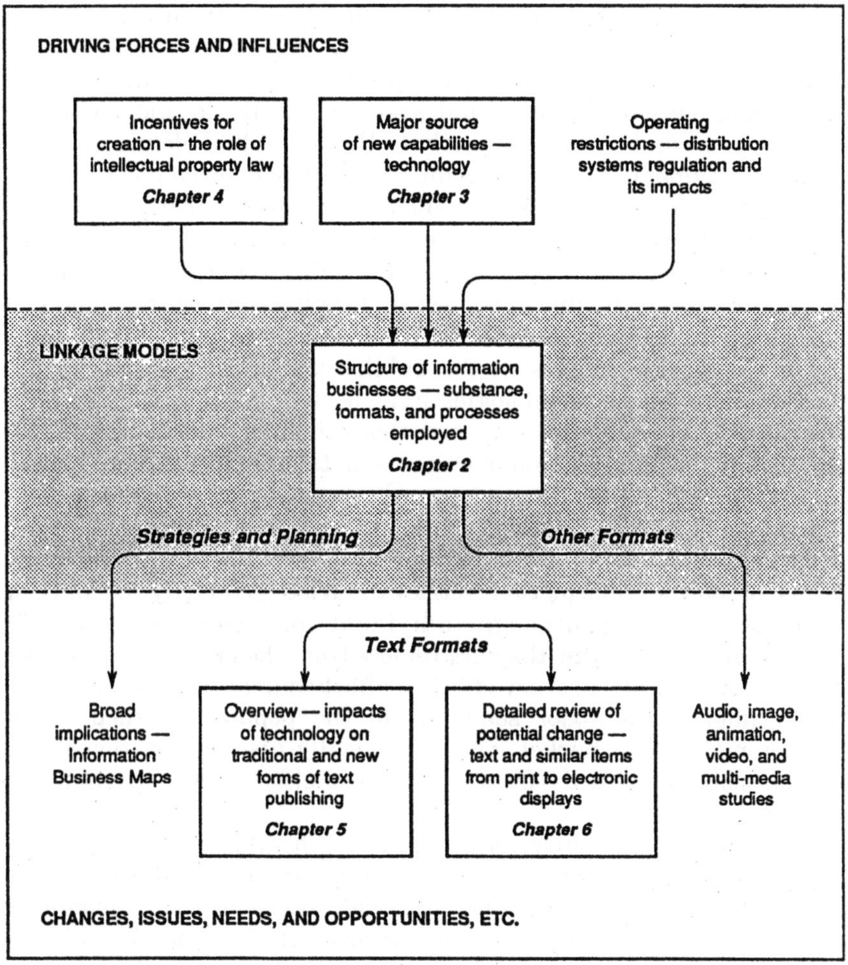

wield enormous influence on the nature of a nation's information businesses. Similarly, economic feedback provided by the marketplace is a primary determinant of what actions publishers (and all other information industry managers) must take to survive. These actions, in turn, establish much of the industry structures that evolve.

The driving factors can be related in many ways to specific subjects of interest—that is, to particular changes of importance that are underway, and to issues, needs, and opportunities being raised or resolved by the changes. The approach used in this book emphasizes the structure of industry output at the detailed level, as established by a few basic elements in terms of which *all types* of information products and services can be defined. This particular approach has many advantages. For example, use of the three defining elements—substance, format, and process—makes it easy to identify commonalities (and thus, potential competition) and differences within and among sets of products and services. Available and emerging technologies can be related directly to the individual elements where their employment may be relevant and, through these defining elements, to existing or possible products and services. And, to at least some extent, specific legal and regulatory subjects also tend to be associated with each element. Thus, this definitional approach makes it easier to unveil the links between underlying sources of change and more specific topics of interest.

On the whole, changes in the publishing industry owing to the introduction of new technologies have been less dramatic and have attracted less public attention than those in other information industry sectors, such as computer systems or telecommunications. Many important changes (for example, word processing, new printing techniques, and satellite transmission for more local printing) take place in process activities invisible to the end users. Others, such as many forms of online information retrieval, arise primarily in narrow business activities; although individual consumers often benefit greatly from the results, they are remote from the production activity. Throughout the 1980s, every effort to effect changes with obvious and direct impacts on major segments of the population, such as by developing a mass market for electronically distributed, text-based information, had failed—even when these efforts were big and well funded.

This pattern of failure may change in the 1990s. New computer equipment has so grown in power that software making these systems much "friendlier" has become practical. An enormous amount of complexity can be incorporated at low cost, all of it made invisible to users. Storage capacities have increased radically, giving electronics a major advantage when large amounts of information are involved. Led by the needs of engineers and graphics designers, and fueled by growing international interest in High Definition Television (HDTV), major improvements in future electronic display quality seem certain. And the experiences of the past—both the failures and the rarer successes—have not been lost on the business world; a lot has been learned the hard way about what is needed and what must be avoided.

At most, these technological advances offer what might be called "enabling capabilities." They suggest that some important conditions are changing in ways that could greatly favor electronic advances in the publishing field; but many barriers remain, some already encountered during previous failed efforts and others introduced (or amplified) by the same technologies that benefit electronic penetration in other ways. It seems timely, therefore, to take a careful look at the situation and the change processes that are arising.

1.2 PENETRATING THE TURMOIL OF CHANGE: STEP-BY-STEP THROUGH THE BOOK

Because of its centrality to all our material, we make our starting point the Linkage Model mentioned in Figure 1-2. Chapter 2, "Building Blocks and Bursting Bundles," overviews the role of information and the underlying structure of all information products and services, sounding a unifying theme for the remaining chapters. At the same time, it introduces concepts of considerable power that can help one understand and analyze the evolution of *all* the information industries, now at such a dynamic stage of development.

In essence, Anthony Oettinger notes that information is a resource that is needed, in combination with materials and energy, for anything useful or meaningful to happen. All the economic, legal, and political questions that can be asked about materials and energy resources also can be asked, in similar or equivalent form, concerning information resources. In particular, shifts in the balances of capital and labor employed in information activities, and in the balances among energy, materials, and information used to create and distribute *all economic goods*, are the sources from which the information evolution derives much of its importance, and the reason it attracts so much attention.

Information products and services are built from a triad of elements:

- *Substance*: Refers to the content of information in a very broad sense;
- *Format*: Concerns the physical materials and/or signals in which substance is, or can be, embodied for subsequent manufacturing and distribution as well as for eventual absorption and interpretation; and
- *Process*: Includes all the energy-consuming means used to create and manipulate substance, embody it in a format, and deliver it to a user.

These elements are the fundamental building blocks; individual products and services simply represent particular combinations, or

Figure 1-3. Patterns of Information-Defining Elements

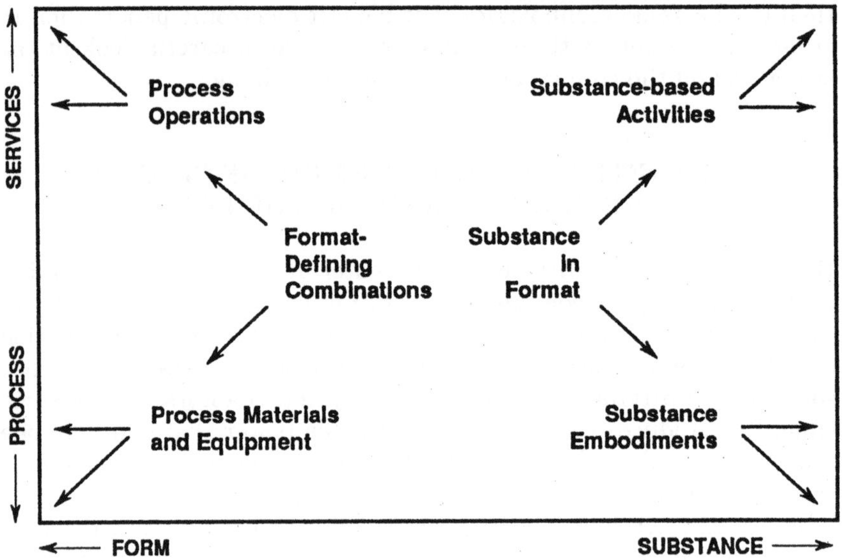

"bundles," of the elements. In terms of the Information Business Map shown earlier, Figure 1-3 indicates schematically how entries in the different portions of the Map contribute to the combining operations.

Evolution can arise whenever one or more of the driving forces or influencers of Figure 1-2 facilitates a change in one or more of the building blocks. Substance can change when new types of content that have potential value to users (or old types that are no longer of interest) are identified. New formats are continually arising as a result of technological or legal/regulatory changes. Sometimes old substance is simply repackaged in the new format; in other cases, new substance is used, or new mixes of different types of old substance are created.

Probably the most frequent effects of technical advances arise through the process changes they often make possible. If the process change is major, one result could be to make a new format economically practical for the first time in its history. Sometimes as a by-product of the change, an old format becomes obsolete or its role in an information industry becomes transformed.

In the flux of changing bundles of information—based on new combinations of old and new substance embodied in a greater variety of new and old formats, and often produced with new processes—old definitions and old industry and legal structures become fuzzy. New words appear, old words become less definitive. The bases for legal actions and regulation erode, sometimes forcing new concepts to be defined before the situation, and likely consequences of using such definitions, are well understood. In this environment, there is great value in having available what amounts to an invariant and impartial set of element definitions—such as those of Chapter 2. Of particular importance, they can help separate the underlying and enduring aspects of a situation from those more easily subject to change. And among the changes, themselves, they can help sort the significant ones from others more likely to be transient and episodic, even if very dramatic.

Having established a perspective on how evolutionary changes arise and propagate in the information industries, we now turn to some forces that drive these processes. The first and most widely recognized of these is technology, the subject treated by Oettinger in Chapter 3, "The Abundant and Versatile Digital Way." The intent of Chapter 3 is two-fold:

1. To provide an understanding of the sources of the capabilities being incorporated into the newer technologies, and the reasons that they are so effective, and
2. To review the basic features of the technologies being employed at a level that nontechnical information industry professionals can understand. (The material also may be useful for reminding the more technically skilled of many of the field's familiar aspects that too easily become taken for granted.)

The structure for presenting the material has strong historical elements, emphasizing the evolutionary processes that dominate much of our thinking about the subjects of this book.

At the heart of the dramatic technical advances made since the end of World War II, a few key paths have enabled much of the progress:

- A growing understanding, at a deep level, of the meaning and technical nature of the communications process; and, from this, a similar understanding of the nature of information.
- The development of both theoretical and practical means for handling *all* types of information in digital form. This includes efficient means for encoding and decoding digital information (e.g., conversion from and to analog form), processing digital information in many complex ways, and identifying and controlling many types of errors when processing or transmitting digital information.
- The embodiment, in very economical hardware, of powerful ca-

pabilities for processing digital information, using low-cost nonlinear materials and techniques that would not operate acceptably with other than digital records.

A major by-product of following these paths has been the convergence of the means we use for computation and telecommunications, with its enormous worldwide impacts on industry and regulatory structures. A far more diffuse (and therefore less explicitly recognized) effect has been an equivalent, widespread blurring of the accepted ideas and boundaries associated with all types of information activities. This blurring has played a large role in enabling and encouraging the splitting and rebundling process described earlier.

Chapter 2 points out that information can acquire value only through being embodied in a physical format—whether a form that uses solid materials or one that is less tangible, such as a pattern of pressure changes in the local atmosphere. However, from the recipient's point of view, the value received in a given "bundle" of information usually is dominated by the substance incorporated in the bundle. So substance quality is critical; to assure the availability of a broad range of high-quality information products, mechanisms must be in place that encourage the efforts of those who create information substance. Although many current information products are based on substance that involves as much or more physical labor as mental labor (for example, all products that record the performing arts), the print publishing origins of efforts to protect the creators' interests have led to the general concept that information substance inputs are a form of intellectual property. The types and effectiveness of means to protect such property are among the main factors that determine how the publishing industry can and does operate.

The concept of intellectual property is relatively new; its use in publishing dates only to the early 1700s. Some cultures view this concept as alien, or even as a mechanism used by the more advanced nations to exploit less developed economies. Partly for these reasons, in many countries the legal structures that protect intellectual property are weak or poorly enforced, and the "losses" that current property owners claim are arising in these nations are very large. Thus, intellectual property issues have many important international elements that must be considered in any realistic proposals for resolving differences of opinion or practice.

Further, few areas of the information industries have felt the impact of technological advances so strongly. Existing definitions of what constitutes protectable intellectual property and of which aspects can be protected by what means have been confused by these advances. Interpretations established by traditional precedents have been stretched and (in the eyes of some) even distorted. The boundaries of ethical standards, used as a basis for determining what constitutes equitable practices, have shifted to at least some degree. Even worse, expectations for continuing technical progress mean that there is no real hope for an early period of greater stability—new and more intractable problems of principle and interpretation, and new and more severe challenges to the enforceability of socially acceptable protective measures will continue to arise throughout the foreseeable future.

In Chapter 4, "Nurturing Creativity in a Competitive Global Economy: Intellectual Property and New Technologies," Anne Branscomb reviews this tumultuous and complex area. She examines the traditional mechanisms in place and identifies their uses and capabilities, their inconsistencies and inadequacies. She considers technologies and business practices, both current and emerging, that challenge the existing laws and have the potential to erode their effectiveness. An important element throughout is the need to continually balance multiple interests that are, themselves, subject to differential impacts from the new technologies.

World attention to intellectual property protection grew rapidly in the 1980s, and this attention has spawned a level of activity that likely will make obsolete fairly rapidly some of Chapter 4's details. However, the expected changes are principally in broadening the geographic scope of coverage of existing laws, rather than identifying new concepts to handle better some of the newly arising problems. This means that the fundamentals described in the chapter will not rapidly disappear, although the details of their implementation will vary in time and by place.

Branscomb's conclusions are far from optimistic. Even though there are no strong new reasons to alter the underlying principles and values built into our legal system, their interpretation into practical answers to real problems will become increasingly difficult. As a result, our problem areas can be expected to grow. There is a good chance that this growth will occur at a rate faster than that to which the current legal framework can adjust comfortably to new needs. Timely resolution of the critical issues will rely, far more than is usual, on actions by the stakeholders that establish an acceptable path for the legal regimes to follow and legitimize.

Chapters 2 through 4 apply broadly to all of the information industries. Chapter 5 moves to a particular segment of information activities: the field of publishing and, more specifically, print publishing. "Publishing as a Creature of Technology" was originally delivered by Jerome Rubin as a keynote address in a symposium entitled "Toward the Year 2000: New Forces in Publishing." The symposium took place on March 14, 1989, in Jerusalem, at the biennial International Book Fair. The symposium was sponsored jointly by the Aspen Institute, the Jerusalem International Book Fair, and the Bertelsmann Foundation.

The authors of the speech, Jerome Rubin and Janet Wikler, were, respectively, group vice-president of Times Mirror, Inc., with responsibility for its professional information and book publishing group, and director, Marketing and Business Development, for that group. As members of an affiliate organization, they have been active contributors to, and critics of, the Program's work. During an even longer period, they have had extensive experience in the intensely practical function of helping their own organizations operate successfully both in traditional print publishing businesses and in moving into new electronic formats. The speech, in many respects, was a distillation of the views they had developed during these years of experience.

Chapter 5 starts with a broad historical overview of the interactions between publishing and new technologies. It then relates this historical experience to the situations faced by publishers as computers were introduced into various functions of the industry. The types of action taken by publishers are noted briefly, and some general features of the more successful publishing efforts in new electronic formats and media are then described.

The final chapter goes to an opposite extreme: rather than providing a broad overview, it examines in detail a seemingly narrow topic of the publishing arena. Martin Ernst examines the competition between print and electronics to become the primary means for the consumption of all types of visual, nonvideo information—that is, text, tabular, graphics, and pictorial information. This competition has been underway for several decades. Periodically, predictions have been made that print faces a dire future; to date, however, this fate never has been approached, much less fulfilled.

The topic appeared important for several reasons. First, concerning these dire predictions that never came true, why were they so incorrect? Were the reasons only transient in nature and, if so, what factors or events could change them? Closely allied to these questions was the earlier comment concerning the failure of all experiments to date that offered electronically distributed printlike information services to mass markets. More broadly phrased, In which markets or functions, and for what reasons, does each of these two fundamental means for displaying information currently occupy the dominant position? What kinds of changes would be needed to radically alter this balance?

A second set of reasons is less obvious and far more difficult to handle. These reasons concern how computer systems could impact the skills required by individuals in the future if they are to be fully participating members of society. In other words, what will be the requirements for effective "literacy" in the future?

Quite clearly, these requirements will be far more complex than the concept, commonly proposed some years ago, of supplementing current literacy capabilities with a little "computer literacy" acquired by learning a few programs and doing a little coding in BASIC. Also, there is more to it than acquiring a high degree of expertise in narrow areas of computer activities, such as word processing, computer graphics, or reservation operations. Individual businesses and trade schools have proven quite adequate at training enough people to meet the demand from businesses and society for these skills. However, the broader social effects have been limited because this type of training has no obviously important carry-over from work to other aspects of life. The lack of more broadly used computer applications—in effect, the popular mass market applications at which computers have failed in the past—means that computer-related skills mostly are left at the office when the worker goes home.

Put another way, computer impacts on broad, literacy-like skill requirements will have importance only when, or if, effective computer uses are available in society as widely as print uses are now. The factors influencing this possibility, and the types of things that have to happen before computer-driven electronic displays could have such widespread use, provide a starting point for considering the possible nature of a significantly different future concept of what it means to be literate.

It should be emphasized that posing the question in the above form, and using an approach that involves determining the "actions whereby electronics can overcome the barriers to its penetration of current print markets," *should not* be taken as an indication of favoritism on behalf of electronics. The selection of a target for study (electronic dominance over print) is not intended to incorporate any judgment about the desirability (or undesirability) of such a situation; it is only a means to examine with some methodological rigor the types of events and actions that reaching such a condition would imply.

Much of the material in Chapter 6 is at a relatively fine level of detail, for reasons foreshadowed in the earlier chapters. The near infinite variety of formats made possible by the flexibility and interactivity potential of electronics raises problems for publishers, as well as offering opportunities for the pioneers among them. For example, the complex mix of benefits and threats arising with regard to the protection of intellectual property suggests publisher caution in exploiting some paths important to more rapid electronic penetration of print markets. Technical partial solutions are available, but at a price in market building. And, as recounted in Chapter 5, the indirectness and subtlety of many of the barriers (and facilitators) to past changes in how information was produced and delivered, and to whom the barriers were applied, indicate that a very wide variety of influences will be involved.[3] All of these possibilities, plus the record of past failures in building mass markets for electronic text products, make it important to dig as deeply as practical into what might appear to be details. There are good reasons to suspect that some of them may grow up to become critical factors.

1.3 ACKNOWLEDGMENTS

Mention was made earlier that PIRP uses the critiquing capabilities of its affiliates. While its Program materials are still in draft form, PIRP asks for reviews of the materials by representatives of its affiliates, which include all stakehohder groups interested in a given subject area, and by others in relevant professions and disciplines. The benefits to the Program have been enormous in assuring better accuracy in presentation, more equity in coverage of controversial issues, and greater general utility of output.

The following reviewers have contributed to this volume: Raymond M. Alden, Lawrence J. Aldrich, Alvin von Auw, John C. Bachman, James R. Beniger, Frederick J. Berghoff, Henry M. Boettinger, Kurt Borchardt, Jack E. Brown, Diane Callan, Benjamin M. Compaine, James J. Croke, Kenneth W. Dam, Garth W.P. Davies, Phillip Erickson, Mihaly Ficsor, Roger Gallois, Matthew E. Gilfix, Dean Gillette, Anthony T. Green, Brian Kahin, Sheila Karr, Joseph E. Kasputys, Milton Katz, Christine Killorin, Steven R. Koltai, Yasukuni Kotaka, Erwin G. Krasnow, Thomas Laukamm, Maurice Lazarus, Thomas M.

[3] For details on two earlier transition periods, see: Altick, Richard D., *The English Common Reader: A Social History of the Mass Reading Public, 1800–1900* (Chicago: The University of Chicago Press, 1957); and Clanchy, M.T., *From Memory to Written Record, England, 1066—1307* (Cambridge, MA: Harvard University Press, 1979).

Lemberg, Richard J. Levine, Alex Makarovitsch, Robert G. Marbut, David Y. McManis, Arthur R. Miller, D. Verne Moreland, Michael Nelson, Alistair I. Omand, E. Gabriel Perle, G. Russell Pipe, Gordon T. Ray, David Z. Robinson, Richard S. Rosenbloom, Lloyd G. Schermer, Elliot R. Siegel, Janice P. Stanton, Jacques Stern, Jerry Wasserman, Norman Weizer, Glen Weston, Robert White, and Charles A. Zraket.

These reviewers and the Program's affiliates are neither responsible for or necessarily in agreement with the views expressed herein, nor should they be blamed for any inaccuracies of fact or misrepresentations of any type.

2

Building Blocks and Bursting Bundles*

Anthony G. Oettinger

Familiar words evoke ideas and things whose time may have gone. Tying thought to the past, they favor the status quo. The new words in someone's visions are unfamiliar at best. Often they are empty; often, the hype of promoters. In times of change, the right concepts, the right tools for those who wish, as Henri Bergson put it, to think as men of action and to act as men of thought must be stable, rich, intelligible, and impartial enough to serve many in more venues than the here and the now.

This chapter sets forth some perspectives and tools evolved by me and my colleagues at the Harvard Program on Information Resources Policy (PIRP) and used by our affiliates in business, government, and academe.

The first perspective is a concept of information resources akin to the familiar concepts of energy and of materials and complementary to these concepts. Information, energy, and materials make up the world.

Information resources in turn are made up of information products or services. These products and services are bundles of substance, format, and process. Substance, format, and process are building blocks; they can be used alone or in an infinite number of combinations, which can be taken apart and put together again. The way the blocks are combined or used depends on convention, namely, on the

---

* This chapter is adapted from Oettinger, Anthony G., *The Information Evolution: Building Blocks and Bursting Bundles* (Cambridge, MA: Program on Information Resources Policy, Harvard University, P-89-5).

fairy tales dominant at the moment. Thinking in terms of these building blocks helps avoid entrapment by conventions that were appropriate to some moment in history but whose time has long since gone. When needed, untying the basic building blocks sets free once again the creative and discretionary possibilities in their multiple potential combinations.

Information *substance* comes in many familiar varieties, among them wisdom, knowledge, data, news, intelligence, disinformation, and folly.

Information *formats* include concrete tokens (like ink on paper) for abstract patterns (like the Roman, italic, Morse, or Braille alphabets) that express still more abstract symbols (like words). Vocabularies vary from person to person and from nation to nation. Different patterns satisfy different practical or aesthetic needs. New technology makes some tokens cheaper, easier to use, or prettier than others.

Information *processes* change as technologies and societies change. The contemporary information evolution is the story of new electro-optical digital compunications (computer-and-communications) technologies competing in late twentieth century societies with printing press technologies born of the steam technology and the industrial revolution of the nineteenth century.

2.1 BUILDING BLOCKS AND BUNDLES

As needs and tastes for substance change and as new formats and processes come to hand, bundles of an earlier time come undone. Familiar products and services come apart. New ones come and go through trial, error, more trials, and more errors until stabler mixes settle in once again.

In *From Memory to Written Record,* M.T. Clanchy gives the following vivid account of changes in the way people thought about the role of substance, process, and format in England between 1066 and 1307:

> Numerous charters of the twelfth century are addressed to "all those seeing and hearing these letters, in the future as in the present" or to "all who shall hear and see this charter"; these two examples come from the charters of Roger de Mowbray who died in 1188. The grantor of another charter, Richard de Rollos, actually harangues his audience, "Oh! all ye who shall have heard this and have seen!" Early charters likewise quite often conclude with "Goodbye" (*Valete*), as if the donor had just finished speaking with his audience. Documents made it possible for the grantor to address posterity ("all who shall hear and see") as well as his contemporaries. In the opening words of the Winchcombe abbey

cartulary, "when the voice has perished with the man, writing still enlightens posterity." Writing shifted the spotlight away from the transitory actors witnessing a conveyance and on to the perpetual parchment recording it. By the thirteenth century, when charters had become more familiar to landowners, donors cease addressing their readers, as Richard de Rollos did, and likewise they no longer conclude with *Valete.* Once it was understood that charters were directed to posterity, it must have seemed foolish to say "Goodbye" to people who had not yet been born. In place of such conversational expressions, thirteenth-century charters are more stereotyped; they are often impersonally addressed in some such form as "Let all persons, present and future, know that I, A of B, have given X with its appurtenances to C of D."[1]

What we now call *snapshots* and *movies* are pictorial substance and photographic processes combined with the celluloid format described by Daniel Boorstin:

In 1873 Hyatt invented and registered the name "celluloid." What he had invented was actually not a new combination of chemicals but a new way of molding the plastic and making it stay hard. For some years Hyatt used celluloid only for making solid objects....

The opportunity for Hyatt's celluloid to help transform the American consciousness came from the collaborating talents of another upstate New Yorker who combined a bent for invention with a talent for organization and for marketing.... George Eastman... saw that the perfection of dry-plate photography would be more than merely a convenience for professional photographers, because now, for the first time, the taking of a picture could be separated from the making and the developing of the plate. But he also saw that a popular market for photography would have to await a substitute for the heavy, breakable, hard-to-ship glass plates. Until the 1880s, of course (because photographs were commonly made on emulsion-coated glass), photography was not especially associated with the word "film." What Eastman needed was some flexible, light, and unbreakable substance that could be coated with the photographic emulsion. In 1884 Eastman patented a way of coating strips of paper so that they would work in a camera, and from this starting point he initiated the popular revolution in photography....

With his new celluloid roll film, easily loaded and easily developed (no need any more for the delicate stripping operation), Eastman opened up the world of amateur photography. The novel features of the Kodak,

[1] Clanchy, M.T., *From Memory to Written Record: England 1066–1307* (Cambridge, MA: Harvard University Press, 1979), 202–3.

as an English historian observed, "enabled the camera, like the bicycle, to enrich the leisure hours of the many."

Now cut to Thomas Edison:

> Edison very early sensed the importance of celluloid. The perfection of a feasible camera and projector that would show moving pictures of considerable duration depended on finding a suitably flexible substance for the film. It is hard to imagine how Edison could have made his movie camera without celluloid, or something like it....
>
> When he heard of Eastman's improved roll film, he urged Eastman to help him make a motion-picture camera by producing the flexible film in long strips.
>
> Could a series of photographs that had been taken on a single film somehow provide the pictures to be viewed in motion? For a feasible motion-picture system this idea was as crucial as Eastman's idea of separating picture taking from picture developing had been in popularizing still photography.[2]

In paragraphs that shine with hindsight, the historian sums up what is, while it happens, a dark maze of complicated actions and reactions—like those of the established information sector bouncing off newcomers stumbling across its paths, or old competitors lurching along new paths, running into roadblocks or sinkholes sometimes visible, sometimes not, set up by government or opened up by the fickle finger of fate.

But what kind of bundles for what ends? In the Information Business Map (mentioned in Chapter 1 and described further in section 2.8 of this chapter), the familiar concepts of products and services cross with form and substance to provide a tool for charting these actions and reactions.

Examples drawn from the mass media illustrate how such a tool can help business people, voters, public officials, or just plain interested persons trying to steer themselves through the dawn of the Information Age. In this transitional period, snapping that "a newspaper company is in the newspaper business, of course" is not a curt and well-deserved put-down of a stupid question. It is mostly wrong. Like *television* or *radio*, *newspaper* is a term for a particular bundle of means, not for general ends.

Yet the means—the formats and the processes—nowadays are precisely the least stable elements in information business bundles.

---

[2] Boorstin, Daniel J., *The Democratic Experience,* vol. 2 of *The Americans* (New York: Random House, 1973), 373–78.

Indeed, describing the ends of information businesses in substance–format–process terms begs the question at the very heart of change, namely: what kinds of bundles are best for what kinds of ends? Instead, four distinct needs that information meets—escape, social connection, surveillance, and opinion formation/decision making—serve as examples of concepts with which to describe ends. This chapter defines and illustrates these concepts in terms of the mass media and from the perspective of evolving information purveyors. The same concepts are also applied to the perspective of evolving information consumers, specifically those who exercise responsibility and authority.

Information resources differ from energy and material resources in that information is the organizing resource that allows people to integrate energy, material, and information resources to achieve their personal ends or, as leaders and managers, those of their organizations. For the fourth concept, opinion formation/decision making, this chapter therefore details how information users' needs might best be matched with alternative substance, format, and process bundles, concentrating on information required for exercising responsibility and authority.

2.2 INFORMATION AS A RESOURCE

Information is a basic resource, like energy and materials. Without materials there is nothing; without energy nothing happens; without information, nothing makes sense.

Looking at information as a basic resource points up what information has in common with energy and materials, not how it differs from them. In particular, all the key questions about the stakes in any resource go for information resources as well: Who has the resources, who wants them, how can you get them, what are the terms of trade, and how are these terms set? The stakes and these questions are timeless; new generations of stakeholders, changing information technologies, and changing social institutions and other conventions change only the answers.

There is no magic in the information, energy, materials trio, no mystical meaning of three. Einstein once speculated that material is energy, and vice versa. Since Hiroshima, everyone knows that material can turn into energy. For peaceful and earthly affairs, though, it is still convenient and common to set materials apart from energy, and to set both apart from information, as the three basic resources that people rely on.

Distinguished from matter, energy looks like patterned matter. Energy is high when a loose rock is poised high on a cliff; energy is low when the rock rests at the bottom. Energy is high when a home run hit streaks off the bat; energy is low when the baseball is still cradled in the waiting pitcher's hand. That's the only way it is in the only universe we know.

Information, likewise, looks like patterned matter. An arrow made with three branches on a path conveys a large amount of information. Three branches just lying there convey a small amount of information. Ink lines laid out as an "A" convey more information than ink lines from a spill.[3]

The patterned relations between energy and materials belong to the innate order of our universe. The patterned relations between information and materials are ordained only by human conventions that quite arbitrarily link symbols to patterns to tokens in the ways that are told in section 2.3. Moreover, the energy it takes to arrange materials into information-carrying patterns like an arrow or an "A" is minuscule compared to the energy it takes to hit a baseball or to move a rock from the bottom to the top of a cliff.[4] As David taught Goliath, brains can overpower brawn. The modern military call this a *force multiplier*. Gains in effectiveness—that is, more efficient use of energy and materials—occur quite often when information resources are employed to organize smaller amounts of energy or materials, or both, to displace larger amounts.

Materials, energy, and information are necessary resources. They are not sufficient. Without information nothing makes sense, but that's not to say that things *must* make sense even with information. This chapter is not about how to make sense. It is about tools with which to make sense when one can. Nor does it claim a greater or lesser worth for different kinds of information. The worth of information is in the mind of the beholder, just as the worth of a loaf of bread is set by his or her stomach. As economic goods, information resources are just like other economic products or services. The differences between information and bread are of neither lesser nor greater importance than the differences between either of them and scrap metal or real estate.

The materials, energy, information trio is not an exclusive resource classification. Every person plays two distinct roles on the information stage. In one capacity (for instance, as subordinate or as pollee), we *are*

[3] For an elaboration of these ideas, see: Odum, Howard T., "Self-Organization, Transformity, and Information," *Science* 242, no. 4882 (November 25, 1988): 1132–39.

[4] Brillouin, Leon, *Science and Information Theory* (New York: Academic Press, Inc., 1956).

information resources. In another capacity (for example, as superior or as pollster), we *consume* information along with material and energy resources. Another convention carves up resources into labor and capital. That partition is no sharper and no holier than the partition into materials, energy, and information. Seen as labor or as capital, people are mostly information and energy resources. People used to be material resources for cannibals, concentration camp keepers digging dental gold, or medical schools as cadavers. Only in recent times have organ transplants lent a positive cast to using people as material resources.

The boundary between labor and capital is fuzzy and socially, industrially, or historically conditioned. But no one doubts that changes in the relative abundance and prices of labor and capital are a major aspect of economic change. Another major aspect of economic change is change in the relative abundance and prices of materials, energy, and information. The story of changing proportions of labor and capital is neither much clearer nor much murkier for information resources than is the same story for materials or for energy. It just has not yet been told, having barely begun to unfold. The invention of practical steam engines in the nineteenth century opened an era of a hitherto unheard of massive abundance of energy resources with equally unheard of massive power. The ensuing shifts in the relative use of material, energy, and information resources are already the stuff of history. So are related shifts in proportions of labor and capital.[5]

The electronic compunications way with information resources is powerful, versatile, and abundant on a massive scale unheard of prior to the twentieth century. The phenomenon is barely adolescent and still far from mature. By providing entirely new formats and processes with the evolution toward digitization, it upsets the stability of the traditional substance–format–process bundles. It calls into question labor/capital proportions within information resources and also the proportions of information resources to energy and material resources.

2.3 THE SUBSTANCE, FORMAT, AND PROCESS SIDES OF INFORMATION RESOURCES

In stabler times, chopping up more or less innocent and useful information goods like newspapers or TV into such seeming fluff as

[5] For details, see: Beniger, James R., *The Control Revolution: Technological and Economic Origins of the Information Society* (Cambridge, MA: Harvard University Press, 1986).

substance, format, and process deservedly might have seemed metaphysical in the most insulting sense. But when the stuff of the real world is coming unglued, *not* going for these stable building blocks quickly gets impractical to the point of dereliction of duty. When traditional ties that have lingered too long continue to bundle substance of specific kinds or purposes with specific means for dealing with that substance, the arrangement gets in the way of grasping and grappling with essentials of change.

Stereotypically, for example, news went with ink on paper and massive presses and with rewrite men, heroic editors with green eyeshades, and little merchants staggering around the block under a Sunday's load. Mass entertainment was live hoofers on sawdust stages in the 1920s, silver grains on celluloid film projecting motion onto the screens of movie palaces in the 1930s and 1940s, and phosphorescent images with commercials on the tubes of home entertainment centers since the 1950s.

Personal communication for many still means ink, paper, envelopes, licking stamps, and the ring of the postman; for others, it is now mainly a finger in the dial or on the beeping buttons, the ring or peep of the telephone and a voice at the other end; for still others, it is the electronic mail boxes in some network of personal or business computers. Dickens' Bob Cratchit and Uriah Heep are ancestors both of the keypunchers of yesteryear's clerical warrens in banks and insurance companies and of the data entry clerks sought in the want ads of the 1980s.

Electronic digital compunications technologies are already powerful, versatile, and abundant enough to take on all of the above functions, certainly in part if not as a whole. In brief, *all* kinds of substance can be put in electronic digital formats, processed by computers in huge quantities at great speed, and sent around the universe riding on electrons or photons at per-unit costs that keep going down compared to the costs of one of nearly anything else. Economic factors alone call into question the bundles based on other formats and processes. How rapidly do bundles actually come apart? When do new ones get formed? These questions are beyond the scope of this chapter, but are addressed for electronic-print competition in Chapter 6.[6]

---

[6] But see also: McLaughlin, John F., "Marketing Megalomania: The Lure of the Information Business," *PIRP Perspectives* (Cambridge, MA: Harvard Program on Information Resourses Policy, 1989).

2.3.1 Substance

From many conventional standpoints, the term *substance* as used here lumps together too much that seems distinctive: knowledge, data, information (in the narrow sense that some treat as synonymous with data), news, intelligence, and numerous other colloquial and specialized denotations and connotations. For instance, some intelligence professionals adhere to Ray Cline's distinction between raw and finished intelligence:

> In its narrowest context, intelligence is simply information. It may be collected in some clandestine manner, that is, secretly and often at some personal risk because the facts sought are being deliberately withheld. In a broader sense, intelligence on foreign affairs includes such additional categories as press reports, foreign radio broadcasts, foreign publications, and—in the government—reports from our Foreign Service officers and military attaches.
>
> In the world of international affairs, intelligence is only useful if it is subjected to evaluation and analysis to put it into the context of ongoing U.S. national security and foreign policy concerns. It must be evaluated for accuracy and credibility in the light of its source or its collection method, for the validity and significance of the content, after being collated with other available data, and for its impact on U.S. interests, operations, or objectives. The result of this total intelligence process is a report intended to assist policy and operational officers in making decisions.[7]

Scientists often distinguish observed fact from theory, what Thomas Kuhn describes as the system of "intertwined theoretical and methodological belief that permits selection, evaluation, and criticism." As he explains:

> If that body of belief is not already implicit in the collection of facts—in which case more than "mere facts" are at hand—it must be externally supplied, perhaps by a current metaphysic, by another science, or by personal and historical accident. No wonder, then, that in the early stages of the development of any science different men confronting the same range of phenomena, but not usually all the same particular phenomena, describe and interpret them in different ways. What is surprising, and perhaps also unique in its degree to the fields we call science, is that such initial divergences should ever largely disappear.[8]

---

[7] Cline, Ray, *Secrets, Spies and Scholars* (Washington, DC: Acropolis Books, 1976), 7.

[8] Kuhn, Thomas, "The Structure of Scientific Revolutions," in *International Encyclopedia of Unified Science* (Chicago: The University of Chicago Press, 1970), 17.

Some business people draw a line between financial accounting and managerial accounting. As one textbook puts it:

> Financial accounting reports on the overall activities of the organization and is always restricted to past events. These include any financial transactions, such as a sale, a payment, or a change in value of something. Financial accounting is based in the past. It is a history of the organization.... [M]anagerial accounting often moves into the realms of speculation and future events. It deals with concepts such as incremental costs, marginal revenue, sunk costs and potential break-evens. For managers the use of managerial accounting information is a very important part of the decision-making process.[9]

But distinctions between raw and finished intelligence, facts and theories, financial and managerial accounting, information and knowledge, or our facts, their facts, and true facts, are incidental, not basic, in sorting out information resources. Rather, such distinctions reflect always relative and mostly subjective judgments. For instance, one person's knowledge is often another person's raw data. What a vice-president for marketing, production, or finance thinks he or she knows is just data to the chief executive officer's staff. What a scientist thinks he or she knows about the merits of a flu vaccine or the safety of a nuclear reactor is just data for presidential politics and policy.

Data, knowledge, and the rest are kinds of information substance—of greater or lesser value, of greater or lesser cost. Out of the broader notion of information resources, the concept of substance brings out the essence of information, the thing that either a picture or a thousand words conveys, the thing evoked when speaking of matters that are substantive rather than formal or procedural. What happens if we pay more attention to generic traits that are common to all varieties of substance than to the differences among particular species of substance and their particular purposes or values? This is a starting point in this chapter.

2.3.2 Format: Discretion and Pattern

Information substance infuses into a wide variety of more or less readily interchangeable forms. Pictures and words are the most common substance-bearing forms. Words come as speech and words come as writing. Written words alone have many incarnations: toe

---

[9] Compaine, Benjamin M. and Robert F. Litro, *Instructor's Manual for Business: An Introduction* (Chicago: The Dryden Press, 1984), 372.

marks in sand, gouges in stone, ink marks on paper, glowing phosphor patterns on television screens, electrical currents in communications facilities, electromagnetic waves from earth stations to satellites and back, quantum states in computer memories, laser beams in glass fibers. The concept of information formats brings these diverse ways of embodying information substance out from the idea of information resources.

Setting substance apart from format makes it plain how discretionary the ties are between specific kinds of substance and specific kinds of formats. News substance, for example, is not inexorably tied to paper format. The anomalous English word *newspaper* suggests such a tie, but, by contrast, French *journal*, German *Zeitung*, and Russian *gazeta* do not confound substance with format. Of course, news can also be gleaned from radio or television, heard over the phone, or, today as in olden times, passed on by word of mouth.

Telling substance apart from format lets creative thinking about the endless possibilities in combining and recombining substance and format off the leash of traditional combinations. Analogies with more familiar resources show why.

Energy and substance are both patterned matter. More explicitly, energy is to materials-in-general as substance is to materials-as-format. Both energy and information substance are abstractions. This very abstractness frees them from bondage to arbitrary incarnations in particular materials. What is gained by speaking of energy in the abstract is the ability to ask intensely practical and concrete questions, such as *Is energy cheaper as coal, as hydro, as solar, as nuclear, or as some other mode? Or safer? Or more convenient? Or whatever?* If energy is coal and coal is energy, how can energy be something other than coal? When energy and coal are one lump, the very question seems absurd. But when something distinct and abstract (e.g., energy) stays put as its embodiments shift from concrete mode to concrete mode, it gets easier to juggle desirable traits—price, environmental impact, convenience, or whatever—secure in the understanding that the essential good, the energy, is unscathed.

That is exactly like being able to talk of the relative cost and effectiveness of getting a political message—a bit of substance—to some intended audience by such different format–process combinations (modes) as newspapers, broadcasts, or phone calls. What is gained by speaking of substance is the ability to pose intensely practical and concrete questions such as, Will this story make more money as a book, a movie, or a TV miniseries? Or, How much campaign money do I put into TV ads, direct mail, or a phone campaign? Or, How much should we budget for flesh-and-blood spies and how much for National Technical Means of Verification, as the treaties put it, to promote arms control?

Abstracting generic information substance from its embodiments in specific format-and-process modes is necessary for avoiding marketing myopia as described by Theodore Levitt in an article so titled. "The railroads are in trouble," wrote Levitt in 1960, "because they assumed themselves to be in the railroad business rather than in the transportation business":

> Even after the advent of automobiles, trucks, and airplanes, the railroad tycoons remained imperturbably self-confident. If you had told them 60 years ago that in 30 years they would be flat on their backs, broke, and pleading for government subsidies, they would have thought you totally demented. Such a future was simply not considered possible. It was not even a discussable subject, or an askable question, or a matter which any sane person would consider worth speculating about. The very thought was insane. Yet a lot of insane notions now have matter-of-fact acceptance—for example, the idea of 100-ton tubes of metal moving smoothly through the air 20,000 feet above the earth, loaded with 100 sane and solid clients casually drinking martinis—and they have dealt cruel blows to the railroads.[10]

Abstraction is not sufficient. Rather, Alvin von Auw, who was close to several of AT&T's board chairmen in the years just before the 1984 breakup of the Bell System, testifies that AT&T management noted the necessity of this rethinking:

> Whatever for good or ill marketing dogma may have contributed to the economy at large, can there at this juncture be any serious quarrel with the conclusion that two at least of Levitt's three basic formulations have contributed significantly and perhaps crucially to the revitalization of AT&T? It is difficult to conceive how AT&T might prosper—or for that matter survive—in the changed and still changing world it confronts in the absence of the redefinition of its business mission that its own marketing prophets urged upon it: "No longer do we perceive that our business will be limited to telephony or—for that matter, telecommunications. Ours is the business of information-handling, the knowledge business. And the market we seek to serve is global."[11]

von Auw also testifies that abstraction from modes is not sufficient. Marketing that "focuses on the customer's needs and shapes the

---

[10] Levitt, Theodore, "Marketing Myopia," 1960. Reprint, in *Harvard Busines Review* (September-October 1975): 26, 176.

[11] von Auw, Alvin, *Heritage and Destiny: Reflections on the Bell System in Transition* (New York: Praeger Publ., 1983), 169.

organization to meeting them" is, von Auw agrees with Levitt, another ingredient of success although catering to every customer whim can also be just another good intention that paves the road to hell.[12] von Auw recollects "the tardiness of AT&T's recognition of the growing diversity of its customers' requirements in the late '60s and early '70s," and adds:

> Still vivid in the memory of at least one of the participants is a 1969 conference of Bell operating vice presidents and the pungently expressed frustrations of some of its veteran members at the cautiously proffered suggestion that meeting the needs of data communications users might require specialized operating organizations, specialized test centers, even special service measurements. Certainly the recollection confirms Levitt's observation that "executives with such backgrounds"—that is, in the operating end of capital intensive industries—"have an almost trained incapacity to see that getting 'volume' may require understanding and serving many discrete and sometimes small market segments, rather than going after a perhaps mythical batch of big or homogeneous customers."[13]

Formats are ultimately material. Ink on paper is material. So is the metallic or plastic lettering that spells out the brand name on the rear of a car. The metallic pattern of an "A" differs from the metallic pattern of a car body: same material, different function, and different pattern. That is why formats are only ultimately material. To be really useful, the idea of format needs the idea of pattern, just as builders need abstract pattern to speak of arches, flying buttresses, or I-beams.

Arches can be made of stone or brick or concrete or plywood or steel. Steel can make arches or I-beams or L-beams or rails or fenders. This flexibility of choice, this broad discretion, is explicit only when pattern is abstracted from material. Dissecting format into a hierarchy of symbols, patterns, and tokens (see Figure 2-1) gives a similarly valuable freedom of choice.

Suppose the substance to be formatted is the idea of a cat. One discretionary choice is whether to express this idea in French, English, or some other language. By this decision one chooses a symbol for the idea of a cat.

Choosing the symbol leaves other useful choices wide open. The symbol can be patterned in lower case or in capital Roman type, in Morse code or in Braille. The respective practical or aesthetic advantages of the different patterns are plain. The same choice among

[12] McLaughlin, *supra*, note 6.

[13] von Auw, *supra,* note 11 at 170.

Figure 2-1. Format for Substance: Cat Symbols, Cat Patterns, and Cat Tokens

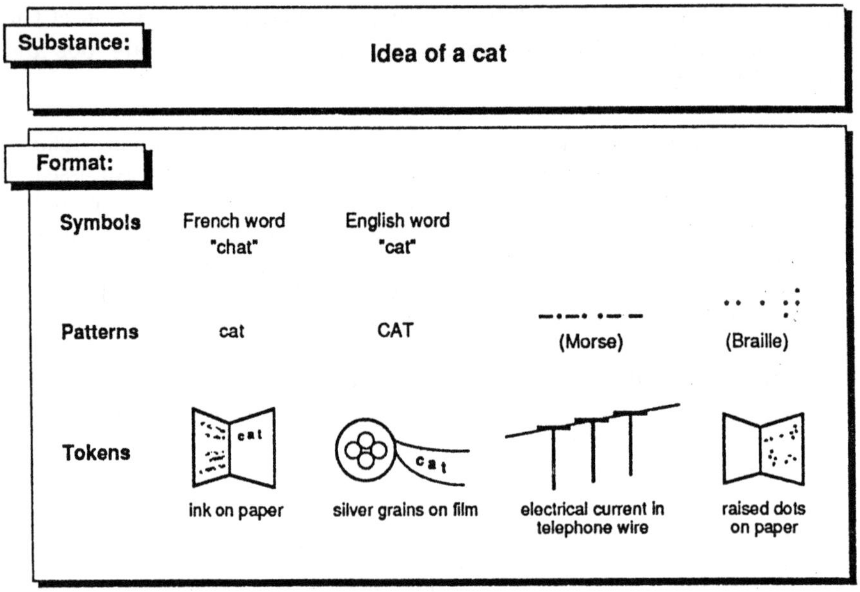

patterns is open whether the French or English word has been picked as the symbol. That all these combinations are possible, and more, is inexpressible if symbol and pattern are not told apart one from another and both told apart from substance.

A symbol and a pattern are both abstract, like an arch-shape or an I-shape or an L-shape or a rail-shape. A token concretely embodies the abstract pattern for the abstract symbol for that abstract chunk of substance, which is the idea of a cat. We sidestep the truly metaphysical questions about how the idea of a cat relates to either one warm purring critter or else to all catdom. An open choice of tokens helps even when the symbol and its pattern are already fixed. The aesthetic and commercial differences between ink-on-paper and silver-grains-on-film as tokens for "cat" are evident. The Morse and Braille patterns show off best when linked with electrical and embossed tokens, respectively. But both the Morse and the Braille patterns had to be infused into ink-on-paper tokens to make the token for Figure 2-1.

2.3.3 Process

Manipulating real-world information substance means applying a process, not abstractly to disembodied substance but concretely to

Figure 2-2. The Process of Making and Using a Newspaper

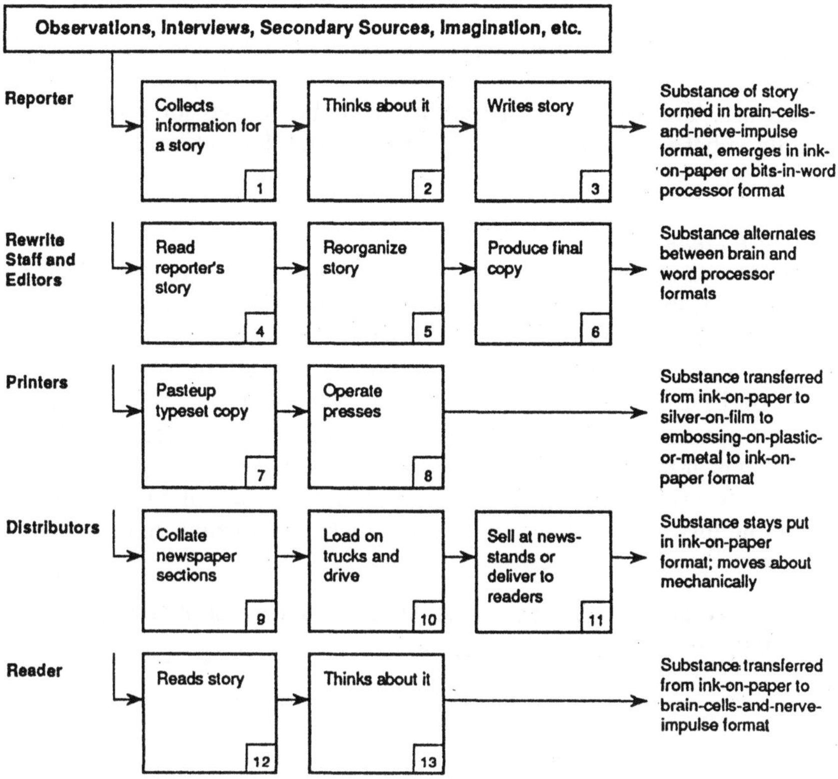

material tokens. The process idea is the third and last element of the dissection of information resources into their substance, format, and process building blocks. Figure 2-2 shows how real information processors (for example, human brains, hands-with-pen-and-paper, and printing presses) together mediate the processes of gathering, storing, manipulating, transmitting, evaluating, and using substance in various formats.

Because abstract substance is, in the real world, always embodied in concrete tokens, modifying substance involves applying energy to some substance's token to change that token into a token for the modified substance. In some ways that's just like applying energy to a steel ingot to roll it into an I-beam for a skyscraper, or like applying energy to sheet metal to stamp it into a fender for a car. A key difference is that working over material-as-information-token normally takes minuscule amounts of energy compared to working over material-as-piece-of-a-building-or-car. How much muscle it takes to erase an "A" typed by mistake, and how much muscle it takes to wreck an A-frame house, give a sense of the relative scales of energy consumption.

In the Industrial Revolution the search was on for new ways to apply new steam technology across the range of energy-consuming human endeavors. The Information Evolution is the search for new ways to bundle substance with new electronic digital formats and processes, displacing, wherever possible, the energy- and material-intensive modes of an earlier era.

These ideas are not new. The myth of wily Odysseus, like the myth of David and Goliath, is the story of brain over brawn, of the clever use of information as a force multiplier. Using their radar better than either the Germans or the British Bomber Command, the British Fighter Command flew their few planes so well in World War II's Battle of Britain that the Germans thought they faced many more. The radar force multiplier ushered in the contemporary electronic manifestations of brain over brawn. Formatting and processing techniques born of wartime intelligence, command, and control needs became available for use in other bundles of substance, format, and process.

Figure 2-3. Information Businesses: Substance, Format, Process, and Their Bundles

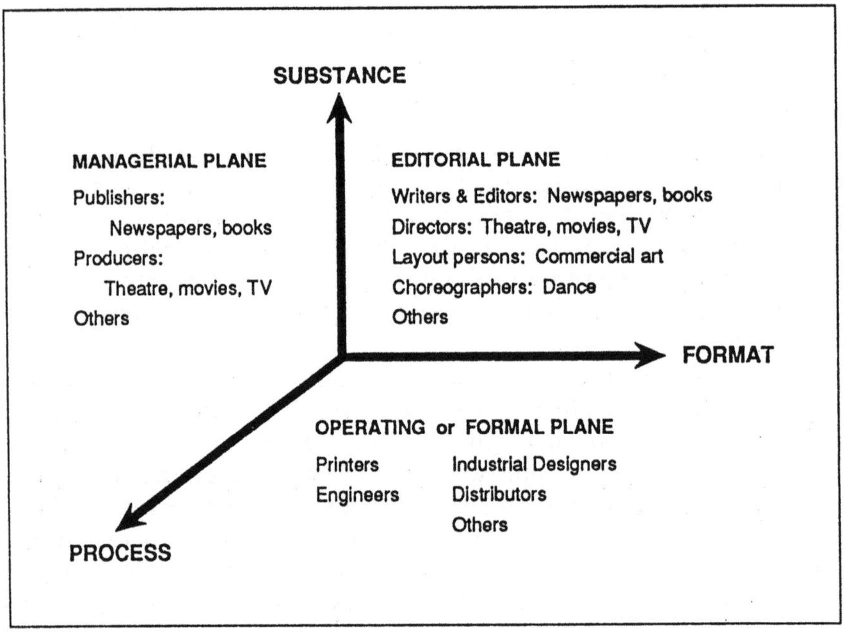

2.4 INFORMATION GOODS AND THEIR PURVEYORS: BUNDLES AND BUNDLERS

Every information product or service is a bundle of substance, format, and process. Newspapers, for instance, bring the substance of national and local news, ads, crossword puzzles, horoscopes, and so on to their readers in an ink-on-paper format through the process in Figure 2-2.

Figure 2-3 provides a basis for visualizing the full range of information products and services as bundles of substance, format, and process. The axes of Figure 2-3 are substance, format, and process. The planes made by the three pairs of axes in turn portray conventional functions within information businesses. Tying substance to process defines a *managerial* plane; infusing substance into format defines an *editorial* plane; and subjecting concrete formats, as materials, to concrete energy-consuming processes defines a formal or *operating* plane devoid of substance. One person or one organization might, of course, do all three bundlings, as in the romantic idealization of the small town editor/publisher with a green eyeshade on his head, black ink on his hands, and a bicycle seat under his rump. In other information businesses people with other titles do the managerial, editorial, and operating functions.[14]

The presence or absence of substance is relative, depending on who's doing what, by what conventions, under what circumstances. A sublime haiku is Greek to one who knows no Japanese, even though nothing has changed in the ink or the rice paper. To Shakespeare, a tale told by an idiot was purely formal, "full of sound and fury, signifying nothing." There is no record of what it meant to the idiot.

I once asked a friend, a violinist in the Boston Symphony Orchestra, what he thought of a performance I had just left enthralled. Said he, "We get paid to play, not to think," much as last night's printer might reply about this morning's news stories.

---

[14] I am indebted to many colleagues and friends for their contributions to the development of both the substance–format–process framework and its graphical representations. Larry Mancini suggested the managerial, editorial, and operating interpretations during a discussion in Kansas City in September 1981 that also involved several of his colleagues at United Telecommunications and several of my colleagues from the Program. Earlier versions are on record in the following works of Benjamin Compaine and Per Ongstad:

Compaine, Benjamin M., *A New Framework for the Media Arena: Content, Process and Format* (Cambridge, MA: Program on Information Resources Policy, Harvard University, 1980), 10–11.

Ongstad, Per, *Information Resources Policy Viewed by an Outskirter* (Cambridge, MA: Program on Information Resources Policy, Harvard University, 1981), 35–37.

Arguments so convoluted that they would confound Talmudists, Jesuits, and Immanuel Kant combined take place in Washington's administrative, legislative, and judicial hearing rooms over whether certain telephone company operations are purely formal or shade over into the substantive. Likewise in Brasilia, New Delhi, Rome, and Tokyo, and in innumerable board rooms. At stake is not abstruse theology or the hereafter but, rather, who may do what kind of business with or without government regulation right here and now: Does this or that piece of market turf belong to local phone companies, AT&T, IBM, or discount warehouses? To Americans, Europeans, or Japanese?[15] For this chapter, something is pure form, innocent of substance, and found in the formal or operating plane whenever the point being made is about a material format undergoing an energy-consuming process, like a violin string being vibrated by the bow, whether the format actually incarnates substance for someone or not. It costs energy either way.

What various media have in common and how they differ can be sorted out by using the ideas summed up in Figure 2-3.

News can be delivered in print or news can be delivered by radio, as shown in Figure 2-4 and Figure 2-5. The bundle in Figure 2-4 is usually called a newspaper section, that in Figure 2-5 a radio broadcast segment. The two figures show the same substance delivered in two distinct substance–format–process bundles made by distinct bundlers. As always, what you make of such a thing depends on who you are and what you might want to prove.

Some will think it plain that there is no difference between the two media: both convey roughly the same news—say, the announcement of the election of a president of the United States—only one does it orally,

---

[15] These arguments and stakes are exemplified in the U.S. by decades of proceedings before the Federal Communications Commission in Computer Inquiries I, II, III, before the courts in the U.S. government's antitrust suit against the Bell System that dismembered it into AT&T and the seven regional holding companies, and in attempts to get Congress to define concepts like information services, electronic publishing, and protocol conversion. For administrative, judicial, and legislative details, see:

USA v. AT&T Co., Modification of Final Judgment, 552 F. Supp. 131 (D.D.C. 1982), *aff'd mem. sub nom.*, Maryland v. USA, 460 U.S. 1001 (1983).

In the Matters of: Amendment of Sections 64.702 of the Commission's Rules and Regulations (Third Computer Inquiry); and Policy and Rules Concerning Rates for Competitive Common Carrier Services and Facilities Authorizations Thereof; Communications Protocols Under Section 64.702 of the Commission's Rules and Regulations, CC Docket No. 85-229: Memorandum Opinion and Order on Further Reconsideration, 3 FCC Rcd 1135 (1988).

H.R. 2140, 101st Cong., 1st Sess. (1989), (Consumer Telecommunications Services Act of 1989).

Figure 2-4. A Newspaper Section as Substance–Process–Format Bundle

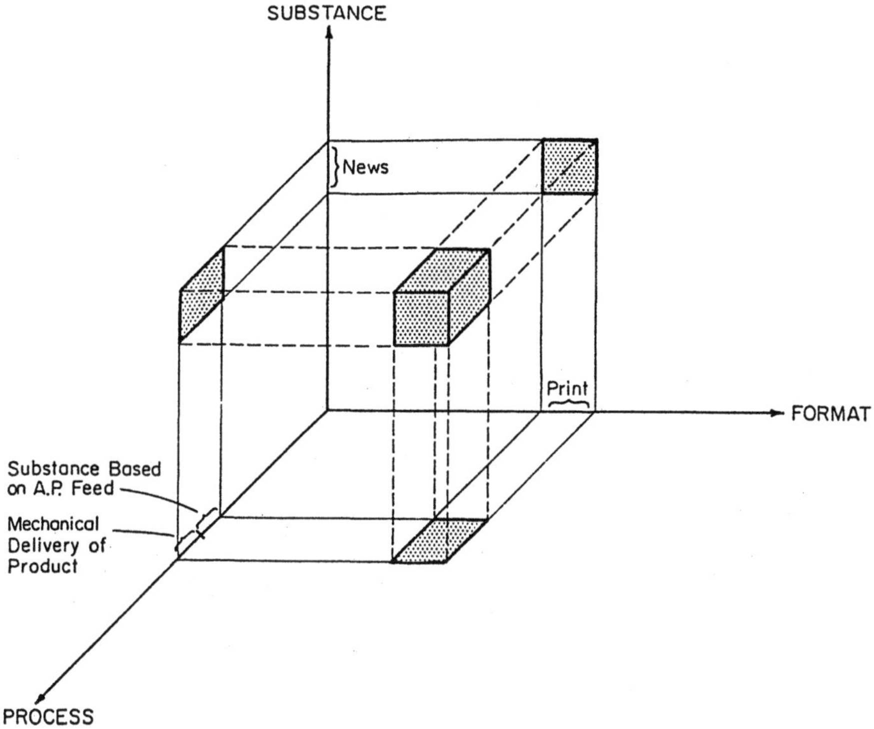

the other in writing. In fact, both newspaper and radio get some of their information from the same wire service. From this standpoint the identical placement along the substance axis in Figure 2-4 and Figure 2-5, and in the overlap at the Associated Press feed on the process axis, overwhelm the differences on the format axis and the differences in delivery processes.

Others will think it just as obvious that the medium is the message. That fairly leaps to the eyes through the different positions of the cubes in Figure 2-4 and Figure 2-5 that denote the entire bundles and likewise through the different positions of the squares that denote the editorial, managerial, and operating contributions to these bundles. Besides, one can point out that the wire feeds to radio and to newspapers are separate. A.P. writes stories for radio that are shorter than the stories it feeds to newspapers. Where a newspaper article might run eight hundred words, the radio announcement runs only fifty. The bare facts may be the same, but the treatment and the impact are something else again. Perhaps that is what Marshall

Figure 2-5. A Radio Broadcast Segment as Substance-Process-Format Bundle

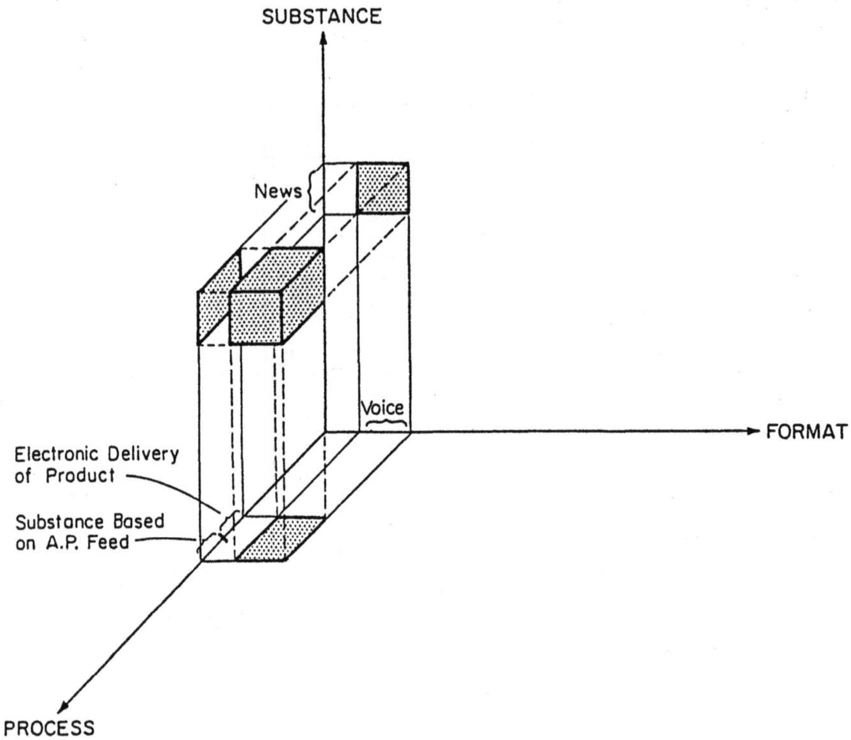

McLuhan meant by his delphic coinage of the "medium is the message" phrase:

> In a culture like ours, long accustomed to splitting and dividing all things as a means of control, it is sometimes a bit of a shock to be reminded that, in operational and practical fact, the medium is the message. This is merely to say that the personal and social consequences of any medium—that is, of any extension of ourselves—result from the new scale that is introduced into our affairs by each extension of ourselves, or by any new technology.[16]

What stays put and what changes in shifts from one medium to another lends itself to differing interpretations. Figure 2-4 and Figure

[16] McLuhan, Marshall, *Understanding Media* (New York: McGraw-Hill Book Co., 1964), 7.

2-5 illustrate the extreme but useful idea that there is something invariant—an abstract and inviolate underlying message or substance—common to both the oral and the written statements that someone has been elected president. The same figures capture another useful idea not at all antithetical to the first, namely, that the flavor of a format–process combination or its temperature—as in McLuhan's controversial hot media, cool media distinction[17]—is somehow substantive and not purely formal. At this extreme, the medium *is* the message. Anything is always at least a symbol for itself, whatever other conventional or unconventional perceptions it might evoke. Arcane arguments in between—say, over whether the smell of the leather and the sight of the gold in a rich binding are or are not part of a book's message—can at least be expressed by the visual metaphor for substance–format–process bundles.

Of course, that does nothing to settle the arguments. At least in one real world, such distinctions are mostly axe grinding. For instance, the concept of the movie rights to a book is respectable, even a legal truth, even an enforceable right, if one believes or at least gets a judge or a legislature to say that there is something—reasonably approximating what is meant here by the disembodied substance of a story—which might be incarnated in both a book format and a movie format and manufactured and distributed through the processes of both Madison Avenue and Hollywood for greater profit than through either alone. This extreme might be tagged as the *alias* view of a story (Figure 2-6A), wherein one and the same story does business as and reaps rewards for its author as both book and movie, for instance *Gone with the Wind-Story* d.b.a. *Gone with the Wind-Book* and also d.b.a. *Gone with the Wind-Movie*. If litigation is war, as some lawyers believe, then controlling presumptions like this is what controlling the high ground is to an embattled Marine.

Under critical pressure, however, either the book's author or the screen writer might take refuge in an *alibi* view of a story (Figure 2-6c). The author's alibi, if the movie bombs, is that he and his story weren't there at all. It was altogether another story, by that scribbler the screen writer, that masqueraded under the book's name. Figure 2-6b suggests the more common "my story, but butchered" that lies between the aliases "my story, the book, and my story, the movie" and the alibi "not my story at all."

After-the-fact justifications of *realpolitik* by such fairy tales and by

[17] Finkelstein, Sidney, *Sense and Nonsense of McLuhan* (New York: International Publ., 1968), 79-84; and Theall, Donald, *The Medium Is the Rear View Mirror* (Montreal: McGill-Queens University Press, 1971), 13.

Figure 2-6. Alias and Alibi: The Story as Book and the Story as Movie

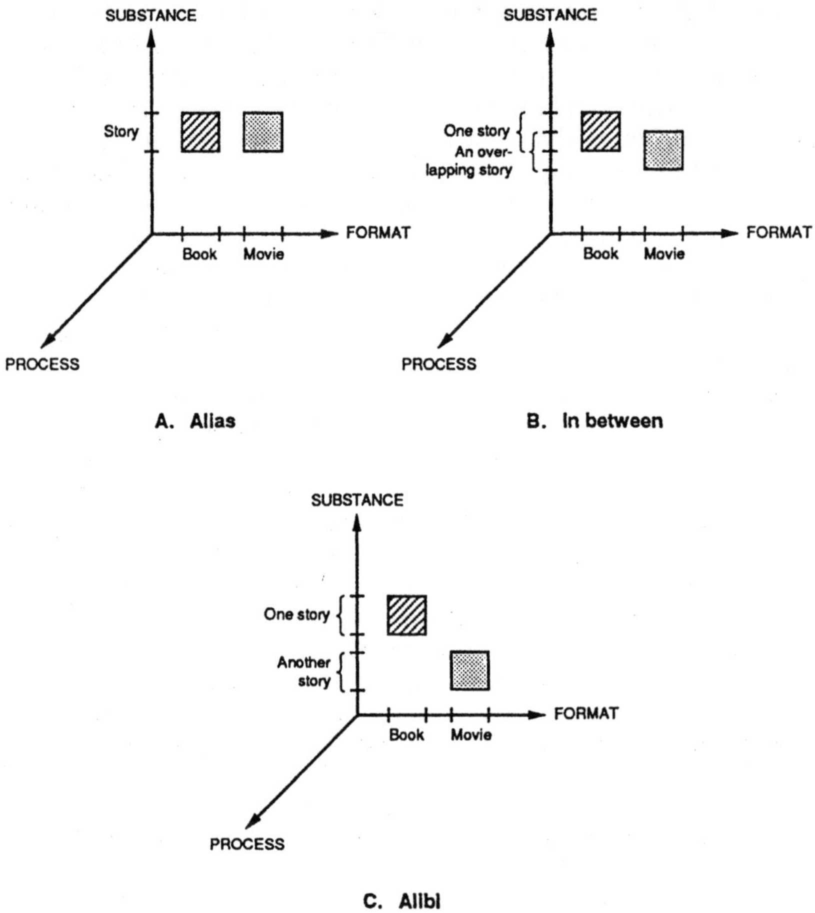

their reification into law are the rule in public and private decision making, not the exception.[18] In part, this is because even now what defines a real-world medium bundle and its bundler's turf is less self-evident and less solid than it seems or than might be sworn to in court.

[18] For details see: Oettinger, Anthony G., "Political, Scientific and Other Truths in the Information World." University of Pittsburgh School of Library and Information Science, Samuel Lazerow Memorial Lecture, November 10, 1988; and Oettinger, Anthony G., *The Formula Is Everything: Costing and Pricing in the Telecommunications Industry* (Cambridge, MA: Program on Information Resources Policy, Harvard University, 1989).

2.5 EVOLVING INFORMATION PURVEYORS: MEDIA COME, MEDIA GO

Many real-world people and organizations tie together many real-world substance–format–process bundles. Among them are the businesses lumped under the *mass media* rubric. Newspapers are among the many familiar products and services that these businesses turn out. Like every other medium, the newspaper is a substance–format–process bundle that came out of its own particular sequence of historical events.

Some bundles are more ephemeral than others; none is a prime mover unmoved or even virgin-born. The dominant newspaper format, for example, issues from an accidental coupling of technology and policy. Many newspaper people express an almost mystical reverence for the size of the standard newspaper exemplified by the *New York Times* or the *Wall Street Journal.* They commonly affect a sneer at tabloids, newspapers sized like the *New York Daily News* or the *National Enquirer.* Indeed, rival papers often hint that the tabloid format connotes pandering to popular if not altogether depraved tastes, while the larger standard format brims over with the truths of responsible journalism.

Few in the trade question all this mysticism. Most act as if the high-class format came with Adam and Eve. The reality is rather prosaic.

When steam-driven presses came out about 1814, they could handle at most a certain size of paper. Until 1855 the British taxed newspapers by the number of pages. It was only natural for newspaper businesses to adopt the largest practicable page size in order to minimize the tax bite. All the rest is snobbery, fueled by the fact that tabloid publishers aim their substance at the lower income mass market.

Essentially unchanged since those days is the *presentation* format that newspaper readers see and feel (Figure 2-2, Box 11), and which annoyingly rubs black ink off on their hands. *Essentially* here means that the casual observer might hardly notice differences that are gargantuan to the cognoscenti of the trade.[19]

The formats used in manufacturing newspapers (Figure 2-2, Boxes 1 to 8) are largely invisible to the reader. They also have changed but

---

[19] Details of newspaper evolution are available in, for example, *Editor & Publisher*, a weekly independent trade journal for the newspaper industry. See also Compaine, Benjamin M., *The Newspaper Industry in the 1980s* (White Plains, NY: Knowledge Industry Publ., Inc., 1980); and Smith, Anthony, *Goodbye Gutenberg* (New York: Oxford University Press, 1980).

little. Prior to the early 1970s, a nineteenth-century newspaper owner would have recognized almost everything that happened at the paper from the time a reporter set his story on paper to the time when that story rolled off the presses. During the 1970s, however, the internal processes of newspapers shifted from hot metal technology to computer-based photocomposition technology, from mainly mechanical to mainly electronic processes, from internal formats based on ink and paper to beeps and bleeps in wires (Figure 2-2, Boxes 7 to 8 and even Boxes 3 to 8). Although unnoticed by the ordinary newspaper reader who, from outside the business, sees only the conventional presentation format (Figure 2-2, Box 11), this change in internal formats and processes typifies how diffusing compunications technologies are transforming not only the mass media but also the information industries in general.

2.5.1 Mass Media: Landmarks

One thing is sure about the future: it begins now. And it is certain that when you don't know where you are it is hard to figure out where you are going. A brief snapshot of mass media during the early 1980s will serve as a sample of landmarks with which to gauge what change has taken place since then and with which to navigate the course of still-evolving change.

As a starting point, at the turn of the eighties, the U.S. mass media industry included:[20]

- ***Newspapers.*** *Editor & Publisher* tabulated some seventeen hundred products listed as English-language daily newspapers. Most were of general interest in a particular geographical area. They depended on advertising for about 70 percent of their revenues and on their readers for the remaining 30 percent. There were also foreign language dailies and special interest dailies, ranging from the *Wall Street Journal* to *Woman's Wear Daily*. Besides these, the *Ayer Directory of Publications* listed approximately nine thousand less-than-daily newspapers, many of them weekly publications in towns too small to support a daily. Usually included under the newspaper rubric, though subject to varying perceptions, were the many "shoppers." Shoppers were usually distributed free and carried some editorial material, but they were primarily if not

[20] The material that follows was adapted from Compaine, Benjamin M., *A New Framework for the Media Arena, supra,* note 14 at 22.

totally devoted to display advertising and classified or even jumbled advertising. Most newspapers were owned by firms that published more than one publication.

- ***Magazines.*** The annual *Ayer Directory* classified more than ten thousand bundles as periodicals. These included some twelve hundred consumer magazines, as well as business, trade and professional publications, scholarly journals, association, alumni, and similar periodicals. Although many such bundles accepted and depended on advertising, others were supported exclusively by circulation revenues, dues, or other subsidies. As with newspapers, most consumer and business magazines were part of multipublication groups.
- ***Broadcast television.*** Three major commercial television networks fed the bulk of the programming of eight hundred VHF and UHF stations. In addition, there were educational or public stations and a loose network to serve them, financed by government appropriations plus private and corporate donations. The networks themselves each owned five VHF stations scattered among the major markets, while other firms also owned chains of local stations. Most programming was purchased by networks from independent film producers and studios. On occasion, *ad hoc* networks came into being for some particular purpose or series.
- ***Broadcast radio.*** The rise of television had already changed the nature of radio from a national- and network-programmed medium to a largely local and independently programmed medium. There were seven radio networks and eight thousand commercial AM and FM stations. The latter were the fastest growing segment of the industry. In addition, there was a relatively small cadre of public/educational stations.
- ***Cable television* (CATV).** Unlike the more established media, cable then functioned mostly as a distributor rather than as a creator of substance. Cable began as a provider of stronger reception of conventional broadcast signals in remote areas. In 1983, five thousand cable systems relied on broadcast television signals from the network affiliates, retransmission of some independent stations, and a growing number of cable programming networks for their fare. In most cases, one or more premium pay-TV services also provided theatrical films and some productions specially produced for this form of distribution. There was little cable operator-originated programming, other than news headlines, weather, and sports scores, often by means of automated displays rather than live announcers.
- ***Books.*** The U.S. Commerce Department enumerated two thousand

book publishers, but this statistic may have understated the true number of small but active publishers. R.R. Bowker Co. identified more than five hundred thousand titles in print, with as many as fifty thousand new titles appearing each year. Books included such diverse segments as trade books, college and elementary and high school textbooks, religious, professional, and university press books and mass market paperbacks. Channels of distribution varied significantly for different types of books and required the participation of wholesalers, jobbers, retailers, and postal services.

- ***Motion pictures***. There were an estimated forty-nine hundred producers and distributors of films, most of them in the nontheatrical end of the business. Theatrical movies were shown on seventeen thousand plus theater screens, many of which were part of "circuits" or chains. Most theatrical films were distributed by nine major firms and, more than any other segment of the media, depended on foreign sales for a major portion of revenue and profit. Nontheatrical films included educational, promotional, and other business films. The federal government was particularly active here, either through its own production or in contracts to independents.
- ***Nonbroadcast video***. The role of video had just begun to grow in both homes and business/government/educational organizations. Business and government spent an estimated $1.1 billion on nonbroadcast television hardware and programming in 1980. Many large firms had their own "networks" that served television outlets in their scattered corporate and divisional offices, using copies of videocassettes prepared in-house or standardized purchased programming. Schools and colleges used closed-circuit and taped programs for instruction. The home market in 1983 consisted largely of recycled theatrical films and a few specially made special interest programs for the 6.3 million home videocassette units. At least eighteen firms were marketing one-half-inch cassette units for the home market, while a handful of firms had entered the licensing and production of programming area. Albeit small, nonbroadcast use of the television set was the fastest growing segment of the mass media. By the end of the decade it had grown enough to justify the re-release of the popular film *E.T.* in the videocassette format for the Christmas trade. RCA was no more, and the NBC network had been sold to GE. Even more important, thousands of videocassette rental stores had arisen across the nation, and already they were being consolidated as this rental business matured by the turn of the 1990s!
- ***Newsletters***. These were distinctive bundles generally regarded as being neither magazines nor newspapers. They were periodicals,

usually devoted to a specialized topic and hence a specialized audience. Most often they were sold on a subscription basis at a relatively high price, with little or no advertising. Although some had a circulation of one hundred copies or less, sometimes they were highly influential among their readership.

- ***Databases.*** The rapid and continuing reduction in the cost of computer storage and processing had stimulated a new form of database storage and retrieval. Vast quantities of data on a broad list of subjects had become accessible from remote terminals, mostly to business, government, and other institutional users who were willing to pay to get timely information. A subindustry of database utilities had also been created to facilitate the dissemination of this information.
- ***Advertisers.*** Most of the media were supported totally or predominantly by income from advertising. Users consequently received the substance for free (in the case of broadcasts or "shoppers") or for less than the full cost of production (daily newspapers, most magazines). Trade books and theatrical films were the two major media that were user supported, although some question whether or not low prices for fourth-class mail were subsidizing mail-order book publishers. In 1982, U.S. organizations as varied as the U.S. Army and Frank Perdue's chicken business spent about $67 billion on advertising, most of that through the mass media. The largest share went to newspapers, followed by television. Advertising expenditures had stayed at a nearly constant 2 percent of Gross National Product since 1940.
- ***U.S. government.*** The U.S. government was in the media business through films and publications for sale. As the State, it supervised media businesses as it does other businesses, subject to provisions, like the First Amendment to the Constitution, that are specific to information businesses. It also consumed media.[21]

---

[21] For examples, see the following:

U.S. Congress, Office of Technology Assessment, *Federal Government Information Technology: Management, Security and Congressional Oversight*, OTA-CIT-297 (Washington, DC: Government Printing Office, 1986).

U.S. Congress, OTA, *Defending Secrets, Sharing Data: New Locks and Keys for Electronic Information,* OTA-CIT-310 (Washington, DC: GPO, October 1987), GPO#: 052-003-01083-6.

U.S. Congress, OTA, *Power On!: New Tools for Teaching and Learning*, OTA-SET-379 (Washington, DC: GPO, September 1988), GPO#: 052-003-01125-5.

U.S. Congress, OTA, *Medlars and Health Information Policy: A Technical Memorandum,* OTA-TM-H-11 (Washington, DC: GPO, September 1982).

- ***Consumers.*** As just noted, users of the media got most of their products for direct expenses on their part that were less than the full cost of production. The major direct expense to receive broadcasts was the one-time investment in the purchase of a television or radio receiver. However, there was also massive investment in VCRs throughout the 1980s. The price of a daily newspaper covered about 30 percent of its cost (including profit margin), while consumer magazines charged readers about 40 percent to 50 percent of cost. Many trade magazines were also provided free of direct cost. Consumers directly covered the total costs of trade books and theatrical films. Many films in the nontheatrical category were sponsored. Cable and premium channel use was supported mostly by users, but cable operators did get some sponsored films and were looking for greater support from advertisers. Nonetheless, at the $44 billion level of 1981, consumers were spending less than advertisers on mass media. What consumers paid indirectly in attention to advertising or through the prices they paid for advertised products is not examined here.

In absolute size, the revenues of the traditional segments of the media, as reported by various trade associations and the U.S. Department of Commerce, were about $58 billion in 1981, or 2.3 percent of Gross National Product (Figure 2-7). By way of comparison, General Motors (GM) had sales of $60 billion, Exxon $97 billion, and IBM $34 billion. Media firms employed a total of about 1.2 million people, compared to 1.1 million people for the Big Three auto makers alone. Even adding the value of consumer electronics shipments (including imports) did not materially change the standing of the overall media industry.

This media industry rested on an infrastructure with a variety of indirect participants (Figure 2-8). For instance, the print media depended on manufacturers of newsprint and of the number 5 coated groundwoods paper used by newspapers and magazines, respectively. About 90 percent of all newsprint produced in the United States and

---

U.S. Congress, OTA, *Federal Government Information Technology: Electronic Surveillance and Civil Liberties,* OTA-CIT-293 (Washington, DC: GPO, October 1985), GPO#: 052-003-01015-1.

U.S. Congress, OTA, *Informing the Nation: Federal Information Dissemination in an Electronic Age,* OTA-CIT-396 (Washington, DC: GPO, October 1988), GPO#: 052-003-01130-1.

U.S. Congress, OTA, *The Electronic Supervisor: New Technology, New Tensions,* OTA-CIT-333 (Washington, DC: GPO, September 1987).

Figure 2-7. Major Mass Media Benchmark: 1981 Revenues

	Value of Product Shipments or Revenue, 1981 ($ Billions)	Percent of Total
Newspapers	$19.5	28.4%
Broadcasting	13.5	19.7
Magazines	9.9	14.4
Cable TV	2.1	3.1
Books	6.9	10.0
Theatrical film	4.4	6.4
Newsletters, databases, spoken word, videocassettes, etc.	1.4	2.0
	$57.7	84.0%
Consumer electronics (television radio receivers, home video recorders, phonograph and hi-fi equipment)	11.0	16.0
	$68.7	100.0%

Canada went to newspapers, while number 5 coated stock was periodically in such short supply that magazines had to import some from West Germany and from Finland. Manufacturers of these grades of papers had their fortunes closely allied with the publishing industry. Ink, a petroleum-based product, was an increasingly large expense for publishers, especially of newspapers, at a time when oil prices had peaked.

Print media also relied on various transportation modes, especially trucks and trains, for both the delivery of their raw materials and the distribution of their products. The magazine industry depended heavily on the U.S. Postal Service—a relationship that many publishers then questioned in light of greatly increased second-class mailing tariffs.

All the media, but print especially, were affected by the cost and the availability of energy. The paper-manufacturing industry was the fourth largest user of purchased energy, while big city newspaper presses used much electricity. Television and radio broadcasters needed electricity to send out their signals and television sets needed

Figure 2-8. Benchmark: The Early 1980s Media Businesses and Their Infrastructure

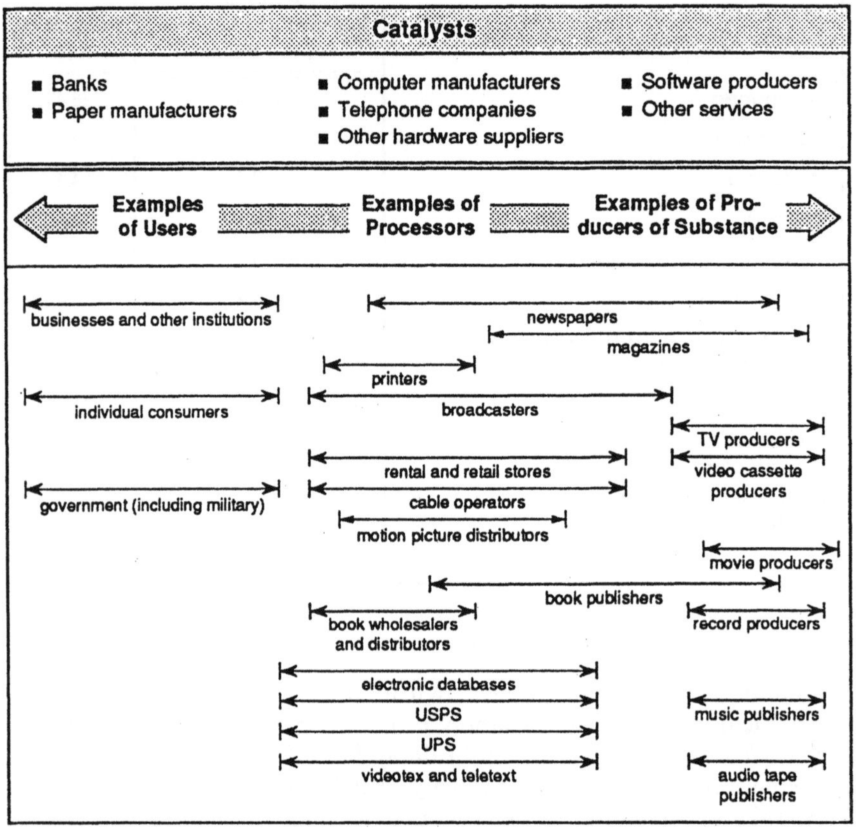

electricity to receive them. Broadcasters also needed hardware such as cameras, editors, and transmitters. Finally, all the media relied heavily on the telecommunications system of wires, microwave, lightguides, and satellites that AT&T and emerging competing telecommunications companies supplied. Relative to the print and film media, the electronic media were less sensitive to the cost of electricity, but they depended more on its uninterrupted availability.

As they went into the 1980s, newspaper publishers faced skyrocketing newsprint costs, but could note that the cost of computer storage had plunged even faster. Magazine publishers, like their newspaper counterparts, had been reaping healthy profits, yet they worried about postal rates and paper costs. Many in the print media businesses were looking at the newer formats and processes. They saw videotex and teletext technologies, video disks, electronic databases for business, electronic games, and personal computers, but were unsure of what it all meant to them.

Their brethren in the electronic media faced the bursting of their own distinctive bundles. For instance, the home television set was being used for private showings of theatrical films or to display computer output; homes with cable service could look at programs unavailable on the old-line networks or, for that matter, anywhere off the air. There was talk of *narrowcasting*, i.e., special interest programming for identifiable market segments rather than the broadcasting which tried to appeal to the greatest mass of viewers.

2.5.2 Blurring Boundaries

Government agencies were having to figure out how regulations and statutes should or could apply to media and technologies which did not exist when these rules were made. The very concepts used to speak of the media world had grown blurry.

Mass communications had often been defined as delivering one message at one time to all of a large, heterogeneous, and unseen audience in different places. The bundlers that purveyed substance that way were termed *mass* media. This tag reflected a traditional distinction between mass communication and media and other types of communication and media, such as point-to-point communication by telephone and telegraph or by individually addressed letters by mail.

Whatever sharpness this distinction once had got lost when a wider variety of formats and processes came on the scene. Personal computers and so-called "dumb terminals" at the office or at home enabled people to pick the substance they wished to get, although they might be drawing on a large common database to do so. Devices had become available for dialing up thousands of phone numbers in order to play more or less identical recorded messages to the recipients. Video and audio cassette recorders enabled people to record broadcasts in order to play them back whenever and how often they wished. Mass mailings often addressed only to "occupant" were not new, and there was speculation that electronic mail might further accent the mass flavor of the once point-to-point mail medium.

In earlier times one could usefully look upon newspapers, magazines, books, movies, radio, and television as the mass media. By 1980 one had to think through again the meaning of *mass* and, even more crucial, one had to confront a blurring of the boundaries among the media, a loss of the stability and the distinctiveness of their product or service bundles. *Television,* for example, had begun to mean something that no longer exclusively displayed broadcast TV signals, but that also displayed signals retransmitted by CATV or originated for CATV, signals from videocassettes or disks played right on premises or even news and other substance sent by telephone lines from a computer.

But the older media descriptions never were, in fact, as clear-cut as it seemed. What is a magazine? It usually has a paper cover, but not always. *Horizon,* like many books, had a hard cover for a time. A magazine is usually printed on glossy coated paper, but some, like *Rolling Stone,* were printed on newsprint. Most magazines carry advertising, but they need not do so to qualify for the label. *Reader's Digest* did not accept advertising until 1955. Magazines are usually thought of as published regularly during the year, but there are many publications that look like magazines but only appear annually or even just once. At what point does a newsletter become a magazine? Why is the tabloid weekly *National Enquirer* treated as a magazine in most compilations of periodicals and by advertisers, although its format is that of many newspapers?

When asked to classify a particular medium, many people ultimately resort to "show me and I'll tell you what it is." But even that can fail. When someone buys a prerecorded videocassette of *Rocky III* and plays it on a television set, is the medium film or television? Someone watching the show on a TV set may not even know and likely will not even care whether he or she is watching a broadcast, a cablecast, a cassette, or a disk. Where the bundler sees a distinctive bundle, the consumer sees a commodity perhaps as fungible as any dollar bill is with any other. And with the bundles themselves having grown unstable as new formats and new processes have come on the scene, it's media come, media go.[22]

2.6 A LANGUAGE FOR CHANGE: BASIC BUILDING BLOCKS STAY

Media may come and media may go, but the basic substance, format, and process building blocks stay on as the tools of choice for expressing change. Thinking explicitly in terms of these building blocks helps avoid entrapment in bundles tied by the exercise of discretion appro-

[22] For an even broader view of the impacts of the new technologies on offerings made to consumers, see Gumpert, Gary, *Talking Tombstones and Other Tales of the Media Age* (New York: Oxford University Press, 1987).

priate to a moment in history but whose time may be long gone. Loosening up the basic building blocks releases yet again all the creative possibilities in their discretionary potential combinations.

Television is one word for what two distinct bundlers, the broadcasters and the CATV operators, deliver to a home set with its tube, generically called a video display terminal (VDT). In the late 1960s and early 1970s, the products of these two distinct businesses spoke roughly the same thing. More precisely, the broadcasting and the cable industries of that time were both in the business of sending the very same substance to be consumed in the very same presentation format. Even their processes were set apart only by differing transmission techniques. The cable business promised better reception by packaging over-the-air reception of the broadcasting bundle by a big antenna on a hilltop with cable retransmission of that bundle.

This commonality, hence the potential for competition between them, was lost on neither the television nor the cable industry. But at the start neither of the two paid much attention to the possibility that both would eventually revert to old conflicts with the telephone industry, by virtue of the latter's latent capability for selling more or less equivalent processes. For example, WNBC, which was NBC's New York City AM-radio flagship until it was sold by GE in 1988, was born WEAF in 1922 at AT&T's headquarters at 195 Broadway. Broadcasting and telephony in the U.S.A. were made to divorce by an agreement reached in 1926 whereby "AT&T was to sell its broadcasting station in New York to RCA with RCA committing itself to utilizing AT&T's lines instead of Western Union's for the purpose of interconnecting the broadcasting stations."[23]

A magazine printed on newsprint and a newspaper are bundles of different substance delivered in similar but not identical formats through similar but not identical processes. Their layouts differ, and so do their delivery schedules.

In terms of the substance, format, and process building blocks, a substance creator—a storyteller, for example—can think about and cut deals with all the alternative operating (format and process) institutions for making and marketing his or her product, and not be locked into the formats and processes of only one among the movie business, the broadcast business, the cable business or the disk or cassette business. Customers for the substance can shop for the

[23] Borchardt, Kurt, *Structure and Performance of the U.S. Communications Industry: Government Regulation and Company Planning* (Boston: Harvard Business School, Division of Research, 1970), 60. See also Barnouw, Erik, *Tube of Plenty* (New York: Oxford University Press, 1975), 44–45.

cheapest distribution process and the most satisfying presentation format available.

In the traditional media, the presentation format from which customers ultimately got their substance was mostly the same as the formats used in production. Except for what took place inside the reporter's head or the typesetter's, all the processes in Figure 2-2 used to rely solely on ink-on-paper formats visible and intelligible to any literate person. Hence the distinctions, so common in the manufacturing industries, between intermediate and finished products, or between production for the final consumption trade and production for the original or outside equipment manufacturer (OEM) trade have been less important in the traditional media businesses. A tomato processor might sell whole, peeled, pureed, sauced, or ketchuped tomatoes directly under his own label, or indirectly under a national brand's, or under a supermarket's label, or in a club's or a restaurant's dish. The same can hold for washing machines and their parts. An information business equivalent is the Associated Press, which cans and distributes print and radio stories for local newspapers and broadcasters to sell or to serve up.

When intermediate electronic processes came into the traditional information industries, they gave more flexibility even to making the same old product. This flexibility makes intermediate formats—and commercial practices analogous to the industrial OEM trade—a possibility starting to be more widely exploited by the media and, indeed, by the information industries in general. By the late 1980s Dow Jones repackaged *Wall Street Journal* substance for its Dow Jones News Retrieval electronic database service. The *Washington Post* was among several newspapers that fed substance, after a brief delay, into Mead Data Central's NEXIS electronic database service.

Processes as they were defined in section 2.3 encompass all the functions of gathering, creating, storing, manipulating, distributing, and otherwise handling substance. This includes a reporter's researching and writing a newspaper article, then storing it in computer memory for editing. It includes a computer's hyphenating and justifying the text for typesetting and makeup. It covers the mechanical printing of the text on a rotary press, loading of the papers on a truck by workers, driving around town and dropping off bundles by someone, and delivery of the papers to neighborhood doorsteps by boys and girls. It encompasses eyeballing the page in a comfortable armchair. Finally, it even encompasses authorized or pirated copying of an article for further processing of all kinds.

The traditional media happened to sort and to name themselves by traditional format or process concepts and labels. The newspaper, book, and magazine businesses are typed and tagged by the presentation format that they sell. More recently, intermediate process names—*radio, cable, videocassette, home computer,* and so on—have been used to denote a medium. This gets confusing. Both cable and videocassette, for example, are merely alternative means of delivering substance in a VDT's video-and-aural presentation format. To a viewer they are still television, so a producer of feature films for theatrical release can, for instance, look to the video presentation format for an increasing share of the market. The universal-optical-fiber-to-the-home world that telephone companies were praying for in the late 1980s is another alternative distribution channel.

Whether the product is delivered by cassette, disk, coaxial cable, optical fiber or broadcast can be vital to form and efficiency but does not of itself necessarily affect substance and effectiveness. As was suggested in section 2.4, this is a matter of emphasis. Arguments over the effect of form (that is, format-and-process) on substance, as contrasted to the effect of form on practical economics, often have the flavor of philosophical arguments over when a quantitative change becomes a qualitative one. The outcomes of such arguments can make or break advertising agencies or conglomerates or presidential image makers.

Just as picture and sound bundlers began to try out new forms, so newspaper publishers began to experiment in the early eighties with the idea that some of what they tied into a bundle on paper, like classified ads or stock prices, might be more efficiently delivered to the VDTs of only those subscribers who requested specific substance from the publisher's or someone else's computer. The newspaper business might therefore turn into a service industry relying in part on ink-on-paper presentation formats and in part on video presentation formats. Increasingly, database publishers have found that computer processing and video presentation of their substance is an efficient and profitable way to offer services—although the substance may be the same as before.

Using the substance, format, process building blocks to describe media can forestall dying asleep in old harnesses. The concept of a magazine, for instance, hitches traditional bundles of substance to a traditional ink-on-glossy-paper form which is but one of the many forms available to the creators of these substantive bundles. Yet traditional magazine publishers rarely see themselves as video producers. But, by understanding that a special substantive expertise is the basis of the printed magazine form, they may come to a generalized view of the business that leads naturally to productions in video form congruent with available editorial substance.

This reasoning also goes for newspaper publishers, broadcasters, book publishers, record producers, and others. The blurring of artificial, formal distinctions traditionally made between substantively similar bundles was evident once CBS's "60 Minutes" referred to itself as a "video magazine" and Westinghouse Broadcasting called its prime time access program "Evening Magazine." Time Inc. tried to translate the fast pace and airy substance of its print *People* weekly directly to a video presentation using the same concept.

Before the substance, format, and process building blocks were made explicit by the Harvard Program on Information Resources Policy, they were implicit in strategic planning in and around the media industry. In the early eighties, some newspaper companies were trying out news services for cable channels or videotex systems. At least one broadcaster was starting to repackage existing news reports for videocassette or video tape sales, and movie distributors had already become accustomed to expanded distribution channels for their theatrical productions via broadcast, pay cable, cassettes, and disks.

These are just a few samples of possible creative outcomes of recombining substance, format, and process building blocks to create or enlarge markets, to reduce costs, to increase profit margins, and so on. Exploiting the new media menu provided by new formats and processes poses both challenges and the opportunities to those in the media businesses.

2.6.1 A Means to What End?

Setting substance apart from process and format allows considering its traits and its uses free from the accident of any particular historical bundling of substance with formats and processes. But substance even with form remains a means, not an end. A fact may be a fact, a theory may be deeply true, and a work of art may be exquisitely beautiful. But if not suited to the needs of the moment they all are tools searching for work, solutions searching for problems, products searching for customers. The ends, the purposes, that substance might serve whatever its form must be described by building blocks other than substance, format, and process and other than the bundles these building blocks make up. To do otherwise courts the circularity of describing news as what is in a newspaper and begs the question at the very heart of the search for appropriate responses to change: What mix of bundles by what mix of bundlers is best for what ends?

Findings have suggested that consumers use the mass media to satisfy four types of information needs: escape, social connection, surveillance, and opinion formation or decision making.[24] Different substance, process, and format bundles can be expected to satisfy different needs in different ways. And consumers use the media differently, depending on what mix of needs they want to satisfy.

- *Escape*: This need is for social and psychological retreat or entertainment. Reading the comics, working the crossword puzzle in the newspaper, or going to a movie theater are among the media uses that meet this need.
- *Social connection*: This need goes along with perceptions of one's social role. The sought substance is apt to be defined by "I know it when I see it." Thus, someone who feels part of the jet set may read newspaper stories about the goings on among the beautiful people or buy *Town and Country* magazine. At other times, a person may think it more important to be up-to-date on a sports star's free agent status.
- *Surveillance*: This need triggers questions more specific than for social connection such as, Did the space shuttle get launched this morning? Are there any houses for sale in that neighborhood? What time do buses leave for New York Saturday morning? Did the Phillies beat the Mets last night?
- *Opinion formation/decision making*: This need is expressed by questions ranging from, How should I vote on the bond issue question? to, What are the features of today's refrigerators that I should be looking for, now that I need a new one? As with surveillance, the substantive need may be relatively well articulated. But the sources for the information may be less sharply defined, requiring a different approach to the search for substance.

These four functional building blocks for articulating user needs, or others like them, are preferable to the traditional substantive and therefore circular categories—news, sports, or advertising, for example—as specifications to be matched against alternative substance, format, and process bundles. Surveillance needs, for instance, might effectively and cheaply be met by random access of an electronic database, but social connection needs would be less readily satisfied by

[24] Urban, Christine, "Factors Influencing Media Consumption," in *Understanding New Media*, Benjamin M. Compaine, ed. (Cambridge, MA: Ballinger Publishing Co., 1984).

that form. In this light, a baseball box score and a bus schedule—both of them substance for surveillance—are seen to have more in common with each other than the box score has with the play-by-play of the same baseball game. Seen in the traditional light, both the box score and the play-by-play are sports substance, but seeking out the box score is surveillance behavior, while reading about the color of the game has more to do with social connection.

Information resources differ from energy and material resources in one truly distinctive way. Substance is the organizing principle with which people integrate energy, material, and information resources to attain their personal ends or, as leaders and managers, the objectives of their organizations. The exploration that follows—of how the needs or wants of information users might best be matched with alternative substance, format, and process bundles—therefore concentrates on substance that is useful in exercising responsibility and authority. The factors that influence choice among alternative formats, so as to use the available substance most effectively, are examined in Chapter 6 for the case of electronic and print modes of substance display.

2.7 EVOLVING INFORMATION CONSUMERS: INFORMATION FOR RESPONSIBILITY AND AUTHORITY

People in organizations create and use the substance of information resources for all four of the building block needs set forth in the preceding section: escape, social connection, surveillance, and opinion formation/decision making.

The *form* of information resources, namely format undergoing process, is the very essence of organization. It shapes and, in its pattern aspect, it *is* the structure that makes organisms or organizations out of energy and materials.

The concrete information formats and processes of an organism or an organization make up its nervous system. Organisms don't have much say over the make up of their own nervous systems, although genetic engineering may some day change that. But the nervous systems of organizations are artifacts, bundles of formats and processes that can be consciously molded, to the extent we know how, for better or worse performance.[25]

---

[25] Generic problems of designing organizational nervous systems are described in the following sources:

Arrow, Kenneth J., *The Limits of Organization* (New York: W.W. Norton, 1974), 53–56.

Simon, Herbert A., "Designing Organizations for an Information-Rich World," in

The organizational nervous system of the moment expresses the organization's needs for substance, assimilates that substance, and, among other functions, mediates the exercise of responsibility and authority within the organization and by the organization in the world outside it.

The nervous system or format-and-process bundle that an organization evolves and the substance which that nervous system makes or picks day by day, make up a substance, format, and process bundle vital to the organization. This bundle differs from the media bundles not in kind but only in aspect. From a producer's vantage point, we looked at media bundles as products or services. Here we see the organizational bundle from its user's perspective. A consulting or software firm might conceive of a management information system, for example, as a product or service. Installed and in use, it is a piece of its buyer's organizational nervous system.

Evolving the nervous system of an organization and the ongoing choices of information substance that this nervous system makes are both vital functions, the one strategic and the other operational. How well does an organization do its daily routine? How deftly does it meet its crises? And, ultimately, will it live or die? That all depends on how well the organization's nervous system works, on how well its people's brains and their words and their pictures and their numbers do their job. It all depends on brain at least as much as it depends on how well the organization's brawn works, on how well its people's muscles and their plowshares and their swords do their job.

Any innovation or any obsolescence in formats and processes, any coming apart and together of substance, format, and process bundles directly affects all information resource markets, not just the media's. The markets of non-information businesses, airlines or hairlines, candy stores or department stores, pin makers or auto makers, are impacted only indirectly. But the nervous systems of all businesses, information businesses among them, are all directly affected.

The information businesses get a double dose as *information* businesses and as information *businesses*, but no business is immune from any opportunity or any threat that change, internal or external, presents to its nervous system, to its means for exercising respon-

---

Computers, Communications, and the Public Interest, Martin Greenberger, ed. (Baltimore: The Johns Hopkins University Press, 1971), 42–44.

Oettinger, Anthony G., "Compunications in the National Decision-Making Process," in *Computers, Communications, and the Public Interest,* Martin Greenberger, ed. (Baltimore: The Johns Hopkins University Press, 1971), 74–76.

Snyder, Frank M., *Command and Control: Readings and Commentary* (Cambridge, MA: Program on Information Resources Policy, Harvard University, 1989).

sibility and authority. What goes for business goes for any organization including government in all its functions from garbage collection to national security.

2.7.1 What Process Does

The workings of the U.S. national nervous system in the first moments of a crisis come alive in the following reminiscences of the 1965 Northeast power failure and blackout. In this 1983 interview, D.H. is Donald F. Hornig, formerly Special Assistant to President Lyndon B. Johnson for Science and Technology; F.A., the interviewer, is Lt. Col. Francis W. A'Hearn:

D.H. The power failure occurred about five minutes of six. At that time the President was driving on his ranch in Texas on an inspection tour, so he heard the announcement on his car radio. That was the first thing he heard. What he did immediately was to call the Secretary of Defense. At that point Bob McNamara had not yet heard about the blackout.

Before I continue this story I must tell you the other half. I had a daughter in Cambridge. When everything went down her reaction was, "My God, there has been a nuclear attack." If so, the family in Washington had presumably been vaporized or something, so she immediately got on the telephone and called my wife. Surprisingly, the call got through immediately. She told my wife that all the power was out and, as far as she knew, everything was out all over the Northeast. My wife fortunately said to herself, "I'd better get hold of Don right away," so they didn't chat. Instead, she called me at my office in the old Executive Office Building. I thanked her and immediately switched on a TV beside my desk.

On the TV they announced that New York had just gone down and that there was no power as far west as Buffalo. It seemed quite clear that it was accidental, but nobody really knew just what was going on.
Just at that moment my phone rang, and Bob McNamara said "Don, I just had a call from the boss, who said that the whole Northeast is blacked out. Do you know anything about it?" I said yes and told him everything I'd just seen and heard on TV!

F.A. At that point your only source of information was what you had seen on TV following your daughter's phone call?

D.H. The only reason I happened to learn it was that my panicky daughter called my wife, who called me and I turned on the TV and got it from there. At that point McNamara—given all his communications—hadn't been informed other than by the President.

F.A. And the President heard it on the radio.

D.H. A funny post script to that whole episode came later. I called the Federal Power Commission to tell Chairman Swidler they had better get on top of this, to which they replied, "We are a regulatory agency, not a technical agency." I reminded them that I figured that by the time the President wanted definitive information from them as to what was happening, the Power Commission had better have some information. About ten minutes later they called me back and said, "Dr. Hornig, it's all under control; we now have an open line to the *Wall Street Journal*."

F.A. Their source of information was commercial, too, then?

D.H. Presumably the *Journal* was on the regular A.P. wire.

F.A. It's interesting to me that President Johnson called his Secretary of Defense, McNamara. Was there any hint, do you suppose, at the time that something other than a natural domestic problem had caused that?

D.H. Not really, but it's the first thing everyone worries about. Is it sabotage? Is it a prelude to something else? Is this Act I in an unfolding drama? There was no hint that there had been any kind of attack, but there was nothing to suggest that it might not have been sabotage. It happened dramatically and quickly, you know.

F.A. I recall it. I guess I was in college at the time. That happened in 1965. Was there any suggestion that President Johnson or McNamara were upset or concerned by the way they learned about it through other than official sources?

D.H. I don't think so. In fact there wasn't much time delay. The whole thing unfolded in about five minutes from when the first breakdown occurred near Buffalo to the time when New York lost power. That places a real strain on communications.

One of the communications failures was to the poor controller in New York who watched his voltage go down and his frequency go down and knew something was desperately wrong. But you know, voluntarily cutting out New York City from the power net is serious business. At that stage, at 6:00 at night when it was dark—remember this was winter—they were borrowing so much power from the outside that anything he did to isolate the city would have blacked it out. That's a great big decision to take. So he tried desperately to call Niagara Falls, at the other end of the big power trunk, where the power was coming from and where the trouble was coming from. He was trying to get the guy in Buffalo on the telephone and all he could get was a busy signal. So, while he was trying to get a phone call through, the whole system collapsed.

This all took minutes, so by the time the President heard it, the news couldn't have been more than a few minutes old. By the time it got through the whole sequence I have described I suppose another five or ten minutes elapsed, so it wasn't as if terrible things had been going on in the country without his being aware.

F.A. It is an interesting story...that the President was first alerted by his own car radio while he was down at his ranch in Texas.

D.H. Right.

F.A. Is your sense that today, for instance, if things went wrong like that, whether by natural causes or...

D.H. My sense is that it would work exactly the same way again because even in military situations it works that way. Once upon a time we looked into the way in which information got back from Vietnam in crisis situations. We looked for an episode which wasn't so big that it just had to get through quickly, and not so small that if you found that things didn't work, you'd say it's probably good judgment on somebody's part not to bother the White House. So, we picked the attack on the consulate in Hue, a middle range episode, and then looked to see how the news got to the White House.

Well, without going through the details, the first message in was a CIA intercept of a Reuters news dispatch which went directly from Hue over commercial cables to London, rather than our transmissions from Saigon which came in something like half an hour later.

Now, again, you couldn't say anything was grossly wrong. There was no national action that had to be taken, but again it illustrates that anytime anything happens in the world, lots of things start happening. In this case a semi-military channel functioned as it might be expected to function.

F.A. That's fascinating. I guess my sense is also that today things pretty much work along those kinds of lines.

D.H. That's all right! I think that's one of the strengths of the system.

I'm on a National Academy Committee which is looking at post-attack situations, and it's called Committee on a Survivable National Communications System. If you ask what the real hope for survivability is, it's probably not in hardness, but it probably is in redundancy, although you still have to make plans to put the remaining pieces together.

F.A. That's an interesting thought. Perhaps having these commercial nets strung out all over is really one of our strengths.[26]

It is plain that the U.S. national nervous system is a rich blend of the public and the private, of flesh-and-blood and artifact. Formats and processes come in people, and they come in things. But the technicalities of format and process, glamorous to some, pedestrian to others, often get blown out of proportion, absent perspective on what substance it is that the formats and processes can really deliver.

Jane, in Donald Barthelme's *Snow White,* writes to a Mr. Quistgaard, whose name she has seized from the telephone book: "It may never have crossed your mind to think that other universes of

[26] A'Hearn, Francis W., *Northeast Power Failure and Lyndon B. Johnson: Interview with Donald Hornig* (Cambridge, MA: Program on Information Resources Policy, Harvard University, 1983).

Figure 2-9. Decision Maker's Information-Seeking Processes

	From Inside Sources	From Outside Sources	From Personal Knowledge
Formal Processes	• Management information systems • Scanning • Special studies	• Media • National Association of Manufacturers, Committee for Economic Development, Harvard Program on Information Resources Policy, and so on. • Consultants • Market research firms	• Schooling • Training
Informal Processes	• "What do you think, Joe?" • "Psst...do you know that...?"	• Golf course • Cocktail parties	• Experience

discourse distinct from your own existed, with people in them, discoursing."[27]

Imagine a Universe of All Possible Discourse (UAPD, pronounced "whopped") that takes in Jane's, Mr. Quistgaard's, Fido's, Socrates', Attila the Hun's, Einstein's and so on, now, then, and forever. The Universe of an Organization's Decision-making Discourse (UODD, pronounced "would") lies within the UAPD, and exchanges new and old substance with it. In changing times, both the UAPD and the UODD are in flux.

The substance that a decision maker has in mind comes from the UAPD in three main ways: through inside the organization, through outside the organization, and through his or her personal knowledge. All three types of process may be either formal or informal. Figure 2-9 gives concrete examples of processes under the six heading combinations. The processes may go on regularly or sporadically, they may have short-term tactical or long-term strategic objectives, and they may produce new substance or confirm old. They occur in neither fixed nor universal mixes or sequences.

The formal processes inside an organization include its new-fangled computerized or its old-fashioned paper-driven management information systems or decision support systems (MIS or DSS—jargon and concomitant hype go in and out of fashion), the scanning activities of a

[27] Barthelme, Donald, *Snow White* (New York: Atheneum, 1967), 44.

corporate planning staff, or special studies made by *ad hoc* task forces set up to respond to some crisis. Informal processes include casual encounters at the water cooler or in the elevator, where you ask Joe and Jane what they think or else they tell you without being invited.

Formal processes outside an organization include the mass media's processes. They also include the doings of consultants, of market research firms, and of organizations like the National Association of Manufacturers, the Committee for Economic Development, Harvard's Program on Information Resources Policy, all the think tanks of various kinds that business people, professionals, and others set up as formal sources for the development of ideas, plus national or industrial espionage nets. Informal outside processes include meeting people on the golf course, over cocktails, or wherever Deep Throat lurks.

Finally, every decision maker pulls more or less substance out of his or her head. Some of this originally came from formal schooling or training of varied kinds. Other bits and pieces came in less formally through more or less deliberate personal experiences.

Formal or informal, these processes are mediated by what General John Cushman portrays as "living webs of systems,...mixes of man-made systems and of man himself, going through a swift, tumultuous, and challenging technological evolution which man must harness for maximum effectiveness in war and in its deterrence."[28] Both the large scope and the occasional informality of the processes are illustrated by Hornig's explicit references to the media and the telephone and by the implied role of other webs.

However pristine and pellucid one might imagine substance to be in the pure precincts of the UAPD, the web of systems through which the

---

[28] Cushman, John H., *Command and Control of Theater Forces: Adequacy* (Washington, DC: AFCEA International Press, 1985), 13–18. See also:

A'Hearn, Francis W., *The Information Arsenal: A C^3I Profile* (Cambridge, MA: Program on Information Resources Policy, Harvard University, 1983), 84–87.

Oettinger, Anthony G., *Whence and Whither Intelligence, Command and Control: The Certainty of Uncertainty* (Cambridge, MA: Program on Information Resources Policy, Harvard University, 1990). [Earlier version in *Proceedings of the 1989 Symposium on Command and Control Research* (McLean, VA: Information Systems Division, Science Applications International Corporation, 1989), 5–21.]

Oettinger, Anthony G., "A Bull's Eye View of Management and Engineering Information Systems," *Proceedings of the 19th National ACM Conference*, ACM Publication P 64 (New York, 1964). Reprinted in Alan F. Westin, *Information Technology in a Democracy* (Cambridge, MA: Harvard University Press, 1971), 250 ff.

Perry, William G., "Examsmanship in the Liberal Arts: A Study in Educational Epistemology," Harvard College, 1963. Reprinted in *Persuasive Writing: A College Reader*, Karl Zeender and Linda Morris, eds. (New York: Harcourt Brace Jovanovich, 1981).

decision maker sees that substance obscures it with the fog of war. Quite literally, as Carl von Clausewitz has observed, "fog prevents the enemy from being discovered in time." Figuratively, there is fog because "a great part of the information obtained in war is contradictory, a still greater part is false, and by far the greatest part is somewhat doubtful."[29] Or, as Donald Hornig's account has Defense Secretary McNamara putting it as he peered through the fog of peace: "Don, I just had a call from the boss, who said that the whole Northeast is blacked out. Do you know anything about it?"[30] Or, in what mercifully was only an exercise during the Jimmy Carter administration:

> Dr. Brzezinski got on the telephone and called the man you all have heard about who carries the little briefcase with all the codes inside, and said, "This is an exercise. I am the President of the United States. We have just gotten warning that a raid of nuclear warheads is en route to the United States. Get me out of here. This is an emergency exercise. We are going to war." The helicopter that is supposed to be on alert at all times, to land on the White House lawn and whisk away the National Command Authority, almost got shot down by the Secret Service. (By the way, this was kept secret for quite some time until it got blown in the newspapers, which is the only reason I am able to tell this story. I think we were ashamed of the horrible state of readiness we were in.) The sum and substance is that the exercise of trying to evacuate the National Command Authority was a nightmare, just a complete disaster.[31]

Beyond the thinkable or the unthinkable seen through a fog of war, of shooting war or of cold, in battlefield or office, marketplace or courtroom, beyond what is known like the fingers of one's hand and beyond even what is known to be unknown, like the number of jelly beans in a jar to be guessed at a fair, there looms much worse. How worse that might be is made plain by the following exchange that took place in a 1975 U.S. Senate hearing on Electronic Funds Transfer Systems (EFTS), specifically on the then new-fangled and controversial automated teller machines of banks. In this exchange, S.M. is Senator McIntyre, A.O. is Anthony Oettinger, and M.C. is Mr. Cox:

S.M. You referred in your statement that the plan to have technology that is being embraced here goes five years back—no, did you say twenty years?

---

[29] von Clausewitz, Carl, *On War* (Washington: Infantry Journal Press, 1950), 51–55.

[30] A'Hearn, *supra*, note 26 at 1.

[31] Rosenberg, Robert, "The Influence of Policy Making on C^3I," *Seminar on Command, Control, Communications and Intelligence, Spring 1980* (Cambridge, MA: Program on Information Resources Policy, Harvard University, 1980), 60.

A.O. I said the ideas for EFTS have been around for twenty years, the technology perhaps for ten.
S.M. Do you know what an Unk-Unk is?
A.O. Excuse me?
S.M. Do you know what an Unk-Unk is?
A.O. No, sir.
M.C. Are you going to tell us?
A.O. You have us in suspense now.
S.M. I am on the Subcommittee on Military R&D. That is known as "unknown unknown." Every time we start off on a research technology, we know there are certain unknowns, but the Unk-Unk is the unknown unknown. I think sometimes people worry about the unknown unknown.[32]

A Perfect Omniscience might have a totally clear and coherent overview of the boundless UAPD, as shown in Figure 2-10. Mere mortal decision makers, however, see only pieces of the UAPD and those only through a fog, dimly. Although capable of surmising the existence of Unk-Unks, a mortal can't act directly on that surmise, since one surely cannot ask a pointed question about what one doesn't know one doesn't know.

One person's piece of the UAPD may not even overlap with another's—"it may never have crossed your mind to think that other universes of discourse distinct from your own existed, with people in them, discoursing."[33] Yet, so long as there is active and intelligent life, each decision alters perceptions of the UAPD, and influences the next decision, in a continuing cycle.

2.7.2 Process and Organizational Survival

Making decisions, setting directions, laying down policy, exercising leadership is just one of the functions, the command function, of organizational nervous systems. Another is the function of intelligence gathering, probing the surroundings to see, to understand, and to evaluate threats and opportunities—in short, to inform before decisions are made. Once intelligence has informed, command ordains autocratically, democratically, collectively, or however. The control

[32] U.S. Congress, Senate, Committee on Banking, Housing and Urban Affairs, *Electronic Funds Transfer Moratorium Act of 1975: Hearings Before the Subcommittee on Financial Institutions*, 94th Cong., 1st Sess., March 14, 1975 (Washington, DC: GPO, 1975), 176.

[33] Barthelme, *supra,* note 27.

Figure 2-10. Unk-Unks and the Fog of War

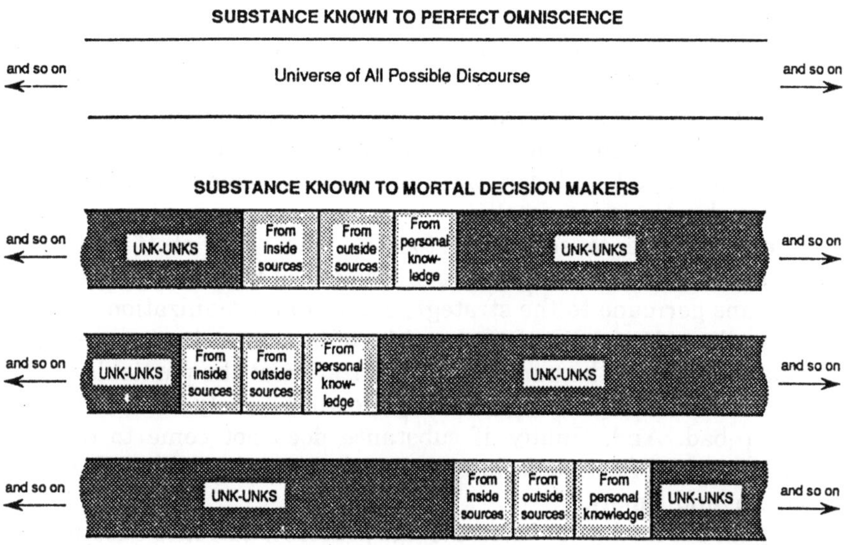

function then monitors what is done, tries to figure out what has happened, and adjusts future actions accordingly. Intelligence, command, and control (I-C-C) functions are essential for any organism or organization, a paramecium or the Pentagon.

This way of tagging the needs at different stages of decision-making cycles and of tagging the nervous system functions that meet these needs is far from a universal language. Business people and business schools might, for instance, put scanning for intelligence, strategic planning for command, and reporting for control. Media-oriented folk see in the intelligence need the finer grain of substance needed for escape, social connection, surveillance, and opinion formation/decision making. Professional intelligence people see intelligence as still much finer grained.[34]

Reality defies these attempts to lay a veneer of order on it. Nonetheless, any organization that wants to survive must keep on getting the "right" information to the "right" people at the "right" time by whatever means are at hand, especially so while its ends are changing. All those quoted rights signify the almost total lack of

[34] Cline, *supra,* note 7; see also Graham, Daniel O., "Quality in U.S. Intelligence," in *Intelligence Requirements for the 1980's: Elements of Intelligence*, Roy Godson, ed. (Washington, DC: National Strategic Information Center, 1983), 21–23.

agreement about what right information might be, who the right people are, and what the right time is.[35] What consensus there is tends to prevail retroactively. For mortals what matters is an edge over nature, competitors, or the enemy—not perfection. Armies, it is said, win wars, not because they are perfect, but because they fight other armies. In business, likewise, it is not perfection that succeeds, but an edge over the competition. And knowing how to make fire gave mankind an edge long before the beginnings of scientific understanding of combustion processes.

There is some consensus as to what the right stuff might be; accurate, selective substance is one element of rightness. Here *selective* means germane to the strategic goals of an organization, and not merely selected according to some whim or by some criterion unrelated to what matters to the particular organization at the particular time. Right also means a process fast enough to allow timely reaction to good news or bad. And, finally, if substance does not come to decision makers in an effective format, it is of no value even if accurate, selective, and timely.

As with the media, new formats and processes call into question the substance, format, and process bundles to which decision makers have grown accustomed, their organizational nervous systems. The informal bundles are affected as much as the formal when the whole world can gather round the water cooler by phone while remote terminals make the home office's formal database accessible from remote branches or outposts. The exercise of responsibility and authority in turn influences what substance, format, and process bundles will be in hand at the next turn of the wheel, if for no other reason than that the nervous system of any organization is always home made.

2.8 CHARTING CHANGE: THE INFORMATION BUSINESS MAP

Information businesses casting about for what to sell next and all organizations with their own evolving nervous systems need means whereby to chart their diverse and often colliding courses.

The makeup, the names, the uses, the legal, business, and social baggage of older bundles of information resources—information products and services among them—can get in the way of fresh, creative thinking. Future possibilities are seen so dimly and usually with so

[35] For a classic description of these dilemmas, see: Wohlstetter, Roberta, *Pearl Harbor: Warning and Decision* (Palo Alto, CA: Stanford University Press, 1962).

little consensus that they alone cannot give a firm base for planning and acting. These conditions are hardly new. Unbundling information goods into their substance, format, and process building blocks helps clarify their history, hence better understand their present state and sort out the key issues to address in charting a course into the future.

Changing information technologies have long served up new formats, new processes, and doubts about the value of their novelty:

> Both to ignorant illiterates and to sophisticated Platonists written record was a dubious gift, because it seemed to kill living eloquence and trust and substitute for them a mummified semblance in the form of a piece of parchment. Henry I's partisans in the dispute with Anselm, who had called a papal bull a sheepskin "blackened with ink and weighted with a little lump of lead," were arguing for the priority of the personal testimony of the three bishops who exercised memory over the mere "external marks" of a writing.[36]

In the realm of the media, the steam-driven printing press made mass-produced books, newspapers, and magazines possible, although it was far from the sole determinant of the details of the makeup and the timing of these developments. Marconi's wireless made possible the radio and the television industries and helped telephony leap across oceans. Celluloid and other inventions ultimately got woven into the motion picture, disk, and tape-recording businesses.[37]

These businesses expanded the variety of ways in which users could get substance. Alone, new formats and new processes create new types of substance only insofar as the medium is the message. They may favor expressing one kind of substance over another. What works in the marketplace for video news is different from what worked in the marketplace for photo stills or for woodcuts.

Mostly, new formats and new processes have made substance more accessible. Film helped move vaudeville, for example, from the immediate experience of only those in the theater at the moment of the show to a widespread audience, all of whom could see the same show both at different times and in various places. Television took this one step further, making such entertainment even more widespread and convenient. Television, at least in the United States, also switched marketing processes from exacting admission prices from audiences to selling audiences to advertisers. Radioed and televised news shows essentially present the substance that was traditionally the news in

---

[36] Clanchy, *supra*, note 1 at 233.

[37] Altick, Richard D., *The English Common Reader: A Social History of the Mass Reading Public, 1800–1900* (Chicago: Chicago University Press, 1957), 318–20.

newspapers and, before that, was spread by personal letter or by word of mouth. The format changed, but not, within limits, the substance. Audio tapes are primarily a variant of the disk recording format. And so on. This leaves aside the by no means self-evident qualitative implications of such changes in scale as from whistle-stop campaigns, where a candidate can touch thousands, to TV campaigns, where a candidate can touch millions,[38] or from Genghis Khan to Stalin, whom Daniel Bell[39] once described as Genghis Khan with a telephone.

Even the hindsight of history has not clearly mapped the highways, let alone the byways, of such evolutions. They certainly were not visible prospectively. Contemporary quandaries over the best way to authenticate compunications-mediated transactions, as with credit cards and other plastic, echo alternatives explored in the evolution of authentication methods during the transition from memory to written records in England:

> Rather similar in function to charters, though different in format, are chirographs. A chirograph recorded an agreement between two parties.... Unlike a charter, each of the parties received a copy of the agreement, usually authenticated by the seal of the other party. The method is described in detail, probably because it was still relatively unfamiliar, in an agreement made before papal judges delegate between the prior of Luffield and John, vicar of Towcester, in c. 1215:
>
> > This composition is reduced into a duplicate writing, made in the form of chirograph, of which writing [*scriptura*] the prior of Luffield is to have one document [*scriptum*] sealed with the seals of the judges and of John, while John is to have the other document sealed with the seals of the judges and of the prior.
>
> The document was thus written out in duplicate and then cut in half. Across the line of the cut, before it was made, was written in capital letters a formula such as JUSTUS DOMINUS ET JUSTICIAS (an extract from Psalms XI, 7) or the word CHIROGRAPHUM. Forgery of one part could thus be checked by aligning the severed formula with its counterpart. As a further precaution, the cut was often made by a wavy or indented line instead of a straight one. This practice grew so common in the later Middle Ages that chirographs became generally known as "indentures."[40]

---

[38] Abramson, Jeffrey B., F. Christopher Arterton, and Gary R. Orren, *The Electronic Commonwealth: The Impact of New Media Technologies on Democratic Politics* (New York: Basic Books, 1988); and Boorstin, *supra*, note 2.

[39] Daniel Bell, Henry Ford II Professor of Social Sciences, Emeritus, private communication 1970.

[40] Clanchy, *supra*, note 1 at 65–66. See also Pool, Ithiel de Sola, *Forecasting the Telephone: A Retrospective Technology Assessment* (Norwood, NJ: Ablex Publishing Corp., 1983), 71–72.

Transposed into a contemporary key, that passage could be from an account of the evolution of smart cards.

The contemporary evolution of media and of all other bundles of information resources continues this age-old evolution. New technologies, such as computers, provide an ever-greater array of formats and processes and hence such new ways of getting substance as by television's showing the first moon landing at the very instant when it happened.

It should go without saying that new technology is born within a social, political, and economic setting; new technology is applied within the norms, stretched or not, of the society, the polity, and the market, and that, when this technology in turn reacts with these social settings, all of them change again in what is, barring a cosmic or a nuclear accident, an endless cycle. But this cannot go without also noting, given the fashion among some to see technology as an end in itself—or at least as leading toward its own inexorable ends—what Alvin Toffler said in his opening lines to *Future Shock*: "This is a book about what happens to people when they are overwhelmed by change...the roaring current of change, a current so powerful today that it overturns institutions, shifts our values and shrivels our roots. Change is the process by which the future invades our lives,..."[41] That debate on the nature of technology is not pursued here.

However, the weave of the fabric must be expressed explicitly here, at least to the extent that Figure 2-8 already has expressed it. No medium, no information business, is an island. Figure 2-8 samples connections among media segments by format along a continuum of producers of substance and of processors.

In addition to the conventionally recognized mass media, there are here as in other industries component businesses that provide specific services, often solely within the industry and not to final consumers. These include producers of programming, of substance, for the video format; they include wholesalers, processors, for books and magazines. Figure 2-8 also shows that the media industry, like any other, needs infrastructure industries that support the media functions without directly participating in these functions, at least in the recent past and in the United States. These catalysts include telephone companies, banks, computer manufacturers and programmers, paper manufacturers, and other suppliers of equipments and services. Competitors for media organizations have also come out of this infrastructure amid conflicts mostly unexpected when they first happened.

[41] Toffler, Alvin, *Future Shock* (New York: Random House, 1970), 3.

2.8.1 Plotting Your Place(s) on the Map

The fundamental question for all information businesses, the media among them, is how best to match substance for which there is a demand (market demand or administered demand) with formats and with processes that can meet that demand in the most advantageous way.

Every organization faces essentially that very same fundamental question, but asked about the organization's nervous system. Some organizations themselves make most of their own nervous system. They run a little inside information business. Other organizations mostly buy outside, both substance and form. But whatever the mix of make or buy, no organization can escape, if not the responsibility for, then at least the effects of, the structure and the performance of their own nervous system.

The Information Business Map (described in Chapter 1) is a tool that was developed to help address that fundamental question from either the purveyor's or the user's standpoint. Translated into Dutch, French, German, Italian, Japanese, and Swedish (at last count), and used on paper and diskette media, the Map has been widely used to chart business plans in information businesses and plans for the internal nervous systems in all kinds of organizations.

The Map helps to chart both the past and the future by laying out relationships among basic building blocks in a way that helps to fend off being trapped in the past or taken in by the future. It does this by blending abstract but conventional economic building blocks with the substance, format, and process components of information resources, and by displaying labels for entities that live and breathe in the here and now and do not just sigh for the past or pant for the future.

The Map's vertical axis (Figure 2-11[42]) ranges from products in the south to services in the north. The polar product–service distinction is common to both business practice and academic economics. At one pole, the idea of service connotes the consumer's continuing interaction with or dependence on the provider of the service. At the other extreme, a product in its purest form implies no interaction—at least no necessary interaction—between supplier and consumer once something has been bought. Interaction is a matter of degree. The sale of products and the sale of services can be combined into mixed strategies—hence a continuum of possibilities between the poles.

---

[42] McLaughlin, John F. with Anne Louise Antonoff, *Mapping the Information Business* (Cambridge, MA: Program on Information Resources Policy, Harvard University, 1986), Figure 3.

The horizontal axis draws on the ideas of substance, format, and process. Format-and-process combined as form define the west end of the horizontal axis. This is in keeping with the idea of a formal or operating plane devoid of substance that was set forth in section 2.4. The east end is pure substance. Figure 2-12 suggests a meaning for the east–west continuum. The five sample substance axes show increasing information value-added in visual metaphors akin to those used to show the radio news bundle and the newspaper news bundle in Figure 2-4 and Figure 2-5.

Books, at the southeast corner of the Map, are substantive products as quintessential as they come. The corporeal forms, the tokens, for items at the east end are of far less consequence than the substantive aspects of these items. Even the pattern of their formats matters not in comparison to their substance. A book is bought mainly for what it says, not for the paper it's printed on.

Of course, real-world books are never disembodied. That means that some can find expensive leather bindings beautiful, they can thrill to the touch of particularly fine rag paper, they may glory in the magnificence of gilt illustrations or, with French-produced books of the old style, they can derive perverse joy from slicing through virgin signatures that no one else has read before. But those aesthetic considerations are, in most instances and for most people, but a small element of what a book is prized for.[43] Likewise, book burning is usually seen as an aberration, a brutish political act, although better the warmth from burning books than death by freezing. These exceptions merely prove the rule. When most of us casually think of a book, we think of what it says, not of how it is made and surely not of the fact that it is an ink-on-paper token. If anything, we are more likely to notice whether the book is hard cover or paperback, which alters the price of a book but not its substance.

Like the word *book,* the other entries inside the Map frame are words that are current as of the Map's date. This means that there is hard evidence of some active business or group of businesses that actually and publicly calls itself by the entry. No entry denotes some configuration that existed in the past or else might be envisaged for the future, but without known instance here and now.

Evidence for the existence of the bundle denoted by a word is its widespread usage in transactions or, at the very least, the existence of a trade association, a newsletter, or some other substantial evidence of a self-conscious and active business group actually selling something,

[43] The "ergonomic" advantages of print over electronic presentations of information, especially for users in certain situations, are discussed further in Chapter 6.

Figure 2-11. The Information Business Map: Placement Aids

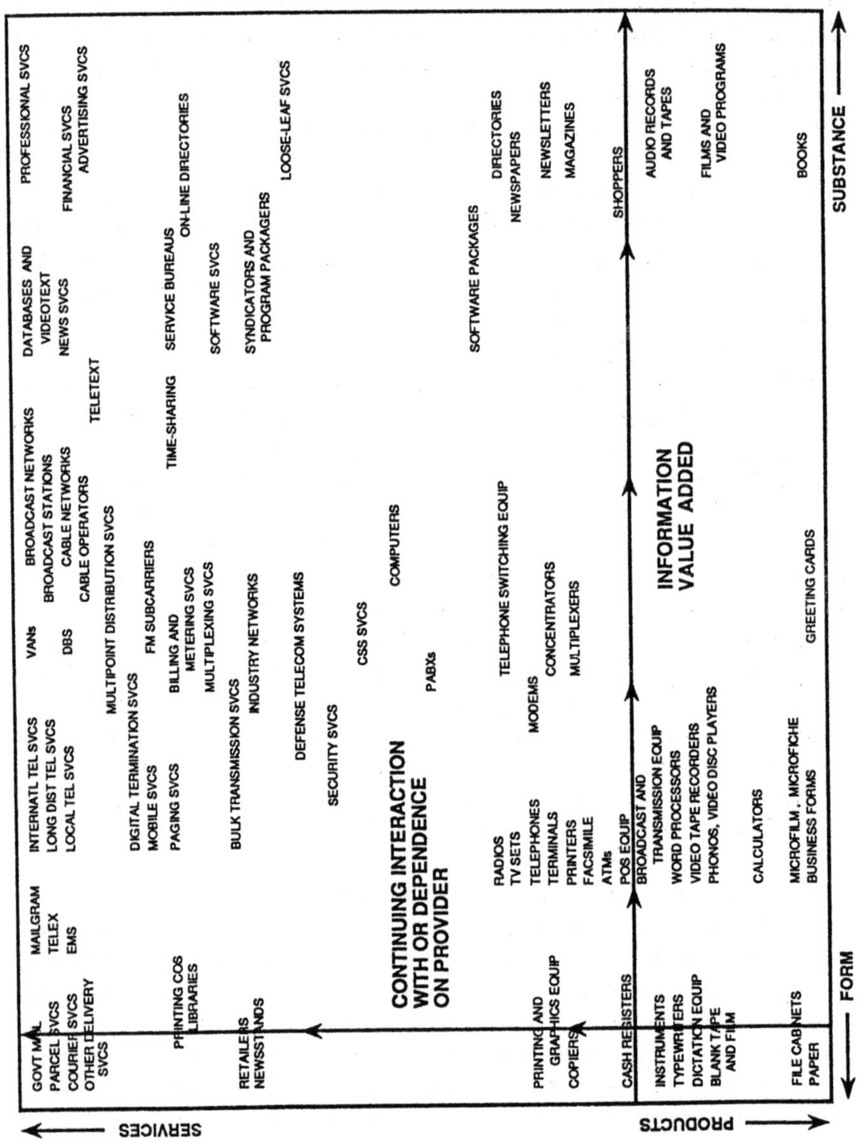

Figure 2-12. The Meaning of Information Value-Added

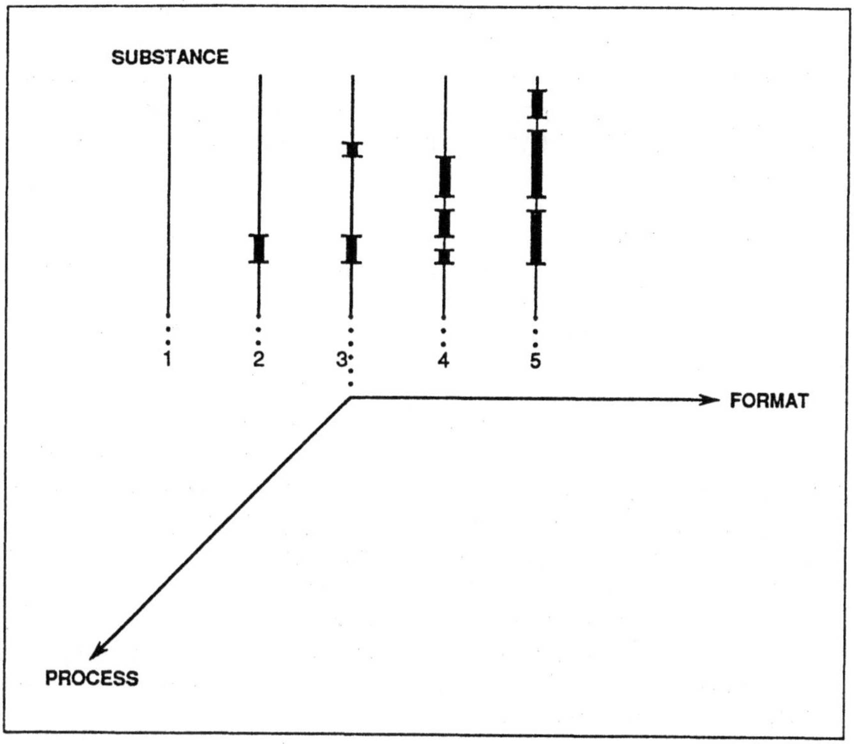

even pie in the sky, for example, a videotex newsletter, an electronic mail newsletter, and so on.

This stress on explicit evidence for active existence accounts for the absence of organizational nervous system names from the Map, despite the claims made about the usefulness of organizational nervous systems to every organization and not just to information businesses. The names used for information resources within organizations are often idiosyncratic, not generic. And insofar as an organization takes its nervous system for granted, it may not even have words for the system or for the system's private parts.

Compared to information suppliers, information consumers are under little pressure to seek common and widely recognized terms. The burden is thus unavoidable for information consumer readers to identify from the supplier labels inside the Map what things they do for themselves, what things they get done for them by outsiders, and what things they don't do at all.

The entries in the Map are names of products or services or lines of business, and not of companies. One company might encompass only one of these products or services among its lines of business, or it might include several. The fact that some of the names coincide with common names of certain types of corporate entities is coincidental. This is the case for *Newspapers,* which means that traditional product and not the corporate entity that produces it. Figure 2-15, coming up shortly, shows why this matters.

Paper, in the southwest corner, epitomizes purely formal products. An empty piece of paper conveys no substance whatever, at least within the convention that substance is only what writing, printing, or drawing denote. A piece of blank paper left as a book mark clearly says "here is where you were," but, like the smelling or the burning of a book, this iconic use of a blank piece of paper is a practice that is noted but not given great significance here.

Business—or government—*Forms* are mapped to the right of blank *Paper* but way to the left of *Books.* This reflects the judgment that forms embody slightly more substance than a blank piece of paper but far less than a book. The headings of a form like IRS 1040 themselves convey some substance. The headings, rulings, and other elements of the form constrain what additional substance might be entered on the form. Here again, we cast aside such common perversions as scribbling on the back of a form or making a paper airplane of it. The Map is a tool for rough and ready reckoning, not for picking a way through the shoals of recondite conundrums.

Up in the northwest corner of the Map, *Government Mail* epitomizes formal services. Government mail is a service. One cannot use it without continuing to interact with, and to depend on, its provider. It is a formal service in that control over substance rests with the consumer of the service, not with its provider. Aberrations such as wartime censorship by the military or peacetime steaming open of mail by intelligence agencies are ignored here. So is the minimal amount of substantive interaction implied by postal use of the address to route the mail. The positioning of *Mailgram* and *Telephone Services* somewhat to the right of government mail reflects the greater economic possibilities for substantive manipulation of information in those businesses. These possibilities touch off much controversy about the evolving roles of the telecommunications and the mail industries, specifically, over how much their activities might or might not be permitted to spill over into the activities of the data processing and the media industries, and vice versa.

Last of the extremes of the Map, *Professional Services* lie in the northeast corner. A doctor in his or her diagnostic or prescription-writing capacity, but not in the meat-cutting capacity, epitomizes purely substantive professional information services. What value there is in the service attaches to the substance gathered or conveyed. Surgeons, by contrast, are valued for combining the know-what-to-do which distinguishes them from the barbers of old with the finely tuned know-how-to-do-it that sets them apart from butchers.

The Map has its limitations. Positioning an entry along either axis is somewhat subjective. As a general rule, items are set in the Map as seen by a customer. But different customers could place the same item differently along either axis. To some degree, providers might place things differently from customers. This may be less a shortcoming of the mapping technique than an accurate rendering of the structural ambiguities of the information business.

Like geographical maps, the Information Business Map is limited by two dimensions. Some items that overlap conceptually show up above, below, or next to one another for visual clarity. The information conveyed is selective and limited, although one might display terms such as *Computers, Mail,* or *Telephone* in large, heavy type and *FM Subcarriers* or *Newsletters* in small type to differentiate their relative annual sales. The differentiations made in Figure 2-13[44] are finer grained than those on the Map; that is, Figure 2-13's entries indicate many more properties (qualities) of a good than where it lies on the product–service axis or the form–substance axis.

These mapping rules do not show numerous components that are integral parts of the information business. *Semiconductors, Optical Character Recognition Devices,* and *Electric Power,* for example, are integral to many of the entries. These items are excluded from the Map, but *Paper* and *Telephone Switches* are in. It is often difficult to tell whether something is a component worthless in isolation, a generic technology, or an end product that belongs on the Map.

Whether a particular item is included and where it is put also depends on the chosen level of aggregation. For simplicity, for example, *Financial Services* is one entry in the basic Map of Figure 2-11. Figure 2-14 shows how further disaggregation of financial services into specific products or services might cause substantial relocations in every direction. *Newspapers* is a single item toward the southeast of the Map. This placement reflects the whole of the traditional newspaper bundle. If the newspaper were unbundled into news, classified ads, horoscopes, comics, crossword puzzles, stock quotations, and so on,

---

[44] Adapted from Oettinger, Anthony G., *Elements of Information Resources Policy: Library and Other Information Services* (Cambridge, MA: Program on Information Resources Policy, Harvard University, 1975), Figure 4; based on earlier work with Vincent E. Giuliano.

Figure 2-13. Differentiating Traits of Information Business

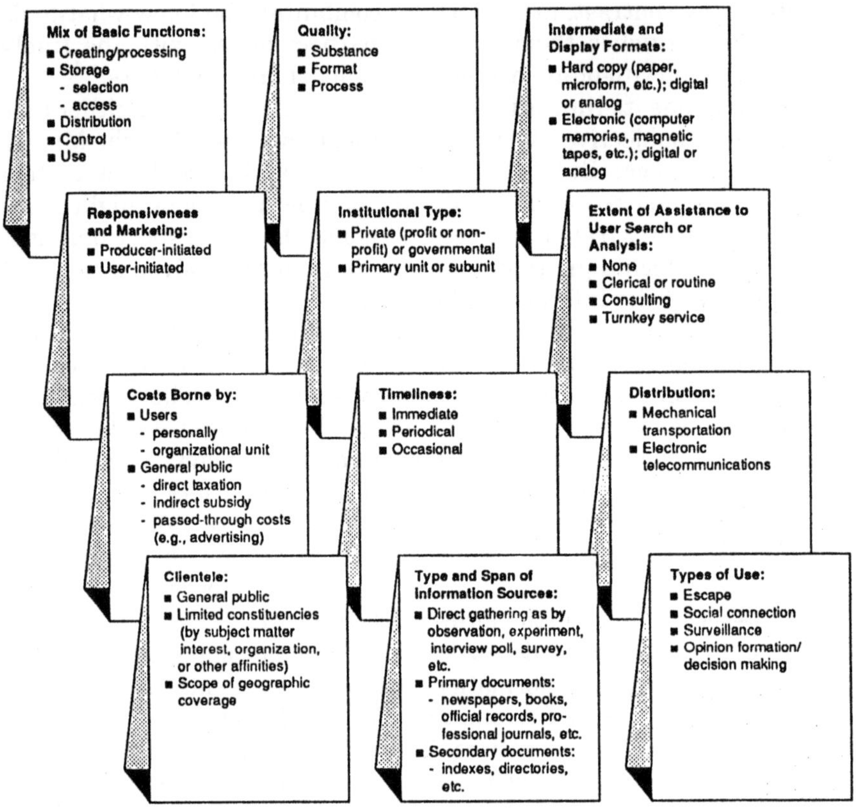

some of these pieces would go closer to *Books,* some closer to *Professional Services,* and so on.

Computers go squarely in the middle, because, if disaggregated, they would literally be all over the Map. Computers are marketed as products or as services with all possible mixes in between. A computer bereft of its operating system, not to speak of its application software, is as emptily formal, not to say inert, as a blank piece of paper. Like the empty paper it, too, has limitless substantive potential. A one-purpose computer, like some of the early game-playing or educational devices trotted out before Christmas, is as set in its substantive repertoire as one book is. The nature and scope of its programming determine where any particular computer falls between east and west.

How a *Newspaper* and a *Newspaper Company* differ leaps out of

Figure 2-14. Map Entry Location Depends on Aggregation Level

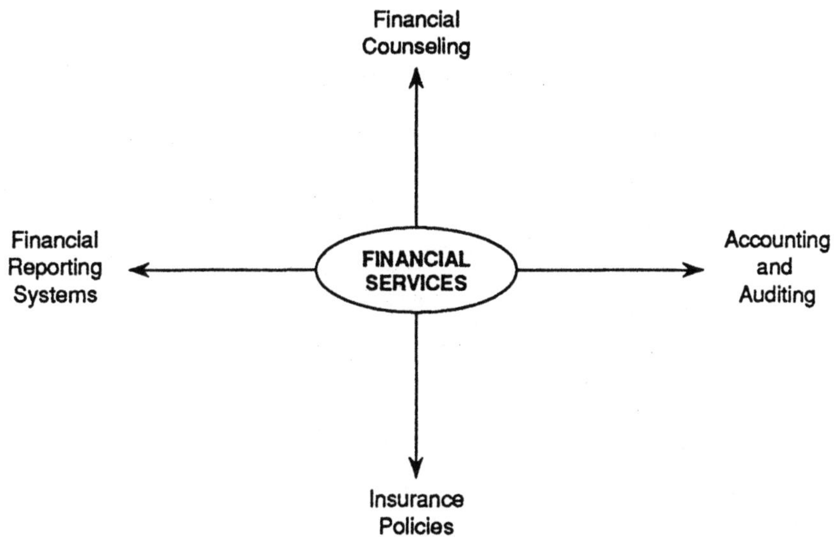

Figure 2-15.[45] The aggregated activities of Dow Jones & Company, Gannett Company, Harte-Hanks Communications, Lee Enterprises, New York Times, The Times Mirror Company, and the Washington Post Company are plotted on this Map. Each company is generally classified as a newspaper publisher. Each indeed publishes at least one newspaper, as denoted by the heavy oval around the newspaper entry. Each company is also in the lines of business marked by the other ovals. As many lines link the *Newspaper* entry with the other entries as there were companies in each of the other lines of business as of 1983–84. Newspaper companies, far from confined to producing newspapers, are literally all over the Map. So, as it happens, are telephone companies.

AT&T's activities before its 1984 divestiture are depicted in Figure 2-16.[46] Under the terms of the settlement of an antitrust suit brought by the United States, the new AT&T company, smaller because divested of its local operating companies, was freed to enter essentially all lines of business shown as entries on the Map.

---

[45] McLaughlin, *supra,* note 42 at Figure 39.

[46] McLaughlin, *supra,* note 42 at Figure 24.

Figure 2-15. Newspaper Company Lines of Business

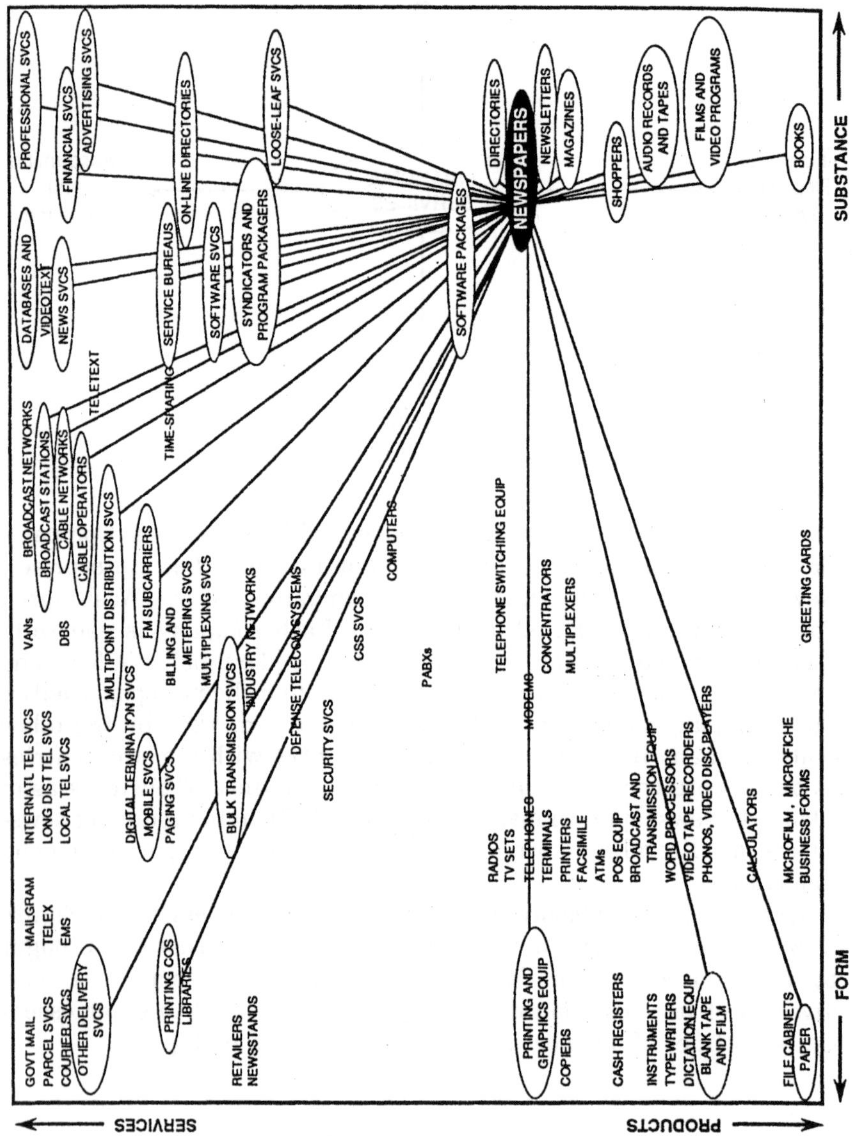

Figure 2-16. AT&T Presettlement Lines of Business

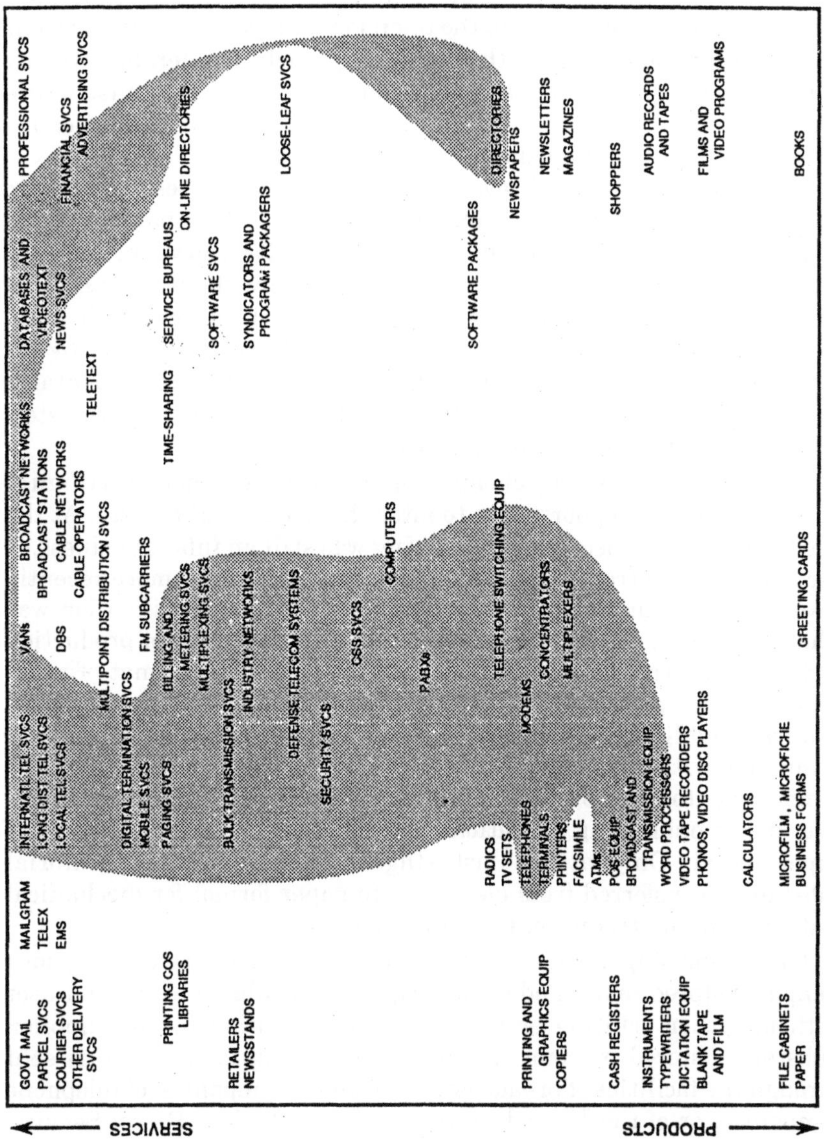

With both newspaper companies and telephone companies all over the map, the possibility of competition, conflict, and compromise among these institutions became actuality in bitter legislative and regulatory debates beginning about 1980. The debates got all the more acrimonious, since the newspaper companies perceived that, because they increasingly depended on the telephone companies to supply their vital telecommunications, they are singularly vulnerable to any anticompetitive actions by telephone companies in those arenas where the two might compete. The Map helps to make this evolutionary ferment visible and immediate.

As noted in Chapter 1, ever since the printing press came into widespread use, the publishing business has encompassed stable bundles from the corners of the Map. Figure 2-17[47] shows the publishing industry through the 1970s and, quite likely, the way much of it will stay for the foreseeable future. This picture differs little from when Benjamin Franklin was publishing the *Pennsylvania Gazette* out of his printing office while serving, perhaps not just coincidentally, first as postmaster at Philadelphia and later as deputy postmaster-general for British Colonial America.

The advent of relatively cheap compunications technologies (Figure 2-18[48]) brought the opportunity to alter the traditional process. At the start of the 1980s, electronic publishing was still an infant business. It used elements of traditional publishing combined with more recently developed and bundled elements. The first stage of modification was wholly internal, affecting the formats and the processes of production and their internal formats, but not the presentation format of products. By 1980, most daily newspaper operations, and many magazine and book publishing operations, had text entered into computers via terminals with video display. Editors retrieved the text from the computer onto their own video displays for editing. Internally, therefore, many publishing operations were already electronic instead of paper based. Only at the last stage of production was editorial substance transferred from electronic to paper format for mechanical distribution and traditional consumption.

The second stage, emerging in the early eighties, was making such computer-stored text—and some graphics—available to the end user without either printing or mechanical distribution by the supplier. Substance, stored by computer in electronic digital formats, is sent through the facilities of broadcasters, of CATV companies, of telephone companies, or of the United States Mail, The United Parcel Service,

---

[47] McLaughlin, *supra,* note 42 at Figure 44.

[48] McLaughlin, *supra,* note 42 at Figure 41.

Figure 2-17. The Traditional Publishing Process

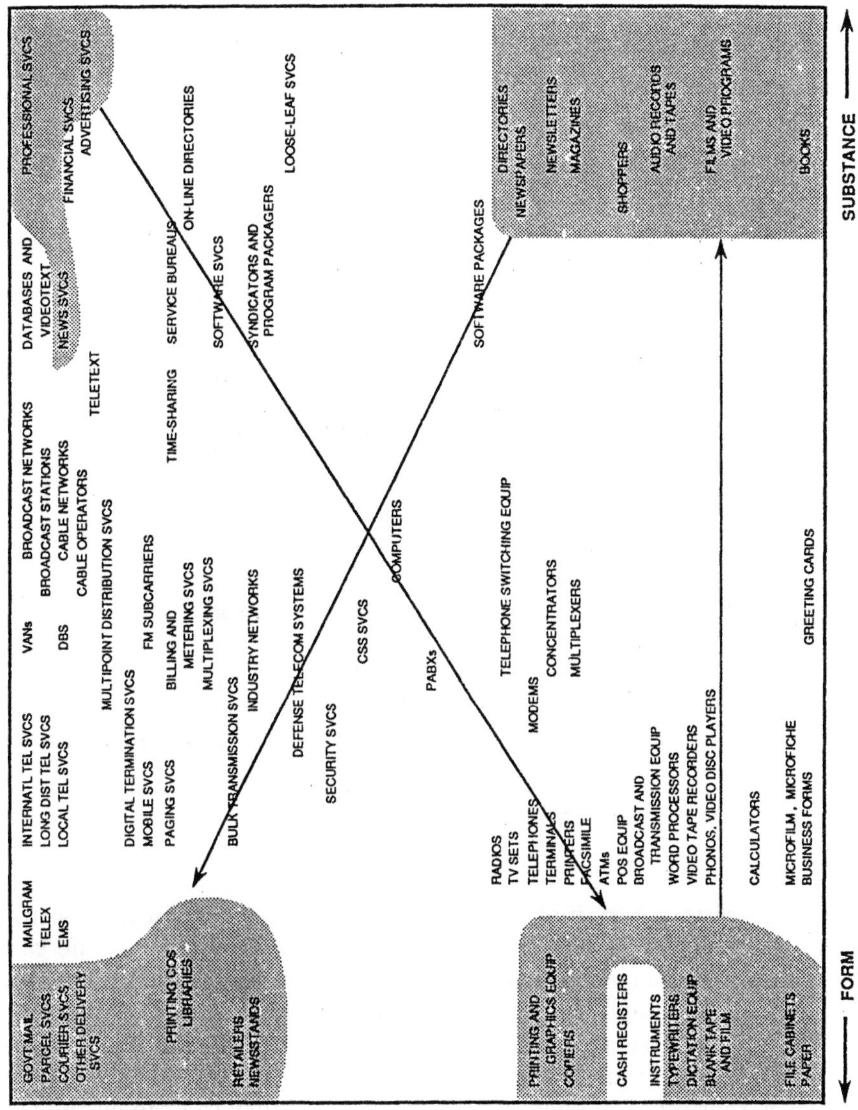

Figure 2-18. Widening Cost Spread Favoring Compunications Technologies over Traditional Information Technologies

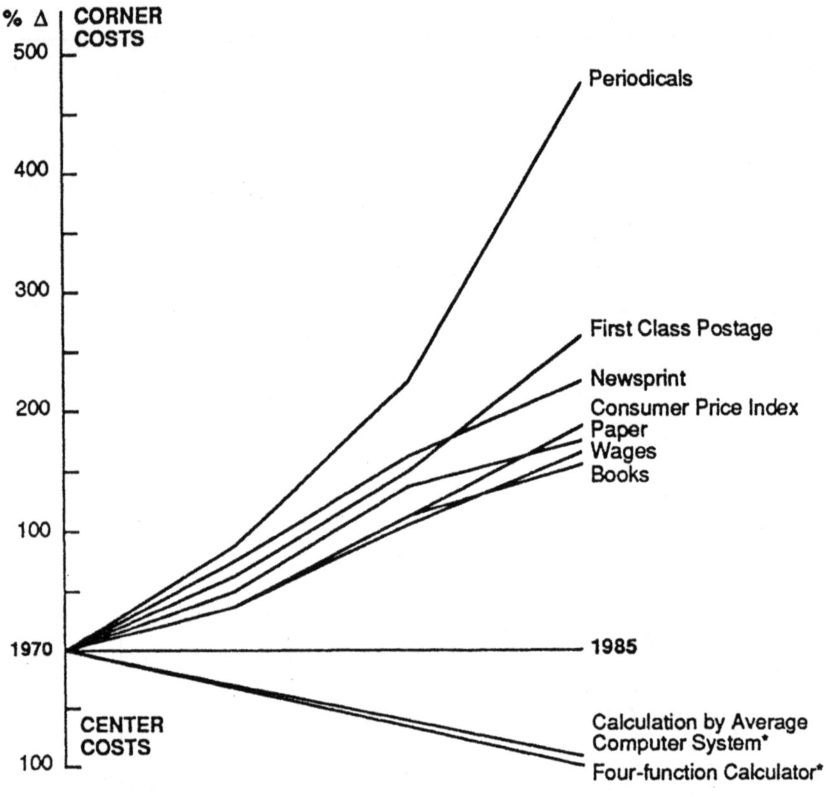

*Program on Information Resources Policy data.

and others to a terminal at the consumer site, either in an institutional setting or, less frequently in the early eighties than by the late eighties, in a home. The effect is a migration from the higher cost corners of the Map toward the lower cost center (Figure 2-19[49]).

A variety of services can be offered. At one extreme, the service might be a continuous offering of a whole database, as in a teletex service that gives the end user at most the ability to grab on the fly one or more frames or pages of substance as it goes by. This is like

[49] McLaughlin, *supra,* note 42 at Figure 42.

Figure 2-19. Corner–Center Cost Differentials

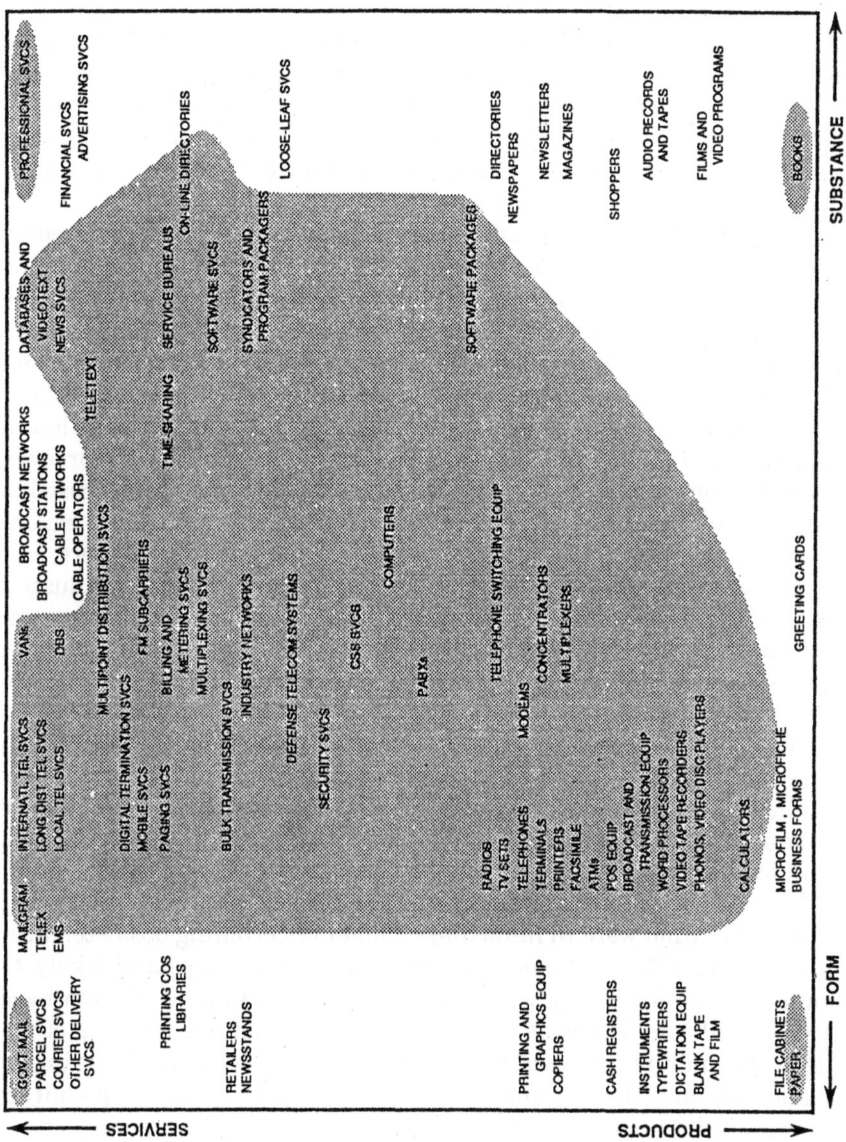

selling a conventional printed database limited in size mainly by the existing technology and the economics of the production and delivery. From such a product, the reader picks and reads only what interests him or her. For example, a newspaper is theoretically expandable to include everything that has been written by local writers, plus all of the wire service and syndicated service copy that has come in since the last edition. The constraints on the size and speed of the presses, the capacity and cost of trucks and of labor, the cost of newsprint, and the like, are what require a more limited product to be made. A teletex service is constrained by acceptable response times for finding a requested frame.

The size of the effective database can be substantially increased by limiting transmission to only what a user actually requests. This mode of operation is an interactive service. In this case, the primary constraint is on the size of the computer needed to store the substance and to handle multiple users simultaneously. Transmission is more elaborate than in a service of the teletex type, since a selection and ordering signal from the user to the supplier is needed in addition to the substantive transmission from the supplier to the user. Moreover, the substance sent from the publisher's computer must be addressed to the specific individual who requested it—a more complex and expensive task than making frames or pages available to all grabbers.

A new set of players started to come into the publishing industry. They included electronic goods distributors such as Tandy Corporation; data processing specialists, such as H&R Block's CompuServe; banks, such as Citibank and BankOne (Ohio); enhanced-service telecommunications firms, like GTE's Telenet and, of course, AT&T. In addition, many firms already in the publishing industry were experimenting with or deploying ventures ranging from pieces of electronic publishing enterprises to full systems. Among these were Times Mirror Company, Dow Jones, CBS, Reader's Digest, Time Incorporated, Knight-Ridder, and Cox Communications.

None of the foregoing implies that traditional hardcopy publishing and distribution were in immediate danger of becoming obsolete. Most of the early efforts at electronic publishing that appeared likely to compete with hard copy were not successful, and many of them have been abandoned. However, for the longer-term picture, the Map of the electronic publishing process (Figure 2-20[50]) shows the blurring of boundaries and the movement toward the center of the Map characteristic of the information business since the 1930s.

---

[50] McLaughlin, *supra,* note 42 at Figure 45.

Figure 2-20. Electronic Publishing

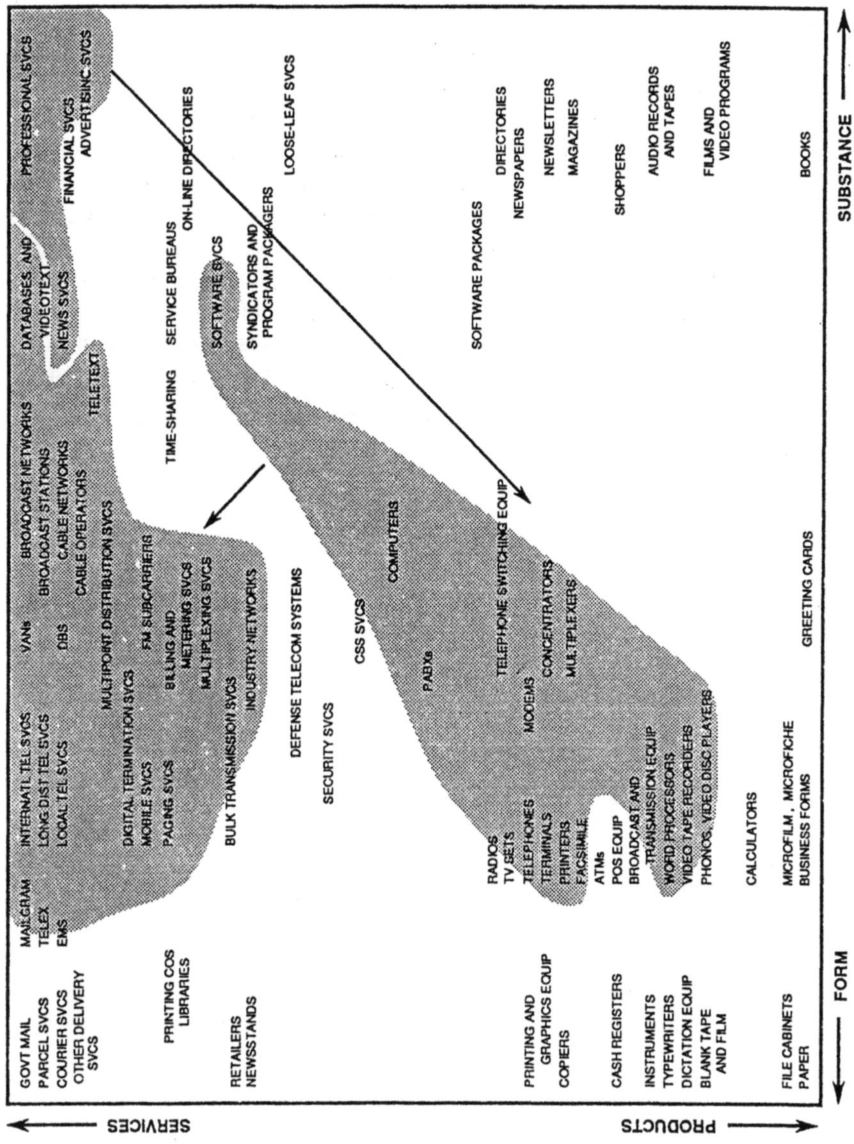

Figure 2-20 shows electronic publishing processors still firmly anchored in human professional services, much as they were in Benjamin Franklin's time. Despite recurrent predictions of revolution, this has remained the stablest of all factors in publishing. The production tools, however, are increasingly compunications based, in combinations determined at least as much by political and policy factors as by technology.

It is not only that processes for creating or gathering substance are changing slowly. The processes of information manipulation, storage, and transmission have been subject to rapid change, along with the formats for both internal production and ultimate presentation to the user. The substance being delivered has not itself changed as rapidly. Consequently, the editorial front end remains relatively unaffected by changes in process and format. Reporters still have to get a story, write it, and have it edited. Photographers, graphic designers, advertising salespeople, filmmakers, and others will continue to perform tasks similar to today's, though perhaps with different equipment and priorities.

3

The Abundant and Versatile Digital Way*

Anthony G. Oettinger

3.1 A CONVERGENCE OF FUNCTION AND FORM: COMPUNICATIONS TECHNOLOGIES

Once upon a time people perceived computing and communications processes as distinct and independent from one another. After World War II, this view gradually shaded into a perception of computing and communications as bundled inextricably into computing-and-communications processes, *compunications* processes for short. The unity of computer and communications science and technology, a commonplace by the 1980s, was still noteworthy in the late 1960s. As I wrote then: "The spectacular growth of *compunications* fortunately has given us powerful tools and techniques for the quick handling of masses of data. (Computers and communications have long since become inseparable. It is time to reflect this union in the fusion of their names.)"[1]

A decade later it was widely understood that the unity of the

* This chapter is adapted from Oettinger, Anthony G., *The Abundant and Versatile Digital Way* (Cambridge, MA: Program on Information Resources Policy, Harvard University, 1985).

[1] Oettinger, Anthony G., "Compunications in the National Decision-making Process," in *Computers, Communications, and the Public Interest,* Martin Greenberger, ed. (Baltimore: The Johns Hopkins University Press, 1971), 74.

For the record, the word *compunications* was coined by my wife, Marilyn, when we were sitting in front of a fire in Harvard's Kendall House, on Sutton Island, Maine, in August 1969.

scientific and technological base[2] had implications for industry structure, and that it had political overtones as well. In 1978, Simon Nora and Alain Minc wrote for the president of France words translated into English by 1980 as: "This increasing interconnection between computer and telecommunications—which we will term 'telematics'—opens radically new horizons." Nora and Minc commented in a note that the neologism *telematics* "closely resembles the term used in the United States, 'compunication.'" They added: "The fact that the American term stresses the computer and ours the telecommunications aspect is not accidental. It expresses a set of power relationships that in France give the upper hand to the latter."[3]

In the 1940s, no one quite likely had seen even the basic unity itself. Claude Shannon, whose pioneering work did much to reveal that unity, described his seminal work as "a mathematical theory of communication." Wrote he: "The fundamental problem of communication is that of reproducing at one point either exactly or approximately a message selected at another point."[4]

The classical 1940s perception of computers shown in Figure 3-1A saw them as bundles of five basic functions, none of them communications.

Processing is the computer's reason for being. Game playing, word processing, and number crunching are familiar examples of particular kinds of processing.

The built-in control function is what makes computers run automatically once someone has programmed them.

Storage plays two roles. Storage serves to remember the substance that is being processed. It also serves to remember the processing commands, the programmed commands that drive the control function. Storage, in short, is for data and programs, both for substance and for process control.

Even if capable of storing substance and of processing it under automatic control, a computer is worthless unless it can also get raw substance from its environment and put processed substance back into that environment. Hence the input function, as done by keyboards, mice, or joysticks, and the output function, as done by printers or TV screens.

---

[2] For more information about how researchers and inventors have transformed the laws of physics into the technology of telecommunications, and about the future of human communications, see: Pierce, John R., and A. Michael Noll's *Signals: The Science of Telecommunications,* a Scientific American Library Book, 1990.

[3] Nora, Simon and Alain Minc, *The Computerization of Society,* a Report to the President of France (Cambridge, MA: The MIT Press, 1980), 4 and 178, n. 1.

[4] Shannon, Claude E. and Warren Weaver, *The Mathematical Theory of Communication* (Urbana: The University of Illinois Press, 1949), 3.

Figure 3-1. Evolving Perceptions of Computer Systems

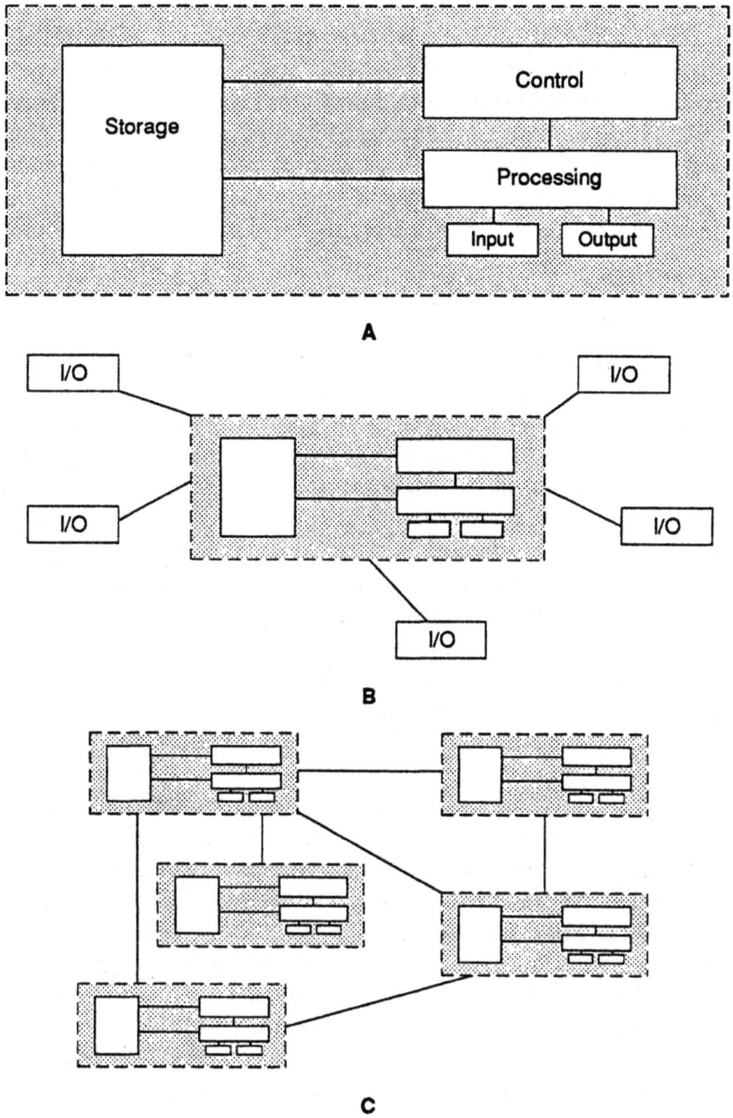

Figure 3-1A shows the processing, control, storage, input, and output functions linked to symbolize the organic unity of these component functions of a computer.

That the links might also denote communications paths among the devices that do the five basic functions was at most an incidental perception in the classical view. The designer who worries about the innards of a machine might see communications paths. But communications paths are irrelevant to someone who is holding a common calculator in the palm of his or her hand, or to someone who is looking at one of the dinosaur-sized early computers through the glass of a museum exhibit. The classical computer was self-contained, except for the private communications between it and the fingers and the eyes of its owner. Then, as now, the communications function was inseparable from the computing function. It was, however, perceived as secondary if perceived at all. In the classical computer, the five functions all happen inside one box. That box fit in one hand or in one room. The hand or the room belong to one person or one organization. Under these circumstances, attention understandably focuses on computing, not on communications.

Computer-related communications became increasingly visible in the early 1950s, beginning with military systems. This perception diffused into the business and the academic worlds throughout the 1960s. Figure 3-1B suggests the focus of the newer perception. A computer mainframe, the classical computer of Figure 3-1A, is seen as the center of the galaxy. Revolving around it are remote input/output devices of a kind that the 1980s came to call *dumb terminals*. These satellites just accept input to the mainframe from a remote site and deliver output from the mainframe to the remote site.

All the smarts—the control functions—are in the mainframe, which is why it is the *main* frame. In this view, as it evolved through the 1960s, the terminals are perceived as doing no processing. Likewise, the communications links between the terminals and the mainframe are perceived as pure transmitters, like a splendidly caring, competent, and inviolate postal service that transports an envelope and delivers it in precisely the mint condition in which it accepted it and, on the way, permits neither eyes nor hands to be laid on the letter inside. Another common figure of speech paints ideal communications links as technically totally transparent: The mainframe and the terminals see each other as if nothing more had come between them than when both of them were inside one box in the Eden of Figure 3-1A. Institutionally, however, the mainframe and the terminals often have different owners. And, in the not so distant past, the communications links were mostly supplied by one or more public utilities. Under these circumstances, attention begins to focus on communications as well as on computing, and the two are seen as belonging to related but different worlds.

By the 1970s the idea of distributed computing had become widespread (Figure 3-1C). Many mainframes are linked to one another. Some of them are smart terminals. *Smart* only means that the terminals are less main than some other frames, the spectrum of available potency by now defying any neat dichotomy between smart mainframes and dumb terminals. Workload is shared among the sites in proportions that depend on the particulars of the services being rendered and of the prevailing costs or prices. Many more parties are involved than just the computer owners and the communications public utilities. Some are hybrids like Tymshare, a company that describes itself as having "since inception,...focused on practical timeshared use of computing, communications, and intricate online software to solve problems, manage information, and bring the intelligence of centralized data to a universe of users."[5] Others, like Dow Jones & Co., Inc., pull together under one corporate roof a variety of means for a variety of ends. Besides the *Wall Street Journal,* Dow Jones "publications and services include the computerized Dow Jones News/Retrieval,...[a] provider of electronically delivered business and financial information; Dow Jones News Service, which operates newswires and delivers information over radio, television, and telephone; *Barron's* magazine, *American Demographics*, and the *National Business Employment Weekly*."[6] Planet-wide and, indeed, galaxy-wide communications links have become essential system components.

Since the 1940s, the view from the communications standpoint has also changed. Classically, communications highlights the links in Figure 3-1, while computing sees mainly the nodes that the links tie together. As late as 1980, approximately 84 percent of the Bell System's annual plant costs of some $40 billion were for links, and only 16 percent for terminals.[7] But this understates and masks the importance of the role of the nodes *within* the system of links that ties together the terminals—the telephones, the computers, or what have you—of the telephone companies' customers.

Coupling computing and communications within the telephone system makes it possible to avoid linking every customer directly to every other. For example, Figure 3-2A[8] shows the sixty-six lines it takes to connect each of twelve terminals directly to every other terminal. It would be economically absurd and physically impractical to hook up every telephone directly in this way to every other telephone. This would take 10 million billion links just within the

---

[5] Tymshare Inc., *1981 Annual Report*, 5.

[6] Dow Jones, *1983 Annual Report*, Introduction.

[7] Weinhaus, Carol L. and Anthony G. Oettinger, *Federal/State Costing Methods: Who Controls the Dollars?*, vol. 3 of *Behind the Telephone Debates*, (Cambridge, MA: Program on Information Resources Policy, Harvard University, 1984).

[8] Figure 3-2 is from: Weinhaus, Carol L. and Anthony G. Oettinger, *At the Heart of the Debates: Costs, Control, and Ownership of the Existing Network*, vol. 1 of *Behind the Telephone Debates* (Cambridge, MA: Program on Information Resources Policy, Harvard University, 1985), Figure 15.

Figure 3-2. Communications Links: Direct and Switched

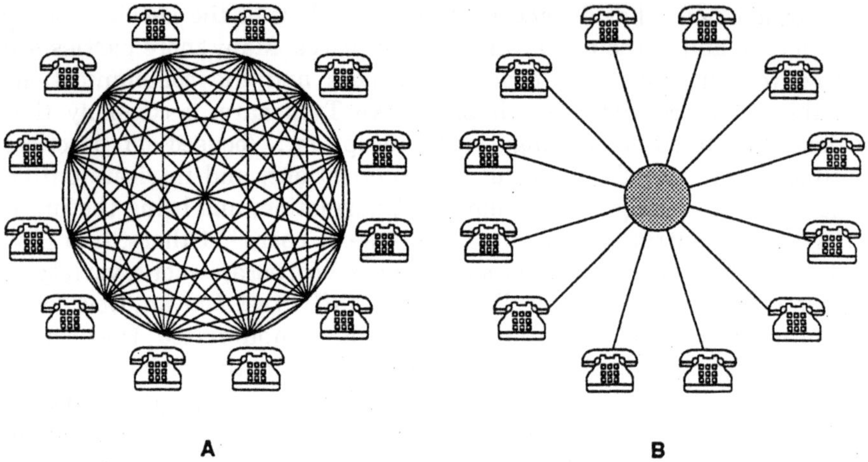

United States. Switches take care of this problem. Running one link from each of twelve terminals to a switch permits connecting any one terminal to any other (Figure 3-2B) with only twelve links, fifty-four links fewer than the sixty-six links of Figure 3-2A.

In its simplest conception, the switch of Figure 3-2B allows only one conversation at a time. One trick in engineering real-life switches is to enable just enough conversations to go on simultaneously. If too few conversations are planned for, some customers trying to make calls don't even get a dial tone. Or, if the switch is over-engineered, most of it will remain idle most of the time, adding an unnecessary cost for customers, stockholders, or taxpayers to bear.

As the number of telephones grows, and with it the amount of traffic and the distance between telephones, the single-switch arrangement of Figure 3-2B rapidly becomes uneconomical and impractical. For economy, telephone networks use many switches interconnected as sketched in Figure 3-3.[9] Actual telecommunications networks have structures lying somewhere between the extremes of Figures 3-2A and 3-3. The precise location ebbs and flows with changing technologies, costs, and government interventions.[10]

In the early days of telephony, the switching took place literally on switch boards. People named *operators* did the thinking to figure out which wire to plug into which hole to make the right connection. They

[9] Weinhaus, *supra,* note 7 at Figure 17.

[10] For more detail on relationships among technologies, costs, industry structures, public policy goals, and government interventions in the telecommunications realm, see Weinhaus, *supra*, note 7.

Figure 3-3. Link and Switch Patterns in Hierarchical Telephone Systems

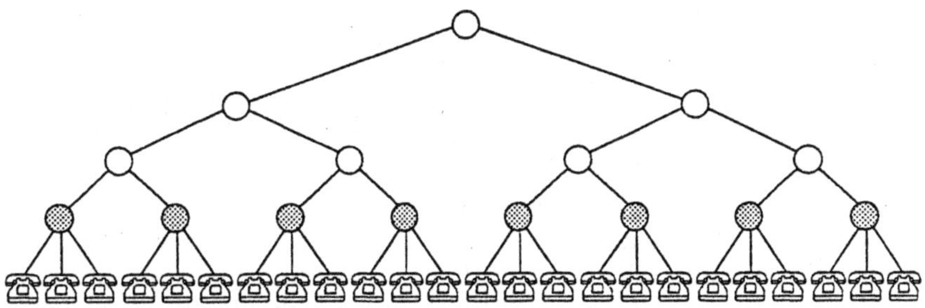

also "forwarded calls to someone's likely location, took messages, and advised callers whom best to call for a solution to a plumbing or medical problem."[11] To Almon Strowger, an undertaker in Kansas City, "these extra services reflected power that invited abuse, pure and simple. (He was not necessarily being paranoid. In the earlier years of phone service, there were many complaints of backtalk, biased service, and eavesdropping....)." This "drove Strowger to such a pitch of exasperation and inspiration that in 1889 he invented what he called the first 'girl-less, cussless telephone,' or, more neutrally, the automatic switch." By 1980, the connections were made almost exclusively by automatic switches, whose generic functions were precisely the generic functions of the classical computer of Figure 3-1A.

The 1980s' telephone switch differs from the 1980s' mainframe or small terminal only in the specifics that define its mission as switching instead of game playing, word processing, air traffic controlling, number crunching, or what have you. Given a phone number as an input, the switching "computer" produces the right connection as its output. Seen in this light, the telephone network of Figure 3-3 looks like a distributed computing system, and the distributed computing system of Figure 3-1C looks like a communications network.

That there is a functional kinship of computing and communications as members of a common compunications species is made evident by Figure 3-3 and Figure 3-1C, either of which evokes the other; whether you see a distributed computing system or a communications network depends only on your mindset. That functional kinship is independent of the details of form. Once perceived, the functional kinship can be discerned as having been there all along, even when the only computers around were mechanical adding machines and when the control element of a switch was an operator's brain. But computing and communications are now kin in form as well as in function. Both

[11] Hapgood, John, "The Connection," *Science* 5, no. 8 (October 1984): 75.

sit on a common technological base of electro-optical digital formats and processes.

Dissonances between the formal and functional coherence of compunications, computing-and-communications, and the fragmented traditional structures of the information sectors of both the economy and the polity account for much of the strife that grew among information businesses in the 1970s and that came to one climax with the breakup of the Bell System on January 1, 1984.

Much of this began after World War II, when the newborn computer industry and the traditional telephone industry both began drawing on the growing base of electro-optical digital technologies, epitomized in the 1980s by transistors and microcomputers.

IBM and AT&T, the giants of these two industries, both were undergoing suits under the antitrust laws. There was, however, a major difference between the companies and therefore between the concerns of these suits. The computer industry had grown up without special government regulation while the telephone industry had become a regulated monopoly some forty years after its birth in 1876. Telephone regulation extended over entry into the industry, over services rendered, and over prices charged.

Until the early 1980s, IBM—already subject to antitrust suits—elected not to do business, at least in the United States, in areas subject to telephone-style regulation (Figure 3-4[12]). IBM was therefore able to avoid this type of government regulation. Thus, a legal boundary was drawn between the unregulated computer industry and the regulated telecommunications industry.

As awareness grew of the functional and formal coherence of the technical bases of both industries, conflicts grew at a legal border that cuts across that common technical base.[13]

Other companies, less visible than AT&T and IBM, began to nibble at and burrow under the legal boundary. By the early 1980s, the boundary had been thoroughly breached; the old order had been undermined. The traditional telephone industry (including AT&T and more than fourteen hundred independent companies), the computer industry, and numerous other information industries, such as the electronics industry and the publishing industry, all faced uncertainty and instability.

Decades of antitrust suits, beginning in the 1950s, culminated in

---

[12] McLaughlin, John F. with Anne Louise Antonoff, *Mapping the Information Business* (Cambridge, MA: Program on Information Resources Policy, Harvard University, 1986), Figure 30.

[13] Weinhaus, Carol L. and Anthony G. Oettinger, *Behind the Telephone Debates*, vols. 1, 4, and Index (Cambridge, MA: Program on Information Resources Policy, Harvard University, 1983).

Figure 3-4. IBM Lines of Business and FCC Regulation, Circa 1978

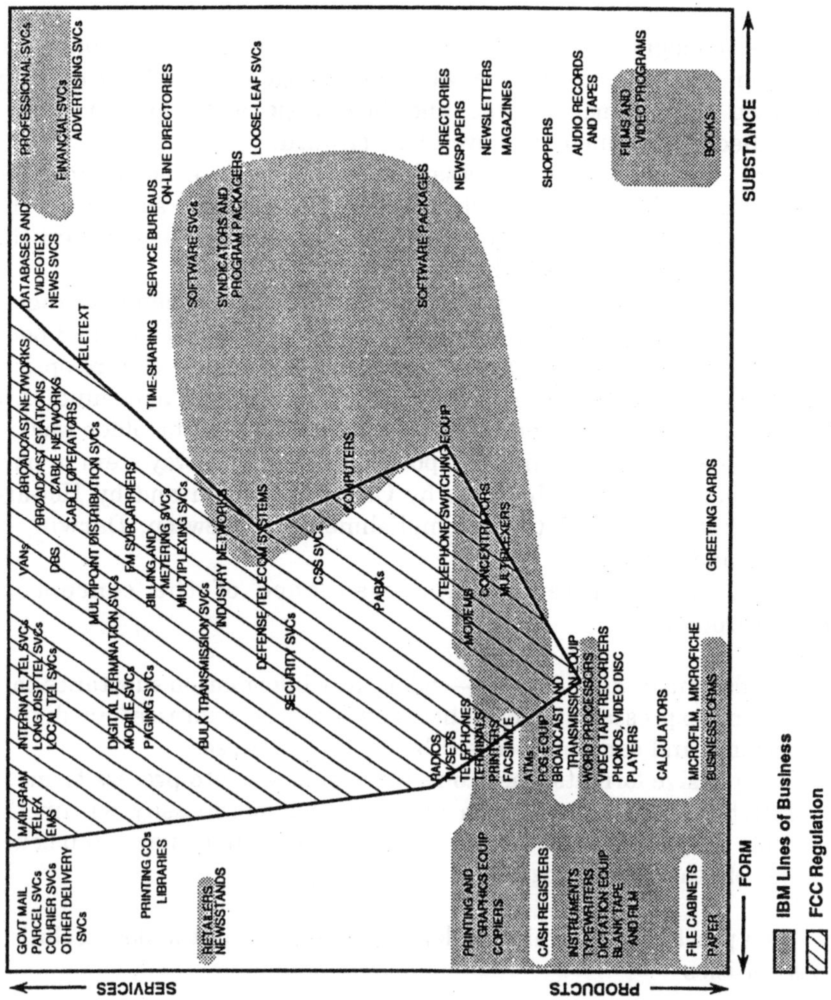

the January 7, 1982, exoneration of IBM and the January 1, 1984, divestiture by AT&T of the Bell Operating Companies and the restructuring of AT&T into regulated and unregulated subsidiaries.

Divestiture left the new AT&T, the new regional holding companies, the independent telephone companies, the other common carriers (OCCs), the computer industry, the newspaper and the publishing industries, and all the other information industries jockeying for position in an environment destabilized by new electro-optical digital technologies, among other factors.

3.2 INSTABILITY: BREAKTHROUGHS BUST BUNDLES

Like seismologists who try to find out why San Francisco quakes on occasion, we can look to see why the information industries keep erupting from time to time and how logic and economics have compelled the technological evolution onward.

More abundant and more versatile than alternative mechanical and analog ways of formatting and processing information substance, the electro-optical digital way has upset traditional balances within the information sector of both the economy and the polity.

Just as in the nineteenth century the potential of then newfangled steam engines loosened up bundles of labor and capital that had been tied up with man-, horse- and water-power, so the new electro-optical digital way loosened up bundles of labor and capital and bundles of information, material, and energy resources tied by the older ways.

The newfound versatility and power of the digital way stem in part from conceptual breakthroughs by Claude Shannon and by Howard Aiken that rank with the accomplishments of Newton, Darwin, or Watson and Crick.[14]

As a practical technical consequence of the conceptual breakthroughs

- Words, music, and pictures—indeed any information substance that can be expressed in any other way—can be expressed in digital formats and can be processed by digital processes.
- Inexpensive formats, easy-to-read formats, easy-to-process formats, reliable formats, and so on are available more easily within the wide range of electro-optical digital formats than they can be eked out of other technologies.

As a practical economic and legal consequence of the new technical possibilities

- Boundaries between information businesses that once were predicated on differences in formats and processes lose that justification for their existence when all information businesses share the flexible and easily altered electro-optical digital formats and processes.

---

[14] For a nonmathematical explanation of the technology behind the telecommunications industry, audio recording, home recording, etc., see: Irwin Lebow's *The Digital Connection* (New York: Computer Science Press, 1991).

3.2.1 Milestones of Innovation

The abundance of the electro-optical digital way stems from technological innovations that came along in time to turn the scientific curiosity of a potential in-principle into a technical potential attractive in actual practice. Figuring out precisely the *what*, *how*, and *how much* of making this or that new or better and cheaper or both is what all the engineering, market research, experimentation, instant millionaires, and abrupt bankrupts in brand new information businesses and in revamped old information businesses are all about.

Beneath the ebb and flow of trial and error in the homes, the laboratories, the factories, the marketplaces, and the cold and hot wars among domestic and international stakeholders, there are a few abiding fundamentals. These fundamentals are stimulating and will continue to stimulate change in compunications technologies for at least another generation or two. This likely will maintain the perceived technical potential at least as high as it has been since World War II, with all the attendant instabilities, opportunities, and dangers that eddy or whirl around fundamental changes.

The aim of this chapter is not to detail either digital science or digital technology. Nor is it to deliver a how-to manual for phone phreaks or computer hackers. The aim is to portray the fundamental technological forces that contribute to channeling the electro-optical digital evolution. That portrait is to be of sufficient depth and clarity to assist readers in making their own judgments about opportunities and risks, whether personal, business, political, or social.

Figure 3-5[15] shows milestones in the post-World War II development of compunications technologies. The entries in Figure 3-5A are selected from an IBM listing, those in Figure 3-5B from an AT&T Bell Laboratories listing. Coming from corporate cultures with traditions that differed historically and that were maintained by the boundaries described at the end of section 3.1, the listings differ, but only on the surface. The common technical base shows through in entries such as "junction transistor," which records the invention of the transistor at AT&T Bell Laboratories, whence it diffused into the computer as well as into the communications industry. Although given a telephony name, the Electronic Central Office (listed as being tried at Morris in 1960) was the first routine computer-as-switch. The Operations Systems entry is a major software system, namely a computer program used for vital telephone operations record-keeping functions.

[15] From: Office of the IBM Chief Scientist; and Bell Laboratories Innovations in Telecommunications, 1925–1977, official compilation.

Figure 3-5. IBM and AT&T Bell Laboratories' Milestones in Compunications Technologies

IBM Computer Technology	Bell Laboratories Innovations in Telecommunications
1946 IBM 603 Calculator—The computer industry's first vacuum tube machine built on a production-line basis.	Research and Electronics Technology 1948 Information Theory Junction Transistor 1950 Error Correcting Codes
1955 IBM 704 (Indexing and Floating Point)—The IBM 704 was the first commercially available computer to incorporate indexing and floating point arithmetic as standard features and to base the software on them.	Customer Systems and Services 1958 Call Director® Telephone 1959 Princess® Telephone 1960 Ballistic Missile Early Warning System (BMEWS)
1957 FORTRAN (Formula Translation)—The most widely used scientific programming language. First high-level language to gain general industry acceptance.	Central Office Systems 1960 Morris Trial-Electronic Central Office 1961 TOUCH-TONE® Calling 1969 PICTURE PHONE® Service Switching
1957 RAMAC (Random Access Method of Accounting and Control)—Invention of the computer disk file, which became the industry's basic medium for on-line transaction processing. The IBM RAMAC 305 was the first disk file system.	Transmission 1971 Data Under Voice 1973 TASI-B 1974 SLC™-40 Systems 1977 Lightware Communications
1962 SABRE (Semi-Automatic Business Environment Research)—Reservation system developed with American Airlines. The first large commercial computer/communications network that operated in "real time."	Operations Systems 1968 CMDS Trunks Integrated Records-Keeping Systems
1964 IBM System/360—First major computer family with upward and downward compatibility, allowing the use of programming across multiple systems. First computer family to employ widespread use of read-only memory for control and the first family with standard input-output interfaces. Extended the addressing range to 16 million bytes of real main memory.	

Figure 3-5. (Continued).

IBM Computer Technology	Bell Laboratories Innovations In Telecommunications
1972 "Floppy" Disk—First flexible magnetic disk or diskette for use with small systems.	
1974 Systems Network Architecture—First widely used commercial computer communications subsystems architecture including Synchronous Data Link Control, adopted throughout the industry by the mid-1980s.	
1980 Densest Circuit Packaging—Complete logic for the large-scale IBM 3081 computer contained in only 26 modules on four printed-circuit boards. This packaging of nearly 800,000 circuits remains the densest yet reported.	
1981 Highest Chip Capacity—Experimental 288,000-bit memory chip, made on manufacturing line producing chips for IBM products, has the highest information capacity yet reported as of 1985.	

Sources: A—Office of the IBM Chief Scientist.
B—Bell Laboratories Innovations in Telecommunications 1925–1977. Official Compilation.

The 1962 SABRE system, described as a "commercial computer/communications network," shows up in the IBM computer technology listing prepared in 1983. Communications is not, however, among the lines of business that IBM reported to the Securities and Exchange Commission in 1975 (Figure 3-6[16]): American Airlines, the buyer of the SABRE system, was responsible for purchasing the computers from one vendor, the communications from another. By 1983, with *Computer Inquiry II* in effect and the U.S. government's antitrust suit dismissed against it, IBM could include telecommunica-

[16] Security and Exchange Commission Form 10-K, AT&T 1975 and 1983, IBM 1975 and 1983.

Figure 3-6. Information Lines of Business Reported 1975–1983

AT&T 1975

...The American Telephone and Telegraph Company...incorporated in 1885 under the laws of the State of New York, is the parent company of the Bell System....

The principal business of the American Company and its telephone subsidiaries is that of furnishing communications services, mainly telephone service, throughout the United States except in Alaska and Hawaii....

Other communications services offered by the American Company and its telephone subsidiaries include data transmission, transmission of radio and television programs and private line voice and teletypewriter services....

IBM 1975

IBM's operations...are in the field of information handling systems, equipment and services....IBM's products include data processing machines and systems, electric typewriters, input word processing equipment, copiers, educational and testing materials, and related supplies and services....

AT&T 1983

On January 1, 1984, pursuant to a consent decree entered on August 24, 1982 by the United States District Court for the District of Columbia and a Plan of Reorganization approved by the Court on August 5, 1983, AT&T divested itself of the exchange telecommunications, exchange access and printed directory advertising portions of the BOCs as well as the cellular advanced mobile communications service business.

...AT&T is now managed as one business with the objective of meeting customer needs, both in the United States and foreign markets, for electronic information movement and management....

IBM 1983

IBM is the largest manufacturer of data processing equipment and systems in the information-handling field....IBM's products include data processing machines and systems, telecommunications systems and products, information distributors, office systems, general purpose and industry-specific workstations, typewriters, copiers, educational and testing materials, and related supplies and services.

Sources: Security and Exchange Commission Form 10-K, AT&T 1975 and 1983, IBM 1975 and 1983.

tions systems and products among the lines of business listed for that year.

3.2.2 Converting Milestones to Money

Figure 3-7 suggests how technological milestones like these get translated into marketplace successes or failures. A shorthand way of looking at the economic value of the substance–format–process bundle

Figure 3-7. Price–Performance Behavior of New Technologies

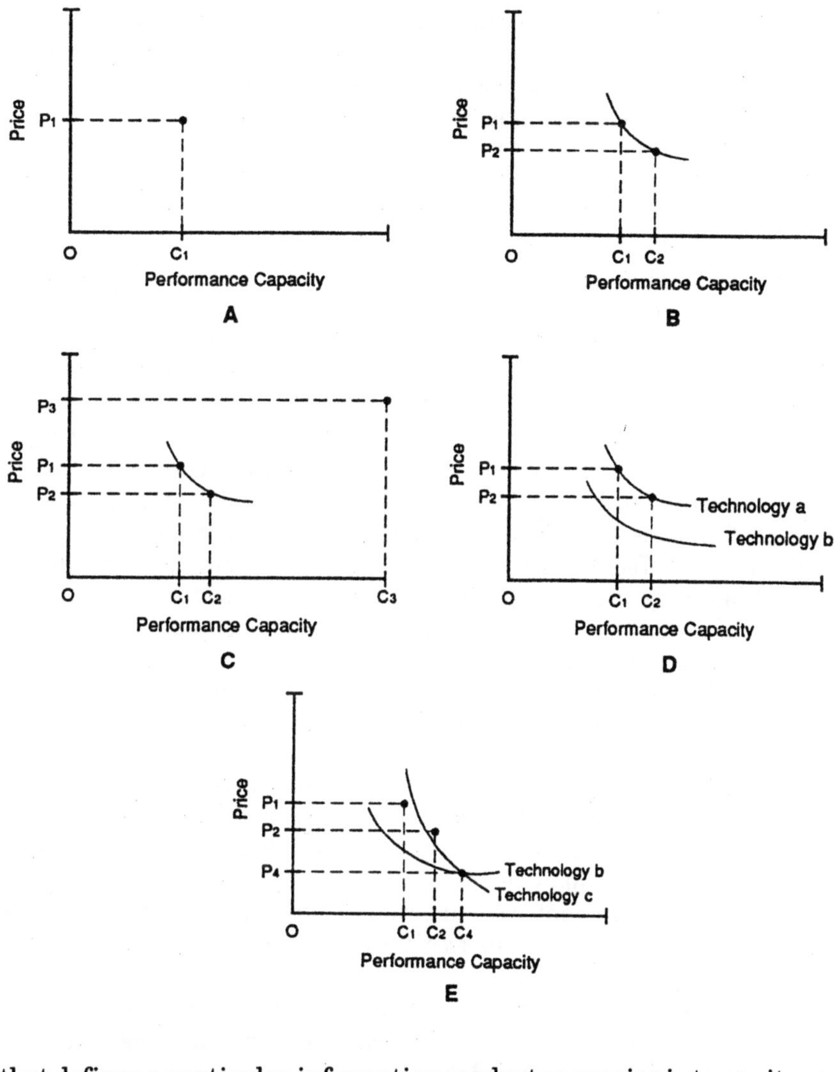

that defines a particular information product or service is to see it as a specific capability obtainable at a specific price, namely a specific cost to the purchaser. Admittedly, vast complexities bedevil specifying both capability and cost to anyone's satisfaction. For now we need merely suspend disbelief in the idea that one can meaningfully and satisfactorily specify both a performance capability, such as C_1 in Figure 3-7A, and the right price P_1 to be paid for a unit of it.

A given technology often has a range of capacity over a range of prices. As suggested by Figure 3-7B, under different conditions the same technology that yields capability C_1 at unit price P_1 can also perform at the higher capability C_2 and at the lower unit price P_2. For instance, C_1 might be produced at unit price P_1 early in a technology's life cycle; C_2 might be produced at unit price P_2 later on. Or the actual capability might depend on market size: the higher capability at lower unit price might be attainable only through mass production. Usually, the practical range of any particular technology is finite: Something inherent in a technology or in available production techniques makes it either literally impossible or perhaps just grossly uneconomical to work above or below a limited range of capability.

Increased technical potential might manifest itself as an increased performance capability, like C_3 in Figure 3-7C, even if at a higher price P_3. This can be attractive when price is subordinate to performance, as when NASA buys a trip to the moon, when the Pentagon buys a new weapons system, or when J.P. Morgan bought a new yacht and advised others not even to think about it if they had to ask how much it cost.

A preferred and more widely useful form of new technical potential is, as illustrated in Figure 3-7D, where a new technology improves on both performance and price. For inching along the price and performance curve of Technology a (Figure 3-7D), improving performance a bit and lowering the price a bit, Technology b substitutes the breakthrough of lower price at every level of performance, plus an extended range of higher performance at lower prices.

Although frequently headlined by newspapers and trumpeted on television, the notion of breakthrough is fuzzy at best. Among the many reasons for this fuzziness are complexities of the kind that Figure 3-7E shows. Technology b is preferable to Technology c below performance capability C_4, and Technology c is preferable above. Which one is better depends on what for. And that in turn depends on guesses made about an adversarial world seen through the fog of war. So research management, venture capitalism, entrepreneurship, and public policy making remain exhilarating adventures, not cut-and-dried routines.

A small company might, for instance, "asphyxiate on its own success." As Tracy Kidder, in *The Soul of a New Machine,* explains about Data General around 1973:

> Demand for its products would be soaring, and the owners would be drawing up optimistic five-year plans, when all of a sudden something would go wrong with their system of production. They wouldn't be able to produce the machines that they had promised to deliver. Lawsuits might follow. At the least, expensive parts would sit in inventory,

revenues would fall, customers would go elsewhere or out of business themselves.[17]

Even in AT&T, when it still styled itself as "the largest business on earth," life at the top was far from channeled. This is how Alvin von Auw depicts what he witnessed for over a decade as assistant to the chairman while the AT&T leadership asked, What is our business? Who are we?:

> Coping with intangibles—the public's mood, the politician's whim, not to mention breakneck changes in technologies and markets—they made their decisions day by day on the basis of their best estimate of an unknowable future and with nothing to assure them that what they decided, even though it represented their most conscientious judgement of what their responsibilities required of them, might not turn out to be egregiously, even fatally wrong.[18]

Only retrospectively does the picture clarify of "the public's mood, the politician's whim" and of the "breakneck changes in technologies and markets."

By 1979, a Data General executive could draw lessons from the experience six years before:

> We were missing our commitments to customers. We just grossly fucked over our customers. We actually put some entrepreneurs out of business and I think some of them may have lost their houses. But we recovered from our shipment problems and never repeated them.[19]

Figure 3-8[20] gives an example of 20/20 technological hindsight. Each point in the apparently inexorable progression of Figure 3-8 stands for the cost and performance characteristics of a large IBM mainframe, of the vintage of the indicated year. Performance in Figure 3-8 means the speed at which an arbitrary benchmark task is done. The task in this example is "an identical mix of 1700 typical data processing operations, involving millions of computer instructions."[21]

---

[17] Kidder, Tracy, *The Soul of a New Machine* (Boston: Little, Brown and Co., 1981), 26.

[18] von Auw, Alvin, *Heritage and Destiny: Reflections on the Bell System in Transition* (New York: Praeger Publ., 1983), xi.

[19] Kidder, *supra,* note 10 at 26.

[20] Adapted from data courtesy of IBM.

[21] "How New Technology Has Lowered the Cost of Data Processing." Personal communication from the office of the IBM Chief Scientist, August 31, 1983.

Figure 3-8. IBM Computers: Speed as Performance Index vs. Cost

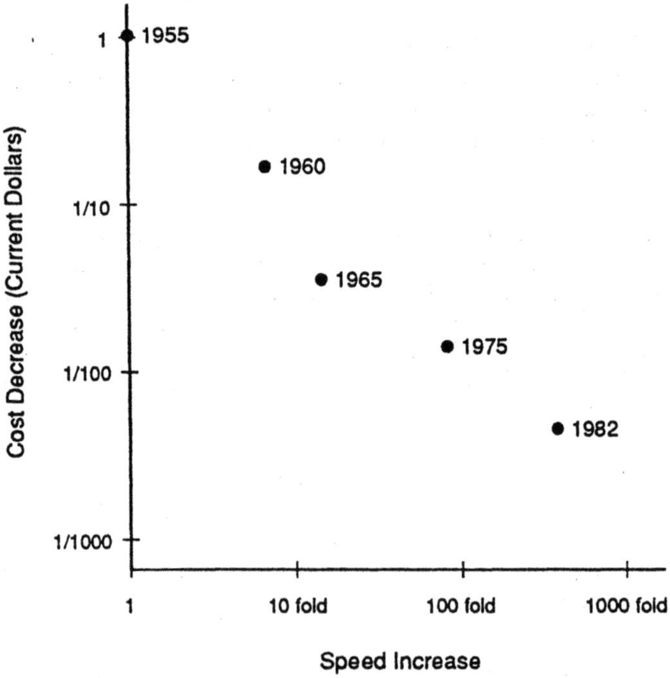

This fixed task took 375 seconds in 1955, 1 second in 1982. The precise performance measure is therefore speed increase over the 1955 speed taken as the yardstick unit.

Cost in Figure 3-8 starts with a dollar amount, in the current dollars of each year; that is, the figures are not adjusted for inflation. It does not matter much here precisely what is included in cost and what is left out. The critical commitment is faith that the IBM staff used at least roughly the same recipe for toting up cost for each year. By their reckoning, the fixed task cost $14.54 in 1955 and $0.07 in 1982. The precise cost measure is therefore current cost relative to the 1955 cost taken as the yardstick unit.

On these terms, performance was multiplied by the hundreds, or improved about two orders of magnitude between 1955 and 1982. Current cost likewise improved by about two orders of magnitude. The joint effect can be expressed as cost times performance improving by four orders of magnitude. Or, since 375 (the speed factor) times $14.54/$0.07, or 208 (the cost factor), is about 78,000, which is almost 100,000, the data of Figure 3-8 can be read roughly as an estimate of almost five orders of magnitude improvement in the cost and performance behavior of large computers between 1955 and 1982.

This amounts to an average current cost and performance improvement rate of more than 50 percent per year sustained for the last quarter century, enough to trigger gold rushes by those willing to risk being "egregiously, even fatally, wrong" and to suffer "the proud man's contumely... the law's delay"[22] for their pains.

The points in Figure 3-8 are not connected. Unlike the two points in Figure 3-7B, they are not perceived as lying on a single technology curve. Instead, they are seen as epitomizing successive technological generations, fruits of breakthroughs that define new technologies with some distinctive break from the preceding technologies. In the workaday world it is not always self-evident what constitutes pushing a given technology to greater performance, namely, staying on one curve of Figure 3-7, and what constitutes jumping to a different technology, namely, going from one curve in Figure 3-7 to another.

By 1955, the electromechanical hardware technology of the pioneering Aiken/IBM Automatic Sequence Controlled Calculator of the forties had been supplanted by vacuum tube and magnetic technology. John Von Neuman and Maurice Wilkes had made explicit the powerful role of software, the programs that direct the hardware's functioning. The 1960 machine in Figure 3-8 used transistors instead of vacuum tubes, plus magnetic devices faster than those of 1955. Machines of that vintage were dubbed "second generation" machines. The 1960 transistor was about the size of a pinky nail and had three palpable wires coming out of it. At first, each wire had to be individually soldered by hand; later, it was done automatically. More important for the progression from 1960 through 1982, more and more transistors and other circuit elements by the thousands eventually got packed and hooked together on the pinky-nail-sized chips of silicon. Along with all these changes in the hardware technology went numerous changes in the software technology. Hundreds of tables and charts describing the detailed characteristics and capabilities of the components out of which systems could be built, like those collected in Montgomery Phister's *Data Processing Technology and Economics* are the sources for change that some choose to see as a forest and others don't.[23]

Technologies in general—among them computer generations and specific media in particular—are bundles of arts and artifacts tied together by loose labels (Figure 3-9). The unity, stability, and distinctiveness of any bundle so baptized is thus more apparent than real. Only in theory, as in Figure 3-7, and in still-lifes seen with hindsight, as in Figures 3-8 and 3-9, does the idea of a technology hold still for examination as a well-defined bundle.

---

[22] Shakespeare, William, *Hamlet,* Act III, Sc 1, Line 56.

[23] Phister, Jr., Montgomery, *Data Processing Technology and Economics* (Bedford, MA: Digital Press, 1979).

Figure 3-9. Radio and Newspaper Technologies as Format-and-Process Bundles

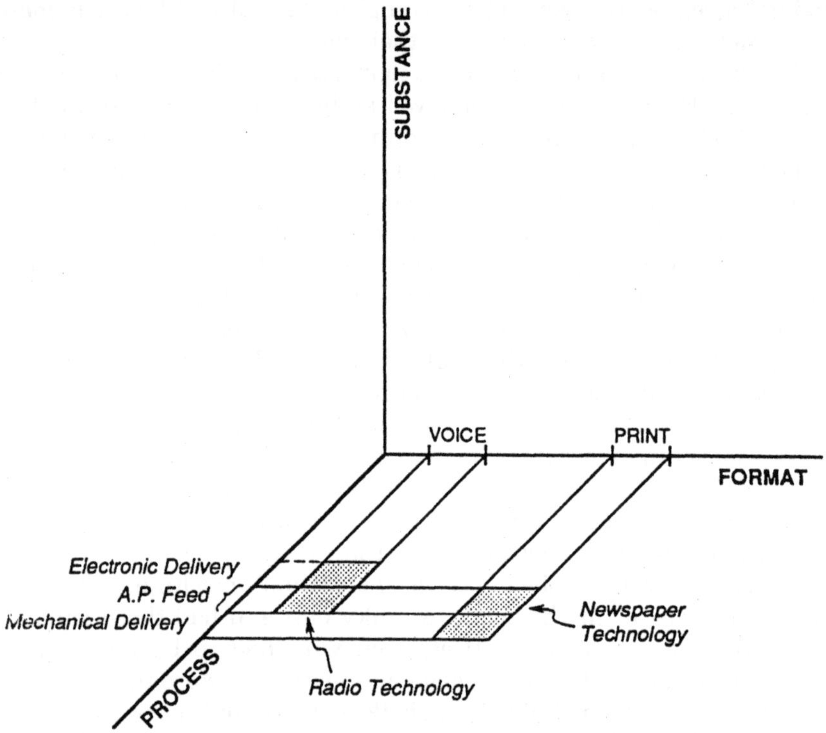

Technologies don't spring up full-grown like Athena from the brow of Zeus. Although they must conform to the laws of nature, they are artifacts. Specifically, tying together some particular bundle of formats and processes and calling that a technology takes an act of volition. It takes, for example, the will to bet a company by spending the capital to tool up for a new production process, knowing that once the capital is locked up in tools it will take years to recover. In the meanwhile, competitors may retain the flexibility to bet on a better technology. One's own bet is made, of course, in the belief that nothing better will come along soon enough for one's competitors to recover from the market gains made by one's new product at their expense.

Even if known accurately and precisely, cost and performance data like those of Figures 3-7 and 3-8 only partially describe useful format-and-process bundles. The mix of 1700 data processing operations that underlies includes "a cross section of payroll, discount computation, file maintenance, table lookup and report preparation."[24] Leaving aside the question of how representative this mix might be of any user's real workload, payroll calculations and all the rest are only a part of the total workload of any user. And the cost and performance of the computer itself are only a part of the total cost and performance of the computer operation. There are, in addition, programmers to program the computer, operators to run it, clerks to prepare input data and more clerks to interpret output data, and so on. The odds are, therefore, that a 50 percent per year cost and performance gain for just a computer vastly overstates the overall cost and performance gain of any format-and-process bundle within which a computer serves as a processor.

In many cases, the situation is more complex even than this. Some computer costs (like those for space or building rent, air conditioning equipment, energy use, and maintenance) have declined fairly rapidly over time, even enough to sometimes justify re-equipping for just these reasons. On the other hand, uses and demand tend to grow, leading to capacity requirement increases that eat up these potential savings.

Figure 3-10[25] shows data for a communications element of compunications technologies. Like the data in Figure 3-7 and Figure 3-8, the data in Figure 3-10 overstate cost and performance gains. Seen in isolation, these data also understate the complexities and uncertainties of overall format-and-process cost and performance gains.

Each plotted area of Figure 3-10 shows the current cost and performance characteristics of a transmission pipe, namely a format-and-process bundle for conveying information across space. Singled out are the cables with wire pairs in them that are still the most common form of first hook up of a terminal into a network; coaxial cables, like those used also for local cable television, but here adapted to conveying information over long distances; and microwave radio links and light guides also commonly used for long-haul transmission, and, increasingly, for short-haul as well.

Performance in Figure 3-10 means the number of conversations (number of circuits) that a typical pipe (cable of wire pairs, coaxial cable, microwave radio transmitter-to-receiver link or light guide) can carry simultaneously. This is labeled as *circuit density*, namely, the

---

[24] *Supra,* note 13.

[25] Weinhaus, Carol L. and Anthony G. Oettinger, *Behind the Telephone Debates* (Norwood, NJ: Ablex Publishing Corporation, 1988), Figure 15.1. Reprinted with permission. Adapted from Eugene F. O'Neil, "Radio and Long Haul Transmission," *Bell Laboratories Record* 53, no. 1 (January 1975), 51–52; AT&T Bell Laboratories.

Figure 3-10. AT&T Bell Laboratories: Conversations per Pipe as Performance Index vs. Cost per Conversation

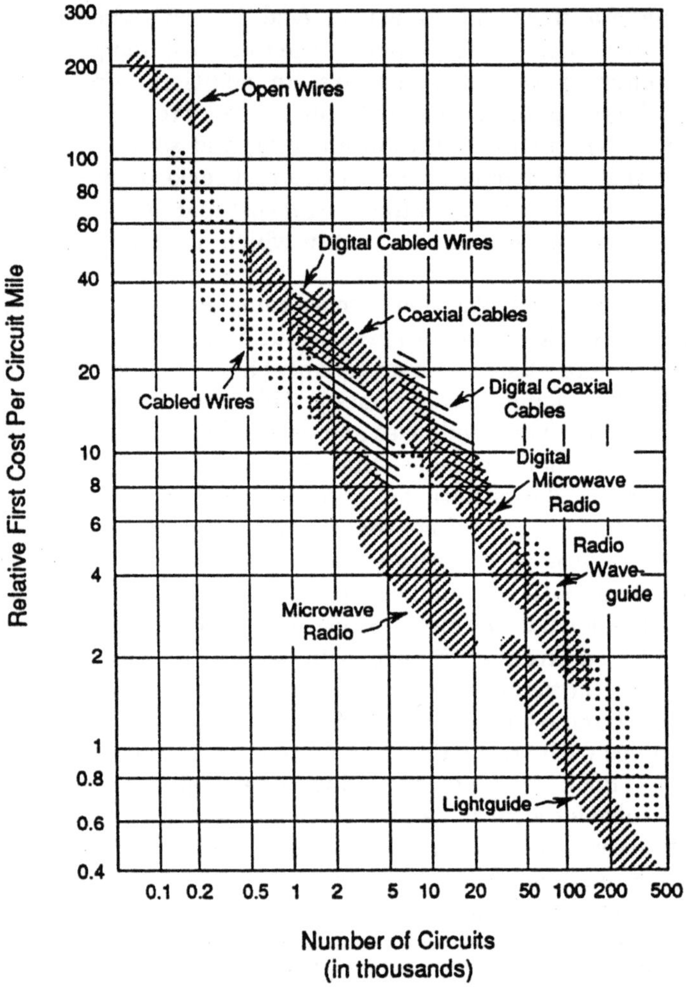

number of circuits per pipe. In absolute terms, circuit density ranges from about one hundred circuits per wire pair cable to hundreds of thousands of circuits per pipe in some of the other technologies. For this exercise, the relative performance measure is the increase in circuit density over the wire pair cable taken as the yardstick unit.

Cost in Figure 3-10 is current cost-per-mile-per-single-circuit. A critical element is once again faith, here faith that the AT&T staff used at least roughly consistent recipes for toting up unit costs for each transmission technology. The absolute values range from $100 per mile per wire pair to less than $1 per mile of circuit in other technologies. In this example, the cost measure is decrease in cost-per-circuit-per-mile over the wire-pair unit cost taken as the yardstick unit.[26]

By the logic applied to Figure 3-8, the overall cost and performance advantage is about four orders of magnitude. But once again, there is less to this than meets the eye.

If for some reason you could run no more than one pipe between Point A and Point B, then a pipe that can carry 100,000 circuits is higher performance than a pipe that can carry only 100 circuits. If you could run as many pipes as you wish without penalty, a thousand small-capacity pipes would do precisely what one large-capacity pipe would do. The cost and performance gain is then purely a cost gain, or just two orders of magnitude, not four. Reality tends to be in between.

If you don't need 100,000 circuits, paying for that total capacity to get a lower unit cost is as absurd as it would be to lay a fire hose from a reservoir just to water your lawn. But it might be worthwhile to cooperate with the neighbors to bring a fire hose to the neighborhood, so that each household might pay only its share of the hose plus a short, small connecting pipe, instead of each neighbor's laying lots of long, small connecting pipes all the way to the reservoir. So a share of the cost and performance gain could be yours if you could work out the politics.

The cost of transmission links, called *outside plant* in Figure 3-11, is only a portion, and a decreasing one at that, of total traditional telephone industry investments. And, finally, the complexity of telecommunications costs is such that each of the elements of total cost must be measured by arbitrary processes; these are defined by conventions handed out from rooms, some filled with smoke, others drenched in sunshine, but none of them atop Mount Sinai.

The path from the promise implied by a casual glance at Figure 3-10 to realized cost and performance gains is thus a foggy one, with many chances to get lost.

Why then the continuing excitement over the potential of compunications technologies? Nominal and partial cost and performance gains of 50 percent per year are attractive, even if skeptically dis-

[26] While the effects of technical advances over time are indicated both by the shapes of the plotted areas and the very existence of some of the areas, all the pipes now co-exist in use. This is in contrast to the case of computers, which have to be examined in terms of changes over time.

Figure 3-11. Cost of Traditional Transmission Facilities (Outside Plant) in Relation to Other Telecommunication Plant Costs

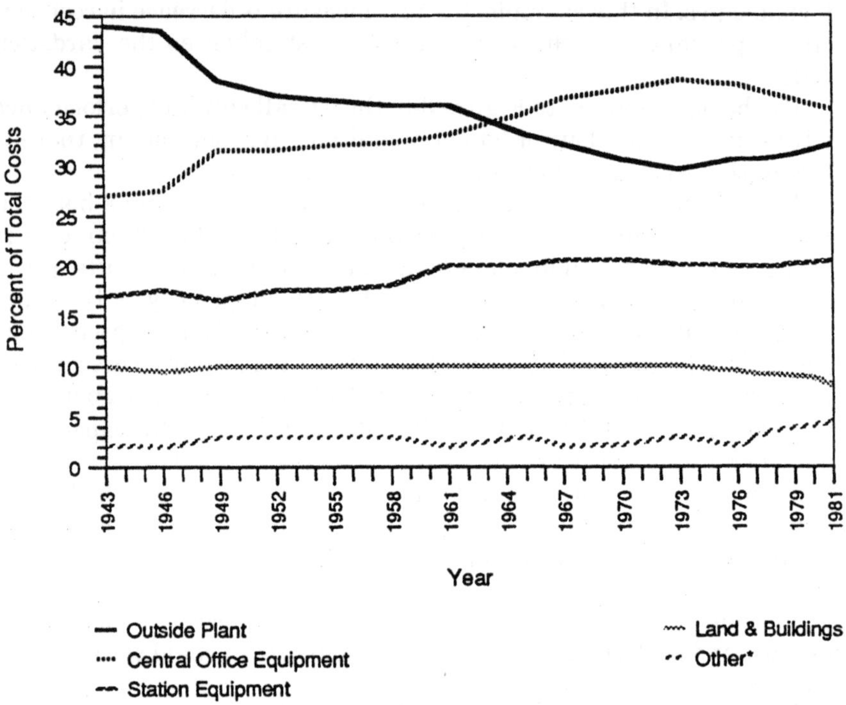

*Other: Organization; Franchises; Patent Rights; Furniture and Office Equipment; Vehicles and Other Work Equipment; Telephone Plants sold and acquired; Unclassified.

counted to much lower realizable gains. And, with the pipeline from laboratory to market still filled by unexploited technological potential, and the promise of still higher potential yet to come, what Cassandra would dispute the possibility that 50 percent per year is on the low side when all the factors are counted?

What mainly underlies this optimism is a still-growing comparative advantage of *electro-optical digital* formats and processes over *mechanical digital* formats and processes and over *all analog* formats and processes. Conceptually, some of that advantage has always been there. It has been explicitly understood, however, only beginning in the 1930s. What is more, the conceptual advantage became amenable to practical exploitation only owing to post World War II advances in electronic, optical, and other technologies. This evolution is still far from being played out. The milestones in Figure 3-8 are mostly electronic digital milestones, and only partly optical. The milestones in Figure 3-10 are electronic but mostly analog milestones. The digital wave in the telecommunications industry has already washed over most switches in place in the field but, in the early 1980s, it had not yet reached most of the fielded transmission plant, most notably, the capillaries fanning out from major centers to myriad places of work and residence. The fully digital network was still ahead. By the late 1980s the wave in the industrialized nations had reached almost all but the "last mile" in the capillaries. And much remained as yet unexploited in compunications laboratories around the world.

The fundamentals of the electro-optical digital compunications evolution therefore remain worth understanding by anyone wishing to influence its course.

3.3 HOW TO TELL ANALOG FROM DIGITAL FORMATS

Analog and digital formats and processes are two distinctive ways of handling information substance. Both are age old. Analog formats directly mimic substance. The drawing of a cat, an analog format, both looks like a cat and refers to it. Digital formats and processes mimic substance, if at all, only indirectly. The word *cat,* a digital format, does not look like a cat at all but nonetheless refers to one.

Both the drawing and the word are meant to evoke a particular cat or the general idea of cats, but each does the job differently and each does it more or less faithfully. Neither an analog nor a digital format necessarily *is* what it evokes; either one just denotes, connotes, or represents, with all the frailties and ambiguities inherent in the tie between a sign and what it signifies.

The analog drawing of a cat and the digital word *cat* demonstrate that both analog and digital formats are familiar and ubiquitous. They have long been so, just as gravity, or rather its effects, was familiar and ubiquitous long before Isaac Newton explained it more profoundly and with greater practical import than anyone before him.

The contemporary attractiveness of digital formats stems in part from a self-conscious and deep understanding, reached only within the last half-century, of the properties of these formats. It stems also from the invention of practical electro-optical processors capable of putting digital formats through useful processes of increasing complexity, at increasing speed and with decreasing cost. The rest of this chapter describes how that came about and why it is likely to go on for the foreseeable future. To pave the way, this section sketches familiar digital formats a bit more, but not much more, precisely than by pointing to the word for a cat and differentiating it from a picture of a cat. More specific details about less familiar but increasingly important digital formats then follow.

All digital formats have in common their foundation of alphabets and arrays. This very text is in a digital format built on an alphabet that includes the familiar twenty-six-letter Roman alphabet, augmented by punctuation marks, spaces, ampersands, and the like. The array of this text—or of any English text—is an imaginary endless sequence of imaginary empty slots. By convention each slot either is empty or else has in it a single character drawn from the alphabet and nothing else. Anything else, like a smudge, is meaningless. In conventional and contemporary Western practice, the imaginary sequence, when filled for real, is broken up into horizontal line segments which are read from left to right and packed into pages which in turn are folded and bound into books. Israelis agree to read their arrays from right to left, and Japanese from top to bottom. Scrolls, not folios, predominated under older Western technologies.

The way we write numbers is another familiar digital format. The set of ten familiar Arabic numerals "0, 1, 2,..., 9" is the alphabet of a digital format built on an array that is an imaginary sequence of empty slots with names like "ones' place," "tens' place," and so on. If the sequence is cut into two pieces, one going to the left of a decimal point and the other going to the right, the integer places to the left of the decimal are named as above and the fraction places to the right are called "tenths' place," "hundredths' place," and so on.

The typewriter is a familiar mechanical digital processor designed to lay out, on sheets of paper, digital formats with slots filled by characters drawn from the literal and numeral alphabets available on its keyboard. The newer electronic word processor is like the typewriter, and then some. Both the word processor and the typewriter supplanted or at least supplemented ball-point pens, fountain pens, goose quill pens, and other processors. But the format of English writing has always been essentially a digital format. For an example of a shift from analog writing to digital writing, one must reach back to the evolution of hieroglyphics from analog pictograms to digital abstract symbols for sounds.[27]

Analog and digital formats are often intermingled, as in analog and digital watches. Both kinds of watches mimic the flow of time. The

---

[27] The *Writing* entries in the *Encyclopaedia Britannica* and in the *Encyclopedia Americana* have as good a summary of the little that is known of the history of writing as may be found anywhere.

Figure 3-12. A Digital Watch Readout

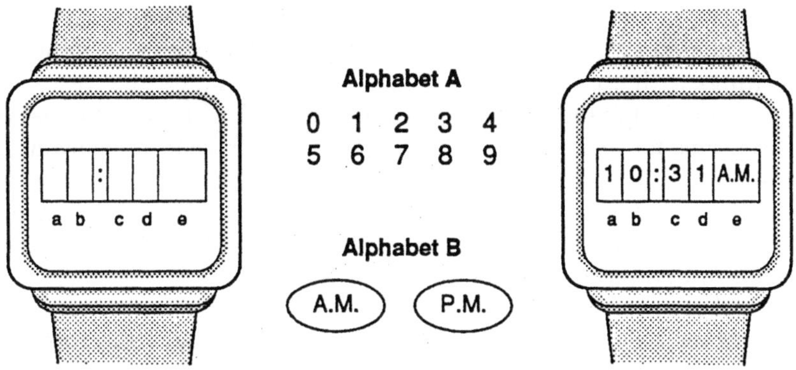

A **The Five Slot Array**

B **The Two Alphabets**

C **The Conventional Digital Time Symbol**

conventional watch does this with a swinging pendulum or a flywheel driving an escapement. More modern watches do it with a vibrating quartz crystal.[28]

In a watch with a traditional analog readout, the time-mimicking process drives two or three hands. The angular position of each hand is analogous to time. For the short hand the dial is read in hours, for the longer hand the face is read in minutes, and for the longest hand the face is read in seconds. In a watch with digital readout, the time-mimicking process drives a digital counter that is faster and smaller than fingers or toes or than the beads of an abacus. Figure 3-12 shows the digital alphabets and arrays that portray a digital count on the watch's face.

Figure 3-12A shows the five-slot array of a simple digital watch face. Slots a and b are for numerals chosen from alphabet A in Figure 3-12B. The prevailing convention is to read that pair of numerals as hours. Slots c and d are also for numerals from alphabet A, but the prevailing convention is to read that pair as minutes. The fixed ":" reminds us of the convention. Slot e is reserved for a symbol drawn from the two-symbol alphabet B (Figure 3-12B). Figure 3-12C shows a complete conventional digital readout.

---

[28] Landes, David S., *Revolution in Time: Clocks and the Making of the Modern World* (Cambridge, MA: Harvard University Press, 1983), 12.

The combinations "A.M." and "P.M." are circled in B to underscore that each is essentially monolithic according to our watch-reading conventions. The components "A", "P", "M", and "." make each symbol self-explanatory, at least for literate folks. Some digital watches tag mornings with an "*" and afternoons with a blank, or vice-versa. The "*," "blank" alphabet is not self-explanatory. Unlike the long-stable conventions for analog watch faces, digital watch-reading conventions were still fluid in the early 1980s and both watch-setting and watch-reading conventions still varied confusingly from watch to watch, even for watches from one manufacturer. By the turn of the 1990s, there was even a return toward conventional hands.

Watches intermingle analog and digital formats and processes in yet another way. The traditional analog watch readout illustrates how. The angular positions of the hour, minute, and second hands are respectively analogous to hours, minutes, and seconds. But, looked at as a whole, the readout appears as a digital array of three slots: an hours' slot, a minutes' slot, and a seconds' slot or position. Instead of being strung out on a line like the letters in this sentence, these three slots are piled one on top of the other, and told apart mainly by the size and speed of their respective hands.

It is each position in this superimposed array that has an analog format. Instead of being filled by a symbol picked from some finite and discrete alphabet of letters or numerals, each position is filled by an infinitely and continuously varying angular position of a hand. The hand position is analogous to the flow of time in units of hours, minutes, and seconds, respectively. Ordinary writing occasionally plays similar tricks. In the linear digital arrays that name t-bar ski-lifts and that name the C-clamps that hold pieces of wood together while the glue dries, the letters "t" and "C" serve as analog pictograms that gradually became treated simultaneously as arbitrary digital symbols.

Perceptions of what is analog and what is digital are relative in still another sense. Typing, as mentioned earlier, is an essentially digital process. Symbols, picked from among the letters of the alphabet available on the keyboard, are strung out in a linear array on the page. But reproducing a typed page in a dry copier or by photography is an analog process. The copier or the camera are made to deliver shapes as exactly analogous to the original as possible. The copier and the camera treat doodles as faithfully as they treat typed words. Where the ink shapes on the page came from matters not when a newspaper is used to wrap up fish. It matters not when the printed page is a graphic object to be copied. It matters only when the printed page is used as a digital format for substance. What a printed page *is* at any given

Figure 3-13. Digital Array to Synthesize Shapes of Numerals

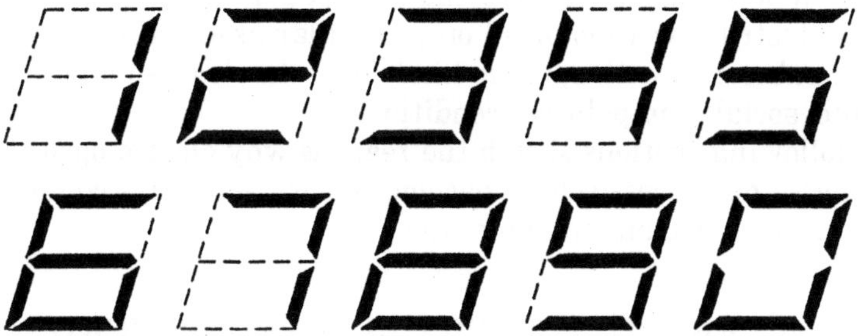

moment depends on what convention you follow when you look at it at that moment.

Pictorial analogies are often approximated by digital processes. The arrays of black dots and white blanks that make up the traditional half-tone pictures in newspapers are one example of digitized analogies. In a digital watch display or a digital calculator display, an analog of the shape of each conventional numeral is synthesized by turning on or off one or more of seven elements in the array shown in Figure 3-13.

Laborious spacing, line-feeding, and key-pecking can produce a crude half-tone picture on a typewriter, a process few people have the patience to carry out. The process gets easier when computer driven. On October 24, 1965, a forgotten hero named H.P. Peterson cranked out "Mona by the Numbers," a half-tone Mona Lisa, at Control Data Corporation's Digigraphics Laboratories. Later on, anyone's picture by the numbers could be had for a few dollars in a few minutes at most any carnival or fair.

Digital formats themselves sometimes incorporate valuable analogies! Moving the decimal point in a conventional arabic numeral one place to the left is like dividing the named number by ten. Moving the decimal point one place to the right is like multiplying the named number by ten. The size of a number expressed in arabic notation is thus easier to estimate at a glance than the size of a number expressed in Roman notation: where the leftmost nonzero digit sits relative to the decimal point tells the story.

Information substance is necessarily always embodied in some material format and processed by some energy-consuming processor. Historically, certain kinds of substance bundles have been linked up with certain format-and-process bundles—that is, with certain technologies. Figure 3-14 lists a sample of such bundles.

In its time, each of these bundles became attractive for some combination of economic, technical, esthetic, political, and other reasons. Whole industries, like the newspaper, radio, TV, movie, or record industries, were founded on particular associations of specific kinds of substance with specific kinds of technologies under specific economic, social, and political conditions.

The following sections sketch the reasons why electro-optical digital formats and processes have become so very attractive compared to other available formats and processes.

3.4 VERSATILITY: WHY ELECTRO-OPTICAL DIGITAL FORMATS ARE BETTER

The following claims—to increasing versatility and economic and other efficiencies—are substantiated in the remainder of this chapter:

- Every intrinsically analog format is sharply limited in its range of application: it must resemble the substance it embodies. Intrinsically, digital formats are based on arbitrary alphabets linked only by convention to what they embody. They are, therefore, in principle more versatile than analog formats. They can be built in arrays not limited to slots strung out indefinitely along a line but laid out in two, three, or more conceptual dimensions. Such digital arrays can be devised to embody any substance whatever, as precisely as desired. Most especially, digital arrays can mimic analog formats as closely as desired.
- In practice, digital arrays can be handled by electro-optical digital compunications processors that have cost and performance characteristics superior to those of mechanical digital processors and to those of both mechanical and electronic analog processors.
- The relative advantage of digital over analog formats and processors is likely to keep growing.

The arbitrary relationship that convention sets between substance and a digital format confers great versatility. A picture of a cat has to look like a cat or it won't work, at least not as an analog format. The convention that the word *cat* means "cat" is arbitrary. Some other digital format would serve as well, like *chat* in French, or *Katze* in German.

It is far from self-evident that arbitrariness necessarily means useful versatility. The Tower of Babel myth testifies to a contrary tendency. One problem is that arbitrary conventions have to be learned. A rose is a rose is a rose. The ability to identify a picture of a cat with a cat, once one has seen a cat, is either innate in people or

Figure 3-14. Historical Combinations of Substance, Format, and Process

SUBSTANCE	FORMAT			
	ANALOG		DIGITAL	
	Processor	**Analog**	**Processor**	• **Alphabet** • **Array**
TIME OF DAY	Traditional watch	Angle of hand to minute or hour	Digital watch	• Numerals and am/pm indications • Four digit positions and one am/pm position
IDEAS (musical)	Record player Cassette player	Depth or width of groove to loudness and pitch Strength of magnetization to loudness and pitch	Digital compact (optical) disk Digital audio tapes	• Bits • Positions in sequence
IDEAS (verbal)	Person speaking	Amount of exertion of vocal chords on air to loudness and pitch	Person writing phonetic transcription Person writing script or print characters	• Phonetic symbols • Positions on line • Letters, numerals and punctuation marks • Positions on line
IDEAS (pictorial realism)	Person painting	Disposition of pigment on canvas to real world color patterns	Newspaper halftone photo processor	• Dot or no dot • Two-dimensional grid
ANY TYPE OF SUBSTANCE	None	None	Compunications system	• Arbitrary alphabet • Multi-dimensional grid

learned in earliest babyhood. But, although every normal child masters the arbitrary conventions or at least the rudiments of spoken language in his or her daily family setting, industrialized nations have had to invest heavily in literacy training.

Literacy training means, among other things, propagating the subtler conventions of standardized spoken language, hammering in the arbitrary convention that "c", "a", "t" is the written format for the spoken English word *cat*, and sorting out the different sounds that convention arbitrarily links to the same letters in *although*, *bough*, and *tough*. These tasks are not easy: Witness the perennial controversies over why kids can't read and over how best to teach them. Industrialized nations invest less heavily, but still substantially, in teaching foreign languages. This means, among other things, clueing English speakers in on the alien conventions that *chat* means *cat* in French but *Katze* means *cat* in German (including the need to use an upper case "K" because *Katze* is a proper noun, and nouns require a capital in German, but not in English or French).

So far we have used the substance–format–process concept primarily for describing products and services—that is, complete systems of some type. However, the concept is equally applicable to all the components of such systems, including the elementary elements of language. In fact, the versatility that comes from arbitrary ties between a digital symbol and the substance it stands for is of net value only if exploring this versatility confers advantages that outweigh the bother of tying and untying arbitrary substance, format, and process bundles. Historical changes in ordinary language give evidence of one kind of recurring perception of a positive net value of versatility. The most frequently used words in all languages ultimately get the shortest strings of phonemes or of letters. The words *I*, *the*, *yes*, *no*, spoken or written, are English examples. The evolution of certain familiar conventional expressions from "horseless carriage" or "automobile" to "car" or "auto" and from "television" to "TV" illustrates how shifts in symbolic conventions mirror shifts in the frequency of reference to the symbolized substance.

In processes based on electro-optical digital formats, the costs of versatility in money or in convenience are down sharply from the costs of versatility in digital processes that rely on flesh-and-blood-brain formats or on mechanical formats.

One case in point is the user friendly personal computers that started to enjoy wide popularity in the mid-1980s. In part, what made them friendly was exploiting the increasingly cheap versatility of microprocessors and their software. For example, with suitable equipment someone could choose to select data or commands by diverse alternative format-and-process combinations such as touching a spot on a screen; pointing at the spot by moving a cursor by key, by "mouse," or even by voice; typing a name in full, using abbreviations, and so on, depending on personal predilections or the stage of developing skills.

The machine, properly programmed, could effectively and affordably track shifts in conventions. Putting the burden of adaptation on the machine makes the shift to its formats as effective and as unselfconscious as the accommodation between one's feet and a really good, not to say foot friendly, pair of new shoes.

Electro-optical digital processes became more versatile and less costly than any others known in the 1980s for three main reasons. First, electro-optical digital processes make it much easier and therefore more advantageous than mechanical or known biological processes, analog or digital, to switch from format to format for best effects at different stages of different processes. Depending on what the process does to the substance embodied in the format, and depending on who or what the processor is, one format can make doing it easier, cheaper, faster, more reliable, more intelligible (or more of many other desirable properties) than some other format. Multiplying by ten is easy in our conventional decimal digital notation, but the Mayan convention was better for multiplying by five or by twenty. Switching back and forth between conventions is not something people like to do. But it's cheap and easy for electro-optical digital processors.

Second, the precision of analog formats is more severely limited by the laws of nature than is the precision of digital formats. Why this should be so is more apparent from the two formats for the number 3.34 in Figure 3-15 than it is from the two formats for a cat. The Arabic numeral "3.34" on the face of the digital calculator makes the value of the number evident at a glance. Estimating where the hairline is between the 3-mark and the 4-mark on the slide rule analog format is not so easy. One could put additional marks between the 3-mark and the 4-mark. If the size of the slide rule is fixed, that tactic quickly founders on how finely the lines can be engraved, or, even if finely engraved, then on how finely they can be seen by the naked eye. In any case, lines finer than the molecular structure of the slide rule are impossible in this world. If, instead, the slide rule is made bigger and bigger, it quickly gets unwieldy.

There is no theoretical limit to the precision of the digital format. In principle, an infinite number of decimal places can be strung on both sides of the decimal point. In practice, too, the number of places can easily be enlarged: writing out a dozen or so decimal places is no great strain on either hand or paper. Practical slide rules are good for three or four places at most. In 1980, eight-place calculators had become common at less than $10, and slide rules had become obsolete. Cost/performance curves like those of Figure 3-8 saw to that. A picture may be worth a thousand words, but thousands of words come easily in both the digital spoken and the digital written ordinary language.

Figure 3-15. Analog and Digital Cats and Numbers

Analog		
Substance:	Idea of Cat	Idea of Number 3.34
Format:		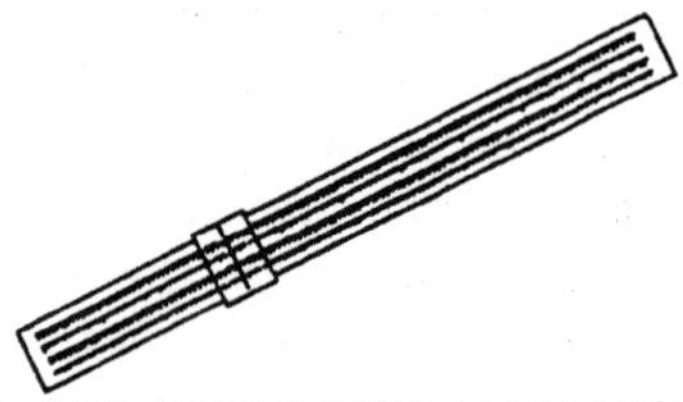

Digital		
Substance:	Idea of Cat	Idea of Number 3.34
Format:	**Cat**	

Speaking another word—in an additional time slot—is easy and cheap. Adding another page—additional slots—to a letter or to a manuscript is also easy and cheap.

The theoretically unlimited precision of digital formats has a more subtle but enormously important and practical value: Their precision enables the creation of digital processes of arbitrarily high reliability, almost independent of the reliability of the physical building blocks that might be used to carry out real digital processes on real material formats with real energy-consuming processors.

Digital processors are far more reliable in practice than analog processors, partly because the real-world building blocks for digital tokens and for their digital processors are intrinsically reasonably reliable. Mostly, however, digital processors are so very reliable because of the understanding, developed after World War II, of how to build up large digital systems that are more reliable than any of their individual parts.

Figure 3-16. Advantages of Electro-Optical Digital Formats

PROPERTIES OF FORMATS		ELECTRO–OPTICAL DIGITAL ADVANTAGE
ANALOG	DIGITAL	
Analogical Relationship to Substance	Arbitrary Relationship to Substance	Versatility
Precision Limited in Practice	Precision Unlimited in Practice	Precision and Reliability
Linear Processes Needed to Preserve Analogy	Fundamentally Non-linear	Abundance and Low Cost

Third—as will be described in detail in the next section—realizing the potential versatility, precision, and reliability of digital processes is possible because digital formats and processes can be realized by exploiting so-called nonlinear materials. Contrasted to the so-called linear materials that are necessary for analog processors, nonlinear materials are vastly more abundant and cheap. In particular, the nonlinear silicon that is at the base of the electro-optical devices of the 1980s comes from a raw material that is found everywhere and that is literally dirt cheap—namely, sand.

The greater versatility, precision, reliability, abundance, and low cost of electro-optical digital formats are, as summarized in Figure 3-16, the practical keys to unlocking the vast and versatile powers of electro-optical digital processes.

Finally, to be both complete and fair, we note that digital systems don't entirely escape from the tyranny of linear requirements. While nonlinear materials and processes are the keys to the flexibility and economy we can achieve with digital systems, an exquisite level of linearity is needed in manufacturing critical parts of these systems, such as processing and memory chips. Photolithographic masks, automated mask-handling devices, and a variety of equipment for etching or depositing materials on the faces of silicon chips are only a few examples of the many areas where "hidden" linearity is needed. The level of technical ability to achieve linearity in these operations often is the pacemaker for progress in digital equipment. It also is responsible for both our ability to make magnificently complex, very small computer chips, and our inability to achieve even somewhat lower densities of complexity on larger substrates. But, fortunately, the requirements for high linearity are largely limited to small quantities of production tools, rather than being needed in each one of the final operating devices. At the turn of the 1990s, however, the ability to make these tools had become one of the important scoring criteria in the economic rivalry between the United States and Japan.

3.5 ABUNDANCE: DIRT CHEAP IS SPELLED "NONLINEAR"

Digital formats have always had one peculiar in-principle advantage over analog formats. This advantage accounts for why ordinary languages the world over ultimately evolved as digital phonemic and graphemic systems, and not as analog onomatopoeic or pictographic systems. But languages got that way by just growing. People have caught on explicitly to the digital advantage only within the last century. The source of this advantage is reliance by digital formats on a ubiquitous property of the physical materials and processes that happen to be at hand abundantly in this, the only universe we know. That very property of physical materials and processes also happens to be disastrous for analog formats.

3.5.1 The High Costs of Linearity

Analog formats and processes must rely on physical materials and processes that are linear in a sense that will be made plain shortly. But most of this world's physical materials and processes are nonlinear. Various *tours de force* can make them seem more linear than they are. But that is usually over a narrow range of usefulness and at relatively high expense. Digital formats and processes thrive on cheap nonlinearity.

Whether, at any given time and for some specific purpose, practical analog formats and processes are preferred over practical digital formats and processes or vice-versa depends on the relative costs of analog and digital systems over the desired range of performance, in the way of Figure 3-7. Theoretical understanding developed since the 1930s and electro-optical materials developed since the 1950s have tipped the balance increasingly in favor of digital systems.

Materials that can be fashioned into physical formats, or tokens, that are appropriately analogous to some given information substance, are not easy to find, not easy to fashion, and not easy to keep faithfully analogous. The history of representational painting from caveman to Leonardo da Vinci attests to that. Only within the last century have techniques been achieved for making sizeable magnifying glasses or eyeglass lenses that will not make straight lines look curved or white paper look like the rainbow. Some rather effective analog formats and processors have nonetheless been fashioned. Many have to work with more than one material and more than one process to do their job.

Figure 3-17. An Analog Transducer

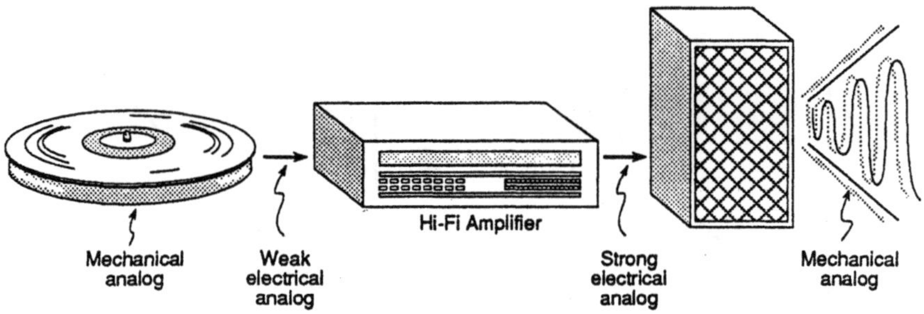

Figure 3-17 depicts how a hi-fi system uses both mechanical and electrical analog tokens and processors.[29] The aim is to preserve analogies so that the music from the loudspeaker is just like the music on the record, only audible. Evanescent sound-in-air is how the music was embodied at the moment when it was recorded as the more stable groove-in-disk token and how it must be embodied once again to be heard. A sound-in-air embodiment expresses substance—musical ideas—by variations in air pressure—compressions and rarefactions—around the normal resting state. A pattern of air pressure variation over time is converted at the recording studio into a mechanical pattern in the grooves of the record, then by the hi-fi tone arm into an electrical pattern, both the latter analogous to the original pattern of pressure variation. If all goes well, what finally emerges from the loudspeaker sounds satisfactorily like what went into the recording.

The ultimate analogy is identity, when two patterns are one and the same. Identity is not only rare but also pretty useless in this instance. Music played loudly is not identical to music played softly. The weak electrical analog produced by a phono tone arm is not identical with the strong electrical analog that comes out of the hi-fi amplifier and is fed to the speakers. What makes the magnified image analogous to the picture seen without a magnifying glass, the loud music analogous to the soft, the strong electrical signal analogous to the weak, and the electrical signal analogous to the sound-in-air is not identity but proportionality. The size of the picture or the size of the sound may

[29] Audiophiles will note that one of the two mechanical analogs, the record, already has succumbed to the optical/electronic digital formats of compact disks and, potentially, digital audiotapes.

Figure 3-18. Proportionality and Linearity

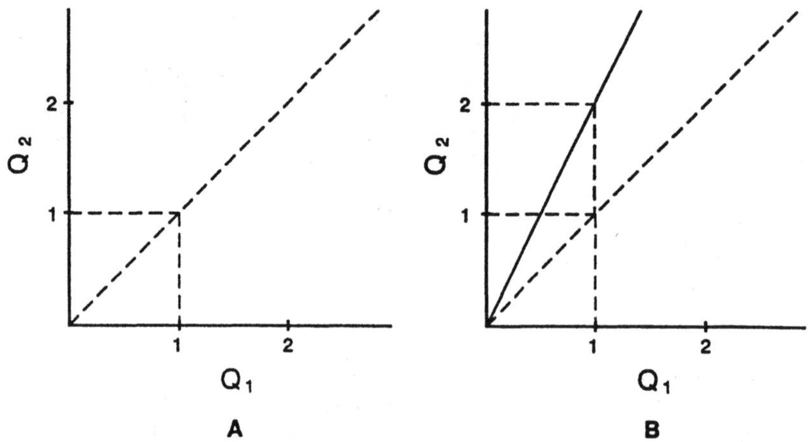

change, but when everything is kept in exact proportion—even through several transmutations, as in going from sound-in-air to mechanical to electrical to sound-in-air—people perceive the result as the same picture, only bigger, or the same music, only louder—not as a different picture or a different music.

Transducer is the name for either an abstract process or else a concrete processor that converts one abstract format or its concrete token to another. The hi-fi amplifier in Figure 3-17 is a transducer that turns weak electrical analog tokens into strong electrical analog tokens. Microphones are transducers that turn sound-in-air tokens into electrical tokens; speakers are transducers that do the reverse.

A not just high-fidelity but perfect fidelity transducer would preserve proportions exactly, no matter what the circumstances: for picture small or large, in light bright or dim; for sound loud or soft, for bass drum or for piccolo. There is no such thing as perfect fidelity in the real analog world, not even at the most exorbitant hi-fi prices. The way our world happens to be built there are, to the best of our knowledge, no materials suitable for making analog tokens and analog transducers that will faithfully preserve proportions under all but a limited range of conditions.

Proportionality can be described in both algebraic and geometric terms. Arithmetic and algebra express the kinship between a quantity Q_2 related to another quantity Q_1 by a proportionality constant P by the multiplication $Q_2 = P \times Q_1$. This kinship is expressed geometrically in the Cartesian plane by a smooth straight line (Figure

3-18A). The greater the proportionality constant P, the steeper the smooth straight line (Figure 3-18B). The phrase "Q_2 is linear in Q_1" expresses the geometric aspect of the relationship between Q_2 and Q_1.

A nonlinear relationship is one where the change in Q_2 is not proportional to the change in Q_1 for at least some values of Q_1. For instance, Figure 3-19A plots what happens to Q_2, \$100 left in the bank at 10 percent a year compounded once a year at year's end, over the time Q_1 that the money is kept in the bank. Q_2 is not proportional to Q_1, so the plot is called nonlinear, even though it is made up of little choppy straight line segments. When interest is compounded continuously, the smooth but nonetheless nonlinear—indeed, exponential—curve of Figure 3-19B expresses the relationship between Q_2 and Q_1. Only a smooth straight line, as in Figure 3-18A and B, expresses a direct proportionality and only a direct proportionality is expressible as a smooth straight line.

Unfortunately, the real world materials at hand for making real world transducers generally have nonlinear characteristic curves in the vein of Figure 3-19. Aeons of ingenuity have brought forth relatively few workable analog transducers.

Figure 3-19. The Nonlinear Behavior of 10% Compounded Annually

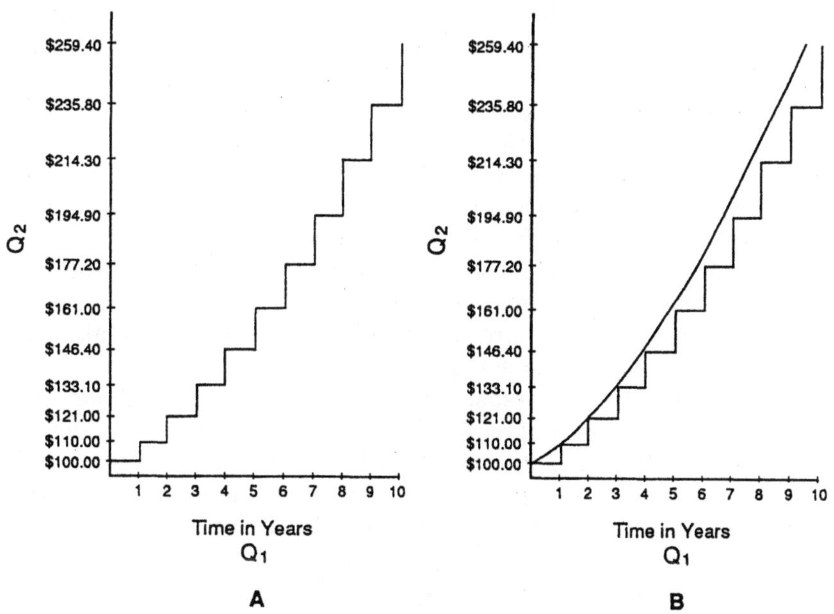

Figure 3-20. Degrees of Nonlinearity

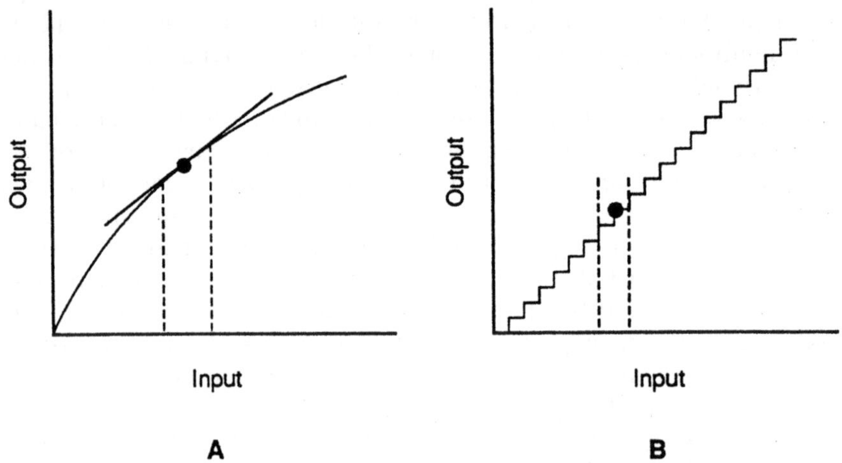

What still saves the day for the practicality of some analog processors is that some kinds of characteristic curves are more linear than others (Figure 3-20). For instance, the characteristic curve of Figure 3-20A is smoother than the characteristic curve of Figure 3-20B. The smoother curve is also less nonlinear than the staircase curve in a sense that is visually evident and that nineteenth century mathematicians nailed down formally. If you happen to be at or near one of the corners of the staircase, it is impossible to approximate the characteristic curve of Figure 3-20B by any straight line that is also faithful to the turning of the corner. With smooth curves like the one in Figure 3-20A, however, the following is mathematically true: for a *small enough* distance around any point on such a smooth curve, a straight line is a reasonable approximation to the curve.

Although most materials that can be considered for building real-life analog transducers or other analog information processors are nonlinear, enough of them are smooth like Figure 3-20A to make some analog devices reasonably serviceable and affordable.

In audiophile terms, reasonable means that you can get hi-fi cheaply provided that you're willing to play it softly. The louder you want to play your hi-fi, the more high quality costs. Everyone has experienced this: a $10 portable transistor radio sounds tolerable, perhaps even good, if played softly enough. If Figure 3-20A is the transistor's characteristic curve, *softly enough* means softly enough for the excursions around the heavy dot in Figure 3-20A to stay within the bounds of reasonable approximation to linearity, for instance between the two vertical dashed lines. Excursions beyond that run

Figure 3-21. Effects of Linear and Nonlinear Amplifiers

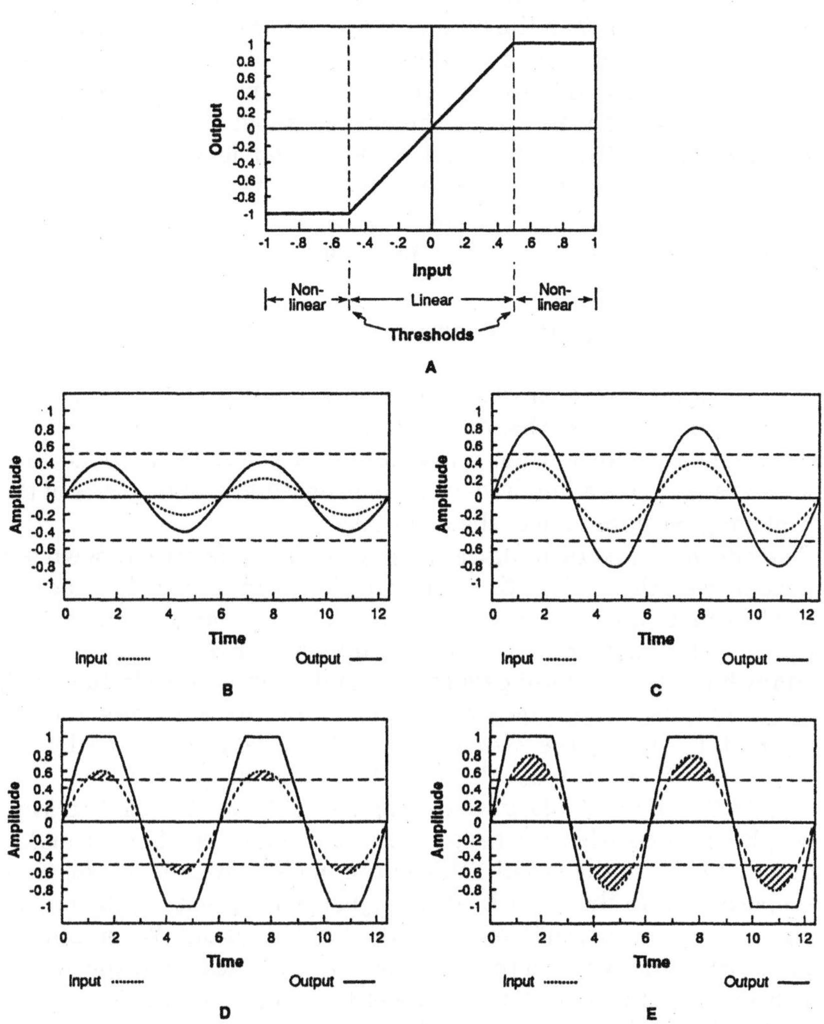

into the region of noticeable nonlinearity, sooner for musicians, later for tin ears.

Within the linear region of Figure 3-21A the output is proportional to the input. One unit of input gives two units of output. Once the input exceeds the threshold in either direction, the output stops being proportional to the input. Indeed, in this extreme example, the output stays put at one no matter how big the input gets.

Figure 3-21 shows what an abrupt departure from linearity does to a pure tone.

In Figure 3-21B and Figure 3-21C, the maximum input amplitudes, 0.2 and 0.4, respectively, are within the 0.5 thresholds. The outputs are therefore bigger than the inputs, but proportional throughout. The ear hears this as a pure tone of the same pitch as the input, just louder.

In Figure 3-21D and Figure 3-21E, the maximum input amplitudes, 0.6 and 0.9, respectively, exceed the 0.5 thresholds. Both outputs are still bigger than the inputs, but they are no longer proportional throughout. It is as if the parts proportioned to the shaded portions of the inputs had been clipped off the outputs. The effect is of a loud and annoyingly rasping noise, not of a pure tone.

3.5.2 Nonlinear Digital Processors at Work

To put together an apparatus that is reasonably linear over a wide dynamic range, namely, that one can play loud and hi-fi as well as soft and hi-fi, is difficult but not impossible. But prices for the loud hi-fi that can range up to a hundred- or even a thousand-fold the price of the soft-playing bargain reflect the difficulty.

The advent of practical digital processors has sharply cut down our dependence on the limited linearities available in nature. Instead, all digital formats and processes glory in the very nonlinearities, like those of 3-21A, that limit the scope of analog formats and processes.

Many humble but useful gadgets are nonlinear, like the light switch of Figure 3-22A. When the switch is open, no current flows and the lamp is dark. When the switch is closed, current generated by the power source flows through the circuit and the lamp glows.

Figure 3-22B and C show what happens as the switch blade travels through positions where it keeps the circuit open to where it makes contact and closes the circuit. While the blade travels from the wide open position a to the point b where it just makes contact, the circuit remains open, no current flows, and the light stays out. When contact is made, current flows and the light goes on, as indicated by the abrupt transition from the lower b to the upper b in Figure 3-22C. The pieces of a switch are flexible, so the blade will travel a bit farther to c. However, since contact has already been made at b, there is no further increase in current flow. The arrows in Figure 3-22C indicate that the reverse happens when the switch is opened.

The circuit of Figure 3-22A is a transducer (Figure 3-22D) that converts a mechanical input, switch blade travel, into an electrical output, current flow, that is further transduced into light by the glowing lamp filament. This transducer has the very nonlinear characteristic curve of Figure 3-22C.

Figure 3-22. The Useful Nonlinear Light Switch

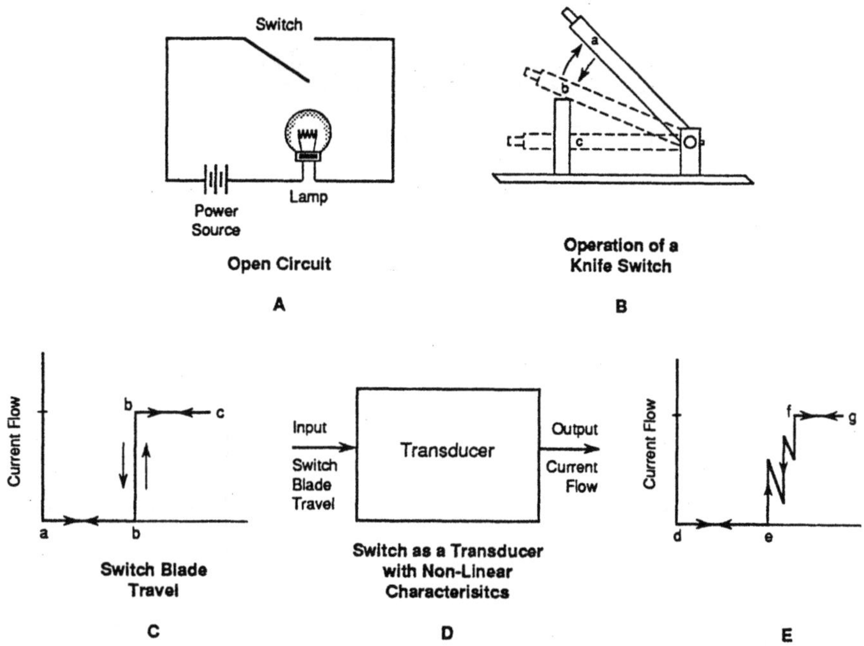

However, real-world switches do not behave precisely as in Figure 3-22C. Instead, as shown in Figure 3-22E, there is apt to be bouncing and jiggling as the blade makes contact or when it opens up. Dust or corrosion on the contacts might cause sparking or intermittent current flow. These accidents are indicated by the jagged transition from e to f in Figure 3-22E. What makes the circuit valuable in spite of the messy transition is the presence of well-defined and stable positions where there is either no current (line de in Figure 3-22E) or full flow of current (fg in Figure 3-22E). Devices with such a characteristic curve are called *bistable* or *two-state.*

Figure 3-23 illustrates a collection of two-state devices that became commonplace in the 1980s, the credit card. Imagine a spot on the card's magnetic stripe (Figure 3-23A) to be magnetized, say in the south/north direction, and quietly sitting there. This state of affairs is depicted by the point marked *1* in Figure 3-23B. Now suppose that a magnetizing force is applied, say by a burst of electric current. The stripe stays magnetized precisely as before until, at point c, the magnetizing force reaches a strength specific to the particular magnetic material used in the stripe. The magnetization of the spot then

Figure 3-23. The Nonlinear Two-State Credit Card

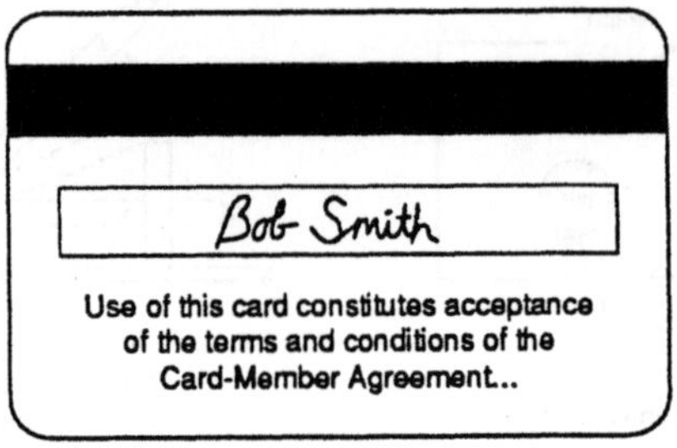

A

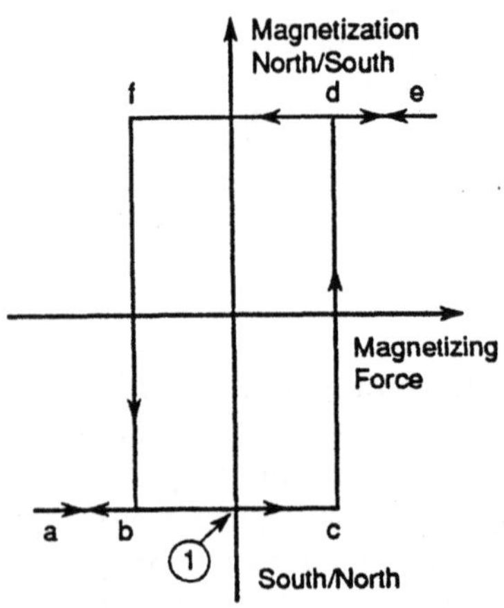

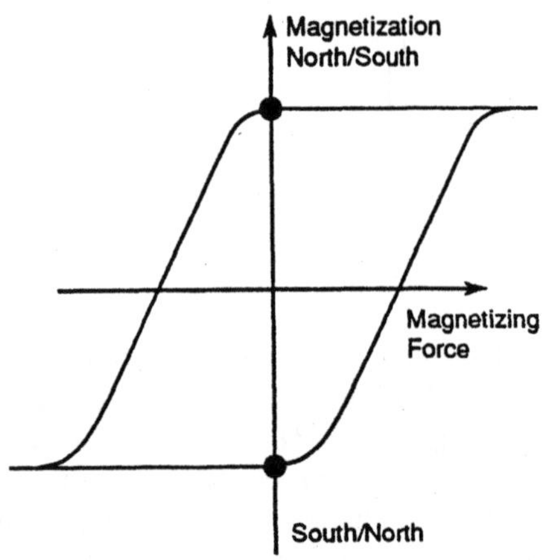

Magnetization of Stripe

B

C

flips from south/north to north/south as shown by the transition to d. Further increase of the magnetizing force causes no further change in the state of magnetization.

Like the switch, which may be opened and closed over and over again, the magnetizing process is reversible over and over again. The process differs from the switch in that the path is not retraced exactly. The magnetizing force has to be fairly strong in the opposite direction before anything happens; so the reversal occurs not at d but at f.

Figure 3-24. A Century of Service: The Nonlinear Punched Card

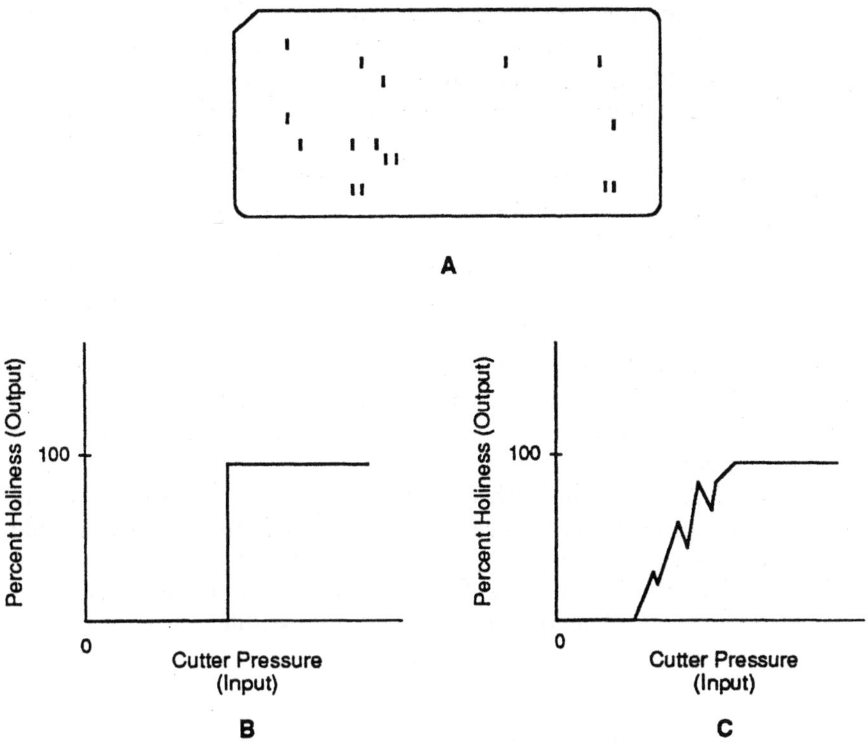

Real-world magnetic materials have sloppier transitions than in the idealized picture of Figure 3-23B. The characteristic curve in Figure 3-23C is more realistic. Allowing for the transitional indeterminacy, it still has the two well-defined and stable resting states shown by the heavy dots. This sharp definition and stability are what count in making two-state devices.

Figure 3-24 depicts the workings of the vanishing punched card, a mechanical input/output format (Figure 3-24A). Figure 3-24B, a characteristic curve relating percent holiness (output) to exerted cutter pressure (input), tells what happens when a cutter presses through the paper to make a hole. Nothing happens until enough pressure is applied. Then all at once the cutter tears through the cardboard and ejects a little rectangle, leaving a hole.

Once again the real-world way is neither quite so abrupt nor quite so clean. Figure 3-24C comes closer to reality.

In principle the process is reversible: one can imagine stuffing the little rectangles back in the holes and gluing them or taping them back in. Except in desperation, however, the process is one-directional, making the venerable punched card an example of what is now called a ROM, from *R*ead-*O*nly *M*emory. Once you've written (punched) in a card, you can only read it again and again, but not write into it anew. The reversible switches, magnets, and transistors can be erased and rewritten over and over again in more practical ways than stuffing little rectangles back into some holes and punching new ones.

Two-state devices abound in nature and in artifacts, and are particularly suitable for digital electro-optical operations. Even with their region of slop or indeterminacy, they are readily exploited both as tokens for two-symbol alphabets and as processors for such tokens.

What makes these devices so useful is the fact, illustrated by Figures 3-22, 3-23, and 3-24, that they are common and readily manipulated. Avoiding slop or indeterminacy and working only with the stable positions is much easier and cheaper in practice than seeking linearity.

Figure 3-25 shows only three of the infinity of possible ways of setting the conventions that associate two symbols with the stable states of two-state tokens. Column 1 shows a dot and a triangle as the associated symbols. Columns 2 and 3 show the possible ways of associating the symbols 0 and 1 with the two stable states.

Figure 3-25. Associating Symbols with Two-State Tokens

Condition	Two-State Token			Arbitrary Symbol		
	Electric Circuit	Magnetic Stripe	Punched Card	Column 1	Column 2	Column 3
Stable State 2	Current Flow	North/ South Magnet	Hole	●	1	0
Region of Indetermincy				Ignored		
Stable State 1	No Current Flow	South/ North Magnet	No Hole	▲	0	1

Figure 3-26. Multistate Optical Tokens

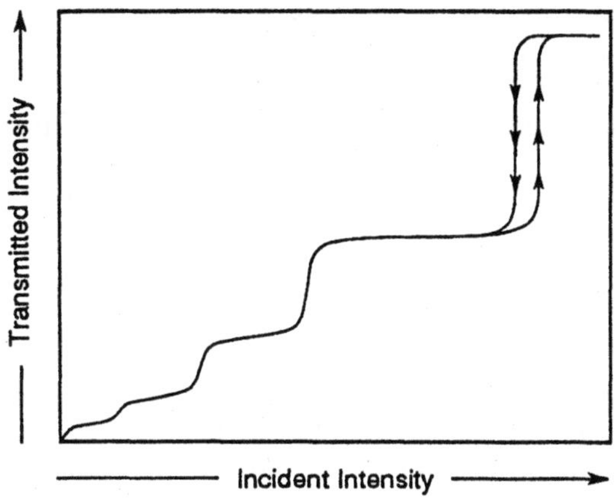

There is nothing magical about using two-symbol or binary alphabets. The important difference is between one and many. Two is just the least among many. Binary alphabets are used because two-state tokens will do, and because two-state tokens suitable for electronic digital processors happen to be handy in this universe and in this epoch. If and when multistate tokens (Figure 3-26[30]) become readily available, multisymbol alphabets will be used. One possibility receiving attention is in the development of optical processors, where there are suitable phenomena to be exploited.

As in any relation between symbols and tokens, the choice of the symbol pair 0 and 1 is just an arbitrary convention. This convention is rooted in the historical accidents of the needs and the tastes of early computer designers, but has no deeper significance.

The punched card, although inherently binary, was mainly used decimally and alphabetically. Any one column could be used to hold one decimal digit as a punch in one of the rows designated 0, 1, 2, . . ., 9. Any one column could be used to hold a letter of the alphabet by double-punching it with combinations of two holes. This scheme best suited the electromechanical clunkers—literally—which processed punched cards in their heyday.

Transistors can be made to behave like the two-state mechanical switch, the two-state magnetic stripe, and the two-state punched card,

[30] Adapted from "The Optical Computer," by Eitan Abraham, Colin T. Seaton, and S. Desmond Smith. Copyright (c)1983 by Scientific American, Inc. All rights reserved. Reprinted by permission.

only much, much faster, not in seconds, but in millionths or billionths of seconds. And transistors can be made much, much cheaper than mechanical two-state devices, at unit costs reckoned not in dollars but in minute fractions of cents. They are usually in circuits that control the current flow through other transistors, not just in circuits that directly turn on a lamp or directly do some other useful thing. Webs of circuits where some circuits control other circuits that control still other circuits are the building blocks of electro-optical digital devices.

3.6 HOW EVERYTHING CAN BE SAID IN DIGITAL

It is easy to make a bigger collection of digital symbols from a smaller one. The trick is familiar. With a few letters you can make up many more words. With those words in turn you make up many more sentences. And so on. By playing with the positions and the combinations of holes in a punched card, the hole/no-hole pair can make up decimal numerals and alphabetic literals. It even is easy to make a digital portrayal of an analog symbol, as mentioned in section 3.3 and in more detail below.

It is not so easy to make analog symbols from digital ones. But it is possible. The why and the how of that come later.

3.6.1 Making Alphabets

In principle, everything that can be done either with analog symbols or with a large collection of digital symbols can be built up from a small digital alphabet. An alphabet with two symbols, a binary alphabet, will do.

Figure 3-27 shows how it is done. The story begins with the bit. A bit is a slot or position that may be filled by, and only by, either of the two symbols in some chosen binary alphabet. A bit is just like the familiar decimal place or like the literal slots filled by the letters of this text. A bit slot differs from decimal slots or literal slots only in the size of the alphabet from which you choose the symbol that fills the slot.

Figure 3-27 makes explicit how the number of bits relates to the number of symbols you can build up from the bits. One bit can express either of two symbols. Since there are four ways of filling two bits, two bits can express any of four symbols (Column 2, Figure 3-27). And, in general, n bits can express up to and including 2^n symbols.

Nothing stops us from using n bits to express fewer than 2^n symbols. Section 3-7 will show how what is lost in apparent waste is often made

Figure 3-27. How Little Alphabets Make Big Alphabets

Number of Bits			
1 □	2 □□	3 □□□	4 □□□□
Number of Symbols Representable			
$2 = 2^1$	$4 = 2^2$	$8 = 2^3$	$16 = 2^4$
0	0 0	0 0 0	0 0 0 0
1	0 1	0 0 1	0 0 0 1
	1 0	0 1 0	0 0 1 0
	1 1	0 1 1	0 0 1 1
		1 0 0	0 1 0 0
		1 0 1	0 1 0 1
		1 1 0	0 1 1 0
		1 1 1	0 1 1 1
			1 0 0 0
			1 0 0 1
			1 0 1 0
			1 0 1 1
			1 1 0 0
			1 1 0 1
			1 1 1 0
			1 1 1 1

up by various kinds of gains. Judicious waste and gargantuan haste are what make for the profitable exploitation of the versatility of the arbitrary conventions whereby digital tokens and representations are associated with symbols.

For the moment, suffice it to say that it is possible to choose digital formats in ways that make this or that easier, cheaper, more convenient, or whatever else might be desired for any substance. This simple fact is the solvent eating up the boundaries between information industries. Figuring out precisely the what and how of making this or that easier, cheaper, or more convenient is what all the engineering, market research, experimentation, instant millionaires, and failures in the information businesses of the 1980s were all about.

Figure 3-28 shows two ways of putting decimal numerals in a binary format: one way is called *pure binary*, the other *binary-coded decimal* (BCD). BCD keeps the familiar decimal slots. There is a ones' place, a tens' place, a hundreds' place, and so on, just as in the ordinary way of writing numerals. The difference is that, instead of using the

Figure 3-28. Different Strokes for Different Folks

Representations of Decimals			
Arabic Numeral	Pure Binary	Binary-Coded Decimal (BCD) Tens Place	Binary-Coded Decimal (BCD) Ones Place
0	0		0 0 0 0
1	1		0 0 0 1
2	1 0		0 0 1 0
3	1 1		0 0 1 1
4	1 0 0		0 1 0 0
5	1 0 1		0 1 0 1
6	1 1 0		0 1 1 0
7	1 1 1		0 1 1 1
8	1 0 0 0		1 0 0 0
9	1 0 0 1		1 0 0 1
10	1 0 1 0	0 0 0 1	0 0 0 0
11	1 0 1 1	"	0 0 0 1
12	1 1 0 0	"	0 0 1 0
13	1 1 0 1	"	0 0 1 1
14	1 1 1 0	"	0 1 0 0
15	1 1 1 1	"	0 1 0 1
16	1 0 0 0 0	"	0 1 1 0
17	1 0 0 0 1	"	0 1 1 1
18	1 0 0 1 0	"	1 0 0 0
19	1 0 0 1 1	"	1 0 0 1
20	1 0 1 0 0	0 0 1 0	0 0 0 0
21	1 0 1 0 1	"	0 0 0 1

ten familiar symbols of the Arabic numeral alphabet in each of those places, BCD uses a binary representation of the ten Arabic digits. Instead of using a single Arabic numeral to fill a decimal place, BCD uses a four-bit byte to stand for a decimal digit. *Byte* is the term for a cluster of bits, a big position or slot made up of little slots.

Figure 3-28 illustrates why one would bother picking one representation over the other. People, for example, find BCD somewhat easier to decipher than a pure binary format. One need only memorize 10 four-bit combinations in order to read BCD as if it were ordinary decimal notation. Deciphering the pure binary notation is harder for people to learn. But pure binary notation is more economical than BCD, because

Figure 3-29. The Alphabet in Bits

An Encoded Alphabet					
Letters	Binary Coding with Five Bits				
A	0	0	0	0	1
B	0	0	0	1	0
C	0	0	0	1	1
D	0	0	1	0	0
E	0	0	1	0	1
F	0	0	1	1	1
G	0	1	0	0	0
H	0	1	0	0	1
I	0	1	0	1	0
J	0	1	0	1	1
K	0	1	1	0	0
L	0	1	1	0	1
M	0	1	1	1	0
N	0	1	1	1	1
O	1	0	0	0	0
P	1	0	0	0	1
Q	1	0	0	1	0
R	1	0	0	1	1
S	1	0	1	0	0
T	1	0	1	0	1
U	1	0	1	1	0
V	1	0	1	1	1
W	1	1	0	0	0
X	1	1	0	0	1
Y	1	1	0	1	0
Z	1	1	0	1	1

it uses fewer bits. This suggests using BCD as a display format and pure binary for processing. But then translation is necessary from one to the other and back, and so on. By such picky tradeoffs are the minds of compunications engineers seized. The success or failure of these tradeoffs influences competitive costs and weights the wheel by whose spins fortunes are made or lost.

Figure 3-29 illustrates how the conventional twenty-six-symbol alphabet may be formatted by five-bit bytes. Some waste is inherent here, since five bits could do thirty-two symbols.

Calling electro-optical digital processors *computers* is a hangover from their earliest limited forms. Specialized forms have gotten other names, like *word processor*, but even the generic name masks the full generality of the generic power of digital processors. Together, Figure

Figure 3-30. Speech from Brain to Brain

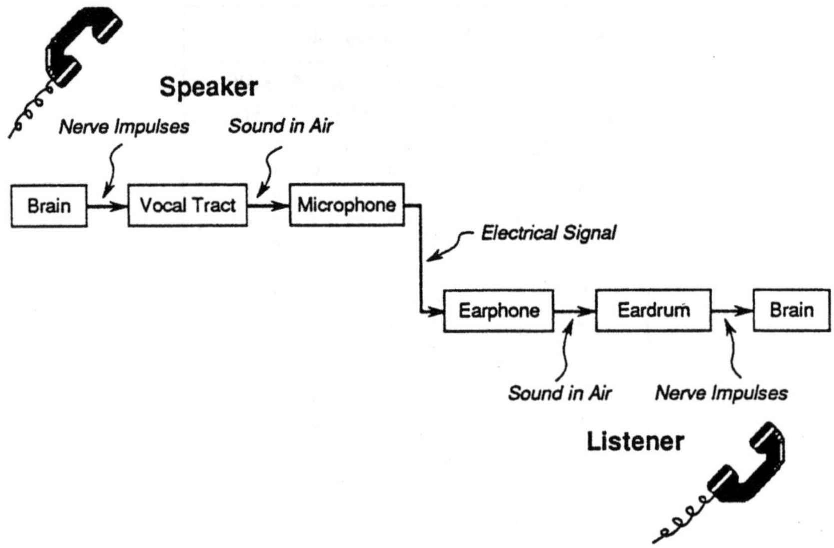

3-28 and Figure 3-29 show why anything done, not only in numbers, but also in words, can be formatted, not only digitally—which the conventional decimal numerals and alphabetic literals already do—but more particularly in the binary alphabets, which happen to be suitable for versatile and abundant electro-optical formats and processors. Thus, absolutely anything that can be said in numbers or words, in numerals or literals, can be formatted in binary digital formats and processed by electro-optical digital processors.

3.6.2 Sounds and Pictures

More remarkably, the same holds for sounds and pictures and indeed for any conceivable kind of substance, no matter how that substance might be represented according to prevalent conventions. Sounds and pictures can be digitized in distinctive ways, some of them of universal applicability but somewhat superficial, others more particular but also more profound.

To help illustrate diverse ways of digitizing sound, Figure 3-30 shows what happens between a speaker's brain and a listener's brain. Telephone transducers are intermediaries here, but the intermediaries might be radio or television systems or some other artifact.

Not much is understood about what goes on in either brain. But whatever does go on in the speaker's brain is nowadays made manifest almost exclusively by the effects of the nerve impulses that actuate the vocal tract, which in turn pushes on the air to make the audible waves that we call sound. All else on brain activity in the process comes either from unreliable introspections and speculations or else from unusual and still very rudimentary laboratory experiments with electroencephalograms, implanted electrodes, and the like. Once sound-waves-in-air hit the listener's ear drum and get transduced into nerve impulses, the brain and its mysteries take over once again.

What people set forth explicitly in digital formats is not what concerns us right here. Writing is digital. So is typing. Written or typed substance comes out of the human brain, nerves, and muscles explicitly formatted in the twenty-six-member alphabet and arrayed in the limitless sequence of digital slots. Music is no problem either when it issues forth from the brain and the hand in conventional musical notation. Staff, clefs, notes, and so on make up a digital format. The mysteries of the composer's brain, nerves, and muscles have embodied musical substance in an explicitly digital format.

What the brain, nerves, and muscles put forth as speech or as music whistled, hummed, or sung is an altogether different matter. Speech, whistles, hums, and songs as sound-in-the-air remain explicitly analog formats by the lights of the scientific understanding of the turn of the 1990s.

Linguists surmise that speech is inherently but implicitly digital. The evidence for this is disarmingly simple. If speech were inherently analog, it would be mostly unintelligible owing to the enormous variations among speakers and hearers that stem from sex, dialect, the health of the speaker's nose or of the hearer's ear. There is no way that a word uttered by one person is simply proportional to or analogous to the same word uttered by someone else, or even by the same person in a different sentence! The prevalent linguistic theory is that the speaker's brain produces—and the listener's brain recognizes—digital phonemes.

Phonemes are supposed to be elements of a small alphabet, not much larger than the alphabet of literals. The speaker produces phonemes and the listener interprets them unruffled by distortions, much as a reader recognizes "a" or "f" however distorted in diverse handwritings or in diverse type fonts. There are more phonemes than there are literals. For example, the "a" phoneme in *bad* is not the same as the "a" phoneme in *bathe*. That the two sounds must be truly distinct and not just distinguished by their different contexts in *bad* and *bathe* is based on such evidence as the pair of words *tack* and *take*.

In *tack* and *take* the sounds that surround "a" are the same. The inference is that since *tack* and *take* are heard differently, the literal "a" stands for one phoneme in *tack* and for a different phoneme in *take*.[31]

But all of this occurs, if at all, inside brains. Try as we might, the evidence for phonemes in speech as sound-in-the-air remains scant. A most convincing kind of evidence, the building of an artifact that would, if not understand speech, at least convert speech into its written equivalent, remains beyond our grasp. In the mid-1980s the results of research in speech recognition fell far short of that goal. Any successes hinged on techniques that have clear commercial possibilities—as in substituting ten spoken digits for the finger in the dial or on the beeping buttons—but that shed only a dim light on the supposed phonemic (digital) nature of speech. So, for acoustic transmissions between brains, speech, or music that start as sound-in-the-air—and not as phonemic or alphabetic transcription or as a musical score—must for the foreseeable future be dealt with as analog symbols. And the same applies to pictures.

It is not entirely self-evident that speech or music as sound-in-the-air, or visual images as light waves, or any other kind of sound or electromagnetic wave, can in fact be given fully faithful digital expression under usefully benign and widely prevalent enough conditions. The familiar half-tone newspaper photo points the way. A half-tone is made up of black and white dots or, if not so binary, of a limited alphabet of discrete shadings of gray. But the quality of the usual half-tone is not what one would choose to mean by a "fully faithful" digital expression. Major mathematical discoveries by Joseph Fourier in the nineteenth century and by Claude Shannon in the twentieth century were necessary to unlock the way to fully faithful digital expressions of a universal but superficial kind.[32]

Not only is the theory far from self-evident, but the fact that Shannon's theoretical possibility could be realized in practice does not at all flow from the theory itself. It just happens—Bell System irredentists would add the aside "but not just by accident"—that the transistor, and, later, its elaboration into increasingly complex and powerful integrated circuits of decreasing cost, provided the practical

[31] Jakobson, Roman and Morris Halle, *Fundamentals of Language* (The Hague, Holland: Mouton & Co., 1971).

[32] Fourier, Joseph, *Analytical Theory of Heat* (Cambridge, England: The University Press, 1878); and Shannon, Claude E. and Warren Weaver, *The Mathematical Theory of Communication* (*supra,* note 4).

Figure 3-31. Water Wave in a Fish Tank

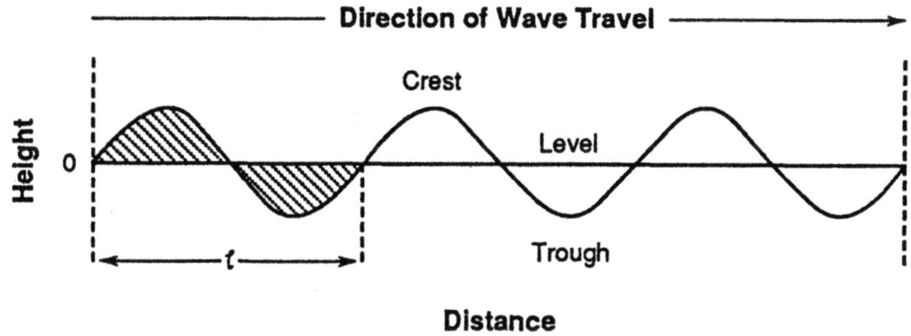

means for carrying out Shannon's processes fast and cheaply enough to be of workaday value, along cost/performance curves as in Figure 3-7.

The story of fully faithful, universal, but superficial digital formats begins with Fourier's decomposition of complex waves, sound waves among them, into simple building blocks.

Some details about the nature of waves—sound waves in particular, but other waves as well—help explain what Fourier and Shannon did that made fully faithful digital encoding of sound a theoretical possibility.

Imagine that you are looking through the glass of a fish tank at a stretch of open water, with your eyes at the level of the undisturbed water. That level is denoted by the horizontal straight line in Figure 3-31. A wave is sweeping across the tank from left to right. At the instant when you are looking, the crests and troughs of the wave are as shown in Figure 3-31. The pattern of crests and troughs is repetitive. Because of the wave's movement, a floating object held in a fixed horizontal position will rise and fall as the wave passes by. The length of one unit or cycle in this repetitive pattern, shaded in Figure 3-31, is the wave length, l, of the wave. The cycle time T of the wave is the time for our floating object to return to the precise position and heading it had at the start of the cycle; and the inverse or reciprocal 1/T of this time is called the frequency of the wave.

Wave phenomena are widespread. They arise in water movements, as just described, in alternating electric current flows, in radio waves, in sound waves, and in many others. The way the phenomenon works in sound, a water crest is like a compression of the air molecules. A water trough is like a rarefaction where the air molecules are farther apart than in the undisturbed air. A pure tone sung by a singer travels from the singer's mouth to the listener's eardrum like the water waves traveling across Figure 3-31. The effect on the listener's eardrum also

Figure 3-32. Sine Equals Opposite Over Hypotenuse

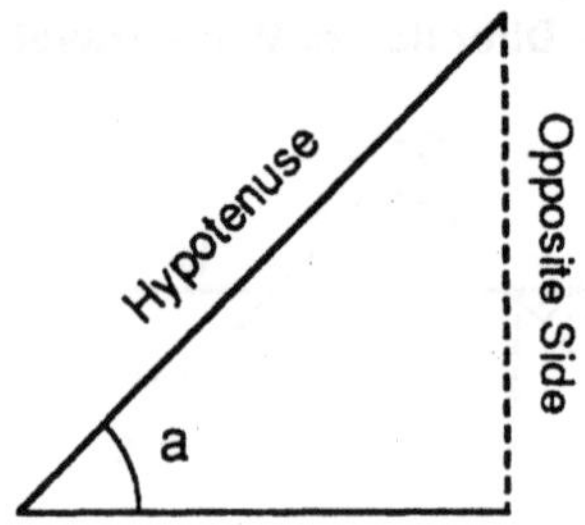

may be visualized as in Figure 3-31. At a crest, the eardrum is pushed away from its resting position toward the inner ear. It then returns to its resting position, only to be drawn toward the outside of the ear as a rarefaction passes by. The resulting vibration of the eardrum thus is a mechanical analog of the compression/rarefaction wave traveling through the air.

Figure 3-31 depicts a shape typical of many kinds of wave, including the wave shape of a pure tone of sound. Waves that convey pure tones are called *sine waves*. Shannon discovered additional properties of sine waves that underlie the methods now more and more widely used commercially for the fully faithful digital formatting of analog sound waves.

Sine waves are named after the sine of an angle. The sine of an angle of a right triangle is the ratio of the length of the side of the triangle opposite the angle to the length of the hypotenuse of the triangle, as in Figure 3-32.

With the length of the hypotenuse taken as the unit of length, the value of the sine of the angle is just the height of the side opposite the angle. As the unit hypotenuse turns counterclockwise and describes a circle, the sine takes on different values—first higher and then dropping to a negative peak before returning to its starting point.

Figure 3-33 shows intermediate values of sin a, the sine of a, as a goes from 0 degrees to 360 degrees or, equivalently, from 0 radians to 2π radians. Figure 3-33 also shows that the value of sine a ranges between $+1$ and -1.

A sin a, which therefore ranges in value between $+A$ and $-A$, thus can represent pure tone waves of any amplitude A.

One additional arithmetic trick completes the adaptation of the trigonometric sine to the description of pure tones. By definition a pure tone goes through one cycle or period in a time interval T. Defining a as $\frac{2\pi t}{T}$ where t is elapsed time and T the period of the wave, is that trick. When $t = 0$, at the beginning of a period, $a = \frac{2\pi \varnothing}{T}$

Figure 3-33. The Sine Waveform

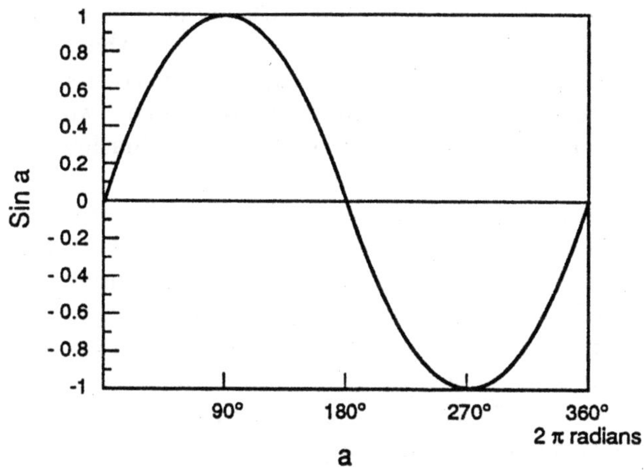

= 0 and sin a = 0, as desired. When t = T, at the end of a T period, a = $\frac{2\pi T}{T}$ = 2 π and sin a = 0, as desired. Likewise at all intermediate values of t. The quantity $\frac{2\pi}{T}$ thus joins the period T and the frequency f = $\frac{1}{T}$ among convenient descriptors of pure tones.

Why pure tone waves happen to be sine shaped has to do with linearity and with how natural vibrations happen in the springs of a harmonica, the strings of a violin, the air in an organ pipe, the membranes of kettle drums or of eardrums, the water in the fish tank, the pendulum of a clock, and so on.

Imagine a violin string that is displaced from its resting position, but not too far. *Not too far* here amounts to asking for enough linearity in the neighborhood of the resting state precisely as in Figure 3-20A. The restoring force F that pulls the string back to its resting position is proportional to the displacement D, namely F = constant × D, if only D is small enough. It then follows from Newton's Laws of Motion that a sine wave precisely describes the vibration of the violin string.

That remarkable conclusion may not impress any musician who knows that real strings or skins are not necessarily displaced just a little bit from their resting position. Indeed, what makes Middle C on the violin differ from Middle C on the piano is that, in each instrument, real fundamental notes or pure tones come with harmonics. These harmonics differ from instrument to instrument and give each instrument its unique tonality. And the sources of the harmonics are the nonlinearities that arise from exceeding linear displacement limits.

But the harmonics themselves can be thought of as pure tones of a pitch or frequency different from the fundamental pitch. True harmonics are of a frequency that is a multiple of the frequency of the fundamental pure tone. What Fourier discovered is that every periodic wave—and, indeed, much more general sound patterns—can be portrayed as made up of sine waves. In particular, such a wave is made up of a fundamental pure tone and various combinations of its pure harmonics.

Figure 3-34 shows how sine waves, added together in systematically different ways, can make up different shapes. The triangular shape is discernible by the third step in Figure 3-34A, the square by the third step in Figure 3-34B. After sixty steps, the only discernible action is at the sharp corners. The sine waves that make up another waveform are called the Fourier components of that waveform.

Describing a waveform by its Fourier components leads to simplifying insights of major practical import as well as of deep theoretical significance. It so happens in this universe that any linear transducer behaves very simply with inputs that are the sums of sine waves. What the linear transducer does to the sum of several sine waveforms is just the sum of whatever it does to each sine waveform by itself. So, if we know what a transducer does to a sine wave of any arbitrary frequency, and if we know what sine waves the input is made up of, then the output of the transducer is just the sum of whatever the transducer would do to each of the component sine waves in isolation. In summary, once you know how a linear transducer treats one sine wave, you know how it treats any wave.

Turning these insights into practical schemes for fully faithful digital formats for sounds hinges on a trait already noted about the universe we happen to live in. Because they are linear enough only over a limited range (Figure 3-20A), real world transducers work well for only a limited range of harmonics. That's why hi-fi sets must have woofers for the low notes, tweeters for the high notes, and, when more expensive, some additional loudspeakers for in-between notes.

Our vocal tracts and our ears are transducers for sounds, the sound of speech and the sound of music among them. Like all materials, throats and ears can handle only a limited range of frequencies. In particular, the ear cannot hear sounds pitched higher than about 20 kilohertz (20,000 cycles per second). Dogs do better than that, which is why we've invented ultrasonic dog whistles with a pitch that is beyond what we can hear but that dogs jump to. Indeed, most of us get anywhere near 20 khz only in youth; as we grow older, we drop off toward 15 or perhaps even 12 khz as the upper limit of our hearing range.

Figure 3-34. How Sines Make Up Triangles, Squares, or You Name It

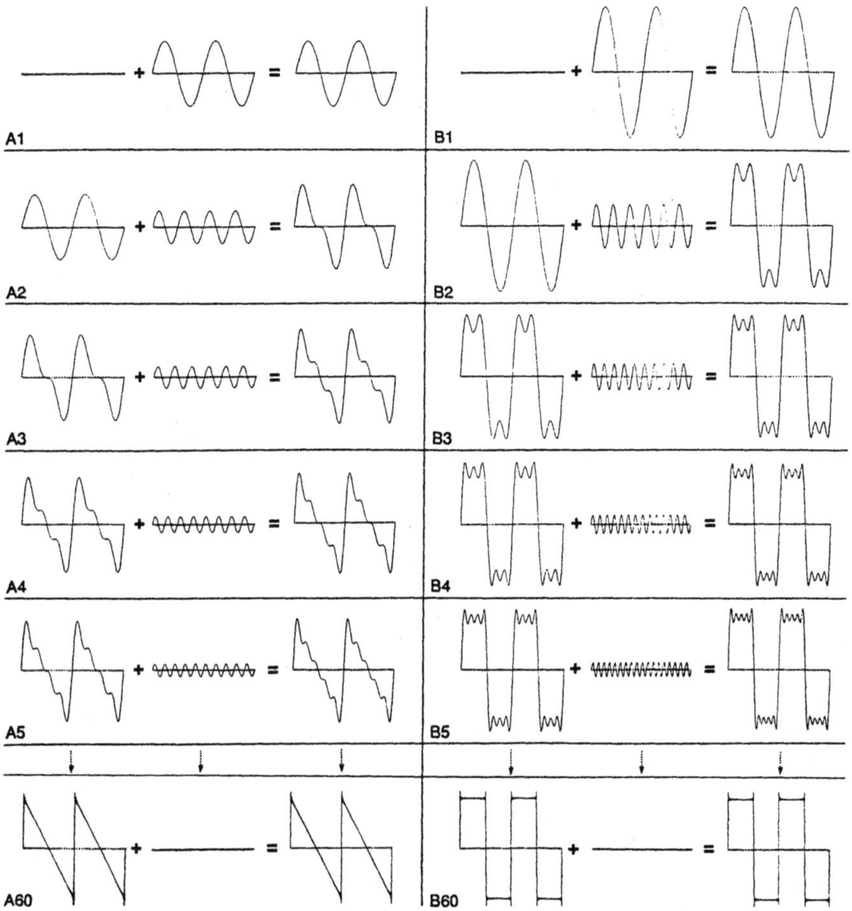

At the lower end of our hearing range, most of us can hear enough of the 60-hertz hum that fluorescent lamps make to get annoyed, but acuity drops off pretty fast below that.

3.6.3 Bandwidth Economics: Matching and Sampling

The range of frequencies over which a transducer functions well enough by someone's lights is called the *bandwidth* of the transducer. Thus, our ears have a bandwidth of about 12 to 20 khz. The concept of bandwidth provides a good way of matching the makeup of waveforms

Figure 3-35. Sampling Sounds for Fully Faithful Reproduction

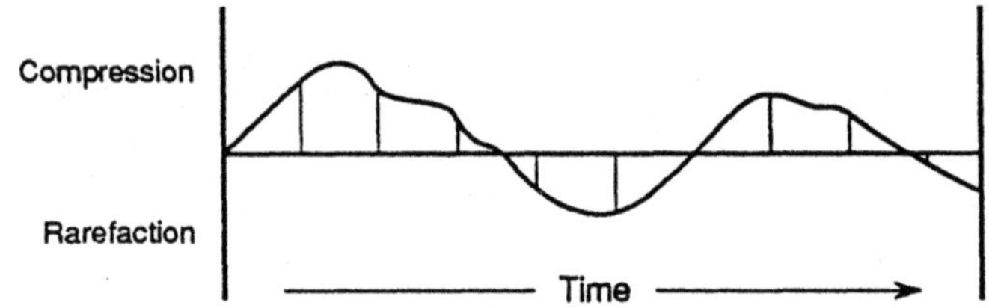

A

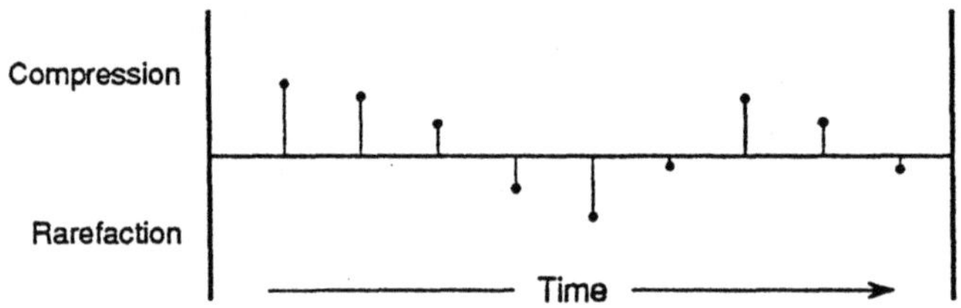

B

with transducers—transmission channels among them—of just the right capacities.

Fourier analysis describes any waveform by listing the pure sine waves that make it up. The range between the frequency of the lowest frequency sine wave in the waveform and the frequency of the highest frequency sine wave in the waveform is the bandwidth of the waveform. A sound wave with lowest frequency component near 60 hertz and highest frequency component between 12 and 20 khz has a bandwidth of about 12 to 20 khz.

A waveform with, say, a 15-khz bandwidth is best matched to a transmission channel of exactly that bandwidth. A transmission channel with less than a 15-khz bandwidth would not provide fully faithful reproduction, because it would not pass through enough of the pure sine waves that make up the input waveform. A transducer with more than a 15-khz bandwidth would waste its capacity for handling sine waves that aren't in the waveform.

Matching a waveform's bandwidth to a transducer's bandwidth is the analog way to efficiency. On a foundation of analog-bandwidth matching, Shannon built a scheme guaranteed to deliver a fully faithful digital format for any waveform of a specified bandwidth.

As a first step, Shannon discovered that just sampling a waveform of specific bandwidth W is good enough to define that waveform with full faithfulness. Figure 3-35 illustrates this. The waveform of 3-35A is sampled at discrete intervals. Shannon discovered conditions under which transmitting only samples as shown in 3-35B and omitting everything else is good enough, in principle, to give fully faithful reproduction of the original signal at the receiving end.

The bandwidth W of the original signal fixes the interval at which samples must be taken. Shannon found that the sampling interval cannot exceed 1/2W seconds for full faithfulness. For instance, if W equals 4 hertz, then 1/2W equals one-eighth second. The samples must be taken no more than one-eighth of a second apart. No faithfulness is lost if samples are taken at shorter intervals, but that's wasteful. If samples are taken at intervals longer than one-eighth of a second, then reproduction will not be fully faithful.

The French have a saying, "C'est simple, mais il fallait y penser," meaning "It's simple, once you thought of it." As a colleague of mine in the early days of the Apollo moon-landing program put it, "This problem, when solved, will be easy." And so it is with the elegant simplicity of the Shannon Sampling Theorem. It is intuitively reasonable. A slowly varying wave form, oscillating no faster than four times a second, can be faithfully described by sampling it every one-eighth of a second. A fast-varying wave form, say one with a 20-khz component at the limit of human hearing, would be described faithfully only if sampled every 25-millionths of a second. Elegant, simple, but not at all practical when first thought of.

The practicality of digital telephones, digital CDs, and so on turns on compromises that make a virtue of human limitations and that exploit cheap fast electro-optical digital technologies.

The bandwidth of our throats and ears is in the 10- to 20-khz range. The experience of the world's telephone companies, however, is that a bandwidth of 3–4 khz is more than adequate for transmitting voices faithfully enough to keep their customers happy. A 4-khz bandwidth makes speech intelligible. Moreover, speakers are recognizable and shades of inflection and intonation are discernible. As anyone knows who has listened to music-on-hold, 3–4 khz is terrible for music. It is, however, an adequate and, in any case, a widely adopted, standard for voice transmission. The tradeoff made years ago was between what it would cost to provide hi-fi telephone service to everyone at all times and what it costs to provide it only to some—notably, to radio and TV networks—at some times.

In the world of real telephones, therefore, convention sets the Shannon bandwidth W equal to 4 khz, or 4000 Hz. By that convention, 1/2W equals 1/8000 seconds as the interval not to exceed between samples for faithfulness no worse than that imposed by the 4-khz bandwidth limit. This is 0.125 thousandths of a second, or 125 microseconds per interval. Eight thousand samples must be taken every second.

A requirement to take eight thousand samples in one second may seem tight on a scale of seconds, and just barely reasonable on a scale of microseconds. It may seem ample or even lavish on the scale of billionths of a second, or nanoseconds: the interval between samples amounts to 125,000 nanoseconds. Counting nanoseconds was unthinkable in the practice of the 1930s and 1940s, when Shannon first proposed his sampling idea. By the 1980s, measuring time and taking samples by the nanosecond had become affordable routine.

Some other hurdles had also been cleared by the 1980s. Were it necessary in practice as well as in principle to measure the heights of sample pulses (Figure 3-35B) with absolute accuracy, Shannon's scheme would nonetheless have remained a mathematical curiosity devoid of practical impact.

Another compromise led closer to practicality. This compromise rests on yet another pragmatic observation. Just as our ears have a limited bandwidth, so our ears are also incapable of hearing very small jumps in loudness. The same kind of scientific and commercial observations that inspire reliance on a 4-khz bandwidth as adequate for intelligible, recognizable, and marketable speech have led to the convention that speech with no more than 128 discrete levels of loudness—that is, 128 discrete levels of wave height—is of adequate quality. Given that convention, measurements of sample heights can be rounded off to the nearest among those 128 discrete loudness levels.

There is just one more step to the end of this trail. A stream of sample pulses coming 125,000 nanoseconds apart and each of a height chosen among 128 discrete levels would still have to be amplified from time to time if it had to travel over more than hundreds of feet. The necessary analog amplifiers would have to be linear over the full range of 128 possible input levels or else the speech would be distorted. The trail could be at a dead end.

Fully faithful transmission of waveforms limited to a 4-khz bandwidth and 128 discernible levels of loudness was achieved by shifting to a digital format that takes advantage of the nonlinearities of nature. Instead of trying to transmit 128 distinct pulse levels through analog amplifiers, the levels are converted to a binary code with a seven-bit byte per pulse.

That encoding is illustrated for an eight-level system in Figure 3-36. Instead of having to find materials linear over the whole range of eight distinct and discrete levels, as in the first column of Figure 3-36,

Figure 3-36. Pulse-Formatted Speech

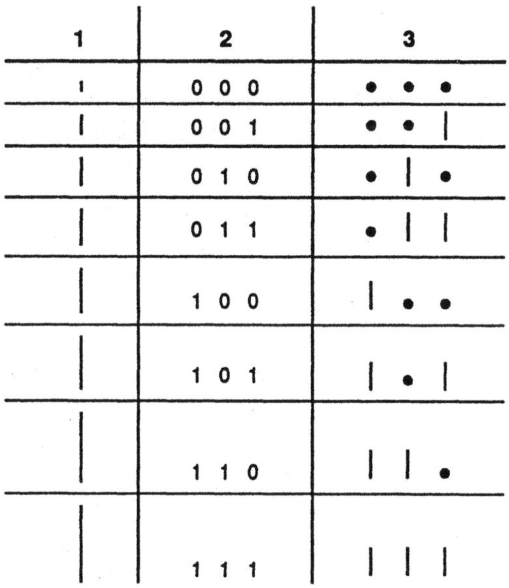

the binary format of the second column can be embodied as a stream of presences or absences of pulses of uniform height. Pulse/no pulse tokens, as in the third column of Figure 3-36, are readily handled by two-state devices of the kind illustrated earlier. A three-bit byte is enough for $8 = 2^3$ levels. A seven-bit byte would be needed for $128 = 2^7$ levels.

What began as an electrical analog of the continuous compression and rarefaction stream in the air has now been transformed into binary digital tokens fully faithful to the original analog tokens. Nothing distinguishes binary tokens that came from a stream of speech, or a snatch of music from tokens for the letters of some alphabet or for numbers. The demonstration that speech can be said in digital, just as numbers and letters can be said in digital, is now complete, at least in principle.

The digital tokens derived by subjecting speech to Shannon's scheme, now a routine scheme called *pulse code modulation*, have no necessary relation to the hypothesized phonemic digital expression of speech in the brain. What that might be remains a mystery. A practical consequence is that the voice-actuated typewriter remains an elusive goal. Just digitizing the wave form does not help us get there from here. Only digitizing speech as phonemes would, if we could.

As of April 1984, the latest in decades of brave words was reported as follows:

> Research on continuous speech recognition has been largely dormant in this country; the sole exception is the ongoing effort at IBM's Thomas J. Watson Laboratories in Yorktown Heights, New York, where the goal is a real-time office dictation machine with a vocabulary of 5000 words. In Japan, however, the so-called "Fifth Generation" project has announced that one of its long-range goals will be a 10,000 word, speech-activated typewriter with the ability to understand hundreds of different speakers. Some observers in the United States believe that, with a substantial application of resources, a limited version of such a system could be available in the 1990's.[33]

More recently, in July 1990, *IEEE Spectrum* noted that Dragon Systems, Inc., had announced

> the first commercial speech recognition system with a large vocabulary of 30,000 words that learns from someone talking fairly naturally rather than from limited sets of words spoken in a preordained order....
>
> The user must pronounce discrete words, separating them by a pause of about a quarter second. He or she also calls for punctuation, such as "comma" or "open quote," just as to a human stenographer.... Once accustomed to the system, users can create text at a rate of 30 to 40 or more words per minute.[34]

Clearly there has been progress; but it still has a long way to go to become an everyday tool for the masses!

In practice, using digital tokens for speech requires not only the initial analog to digital conversion. Eventually, the digital bit stream must be turned back into a continuous stream of compressions and rarefactions that can move our eardrums. The formula that Shannon elaborated, when he discovered how to do the sampling, envisages restoring the original continuous speech wave form by a complicated process of weighted averaging of the samples. That process, like most aspects of Shannon's scheme, would have been impossible in practice at the time Shannon proposed his theory. Versatile and abundant electro-optical digital formats and processors have made it practical.

What can be done for speech can also be done for pictures, with color and all. The not-so-faithful dot/no dot two-state tokens used in the

---

[33] "Natural Language Understanding," *Research News Science* 224, no. 4647 (April 1984): 373.

[34] See "Innovations," *IEEE Spectrum,* July 1990, 50.

familiar half-tone pictures in newspapers thus foreshadow the more general Shannon process for practical, fully faithful binary formatting of any analog symbols whatsoever.

3.7 SHAPING DIGITAL FORMATS FOR EFFICIENCY

Although hardly ever a front-page headline matter, the search for formats that are efficient in various stages of business information processes is important to all information suppliers and consumers struggling for competitive advantage. Making it with profitable data bank services, for example, depends in part on finding format-and-process combinations that are more efficient than the competition's in delivering comparable substance to customers. Here, like anywhere else, the bottom line depends on both the product—substance in some format—and the process for making, selling, delivering, and using it.

In the extreme, a format that is just dandy for substance undergoing one process may be worthless for another process. When standing next to me, you can tell me in plain spoken English that the British are coming by land or else by sea. But if I'm about to go farther away than your shouts will carry, plain shouted English won't do. We have to arrange for you to hold up one lantern in the Old North Church steeple for one message, or two lanterns for the other. In this familiar early American epic, changing the format to accommodate the process was the key to conveying any substance at all.

There are cases in between. If you are paying for a message by the word, as in the bygone days when telegrams were the only form of rapid communication at a distance, you might be quite interested in conveying any given substance with as few words as possible. To one familiar with New England, the message "New England winters are cold" at $10 a word might seem like the epitome of gouging for worthless substance. If you're about to board a plane in Sydney, Australia, bound for Boston, the message "Boston just suffered a minor earthquake" at $10 a word might seem more worthwhile. There is a strong intuitive sense that one of these messages conveys more substance and is of greater significance than the other. It therefore ought to cost less to send less substance.

No one has yet managed to capture in any formal, global, and also useful way all that we lump within the vague ideas of "amount of substance" and "appropriately matched format." There is one particular sense, however, in which the idea of amount of substance has been made explicit in a way that permits precise matching of substance and formats. Here again the theory was pioneered, in the 1940s and 1950s, by Claude Shannon. Shannon's way of measuring amount of substance starts with a universe of discourse. It builds on the notion that how much substance there is in some message is not an absolute but, rather, depends on the universe of discourse from which that message is drawn.

3.7.1 Measuring Substance

Out of the many ways in which one might construe the common sense notion of universe of discourse, Shannon singled out one far less grandiose than the Universe of All Possible Discourse of section 2.7 of Chapter 2. How many messages are in a given universe of discourse and how likely each message is to be sent fully describes a universe of discourse in Shannon's scheme. This simple idea is very useful in assessing the efficiency of digital formats.

Shannon's measure of substance serves the digital world the way bandwidth serves the analog world. Within this measure's limited sphere, it gives benchmarks for matching media with messages. This measure also sheds light on the relative costing and pricing of messages, again within its limited coverage of the scope of the intuitive idea of value of a message.

That is, let's say Shannon's universe U_1 has one message in it; U_2 has two messages in it; U_3 has three; and so on. The universe U_n has n messages in it. When each message is as likely as any other message in a universe, the universe is fully defined by that number of messages in it. How much substance a message conveys when drawn from one of these universes or another is fully defined once you grant the following three propositions that Shannon enunciated about amount of substance.

The first proposition is that getting a message M from a universe of discourse U_1 in which M is the only possible message conveys no substance whatever. If this strikes you as paradoxical, because you think that a message is a message and conveys substance no matter what, consider the following. Suppose you always cry wolf. Since that's the only message I ever get from you, I'll pay no attention to it, and be none the worse off, since your message is without substance. A message out of a universe of discourse with only one message in it is worthless.

If, on the other hand, we have agreed that no news is good news, and you call me to tell me that the sky is falling, then this conveys some substance to me because there is an alternative. In this illustration, the universe of discourse has two messages in it. The format for the first message happens to be the English sentence, "The sky is falling."

The format for the second message happens to be your failing to send the first one by an agreed upon time. "No communication" is used to convey substance in this instance in much the same way that Sherlock Holmes milked substance from observing that the dog did not bark.

In summary, just as the presence of a pulse and the absence of a pulse at a particular time are two possible tokens that may be used to format a binary alphabet (Figure 3-36), so, in a specific context, the uttering of a sentence and the absence of any sentence may be the tokens for two messages.

Shannon's second proposition generalizes the foregoing observations. It asserts that, if a message comes from a larger universe of discourse, say U_n with n messages in it, then that message conveys more substance than a message coming from a smaller universe of discourse, say U_{n-1} with n-1 messages in it.

Together, the first two propositions rank the universes of discourse. In that ranking, the message from the universe with only one message in it conveys no substance, while a message selected from each succeedingly larger universe conveys increasingly more substance.

The third proposition looks a bit more complicated than the first two propositions because it focuses on the process for picking a message. The third proposition asserts that how a message is picked from its universe makes no difference in the amount of substance that the message conveys. Specifically, given a universe of discourse U_n, just picking a message and getting it over with conveys exactly the same substance as first coyly asserting that the selected message is among a group of i messages in U_n (hence, not among the other n-i messages in U_n), and only then telling which one it actually is among the i messages in the group.

Since the coyness could be repeated in picking the one message from among the group of i messages, this proposition clears away quite a bit of underbrush. It asserts that all that matters in this view of substance is the total quantity of messages from among which a particular message is drawn. The details of formats or processes do not affect the amount of substance that is conveyed. No matter how tortured or hidden my procedure for picking which one out of n messages I will send you, and no matter how plain or how bizarre the format of that message, the only thing that ultimately influences the amount of substance that this particular message conveys is that it is this particular message I sent to you from among the n messages in U_n, and not some other.

The image of the communication process implied by these propositions is somewhat as follows. You and I agree about a universe of discourse with some number n of messages in it. That sets up the

Figure 3-37. Information per Message from Universe U_n

No. n of Messages in Universe U_n	H_n = INFORMATION PER MESSAGE Scale:							
	$\log_2$	$\log_3$	$\log_4$	$\log_5$	—	$\log_{10}$	—	$\log_{26}$
1	0	0	0	0	—	0	—	0
2	1	0.63	0.50	0.43	—	0.30	—	0.21
3	1.58	1	0.79	0.68	—	0.48	—	0.34
4	2	1.26	1	0.86	—	0.60	—	0.43
5	2.32	1.46	1.16	1	—	0.70	—	0.49
6	2.58	1.63	1.29	1.11	—	0.78	—	0.55
7	2.81	1.77	1.40	1.21	—	0.85	—	0.60
8	3	1.89	1.50	1.29	—	0.90	—	0.64
9	3.17	2	1.58	1.37	—	0.95	—	0.67
10	3.32	2.10	1.66	1.43	—	1	—	0.71
11	3.46	2.18	1.73	1.49	—	1.04	—	0.74
12	3.58	2.26	1.79	1.54	—	1.08	—	0.76
13	3.70	2.33	1.85	1.59	—	1.11	—	0.79
14	3.81	2.40	1.90	1.64	—	1.15	—	0.81
15	3.91	2.46	1.95	1.68	—	1.18	—	0.83
16	4	2.52	2	1.72	—	1.20	—	0.85
—	—	—	—	—	—	—	—	—
26	4.70	2.97	2.35	2.02	—	1.41	—	1

conditions of communication, the context in which the messages are significant. It also fixes the amount of substance conveyed in this particular situation by one specific message out of the universe of discourse, hence the value of the message in the given context. The idea is that, prior to receiving a specific message, there is uncertainty about the state of the world. Receiving a message reduces that uncertainty or, in other words, conveys substance. In Shannon's approach, the amount of substance and the amount by which uncertainty is reduced are identical ideas. Both grow with the number of possible messages.

Remarkably, these three propositions determine a unique and useful numerical measure of the amount of substance conveyed by the sending and receiving of a particular message from a universe of discourse U_n with n messages in it. That measure, H_n, is the logarithm of the number of messages in U_n (Figure 3-37).

If the number n of messages is 100 then, since $100 = 10^2$, the logarithm to the base 10 of 100, written as $\log_{10}100$, is 2. In general, if a number $n = b^p$, then p, the power to which the base b is raised to generate n, is the logarithm to the base b of n. Figure 3-37 shows logarithms to bases 2, 3, 4, 5, 10, and 26, and universes with from 1 to

Figure 3-38. Alternative Ways to Pick a Message

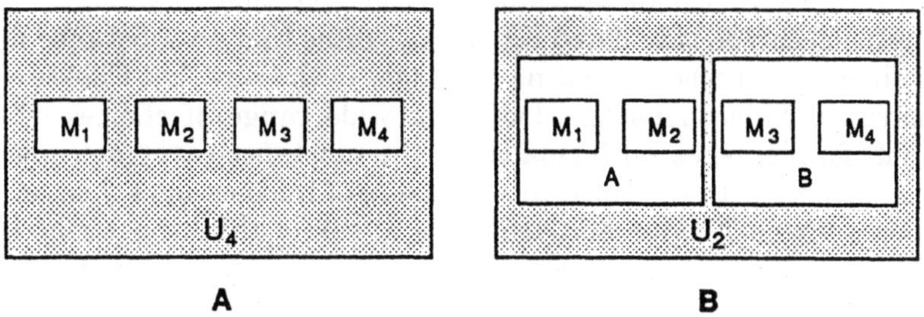

16 messages in them. The logarithms to the various bases are proportional to one another, so choosing a base is just choosing a convenient scale. For instance, the boldface "1"s in Figure 3-37 show that, if there are b messages in a universe of discourse, then, on the scale of logarithms to the base b, one message picked from that universe of discourse conveys one unit of substance. How message formats influence the choice of scale is touched on below.

Figure 3-37 shows how H_n satisfies the three propositions. H_n is 0 on every scale when n = 1, namely for the universe U_1. H_n increases as n increases. That takes care of the first two propositions, but any sequence of numbers that goes up from 0 would do that. The logarithmic measure also satisfies the third proposition, and, although we don't prove that here, nothing but the logarithmic measure satisfies the third proposition.

Suppose, to make all this concrete, that, instead of picking a message directly from the universe U_4 with four messages in it (Figure 3-38A), the message is picked in two steps. The first step picks group A or group B (Figure 3-38B). The second step picks one of the two messages in the selected group. The first step is visualized as selecting one of the two messages A and B in a universe U_2. Either message conveys 1, 0.63, 0.50, 0.43, 0.30, or 0.21 units of substance depending on the scale (Figure 3-37). The second step, say if group A has been picked in the first step, consists of picking one of M_1 and M_2. Either way, this second selection is once again from a universe U_2, A in this example. The second selection therefore also conveys 1, 0.63, 0.50, 0.43, 0.30, or 0.21 units of substance depending on the scale (Figure 3-37).

Fully elaborated, Shannon's third proposition asserts that the total substance conveyed is the sum of the substance conveyed at each step. In this instance the sum is 2, 1.26, 1, 0.86, 0.60, or 0.42 depending on the scale. But, as Figure 3-37 makes plain, that sum is just the amount of substance conveyed by a message picked in one step from a universe U_4.

Although couched in terms of message selection, Shannon's third proposition can be translated into a guarantee that no substance need be gained or lost when encoding messages in the way that Figure 3-27 illustrates. This opens the door to a wide range of choices of the formats for messages, while matching the substance-carrying capacity of the formats with the substance measure of the messages, just as, for analog signals, Fourier analysis gave a way of thinking about efficiency as the matching of a waveform's bandwidth to the bandwidth of a transducer.

For a concrete instance of those ideas, think once again of the universe of discourse U_4 with four messages in it. These four messages can be formatted in the two-bit formats "00", "01", "10", and "11" in the manner of Figure 3-27. Each of these two-bit formats can also be seen as a sequence of 2 one-bit formats, but for what messages? Figure 3-38B suggests viewing "0" in the left (first) bit position as a format for, say, "the message is in group A of U_2" and "1" in the first bit as a format for "the message is in group B of U_2." The interpretation of the symbol in the right (second) bit depends on what is in the first bit. If there's a "0" in the first bit, then the second bit is a format for either M_1 or M_2. If there's a "1" in the first bit, then the second bit is a format for either M_3 or M_4.

Each bit is a format for a message selected from a universe U_2. Figure 3-37 shows that the measure of the substance conveyed by a message from U_2 is 1 unit, 0.63 units, 0.50 units, and so on, depending on the choice of scale. Picking the $\log_2$ scale for U_2 gives a nice round number, namely, one unit. Since a one-bit position has the capacity to format one out of two possible messages and such a message conveys one unit of information on the $\log_2$ scale, this unit is also called a bit. In our example, a one-bit position holds exactly one unit of substance.

It therefore seems natural to use *bit* for the name of the unit of substance on Shannon's logarithmic scale as well as for the name of a slot that can hold either of the two symbols in a two-symbol alphabet. A one-bit slot, in our example, holds one bit of substance. In this limited context, at least, that is the most efficient possible use of a bit slot.

3.7.2 Gaining Efficiency

At first blush, such maximum efficiency is the exception, not the rule. Figure 3-37 tells us that a message from a universe of discourse U_3 conveys only 1.58 bits of substance. Unfortunately, there is no such thing as 1.58-bit slots. A one-bit slot can format only one of two messages. Two one-bit slots are enough for one out of four messages. The obvious thing to do is to use the two-slot binary code, even if you employ only three of the four possible combinations. The inefficiency of doing so is also evident: allowing two one-bit slots for only 1.58 bits of information uses only 1.58/2, or 79 percent, of the available capacity.

Figure 3-37 shows that in these simplified illustrations the only 100 percent efficient binary formats are those for universes with a number of messages in them that is a power of 2. Decimal formats are fully efficient only for universes with numbers of messages that are powers of 10, and alphabetic formats only for powers of 26. The gaps between 100 percent efficient formats are smallest for binary formats, so, in that limited sense, binary formats are more efficient than any other format. Along with the ubiquity of two-state devices noted in section 3.6, this fact helps to account for the popularity of binary formats for digital processors.

Why not for all processors? There are concepts of efficiency other than the one we have just explored that favor formats other than binary.

One way to format the n messages in U_n is by representing each of them by one distinct element chosen from an alphabet of n elements. That is straightforward enough.

In theory, it also maximizes efficiency by using exactly one format position for one unit of information. But it has two drawbacks. One is that, in the absence of natural n-state devices, the n symbols of the alphabet themselves have to be built up from some alphabet based on whatever number-of-state-devices are economically available. In most instances this synthesis introduces inefficiencies; witness, in Figure 3-28 and Figure 3-29, the binary formats for the decimal digits and for the twenty-six letters of the conventional alphabet.

More important than these technical inefficiencies is the tradeoff for people, expressed as follows by the logician Willard Quine:

> In logical and mathematical systems either of two mutually antagonistic types of economy may be striven for, and each has its peculiar practical utility. On the one hand we may seek economy of practical expression—ease and brevity in the statement of multifarious relations. This sort of economy calls usually for distinctive concise notations for a wealth of concepts. Second, however, and oppositely, we may seek economy in grammar and vocabulary; we may try to find a minimum of basic concepts such that, once a distinctive notation has been appropriated to each of them, it becomes possible to express any desired further concept by mere combination and iteration of our basic notations.[35]

[35] Quine, Willard Van Orman, *From a Logical Point of View: Nine Logico-Philosophical Essays* (Cambridge, MA: Harvard University Press, 1953), 26.

Figure 3-39. Messages with Different Probabilities

	1	2	3
M_i	P_i	P_i	P_i
M_1	1/4	1/2	1
M_2	1/4	1/4	0
M_3	1/4	1/8	0
M_4	1/4	1/8	0

M = Message
P = Probability

Since people find it difficult to memorize large alphabets, we have evolved ways of avoiding large alphabets by synthesizing formats for each of the many messages in large universes as arrays of formats for smaller universes. The universe of all possible English sentences is formatted by representing each sentence, not as a unique alphabetic symbol in one slot, but as a collection of many slots filled by words drawn from the "alphabet" that is the English dictionary. Each word, even, is not formatted as one slot filled by a single alphabetic symbol unique to that word, but as a collection of slots filled by letters drawn from the bedrock twenty-six-member Roman alphabet of conventional English writing.

So far we have assumed that each message is as likely as every other message in the particular universe of discourse. For the universe of discourse U_4 with four elements, this amounts to assuming that each message is selected with a probability of one-fourth, as shown in Column 1 of Figure 3-39.

Another possibility, illustrated in Column 3, is that one of the symbols has probability 1, while all other symbols have probability 0. If this is not to make a mockery of Shannon's second proposition, then a useful extension of the logarithmic measure must give an amount of substance per message that, in this case, is precisely equal to the amount of substance per message in a one-message universe, namely a zero. Put another way, Column 3 is a one-message universe masquerading as a four-message one.

Figure 3-39, Column 2, suggests the most common case, and Figure

3-40[36] illustrates it. The letters of the alphabet do not occur with equal frequency in English texts, nor does only one letter occur to the exclusion of all others. Figure 3-40 displays the probabilities of letters in English text as estimated by Godfrey Dewey in 1923. Not surprisingly, "e," "t," "a," "o," "i," and "n" were the six most probable letters.

As we have noted, English sentences are not each formatted as a monolithic symbol. They are instead strung together with words, which, in turn, are strung together with letters, the letters, in turn, being picked from the Roman alphabet with the probabilities shown in Figure 3-40. That way of formatting messages as strings of elementary messages lends itself to ways of formatting that ultimately can approximate 100-percent efficiency as closely as desired. For instance, it is even possible to format messages strung together with symbols drawn with equal probability from a three-symbol alphabet so that precisely 1.58-bit slots are used per message on the average, and not the inefficient two-bit slots per message suggested earlier.

When messages have unequal probabilities, like the letters in Figure 3-40, the amount of information to be matched with the capacity of a letter slot in an English text strung together with these letters is the weighted average of the amount of information per letter.

Shannon has shown that the amount of information per letter is log(1/p), where p is the probability of the letter. If all letters have equal probability, as in Column 1 of Figure 3-39, the weighted average is $(p \cdot \log(1/p))$—the amount of information per letter weighted by the probability of the letter—multiplied by n, since all n letters have precisely the same probability. But, since p is just 1/n, when all probabilities are equal, then $n \cdot p$ is $n \cdot 1/n = 1$, so the average amount of substance per letter is just log(1/p) itself. In this instance, since $p = 1/4$, hence $1/p = 4$, $\log(1/p) = \log 4$ or two bits of substance per message, the logarithm of the number of messages as before. Two-bit slots match this exactly, as we already know.

When the probabilities are unequal, the weighted probabilities have to be added together one by one, as in $p_1 \cdot \log(1/p_1) + p_2 \cdot \log(1/p_2) + p_n \cdot \log(1/p_n)$. For $n = 2$, p_2 is $1-p_1$, so the average amount of substance per message is $H_2 = p \cdot \log(1/p) + (1-p) \cdot \log(1/(1-p))$. Figure 3-41 plots the values of H_2 as the probability of the first message ranges from 0 to 1. When either message has probability 0, the other has probability 1

[36] Godfrey Dewey, *Relativ Frequency of English Speech Sounds* (Cambridge, MA: Harvard University Press, 1923), Table D2. Reprinted by permission.

Figure 3-40. Probabilities of Letters in English Text

TABLE D2 RELATIV FREQUENCY OF LETTERS IN ENGLISH, ARRANGED IN ORDER OF FREQUENCY, WITH ANALISIS OF POSITION OF OCCURRENCE IN WORDS

Letter	%	Occur rences	Items	Initial	Medial	Final	Word	Letter
e	12.68	55,465	9,493	2,123	32,472	20,870		e
t	9.78	42,815	5,366	17,182	15,210	10,423		t
a	7.88	34,536	5,352	9,477	22,791	148	2,120	a
o	7.76	33,993	4,305	7,764	21,608	4,617	4	o
i	7.07	30,955	6,058	6,691	23,094	15	1,155	i
n	7.06	30,902	5,480	2,317	20,521	8,064		n
s	6.31	27,642	6,069	6,119	9,508	12,015		s
r	5.94	26,051	5,569	2,165	17,734	6,152		r
h	5.73	25,138	1,634	4,916	17,772	2,450		h
l	3.94	17,261	3,668	2,118	12,155	2,988		l
d	3.89	17,046	3,394	2,756	4,227	10,063		d
u	2.80	12,285	2,448	1,214	10,278	793		u
c	2.68	11,747	3,148	4,327	7,170	250		c
f	2.56	11,199	1,164	4,037	2,550	4,612		f
m	2.44	10,678	1,916	4,010	5,198	1,470		m
w	2.14	9,396	712	6,839	1,604	953		w
y	2.02	8,837	1,189	1,454	971	6,412		y
g	1.87	8,191	2,079	1,588	3,588	3,015		g
p	1.86	8,162	2,154	3,476	4,213	473		p
b	1.56	6,838	1,207	4,788	2,006	44		b
v	1.02	4,481	907	537	3,944			v
k	0.60	2,610	526	436	1,373	801		k
x	0.16	687	214		626	61		x
j	0.10	421	117	256	165			j
q	0.09	403	122	171	232			q
z	0.06	284	131	15	265	4		z
Totals	100.00	438,023	74,422	96,776	241,275	96,693	3,279	
		674 28	159 9	17	644 25	13 3		

Figure 3-41. Average Amount of Substance per Message in a Two-Message Universe

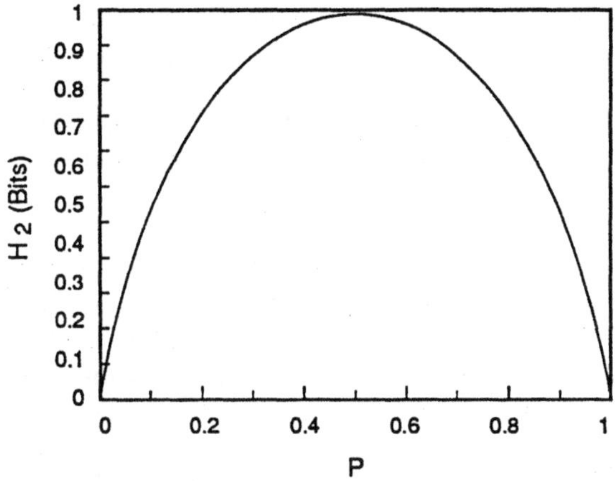

and, for all practical purposes, this is like U_1, the universe with only one message in it. The amount of substance per message is 0. The average amount of substance per message grows as the probabilities get more nearly equal, coming to the not unexpected maximum of one bit of substance per symbol as the probability of each of the two messages reaches 1/2. It is intuitively satisfying that the amount of substance per message is greatest when either message is as likely as the other and that the amount decreases as the likelihood that one message will be forthcoming rather than the other increases.

Now, to make good on the promise to match fractional amounts of substance per symbol with symbol slots that come only in whole numbers. In a literal sense this is impossible. For example, a single message from a universe of discourse U_2 (Figure 3-41) that conveys only a fraction of a bit of substance still must take up at least a one-bit slot. Bit slots come only in whole numbers.

However, on the average, fractional capacities can be made up to match fractional bits of substance. Figuring out how to do this takes an explicit understanding and exploitation of a way to pick formats that is always informally at work in the evolution of ordinary language.

The very short formats that the informal evolution of English language conventions assigns to the very frequent articles and prepositions *a*, *the*, *in*, *to*, and so on are consistent with modern formal understanding. So is the assignment of the shortest Morse code symbols, dot and dash, to the most frequent letters "e" and "t" in the writings of North American and Western European countries.

The formatting scheme illustrated by Figures 3-27, 3-28, and 3-29 does not take into account the probabilities of the messages in the universe of discourse being formatted. For a universe U_4 with messages M_1, M_2, M_3, and M_4 in it (Figure 3-39), this approach uses the four two-bit formats "00", "01", "10", and "11" regardless of whether all four messages have equal probability 1/4 or whether the probabilities $p(M_i)$ are different, say $p(M_1) = 1/2$, $p(M_2) = 1/4$, and $p(M_3) = p(M_4) = 1/8$. But in the first instance two bits, the average amount of substance per message, is precisely equal to the number of bit slots and the formatting is as efficient as it can be. In the second instance, the average amount of substance per message, namely the quantity $p(M_i)\log(1/p(M_i)$ summed over the four messages, is only 1.75 bits, or 1.75/2, for 87.5 percent efficiency.

A different formatting scheme, invented by David Huffman in 1952, leads on average to an exact match between substance per message and slots per message.[37] Huffman's method is a variation on the approach of Figure 3-38. In the first step, the universe of discourse is divided into two parts selected to make the sum of the probabilities of the messages in each part as nearly equal as possible. In the example of Figure 3-39, Column 2, the partition is not as shown in Figure 3-38, but rather into a universe U_1 with M_1 in it, for a total probability of 1/2, and a universe U_3 with M_2, M_3, and M_4 in it, and probabilities that add up to 1/2.

The one message in U_1, namely M_1, is assigned the first—and, it turns out, the only—format digit "1". All three messages in U_3, namely M_2, M_3, and M_4, are assigned the first format digit "0". For U_3, however, the process does not end, since it remains to tell M_2, M_3, and M_4 apart one from another. The partitioning process is, therefore, repeated for U_3. U_3 is divided into U_1 with M_2 in it and total probability 1/4, and U_2 with M_3 and M_4 in it (and total probability also 1/4). To the first format digit "0", which all messages in U_3 have in common, this second partitioning adds the second format digit "1" for M_2 and the second format digit "0" for each of M_3 and M_4. Since M_3 and M_4 remain together in their U_2, they need a third format digit to tell them apart, say "1" for M_3 and "0" for M_4.

The outcome is a one-slot format "1" for M_1 with its probability 1/2, a two-slot format "01" for M_2 with its probability 1/4 and, for M_3 and M_4

[37] Huffman, David, "Method for Construction of Minimum Redundancy Codes," *Institute of Radio Engineers–Proceedings* 40, no. 9 (September 1952): 1098–1101.

with their probabilities of 1/8 each, the three-slot formats "001" and "000", respectively. The average number of slots per format is 1.75, precisely the average amount of substance per message.

Formally, the possibility of the Huffman scheme is accounted for by a sharpening of Shannon's third proposition to take account of unequal message probabilities: the amount of substance per message in a one-step message selection is the weighted sum of the substance per message in each step of a two-step selection. Even where the probabilities aren't as neat as the 1/2, 1/4, 1/8, and 1/8 of the exemplary universe U_4, extensions of Huffman's process[38] can fit slot capacity to amount of substance with an efficiency that, on the average, can be brought as close to 100 percent as desired. The continual creation and testing of acronyms and abbreviations, only some of which make it into the mainstream of language, is one phenomenon that reflects the evolutionary equivalent of the Huffman process at work.

The match between format slot capacity and the amount of substance is only one measure of efficiency. There is also a tradeoff between the efficiency that comes from having a unique monolithic symbol for every message in a universe and the alternative efficiency that comes from building up each message as a sequence of more elementary messages. At the level of words as the universe of messages, Chinese is at the one extreme of this tradeoff and English is at the other extreme, among contemporary languages. The Chinese "alphabet" is hell to learn but economical in use. The English alphabet is easier to learn, but it takes many more characters in English than in Chinese to express a given message, and English spelling is hell to learn.

Identifying and expressing key efficiency measures for formats and for the tradeoffs among formats remains a lively challenge to the digital arts and sciences and to the world of competitive digital enterprises. The square-offs between the proponents of keyboards and mice in the microcomputer marketing world in the early eighties and between bit-mapped and character-based displays in the early nineties are but two examples of the search for format-and-process efficiency in various contexts.

3.7.3 Gaining Effectiveness

There is also a parallel search for effectiveness. To be effective in real-world processors, real-world formats have to stay what they are meant

[38] McEliece, Robert J., *The Theory of Information and Coding* (Reading, MA: Addison-Wesley 1977), 243–48.

to be and not become something else. If I wire a payment of $100, I don't want $1000 to be paid at the other end just because an extra "0" got put in the format. But accidents in real-world processors can change a collection of physical tokens in random or systematic but always unwelcome patterns. The effects of such accidents are generically called *noise*. Noise degrades the effectiveness of formats.

Effectiveness here refers to the effectiveness of formats, not of substance. Substance might be graded from positive values, as in a timely warning not to step off the curb in front of a truck, through negative values, as in disinformation meant to make mischief, like a scurrilous rumor. Whatever the intrinsic quality of substance, its intended effect is not achieved if the format or formats intended to convey it fail to do their job. Noise is anything that leads to such a format failure.

Figure 3-42, where the signal gets noisier from left to right, gives an analog example that illustrates the origin of the noise metaphor. A pure tone, as we have already seen in Figure 3-31, gives a sinusoidal trace, as shown on the left side of Figure 3-42. What is heard when a pure tone is played next to a buzzer might look like the trace at the right of the diagram. Describing the signal at the right as noisy implies that the buzzing sound was unintended. Otherwise, the trace at the right would itself be a good format. Like weedy lawns, or slops on a dinner plate, noisy formats are noisy in the mind of the beholder because they include something unwanted. Dandelion grown for salad is not a weed, the buzzer announcing someone at the door is a signal not a noise, and the last mouthful is good food and not slops when you're still hungry. In a Bach cantata, the trace on the right would be noisy!

Noise is best avoided whenever possible. FM radio, for example, is inherently less vulnerable to the kinds of noise that afflict radio transmission than is AM radio. Even once it has intruded into analog signals, noise often can be eliminated from them, especially when the noise is random. Generally, a little noise, as in the middle of Figure 3-42, is as tough to eliminate as a lot of noise, as on the right of Figure 3-42. The Dolby circuit in expensive tape recorders is one widely known noise suppressor. Once again, however, digital trading on nature's nonlinearity makes noise control and even noise suppression relatively easier and cheaper in the digital world than in the analog world.

Figure 3-43A shows the characteristic of an amplifier for a digital format wherein no-pulse is the token for "0" and a pulse is the token for "1". Any input pulse lower than the threshold value 0.25 marked by the left-dashed vertical is output as no-pulse. Any input pulse higher than

Figure 3-42. Analog Signal and Noise

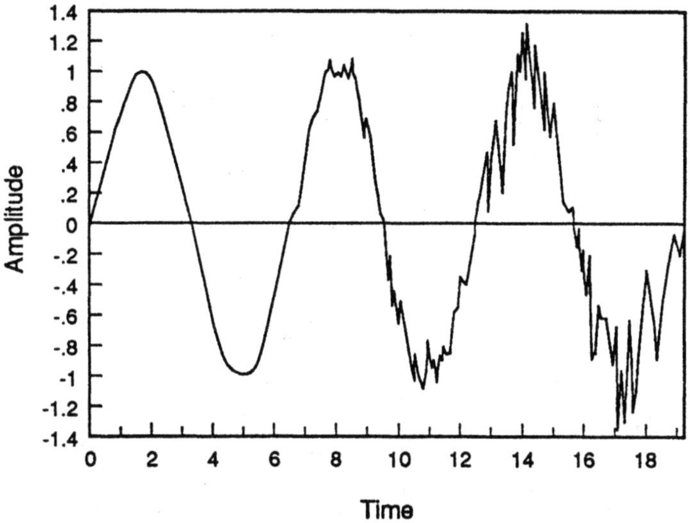

the threshold value 0.75 marked by the right-dashed vertical is output as a pulse.

In low-noise conditions, a digital message should produce no signals in the intermediate, uncertain range. Figure 3-44B shows how perfect input pulses (diagonally lined) pass through the transducer unaltered to become perfect output pulses (dotted). In the digital world, a small amount of noise is as good as no noise at all. The input signals in Figure 3-44C (below) include some no-pulses that noise has perverted into palpable pulses. The input signals also include some pulses that noise has degraded to a fraction of their original height. But the former never got above the 0.25 threshold and the latter never got below the 0.75 threshold, so the effect of the nonlinear transducer characteristic is a perfect restoration of the intended signal, free of any noise.

But, as the noise level increases (Figure 3-43D, E), more and more no-pulses creep up above the lower threshold and cannot be told apart from pulses that have crept down below the upper threshold. When there is good discrimination between perfect pulses and the degraded ones, as there happens to be in Figure 3-43D, some digits are lost but no error creeps in undetected. In Figure 3-43E, however, the noise level is high enough to make one no-pulse creep above the upper threshold and therefore be turned into what seems to be a perfect token for "1" when it is really a token for "0" gone wrong.

Figure 3-43. Digital Signals and Noise

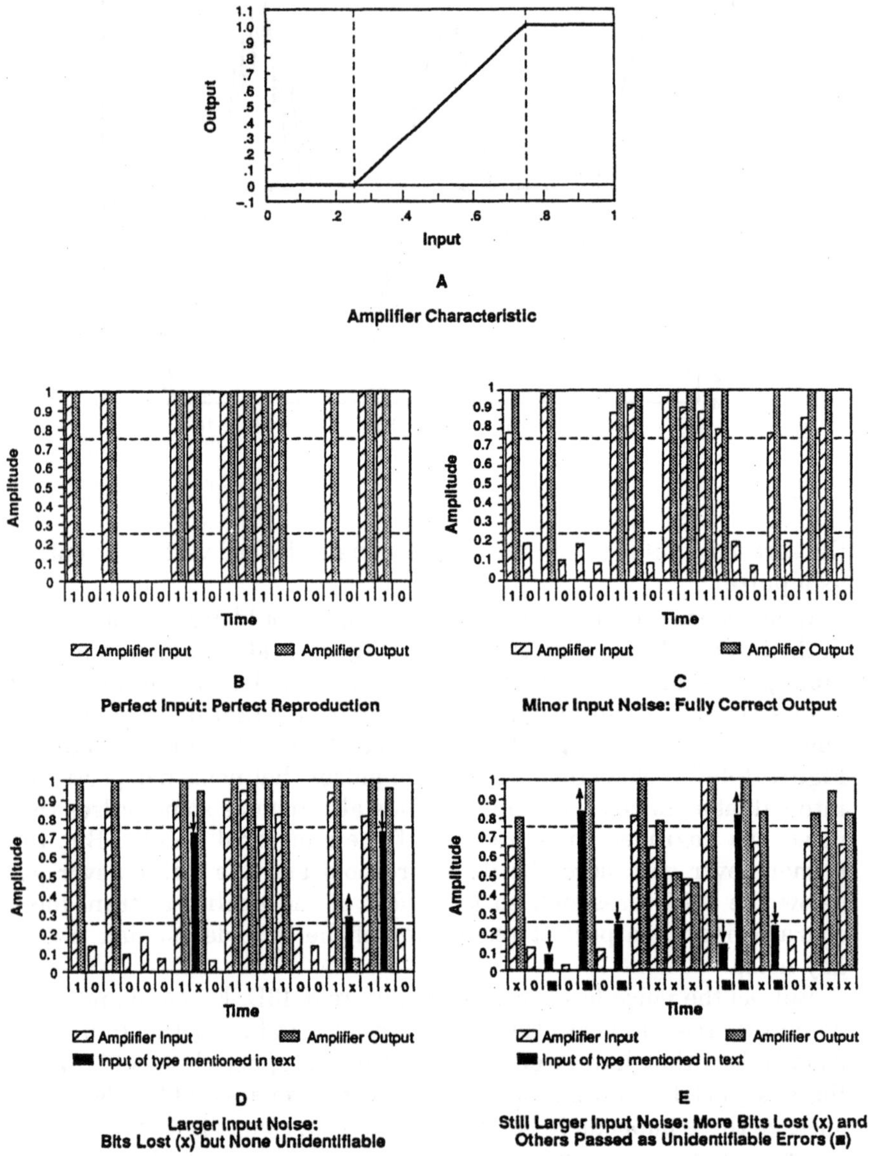

But even a degraded pulse masquerading as a perfect one can be caught—at a price! In 1950, Richard Hamming systematized the design of digital formats that can detect and even correct errors.[39]

The relationship between digital formats and the substance they stand for is arbitrary. Different digital formats behave differently under noisy conditions. It is therefore possible to pick formats with behaviors more or less effective under various conditions.

Figure 3-44A shows a four-message universe with the messages a, b, c, and d. These four messages are shown formatted in a two-bit-per-message format and also in a variable-length format. The two-bit format is called a *block code*, because each message is formatted as a block of bits with the same number of bits in each block. The variable-length formats are called *prefix* formats and are the formats described earlier as invented by David Huffman. In this case, no format is the prefix of a longer format. Note, for example, that since the binary digit "1" formats the message "A", it does not occur as the first digit in any longer message. Neither does the two-bit combination "01" occur in any three-bit combination.

These different traits of block and prefix formats give them different behavior under noisy conditions.

Column 1 of Figure 3-44B shows the message "BAD" formatted first in a block format and next in a prefix format. Column 2 shows the effects of two types of noise. The first type makes the first bit get lost altogether. The effect on the message (shown in the third column) is quite different, depending on the format. In the block format, the first two bits are paired to yield the erroneous message c, then the next two are paired to yield an erroneous b, but one bit is left over. That unpaired bit gives a clue that something is awry. In the prefix format, however, the first "1" is erroneously interpreted as "a", the second "1" is correctly interpreted as "a", and the last three bits are interpreted correctly as "d". There is no clue that the message as a whole is in error. In the second case, shown in the lower part of Figure 3-44B, the noise manifests itself as a reversal that puts a 1 where there was a 0. In this instance, both the block format and the prefix format yield erroneous messages. Neither gives a clue that an error has occurred.

We saw earlier that the prefix format is more efficient than the block format when not all the messages in a universe of discourse have equal probabilities. Here we see that this efficiency is gained at a price. In no instance did the prefix-formatted text give any clue about

[39] Hamming, Richard, "Error Detecting and Error Correcting Codes," *The Bell System Technical Journal* 26, no. 2 (April 1950): 147–60.

Figure 3-44. Effectiveness of Binary Formats

A

Message	Format	
	Block	Prefix
a	00	1
b	01	01
c	10	001
d	11	000

B

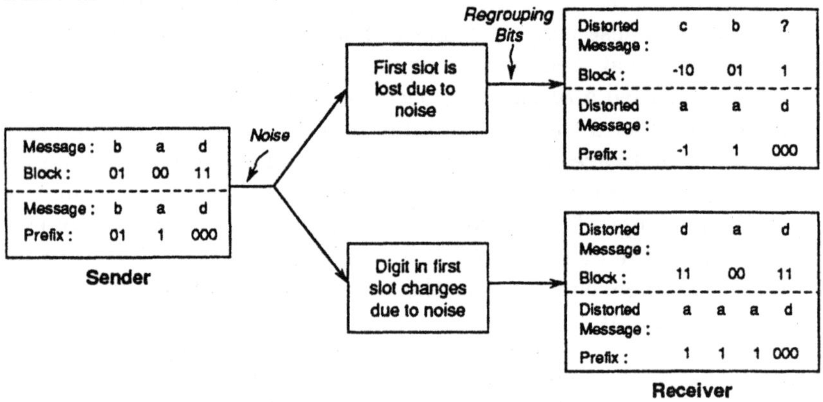

C

Message	Format	
	Block	Parity
a	00	0
b	01	1
c	10	1
d	11	0

D

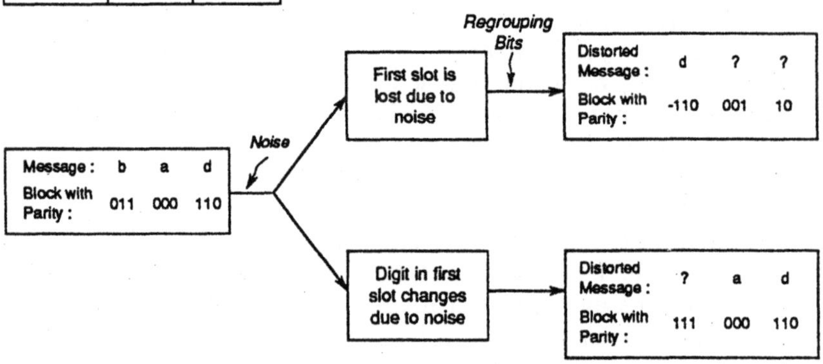

an error. But in one out of two instances of degradation, the block-formatted text indicated that the message was in error. This hints at the possibility of tradeoffs between efficiency and effectiveness. These tradeoffs have been systematized over the years in an elaborate theory of formatting, called *coding theory* by its practitioners.

Coding theory[40] systematizes an art that all people have unconsciously practiced over the centuries. Told that "Noe ia thr yime fpr alk hood mwn ti cone to thw aud if tjeir partu" is supposed to be English, most every English speaker is instantly able to tell that, if the text is English, then it must be egregiously misspelled. Almost as instantly, most people are able to correct the spelling errors, even without being told that each of them stems from a finger hitting a neighboring key on the typewriter instead of the intended one. This capability stems from the redundancy built into the formatting of English messages in the conventional twenty-six-letter alphabet and the fact that not every possible sequence of letters is used to format English words. It is therefore child's play to see that "thr" and "thw" are wrong, at least in ordinary text without chemical abbreviations or British or Canadian zip codes. There is a tradeoff here. A redundant format is not as efficient as one without redundancy. More messages could be represented in three alphabetic positions than actually are represented in English. It is wasteful to resort to four-letter words when three-letter combinations like "thr" and "thw" go unused, "wasted."

Figure 3-44C and D shows one widely used way of systematizing the tradeoff between efficiency and effectiveness. Starting with the block format, a bit is added that makes the number of "ones" in each three-bit format an even number. This uses only four out of the eight possible three-bit combinations. The four other three-bit combinations, each with an odd number of ones in it, are unused.

Adding a parity bit changes behavior under noise. The loss of the first slot bit still lets an erroneous block-formatted message through, but the next block is recognized as incorrect, since it is of odd parity and, as before, the two-bit block can be recognized as not a format at all. Under a digit change, the loss of parity is immediately recognizable, and the error is detected right in the area where it occurs.

In general, a block format of any length with a single parity bit lends itself to the unfailing detection of the presence of a single reversal error. This follows from the fact that any single error in a parity bit block code changes the parity and thus leads to an unused bit combination.

Figure 3-45 shows a parity bit for single error detection added to the three-bit code used to represent the eight levels of quantization in a pulse code modulated voice signal of Figure 3-45. The American Standard Code for Information Interchange (ASCII) format used by

[40] Peterson, Wesley and Edward Weldon, *Error-Correcting Codes* (Cambridge, MA: The MIT Press, 1972).

Figure 3-45. Binary Format with Error-Detecting Parity Bit

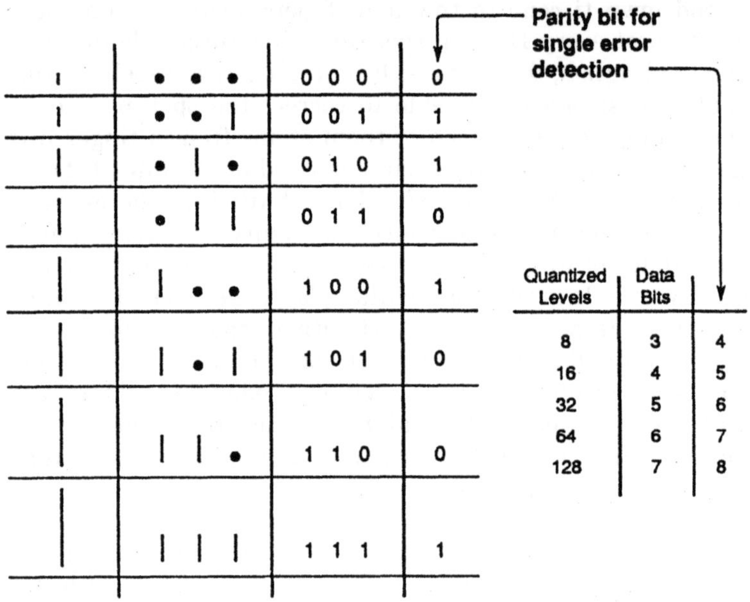

telephone companies and computer manufacturers worldwide to format numerals, letters, punctuation marks, and digitized speech is a seven-bit code with an eighth bit added for parity. Other, more complex error detection *and correction* schemes are available for more critical situations, each with its own special capabilities and its own price in efficiency losses.

In accuracy, flexibility, capacity, and economy, the capabilities of the digital format/electro-optical equipment combination exceed the wildest dreams of just a few decades ago. And they still are far from fully exploited. During a period of continuing, rapid technological change, an understanding of their possibilities and range of applications is one of the important factors affecting the survival or the success of old and new competitors.

4

Nurturing Creativity in a Competitive Global Economy: Intellectual Property and New Technologies*

Anne W. Branscomb

4.1 INTRODUCTION

During the summer of 1986, I arrived in Seoul, Korea, with a damaged suitcase. To replace it I went to the street near the U.S. Air Force Base where inexpensive luggage is readily available. Finding a reasonably priced Louis Vuitton "look-alike" with the familiar LV trademark and conspicuously marked "Made in France," I was assured that it was, as I had suspected, made in Korea. Satisfying my immediate needs, I thought nothing of the purchase until I returned to clear U.S. Customs, where I dutifully reported the full price of my purchase (about one-tenth the price of Louis Vuitton originals). The Customs officer looked at me with scorn and announced that I could not buy Louis Vuitton luggage for such a price. I assured her that it was not LV luggage. She called in the counterfeit products expert, who spent thirty minutes proving to her that it was not Louis Vuitton luggage. Then he turned to me and announced, "Of course, you know that it is illegal to import these counterfeits into the United States."

For a moment I was stunned, expecting the official to pour my

* This chapter is adapted from Branscomb, Anne W., *Nurturing Creativity in a Competitive Global Economy: Intellectual Property and New Technologies* (Cambridge, MA: Program on Information Resources Policy, Harvard University, 1988).

personal possessions onto the floor and to confiscate the offending product. However, he soon chuckled and said, "We only take legal action when the purchase is for commercial resale." I was relieved but not satisfied and went to the trouble of attending a legal symposium on the subject of counterfeit products at the Franklin Pierce Law School in Concord, N.H., soon thereafter. There I discovered that the statute (enacted in 1984)[1] required that I be "trafficking" in the offending product. To confiscate would require a court order.

This personal story highlights the efforts of the United States to protect the intellectual property of companies with valuable assets. It also underlines the difficulties of dealing domestically with a problem that is global in scope and growing more complex as technological progress brings more and more complex intellectual products to market. Although the U.S. Customs might be able to stem some of the tide of illegal and offending copies of our own most desired products, it has no authority over the importation of such products into the multitude of nation states around the world. Our officials must cajole or threaten others through negotiation, reciprocity, and retaliation to protect U.S. interests in its own creative products.

My purchase is replicated worldwide thousands of times a day as computer clones, watches, agricultural chemicals, pharmaceuticals, clothing with designer labels, jewelry, records, tapes, leather goods, auto and aircraft parts, and countless other copies of popular proprietary products make their way into the international markets. Not only is there a financial loss to the originators of the copied products, but there is also danger of legal liability from the inadequacies of the products that are held out to be "originals" of a trademarked item. Further, the products often disappoint customers who purchase clones that purport to function in a manner identical to or compatible with the originals but do not meet the design specifications.

Intellectual property laws establish certain proprietary rights in works generated by intellectual productivity such as books, films, inventions, trademarks, industrial and artistic designs, and computer software. This chapter assesses the status of intellectual property with respect to the impact of new information technologies by

- Taking a whirlwind trip through the maze of legal regimes used to protect the economic value of intellectual property on the global market;
- Examining the inconsistencies in the various intellectual property systems;

[1] Trademark Counterfeiting Act of 1984, Title 18 U.S.C Chapter 113 §1502(a) as amended by §2320.

- Identifying the challenges to established law from the impact of new information technologies;
- Locating forums in which discussions of public policy are taking place; and
- Identifying targets of opportunity where action is needed to modify, reconcile, and harmonize the laws of our own and other countries. For the above, this chapter focuses on developments through 1988.

It is never too early to contemplate changing the laws that govern intellectual property. As Woody Allen has so aptly characterized the problem confronting us, "'Our technological capabilities are far in advance of our intellectual development and our moral development.'"[2]

4.1.1 Size of Problem

Opening the technological Pandora's box releases economic consequences as well. Global trade in engineered products has grown fifteen-fold over the last twenty years to $500 billion in the early 1980s—25 percent of this is for high-tech products in which the U.S. excels. There is an even greater growth to $700 billion in the "invisible trade" that includes consulting, data processing, insurance, and other financial services.[3]

The International Anticounterfeiting Coalition estimated that some $20 billion, or about 18 percent, of world trade in 1980 was lost to unauthorized copies of U.S.-originated works.[4]

A study by the International Trade Commission reported a $23.8 billion loss in world trade in 1986. As only 431 responses were received from the 736 companies sent the questionnaire, U.S. Trade Representative Clayton Yeutter estimates the loss from inadequate protection of intellectual property to be somewhere between $43 billion and $61 billion.[5] The study included 47 computer firms and 52 software firms, which reported some $4.1 billion in lost trade.[6]

---

[2] Miller, Michael W., "Creativity Furor: High-Tech Alteration of Sights and Sounds Divides the Art World," *Wall Street Journal,* September 1, 1987, 1.

[3] Szuprowicz, Bohdan O., "Battle Lines Being Drawn for Global Technology Markets," *High Technology* (October 1984), 59.

[4] Koff, James B., Baker & Hofstetler, Washington, DC, past president, International Anticounterfeiting Coalition, presentation at conference on "Counterfeiting of Trademarks, Copyrights, and Patents: What Lawyers Should Know," March 20, 1987, Franklin Pierce Law Center, Concord, NH.

[5] Raum, Tom, "Trade Panel Decries Piracy of Patents, Trademarks, Copyrights," A.P., February 26, 1988.

[6] Betts, Mitch, "High-tech Pirates Said to Reap Billions," *Computerworld* (March 14, 1988), 79.

Lotus Development Corporation, makers of Lotus 1-2-3, the most successful electronic spreadsheet, claims that over half of its potential sales are lost to pirated copies ($161 million worth pirated, in contrast to $157 million in sales worldwide).[7]

The makers of WordStar, the most copied word processing software, estimate that, in 1984, $177 million in sales were diverted to unauthorized copies compared with $67 million in revenues.[8] Overall, the software industry estimates that at least one unauthorized copy exists for every authorized sale. According to Ken Wasch, executive director of the Software Publishers Association, " 'The industry would be fifty percent larger if it were not for piracy.' "[9]

Videotaped copies of Hollywood films are often released in foreign markets, even before the U.S. release, at an approximate annual loss of $6 billion, according to the Motion Picture Association of America.[10] Computer clones are marketed in Hong Kong and Singapore simultaneously with their general availability in the U.S.[11] Moreover, they are loaded with pirated software for which no payment is made.

An estimated 17 million "Eveready" batteries are marketed in China without licensing or authorization.[12] Pharmaceuticals in twenty-six countries have been identified by the U.S. Department of Commerce as a serious problem.[13] The American Association of Publishers estimates 560 titles of unauthorized reference books (primarily technical) are published in Taiwan. John Wiley & Sons, Inc., which derives one-third of its revenues from exports, has identified 350 of its titles among more than two million pirated text books in Korea.[14]

During August 1988 Senator Orrin Hatch held hearings in Provo, Utah, on his proposed amendment to the Copyright Law, called the

---

[7] Kiang, Lindsey, former general counsel of Lotus Corp., presentation at conference on "Counterfeiting of Trademarks, Copyrights, and Patents: What Lawyers Should Know," March 20, 1987, Franklin Pierce Law Center, Concord, NH.

[8] Kiang, *supra,* note 7.

[9] Antonoff, M., "Can We End Software Piracy?" *Personal Computing* (May 1987), 144.

[10] Blair, Homer, statement given at "Counterfeiting of Trademarks, Copyrights, and Patents: What Lawyers Should Know," March 20, 1987, Franklin Pierce Law Center, Concord, NH.

[11] Computer clones may be "reverse engineered" by manufacturing the product from design specifications, rather than "copied" with direct access, and are not necessarily illegal.

[12] Blair, *supra,* note 10.

[13] Rozynski, Edward, Far East regional director, Pharmaceutical Manufacturers, Assoc., Washington, DC, "Counterfeiting of Trademarks, Copyrights, and Patents: What Lawyers Should Know," March 20, 1987, Franklin Pierce Law Center, Concord, NH.

[14] "Senate Subcommittee Hears Views on Berne Adherence Legislation," *Daily Report for Executives,* Bureau of National Affairs, March 4, 1988.

Computer Software Rental Amendment of 1988. Computer software manufacturers claimed that as many as ten unauthorized copies (on the average) of every legitimate software copy sold are made by pirates or renters. They also claimed that software rental houses serve primarily as a conduit for users to rent, duplicate, and return the software while paying a fraction of the cost of a purchase, none of which redounds to the benefit of the manufacturers.[15]

Pirated works are often more profitable than legitimate sales, which necessarily reflect research and development costs. Pirates do not pay the cost of research and development. They piggyback on the R&D budgets of others. In the pharmaceutical industry, an estimated 16 percent of the sales are invested in the R&D budgets.[16]

4.1.2 Hazards Other Than Financial Loss

There are more serious problems than mere economic loss, as there is no quality control over the unauthorized counterfeits that bear the name of the original product. Jeans, for example, fall apart after one washing, disappointing the purchasers who thought they had bought a bargain. Computer software does not function as advertised, and there is no team of experts to provide support to the user.

For jeans or a software package, the financial loss may be small; however, if the product is an expensive piece of heavy machinery or the driving force of a mainframe, lack of quality control may mean the loss of millions of dollars of productivity or the destruction of valuable data. Even more distressing, there can be physical disaster. A helicopter crash in Peru was attributed to a worn-out rotor blade that was a counterfeit version of a U.S.-made blade. G.D. Searle was forced to recall its Ovulon product because counterfeit "Ovulon" pills were causing excessive bleeding.[17]

Thus, the ramifications of unauthorized copying of intellectual property can be far more devastating than the mere financial loss to the creator, developer, and producers of the product.

4.1.3 Pirating Is on the Increase

The world market for computer communications is expanding rapidly. In 1986 approximately 15 million computers were available, but this

---

[15] United Press International, August 24, 1988; *Infoworld* (September 5, 1988), 4; *American Banker,* September 7, 1988.

[16] Rozynski, *supra,* note 13.

[17] Blair, *supra,* note 8.

number was expected to double by 1990 and continue to increase thereafter at about 15 million annually.[18]

The new technologies of copying (videocassette recorders, computers, reprography) have become widely available even in countries that prohibit their use; in fact, network terminals worldwide are doubling every four years.

Ethical standards, in the application of the new information technologies, are still in an early state of development. Public sympathy seems tilted in the direction of considerable leniency in the utilization of the work products of others. A public opinion poll conducted by the Office of Technology Assessment of the U.S. Congress found 70 percent of those questioned thought copying of a record, tape, TV program, or software program in one's personal possession was permissible. Most thought trading of such personal copies among friends was acceptable. On public accessibility—for example, whether such videocassettes and computer software should be available, as books are, in libraries—those questioned were equally divided. However, some 80 percent deplored circumventing commercial offerings such as pay TV, cable television, or concerts, and 100 percent deplored accessing databases for resale or personal gain.[19]

4.2 TYPES OF LEGAL PROTECTION

There are numerous legal frameworks within which protection of intellectual property can be obtained. There are also inconsistencies and incompatibilities among the various legal regimes. Armies of well-trained patent, copyright, trademark, and trade-secret lawyers are required to sort out the optimum form of protection. Often, none is appropriate. However, each group of legal specialists has a vested interest in carving out a larger and larger area of protection for its special kind of expertise. The various types of protection include the following:

1. Patents and licenses
2. Copyright royalties and penalties
3. Trademark registration
4. Trade secrets
5. Sui generis legislation (e.g., the Semiconductor Chip Act)
6. Export Administration Act restrictions

---

[18] Kiang, *supra,* note 7.

[19] U.S. Congress, Office of Technology Assessment, *Intellectual Property in an Age of Electronics and Information* (Washington, DC: GPO, April 1986).

7. Contractual arrangements (such as performance rights of actors and artists for reproduction or replaying of recorded performances)
8. Unfair competition and misappropriation (based on equity and fair play, the notion that one should not reap where one did not sow), and
9. Neighboring rights (rights which are similar to copyright but cover performances, recordings, and broadcasts rather than literary and artistic works).

4.2.1 Patents

Patented works—which include tangible objects, processes, and designs of a utilitarian nature—must be novel, nonobvious, useful, registered, and they may take too long to get approved. The protection obtained is a monopoly for seventeen years (if utilitarian) or fourteen years (if a design). In the U.S. a patent holder must be the first to invent, whereas in some other countries it is necessary only to register first. Therefore, the first inventor may not hold the patent rights.

4.2.2 Copyright

On the other hand, copyrighted works need not be novel but must be original "works of authorship"; these are protected against copies for the life of the creator, plus fifty years. However, basic ideas are not protected—only the manner in which they are expressed. The work must be "fixed" in order to be copied. Reverse engineering (replicating the program from performance specifications without access to the product) of computer software is permitted so long as the exact work is not copied.

Multilateral copyright conventions (agreements adhered to by a number of nations) and bilateral treaties do permit coverage in other countries from a single registration in one of them. The United States is a signatory to the Universal Copyright Convention but not to the Berne Convention, which has the largest membership and is administered by the World Intellectual Property Organization (WIPO). Artists and writers in the U.S. are urging Congress to enact "moral rights" that permit copyright owners to maintain control over the artistic integrity of their works in re-use, in order to permit the United States to become a signatory to the Berne Convention, as required under its terms. However, some legal scholars have argued that new legislation is unnecessary because case law in the United States provides much of the protection made available in other countries under the rubric of "moral rights."

4.2.3 Trademarks and Servicemarks

A trademark is not an invention, a discovery, or a writing. Trademarks protect only the quality and origin of a product against mistaken identity and misunderstanding. They are designed to protect the customer as well as the trademarked producer from sleazy copies. Tiffany, the jeweler, has succeeded in prohibiting a Tiffany Bar. Similarly, seeking to protect the value of their city's name as a mark of quality, citizens of St. Moritz, Switzerland, have sued other users of the name "St. Moritz" as a trademark. Johnny Carson was able to protect "Here's Johnny" as a servicemark. Trademark and servicemark protection, however, is based upon appropriation by use and securing that right by registration. A company like General Motors could expend considerable amounts of money in the development of SATURN prior to manufacture and distribution and yet be preempted by a third party. Indeed, some small companies are engaged in the practice of registering such names in foreign countries and selling such rights to the multinationals, which cannot afford to lose their prior investment in the name.

There are conflicting schools of thought on the value of trademark protection. Harvard University theorists, such as Edward Chamberlin and Joan Robinson, see trademarks as a significant barrier to market entry causing excess concentration of control and higher costs. Chicago theorists, such as A.E. Alchian, W. Allen, and Y. Brozen, argue, alternatively, that part of a product's cost is the information to make comparison shopping possible.[20]

Thus, trademarks and servicemarks encourage maintenance of high quality by identifying the source of goods marketed.

The International Trademark Registration Treaty of Vienna, promulgated in 1973, has remained ineffective because there were too few signatories. More recent efforts to rationalize and harmonize trademark registration are taking place under the Trademark Cooperation Treaty administered by WIPO.

[20] McCarthy, J. Thomas, *Trademarks and Unfair Competition*, 2d ed. (San Francisco: Bancroft-Whitney, 1984), 63–64; Alchian, A.E. and W. Allen, *Exchange and Production: Competition, Coordination & Control*, 2d ed. (Belmont, CA: Wadsworth Publishing Co., 1977), 193; Brozen, Y., "Entry Barriers: Advertising and Production Differentiations" in Goldschmid, H.J., H.M. Mann, and J.F. Weston, eds., *Industrial Concentration: The New Learning* (Boston: Little, Brown, 1974), 115; Chamberlin, E., *The Theory of Monopolistic Competition* (Cambridge: Harvard University Press, 1956); Robinson, J., *Economics of Imperfect Competition* (London: Macmillan, 1938).

4.2.4 Trade Secrets

The oldest form of protection is just plain secrecy. Trade secrets are protected by maintaining confidentiality and by securing a contract with each licensed user. In order to be enforced, they must be used in business to achieve a competitive advantage and must be kept secret. If no one else knows the formula (e.g., Coca Cola Classic has been kept under lock and key for almost a century) or the method (the doctor who developed forceps for delivery of babies was successful in suppressing the distribution thereof for a long time), then the economic value is protected.

However, the case of the forceps highlights the social pressure to share the knowledge in the interests of saving countless babies and their mothers worldwide rather than permitting the originator to hold a monopoly over the new technique. There is less social compulsion to circulate artistic works widely. Yet even there, sharing the pleasure dictates an interest in society in the widespread distribution of creative endeavor. Moreover, artistic and literary talent thrives on public recognition and acclaim.

In both patent and copyright, originators of new products and processes or artistic and literary works are encouraged to disclose their intellectual offspring in exchange for monopoly license fees or royalties. Patents require disclosure upon application and copyrights upon registration and/or publication.[21]

4.2.5 Sui Generis Legislation

In some cases where lawyers and their clients find it too difficult to fit their facts into existing law, they urge legislative bodies to enact sui generis statutes intended to cover the particular circumstances. This was the case with the Semiconductor Chip Protection Act of 1984, which extended protection against unauthorized copying to original mask works (the three-dimensional pattern of layers of electronic circuits contained on a silicon wafer) for a ten-year period. To secure the right, the manufacturer must register the mask works within two years of commercial exploitation.

---

[21] Copyright registration permits disclosure of computer code sufficient only to identify the software while maintaining trade secrecy protection of critical components.

4.2.6 Export Administration Act

Technology transfer that may be damaging to national security is protected from export by the Export Administration Act. This purports to control technical expertise, which is considered to be a national asset, as well as the products in which it is imbedded. However, the effort to control the export of expertise has evoked as much opposition as support. Scientists consider this control an inhibition that could suppress innovation by cutting off the exchange of scientific data and research, which has characterized early stages of intellectual discovery.

4.2.7 Contractual Agreements

Where there exists no statutory or common law remedy, parties may protect their interests by negotiating contracts delineating certain obligations upon which they have reached agreement. The entertainment industry has been resourceful in devising standard contracts that govern the division of earnings to the various types of talent necessary to produce the works on radio, television, and videotapes. Collective agreements are negotiated by the "talent guilds," such as the American Federation of Television and Radio Artists (AFTRA), which provide for "residual rights." These are payments to performers and other skilled personnel for reproduction and reuse of video or audio works. The talent pool is a third-party beneficiary to the terms negotiated on its behalf by the guilds. Advertisers, who also are not parties to the contract, bind themselves to follow the terms by "letters of adherence." Thus, it is clear that ingenious alternatives to legislation can be effected by parties with a strong economic interest in the outcome.

4.2.8 Unfair Competition and Misappropriation

Although trade secrets law is in actuality a subcategory of unfair competition law, it is usually treated separately in discussions of intellectual property rights. However, other aspects of unfair competition law are used as a catchall to pick up the cases that fall between the cracks of trade secrets, patents, copyright, and trademark statutes. It is an equitable remedy which purports to establish a procedure for righting every wrong. Thus, legal principles can be developed under the common law practice to cover new fact situations as they arise, and to set the bounds of propriety and morality within which the marketplace operates.

Misappropriation is based upon the notion imbedded in early American philosophy and borrowed from the English philosopher John Locke: "Every man has a property in his own person. The labor of his body and the work of his hands we may say are properly his." Misappropriation is invoked in situations where an intellectual product that is unprotected by statute is, nonetheless, unfairly pirated by a nonoriginating party and commercialized to the latter's benefit without compensating or acknowledging the work of the former. For example, the International News Service was enjoined from taking Associated Press articles off the "ticker tape" and publishing them as its own.[22]

Attorney C. Owen Paepke has written a provocative journal article advocating an increase in litigation against "free loaders" using the rubric of misappropriation law as a device for protecting investments in innovative products where traditional legal regimes do not adequately discourage stealth of inventions.[23]

4.2.9 Rights of Privacy, Publicity, and Moral Rights

A number of neighboring rights are closely related to traditional intellectual property rights. These include

1. The right to prohibit disclosure or commercialization of information about oneself;
2. The exclusive right to authorize release of or to derive benefit from the commercialization of information about oneself;
3. The right to be acknowledged as the originator or creator of an intellectual work product, sometimes called a "paternity" right; and
4. The right to maintain control over the reuse of the product to prevent mutilation, distortion, or modification, known in some legal systems as a "right of integrity."

Collectively, these are really "merchandising rights" rather than personal rights or merely "moral rights," for the law is seldom used in the United States to protect intellectual interests that are not of a commercial nature.

---

[22] International News Service v. Associated Press, 248 U.S. 215 (1918).

[23] Paepke, C. Owen, "An Economic Interpretation of the Misappropriation Doctrine: Common Law Protection for Investments in Innovation," *High Technology Law Journal* 2, no. 1 (Spring 1987): 85.

4.3 RESTRICTIONS ON PROTECTIVE LEGAL REGIMES

4.3.1 Fair Use

The taking of intellectual property without compensation also finds legal doctrine in support. The "fair use" doctrine—an avoidance mechanism that protects innovation—permits lifting portions of a protected work for critical or academic purposes. The more recent doctrine of "passive reproduction" permits copying of an entire work for personal use but not for resale or commercial exploitation.

Domestically within the U.S. there is still a great deal of turmoil concerning what constitutes permissible use of protected materials. Under the "fair use" doctrine, use of portions of protected materials for scholarly and research purposes is permissible under a long-standing legal interpretation now incorporated into the law in Section 107 of the 1976 Copyright Act.

A former registrar of copyrights once commented: "It is too often easy to convince people that the public interest is always served when someone else's property can be had for free."[24] Therein lies the dilemma confronting American ingenuity and creativity in an economy that favors the marketplace to allocate resources but encourages widespread sharing of intellectual output. American artists, scientists, and engineers are among the most productive in the world. This is due more to an open immigration policy, which welcomed fugitives from less affluent and more authoritarian societies, than to an innate ability. This high level of productivity may also be related to the frontier mentality and pioneering urges which may have migrated toward the newly invigorated Asian societies such as the Japanese, Taiwanese, Koreans, and Chinese.

Creativity, wherever it exists, is coveted especially when its fruits could be beneficial to all of mankind. How that creativity can be compensated equitably is more difficult to determine as technology is transferred across national boundaries. Furthermore, the dilemma is built into the U.S. Constitution, where support can be found for protecting and rewarding talented intellectual productivity as well as for promoting wide dissemination of the fruits of innovation.

---

[24] Gervaise, Davis G., "Fair Use of Software and Databases with an Emphasis on Education," paper prepared for the Computer Law Association conference, "Update on Computer Software," November 3–4, 1986, Washington, DC.

4.3.2 Passive Reproduction

The "fair use" doctrine, which permits uses for academic or critical purposes, has been expanded by the Supreme Court in recent cases. Formerly applicable only to use of portions of work, it is now used to cover "passive reproduction" for personal use. The Sony-Betamax case,[25] which condoned copying "off the air" for the purpose of watching a program at a later time, could be used as a legal precedent to justify copying of computer software for personal use only or for downloading from an online database to shift the time for viewing. Such a case has not come before the courts, nor is one likely to do so. The software firms seem to have conceded the argument by pursuing their legal remedies only against large companies with multiple users of software products.[26]

Several suits have been settled among the litigants, and judgments have been obtained to enjoin resellers of protected software.

The reason why the Court found this exception for personal purposes while holding the line at commercial exploitation is not hard to ascertain. The behavior cannot be monitored without invading the privacy of individuals. Therefore it would be obtrusive and unacceptable in a free society to outlaw such conduct. Furthermore, current ethics seem to approve of such copying. The rationale seems to be this: If you can loan your friends a book, why not loan use of a software program, or a musical tape, or, easier still, give them copies of the disk or tapes? If we were to judge the behavior by whether or not the loan (which is legally permissible) or copy (which is not) is displacing a purchase, the decision might well be otherwise. However, the choice is an economic one, which may be more equitably made by legislative enactment than adjudication.

Where the philosophy and political consensus currently seem to rest is on encouraging and rewarding innovation and product improvement while discouraging those who seek to reap financial benefits where they have not sown the seeds or invested their own intellectual capital. More often, however, lawyers and their clients are beginning to realize that public awareness and sympathy must be cultivated as a necessary foundation to the protection of capital investment. The law cannot enforce what the majority of citizens choose to ignore, regardless of the many complicated legal systems designed to protect against

---

[25] Sony Corporation America v. Universal City Studios, Inc., 464 U.S. 417 (1984).

[26] It would not be cost effective to pursue legal remedies against individual offenders even if the evidence were easily obtainable.

nefarious practices. The courts as well as the legislative bodies are slowly recognizing the force of public behavior in the protection or lack thereof of intellectual property. This judicial and legislative wisdom has been exercised in two important developments—one by the Supreme Court, the other by Congress.

In the Sony Betamax case before the Supreme Court, the justices recognized that it would be fruitless to try to turn the tide against the massive purchases of videocassette recorders (VCRs), which are used both to record television programs for later playback (which the Court recognized as permissible copying) and to archive copies of such programs for private libraries or videoarchives (which arguably might be in violation of the Copyright Act, although difficult to document and litigate). Today, more than half the homes in America are equipped with these copying machines. Thus, the Supreme Court created a theory of copying for "private use" as distinguished from copying for commercial exploitation.

Congress in the Cable Communications Act of 1984[27] also recognized that the million owners of satellite dishes were a potent political force. The statute declared that signals that were broadcast into the radio spectrum without scrambling could be received by satellite dish owners without compensating the copyright owners of the programs so long as there was no commercially viable way of marketing these programs to the consumers. Cable operators who depended upon the sale of their programs to subscribers quickly turned to scrambled signals and the sale of decoders.

Thus, the law creeps along, recognizing that it cannot move mountains but must cope with the political and economic realities.

4.4 TYPES OF REMEDIES

The manner in which intellectual property rights are administered and require recompense varies as markedly as the different rights. These include (1) licensing of patent rights for a fee for a term determined by the parties, (2) negotiated as well as statutory and compulsory royalties payable for use without requiring the permission of the copyright owner, (3) injunctions to require infringers to cease and desist, and (4) confiscation of imported goods that infringe copyrights or patents. The Trademark Counterfeiting Act of 1984 makes "intentional trafficking" (purchase with intent to resell) a

---

[27] 47 U.S.C. §§521-59 (1984).

criminal violation and imposes civil sanctions as well. Loss of import/export privileges may be imposed for offenders to the Export Administration Act. Money damages may be awarded by the courts according to the nature of the offense.

Voluntary compliance obviously is the most desirable and least expensive course of action for any society, but it requires the cooperation of the potential offenders. However, numerous trade organizations are selecting that route and spending their dollars on public education rather than on litigation. The Association of Data Processing Service Organizations (ADAPSO) has initiated a "Thou Shalt Not Dupe" campaign,[28] and the cable television industry is spending millions of dollars advertising the impropriety of tapping into cable lines as well as lobbying for state laws to outlaw such conduct. Some fifty software manufacturers committed $500,000 to a Software Protection Fund to combat software piracy.[29]

The carrot is often more persuasive than the stick, if the financial incentive is sufficiently attractive. The Trade and Tariff Act of 1984 (PL 98-573) permits intellectual property protection to be considered in determining the applicability of trade preferences. The Trade Act of 1988 strengthens the sanctions that can be applied by trading partners to curb unauthorized exploitation of U.S. intellectual property. It also explicitly authorizes the U.S. special trade representative to investigate the adequacy of protection afforded holders of U.S. patents, copyrights, registered mask works, and registered trademarks. Moreover, the Caribbean Basin Economic Recovery Act (PL 98-67) permits consideration of compliance with copyright laws in determining how much economic aid will be granted.

International agreements are but another route for reaching harmonization of laws protecting intellectual property, and the General Agreement on Tariffs and Trade (GATT) has placed the discussion of such an agreement on its agenda for the next trade round. Such multilateral agreements save considerable time and personnel necessary to negotiate multiple bilateral agreements and have the advantage of uniformity of application. However, they also have the disadvantage of smaller nations joining forces against the interests of large nations in forums where majority voting does not reflect economic and political realities.

The Office of the Special Trade Representative in the United States has been instrumental in forwarding a draft proposal to the GATT

---

[28] Antonoff, *supra,* note 9 at 147.

[29] "Maryland Firm Agrees to Pay in Computer Software Piracy Suit," *Washington Post,* March 19, 1984, 15.

putting forth the recommendations of affected U.S. industries. These include efforts to harmonize the national intellectual laws, to develop efficient sanctions for noncompliance, to eliminate trade distortions resulting from the lack of a multilateral mechanism for settling disagreements over the application of intellectual property laws, and to promulgate some mutually agreeable procedures for curtailing trade in infringing products.[30]

The Council of Europe is a regional forum for the discussion and resolution of conflicting views on intellectual property protection. The advent of cable television and direct broadcasting satellites has served as a major impetus for promulgating recommendations for new media applications. In addition to urging compliance with earlier recommendations and existing treaties and conventions, the Committee of Ministers issued two new recommendations—No. R(88)1 and No. R(88)2 on Sound and Audiovisual Private Copying and Copyright Piracy, respectively—in January 1988. The former urges member states to "carefully examine whether sound and audiovisual private copying in their respective countries is not done in a way and to an extent that conflicts with the normal exploitation of works or otherwise unreasonably prejudices the legitimate interests of rights owners..." and urges that authors, performers, and producers be protected. It also suggests careful consideration of the levying of royalties on blank media or recording equipment as a viable solution already in operation in several of the member states.

The second recommendation addresses piracy of video, print, and computer media for commercial purposes and urges national consensus criminalizing the practice, authorizing search and seizure as well as destruction of the infringing products, and forfeiture of financial gains.

In early June 1988, the Commission of the European Community issued a call for comments on the challenges of technology that require "immediate action" to curb rampant piracy of community "goods to which considerable value has been added through the application of technology, skill and creativity." Noting the special vulnerability of service industries to economic loss from misappropriation of this "value added," the Green Paper observed astutely that "technological

---

[30] In May 1990 the U.S. Special Trade Representative tabled a comprehensive proposal seeking agreement on trade secret protection, applicability of copyright principles to computer software and the assurance of due process with adequate sanctions to assure compliance.

innovation itself paradoxically generates both the possibility of new economic activity and its misappropriation."[31]

4.5 DIFFICULTIES IN RESOLVING THE PROBLEMS

Numerous difficulties affect efforts to protect intellectual property.

4.5.1 Conflicts in Legal Regimes

There is confusion over which regime applies to new technologies. It has taken decades of litigation and some legislation to sort out whether patent or copyright or trade secret protection would apply to computer software. The lawyers and judges are still in dispute concerning the availability of copyright protection for the user interface or screen display (the "look and feel") of computer software. None of the current legal regimes is quite a happy fit. Keeping a trade secret in a product sold to millions of users is difficult. Although a dynamic database may be "fixed" sufficiently to meet the requirements of the copyright law, it may be difficult to determine which version should be registered. Many database providers, such as Dow Jones, which keeps its stock market quotes current, offer material that is in a constant state of flux.

The "shrink wrap license" on computer software is a prime example of the law trying to cope with application of a legal principle which makes no sense to rational intelligent analysis. The "shrink wrap license" is the document printed on the cover or inserted underneath the outer protection of computer software diskettes. This is a long and complicated agreement to which the purchaser supposedly agrees upon opening the package.

The words are usually set in type too small for most of us to read (and most of us do not). If read, they convey a warning that the license to use is limited to the purchaser who may not "use, copy, modify, merge, translate or transfer...except as expressly provided in this agreement." That so much copying and redistribution takes place is testimony enough that most customers do not read or do not take seriously the admonitions in the "shrink wrap license." The Fifth

---

[31] Commission of the European Community, "Green Paper on Copyright and the Challenge of Technology: Copyright Issues Requiring Immediate Action," Com (88) 172 final, June 7, 1988.

Circuit found the Louisiana Software License Enforcement Act[32] to be unenforceable. Thus, the prohibition contained in the plaintiff's "shrink-wrap" license against decompilation or disassembly had no legal efficacy.[33]

Moreover, common sense is offended by relying upon trade secret law to protect consumer products that are marketed in the millions all over the globe.

Equally incomprehensible to the ordinary user is the attempt to "license" large numbers of consumers for particular uses under circumstances that, for all practical purposes, are perceived by the "purchaser" (or licensee) as a "sale" rather than a license. In addition, most software also often claims copyright protection, which is statutory and assumes widespread distribution to the public. To distribute so widely and yet require secrecy or restricted use is a legal anachronism that defies normal human expectations. However, lawyers eager to protect the interests of their clients grasp at whatever legal string they can pull. They argue that claiming copyright protection does not destroy whatever trade secret protection they are claiming, as the two legal regimes protect different rights. The dual protection has become possible because current copyright registration procedures do not require full disclosure.

4.5.2 Magnitude of the Problem

If estimates of computer software firms, movie houses, and publishers (see section 4.1.1) are to be taken at their face value, the economic loss to creators and distributors of intellectual property is quite immense and increasing.

4.5.3 Changing Nature of the Work Force

The most effective skills, and the competitive edge, of the U.S. labor force are in problem solving. Moreover, the jobs being lost in the U.S. are in the manufacturing industries. The jobs being gained in the U.S. work force, as in other information-oriented societies, are in intellectual activity rather than in manual work. Thus, all such emerging "information societies" have a vested interest in the promulgation of better international intellectual property protection.

---

[32] La. Rev. Stat. Ann. Sec. 51:1961 (West 1987).

[33] Vault Corporation v. Quaid Software-Limited, 847 F.2d 255 (June 20, 1988).

4.5.4 Adaptation of the Law

Rather than enact new laws, there is a preference for adapting the existing laws in order to accommodate a new technology. The copyright law, for example, which was intended to protect literary and artistic works, has been extended to cover computer software—even though software is substantially a utilitarian product which patent laws were designed to protect. Yet software, according to earlier court decisions, does not comply with patent law unless it is imbedded within the hardware. Nonetheless, the patent office is now becoming more lenient in interpreting patent law so that it can cover some software that meets the more stringent requirements for patents where uniqueness is necessary rather than mere original expression.

Registration procedures for computer software have modified the requirement of disclosure upon copyright registration. Since secrecy often is felt to be the only protection computer software firms can rely upon, software programs are registered at the copyright office with only the first and last twenty-five pages of source code and can be partially blocked out, so that registration copies can contain sufficient identification without disclosing the critical program algorithms. Thus, the administrative regulations have been modified to accommodate the needs of the new registrants.

Many copyright lawyers enthusiastically endorse the ease with which copyright law has incorporated computer software, whereas some lawyers representing software firms remain skeptical and continue to rely heavily upon trade secret law.[34]

Many lawyers are seeking the more stringent protection offered by patent law now that the patent has become more accessible. However, not a few fear success with patents may stifle the rapid innovation that has heretofore flourished in the development of computer software.

4.5.5 The Conflict between Company Loyalty and a Proprietary Interest in Personal Knowledge and Skills

There has been a considerable abandonment of company loyalty, in the software industry especially. Individuals desire to carry with them whatever intellectual advantage they may have gained as an employee in one company to their new employment environment, whether a new company or an entrepreneurial enterprise of their own. Law suits for

[34] Ware, Donald R., "Trade Secret Protection of Computer Software: The Common Law Encounters High Technology," *Boston Bar Journal* (November–December 1985), 6.

misappropriation of information are as rampant in Silicon Valley as is the pirating of personnel from the more established to the start-up firms. The interests of the employer and employee in these situations no longer coincide as they did when company employment was usually for life.

4.5.6 Technology Transfer as an International Obligation

International competitors have different attitudes about borrowing our technology or even feel that we are obligated to share it with them. We cannot be too critical of this attitude, since the United States refused to protect British authors during the nineteenth century. Much of the English language literature was copied by U.S. publishers without paying royalties, much in the same way that the Chinese are adopting our own scientific and technical literature today.

Especially in medical innovations, third world countries are concerned that they have access to new pharmaceuticals as soon as they are available in the laboratories of the more advanced countries. This they consider a matter of basic human needs. Patent protection for new seed varieties also irks third world farmers, who call it "genetic imperialism."

4.5.7 Technology Transfer as a National Imperative

In the late 1970s, it was discovered that many patents that were developed under government contract were languishing for lack of interest by the private sector. As a consequence Congress passed the Stevenson-Wydler Act in 1980,[35] directing the secretary of commerce to establish an Office of Industrial Technology, whose mandate was to promote industrial competitiveness and stimulate entrepreneurship. The Department of Commerce was authorized to transfer patents developed with federal funds to Centers of Industrial Technology comprised of university–industry joint ventures. Further amendments to the Act, in 1986, authorized government-operated federal laboratories to accept funds from royalties or to waive any rights of ownership and to encourage employees or former employees "to participate in efforts to commercialize inventions they made while in the service of the United States."[36]

However, due to a quirk in the application of intellectual property

[35] National Technology Innovation Act of 1979, Public Law 96-480,October 21, 1980.
[36] Federal Technology Transfer Act of 1986, Public Law 99-502.

laws which have favored copyright rather than patent protection for computer software, neither act extends the privileges for transfer of federal interests in computer software to the private sector, and Section 105 of the copyright statute prohibits the federal government from holding any copyright interest in copyrightable material developed by agencies of the U.S. government. Despite this prohibition, the National Library of Medicine has successfully protected a proprietary interest in the MEDLARS system against disclosure under the Freedom of Information Law on the narrow ground that the computerized bibliographic data about medical research were not agency records.[37]

However, the decision has been roundly criticized by scholars and Congress alike.[38] Yet government computer experts are thwarted from cooperating with the private sector in effecting a transfer of their technical expertise in a manner that is consistent with the Stevenson-Wydler Act and with the best interests of the country in honing its competitive edge within the global marketplace. The interest of the federal government in its direct investment in new intellectual assets in a period of severe budget restrictions is in sharp conflict with the interest of the same government as a mechanism for sharing expertise to enhance the private sector's capability. Furthermore, the prohibition against a government copyright facilitates transfer of government-funded research to foreign companies through publications designed to serve U.S.interests. This is a controversy in which the National Technical Information Service has found itself in the center as agitation persists to transfer that service to the private sector.

Nurturing national creativity and enhancing the competitiveness of U.S.-based companies is a difficult task to achieve without at the same time assisting international competitors to enhance their skills and knowledge. Developing nations also benefit from technology transfer that recognizes no national boundaries, and some consider sharing of expertise and knowledge an international obligation or basic human right.

4.5.8 Conflicts of Philosophy

The United States Constitution contains the conflicting philosophies of sharing information to promote the public good while using private

[37] SDC Dev. Corp. v. Mathew, 542 F.2d 1116 (9th Cir. 1976).

[38] U.S., House Comm. on Government Operations, H. Rep. No. 560, 99th Cong., 2d Sess., *Electronic Collection and Dissemination of Information by Federal Agencies: A Policy Overview* (1980).

enterprise as a methodology for stimulating market innovations. Article I, Section 8, provides:

> The Congress shall have Power To promote the Progress of Science and useful Arts, by securing for Limited Times to Authors and Inventors the exclusive Right to their respective Writing and Discoveries.

There is a real tug of war between the concept of exclusive exploitation of creativity as both a reward for and a stimulation of creativity and the concept of shared intellectual progress for humanity. This internal conflict is not limited to the United States but pervades the world. The third world particularly objects to the patent protection provided new grain seeds, since the farmers there always have believed that they should pool their knowledge in the interests of all. Pharmaceuticals that can ease pain and stop disease are thought to belong to "mankind," and Indian philosophy as well as several theologies are beset with the notion that "God-given talents" should be dedicated to the betterment of the general welfare and not be the subject of proprietary claims.

A good example of the divergent philosophies can be found in recent history.[39] The case in point is that of Visicalc—the first electronic spreadsheet made available for personal computers—and its successor, Lotus 1-2-3. No one other than the proprietors of Visicalc would have wanted to give Visicalc a seventeen-year stranglehold on the further development of such spreadsheets, especially after it became obvious that Lotus 1-2-3 was a superior product. Yet, not only a direct descendant of Visicalc, Lotus 1-2-3 also was developed by former employees. Now that similar products are being offered by competitors, however, Lotus Corporation is the most aggressive litigant against look-alikes. Indeed, Lotus' most recent case involved a competitor that advertised:

> VP Planner is designed to work like Lotus 1-2-3 keystroke for keystroke...[and] is a feature-for-feature workalike for 1-2-3....[U]sers familiar with 1-2-3 can skip this chapter.[40]

Thus, there is always a conflict of interest between the creators and users of new intellectual products in a market-oriented economy. If the originator must derive sole benefit from the purchase thereof, compensation must awarded. However, society will be benefitted by fostering

---

[39] Pollack, A., "How a Software Winner Went Sour," *New York Times,* February 26, 1984, 1.

[40] Sanger, D.E., "A Divisive Lotus Clone War," *New York Times,* February 5, 1987.

improvements and widespread circulation. Furthermore, marginal users are anxious to obtain access at the lowest cost. Thus, the widespread sale of clones accelerates the distribution and transfer of technology but unfairly disadvantages the originator who bore the cost of creation and provided the labor.

4.5.9 Need for User-Friendly Interface

The VP Planner advertisement, citing its compatibility with Lotus products, highlights another problem facing those who would design public policy for innovation. There is a genuine need for the "user interface" in computer software to be standardized for the training and human factors to be transferable from one software program to another. Otherwise, there is a serious economic loss to the companies that have invested in training employees in the outmoded system. If they do not transfer over to the newer technology, they may lack competitiveness in products produced using the old technology.

This is one of the greatest worries about the so-called "look and feel" cases, which seem to be holding that the "user interface" can be copyrighted and protected. A recent case involved a software program whose major intellectual contribution was an understanding of the dental profession and its mode of operation. To protect this intellectual contribution, the courts found such "look and feel" designed for the dental profession to be copyrightable.[41]

An equally interesting and provocative case has been filed by Apple Computer, a pioneer developer of personal computers, against Hewlett Packard and Microsoft for infringement of Apple's popular Macintosh computer screen arrangement of "visual displays and graphic images." According to the complaint, Apple has "expended millions of dollars and years of creative effort" in making this interface "user friendly" and, therefore, uniquely attractive to consumers.[42] The defendant, Hewlett-Packard, turned down by Apple for a license to use the screen display program, is marketing its own version entitled New Wave, which, to an unsophisticated observer, seems strikingly similar. However, to sophisticated computer professionals, with elephantine memories, both displays seem reminiscent of the Xerox Star system developed by the Xerox Corporation. For a long time Xerox took no steps to claim a legally enforceable interest in its earlier version of the

---

[41] Whelan Associates v. Jaslow Dental Laboratory, 79 F.2d 1222 (3d cir. 1986), *cert. den.* 479 U.S. 1031 (1987).

[42] Apple Computer, Inc. v. Microsoft Corp. and Hewlett-Packard Co., No.C-88-20149-RPA U.S. District Court, Northern District of California, filed March 17, 1988.

windows and icons, which are attracting so much interest. Then, a case was filed by Xerox against Microsoft but dismissed by the judge.

Neither has the Stanford Research Institute (SRI) claimed a copyright in the pioneering work it did on windows and icons in previous years. However, SRI may have been prohibited by federal funding from copyrighting the software it developed.

No doubt each company has a claim for the original expression or value added. However, we must devise better ways of protecting economic value than to tie the hands of future software designers from using protocols or interfaces that are found to be compatible with the practices of a particular profession. To do so may inhibit rather than encourage innovation.

4.5.10 Conflicting Legal Theories

There is no agreement on the basic underlying rationale for regulation. A recent Office of Technology Assessment report on intellectual property[43] distinguishes between works of art, works of fact, and works of function. It also distinguishes between the legal theories of "property" as a right to derive benefit from any use of the protected work from the "regulatory" system as a right to control use for commercial purposes. In practical terms, the latter is a means of capturing compensation from users of a product rather than from mere purchasers of a product. The basic theory underlying the law has not yet been clarified in this respect, and the OTA concepts are a reasonable point from which to begin the appropriate analysis.

Where the law currently stands, there is no guaranteed protection to the creators of intellectual property that they will benefit from subsequent uses. Where the case law seems to fall is at the point of not permitting unconscionable exploitation of the commercial value of another's work product. However, even that legal distinction fails to protect innovators from infringing uses of their work products when the reprehensible behavior occurs outside the jurisdiction of courts accessible to the innovator.

4.5.11 Technological Fixes Seem Doomed to Failure

In some cases the technology itself seems to offer a solution to protection. For example, in the case of satellite-delivered television

---

[43] *OTA Report, supra,* note 18 at 85.

programs, scrambling the signal appears to deter unauthorized usage. However, in the case of computer software, the imbedding of "worms" or "bugs," which destroy the disk upon copying or "eat up" the data, only angers users and discourages purchase of such programs. Similarly, software that cannot be used without a copy-protected disk being placed in the disk drive discourages sales. Therefore, the software industry has by and large abandoned such practices in the hope of selling enough programs to pay for their own costs. Also, many users discover that they need or want the help of documentation and technical support teams, which comes with the legitimate purchase of the programs.

4.5.12 Mores of the Scientist/Entrepreneur

Scientists have become entrepreneurs and want to share in the dollar rewards of their inventions. In Louis Pasteur's France, scientists would have considered that they lowered themselves in the eyes of their colleagues by doing so. This is not so today, when young computer wizards have become multimillionaires in their late twenties and early thirties.[44] The scientist/entrepreneur is no longer an oddity. The university professor often has a small business venture or a major consultancy on the side.

This trend has its disadvantages as well as its advantages, since the major function of the university as a protected environment for pure research may be eroded. The budgetary crunch for education and research may dictate more and more short-range development activities than pure intellectual analysis, but that is the subject of another paper. However, the impact of these changing mores on the support structure for scientific creativity needs to be better understood and accommodated.

4.5.13 Time Required for Resolution of Applicable Law

It has taken several decades for the computer industry to engage Congress and the judiciary in an effort to analyze and apply existing law. Only in 1980 did Congress finally amend the 1976 Act to include

---

[44] These include William Gates, Microsoft; Mitchell Kapor, Lotus; Fred Gibbons, Software Publishing; William Baker, Information Unlimited Software; Steven Jobs, Apple Computer; Steven Wozniak, Apple Computer; and W.J. Sanders III, Advanced Micro Devices. "Richest are a Diverse Group," A.P., October, 13, 1987; "Another Kid Goes Fortune Hunting," A.P., May 21, 1982.

computer software as a "literary work." It has taken seven years since to define the nature and scope of this protection, because computer software is not really a literary work. An extended legal fight ensued to obtain protection for object code. Until 1986 it was not possible to protect internal flow diagrams (the logic and sequence of computer programs) under the copyright rubric.[45] In late 1987 there was still a confrontation over the newly acquired protection for the "look and feel" of software. Some critics consider "look and feel" to be the essence of the innovation. Others consider this protection an inhibition to the compatibility of user interfaces upon which the future economic health of the industry depends.

4.5.14 Privatization of Public Information Resources

One of the more interesting pieces of litigation in recent history is the case filed by West Publishing Company (hereinafter West) to enjoin Mead Data Central (hereinafter Mead), developer of the LEXIS legal database, from citing internal page numbers (called star pagination) to the published volumes of West's extensive case records from most of the major U.S. courts. Although West obtains the cases directly from the public records of the courts in question, they are the primary or sole source of many opinions and have become the official reporter for many states. As a consequence, West page numbers are uniformly cited by lawyers and judges alike, creating a standard system of reference for legal research and adjudication. While conceding that citation to the first page was "fair use,"[46] West convinced the district court[47] and a majority of the judges on the Eighth Circuit Court of Appeal[48] that the internal page numbers represented a critical component of the copyrightable organization and sequence of the opinions as published in the West volumes.[49] Thus, a temporary restraining order was obtained pending the trial on the merits.

However, Mead has filed suit in another jurisdiction against West on antitrust grounds that West is operating "an essential facility" unlawfully in constraint of trade.[50]

---

[45] Sanger, *supra,* note 35.

[46] This was arguably because a primary use of the LEXIS database is to procure legal citations to quickly find the appropriate West volumes for review.

[47] 616 F.Supp. 1571 (D. Minn. 1985).

[48] 799 F.2d 1219 (8th Cir. 1986), *cert. den.,* 107 S. Ct. 962 (1987).

[49] Interestingly enough, this resembles the arguments made by Lotus against allegedly infringing software programs that capture the on-screen presentation that is user friendly and attractive to the consumer.

[50] Mead Data Central, Inc. v. West Publishing Co., Case no. C-3-87-426 (U.S. Dist. Ct., S. D. Ohio).

This litigation between Mead and West does not represent an entirely new situation caused primarily by the introduction of new technologies, for courts have consigned the job of court reporter to private entities for a long time. Earlier cases can be cited by both sides to support their respective arguments that page numbers are mere Arabic numerals, which are not per se copyrightable or, to the contrary, that page numbers are an essential element of the sequence of cases as organized by the publisher.[51]

As a practical matter, if Mead and West (and other database providers) assign new page or document numbers to the words as they appear in the database, these will be different from the published West opinions, and this will confuse lawyers and judges alike and add to their work load. Alternatively, if the page numbers are copyrightable, then courts may be petitioned to assign the page numbers of their original opinions in some manner that provides equal access to all commercial comers.[52] There is no question that access to the judicial opinions is secure in the law as a prime goal for public policy.[53] Fortunately for the litigants as well as the public, in July 1988 Mead Data Central, Inc., and West Publishing Co. agreed to settle their dispute over the use of "star paging." West agreed to license the use of West page numbers in LEXIS, thus voluntarily acceding to the needs of the judicial system for uniformity in citation of opinions in computerized databases.[54]

However, the two cases and the dilemma presented are a good indication of the difficulties remaining to be sorted out as the introduction of new technologies creates strains upon established institutions. The cost of transferring information to machine-readable form is enormous, and the economic interests of private sector information providers is easily measured. The advantages of delegating the publishing responsibility to private industry are quite tempting. The desire of public institutions to obtain financial support from user fees is quite understandable.[55] Yet the necessity to make legislative, administrative, and judicial information available to the public at reasonable costs is an essential element of democratic government.

---

[51] See: Wheaton v. Peters, 33 U.S. (8 Pet.) 591 (1834); Banks Law Publishing Co. v. Lawyers' Coop. Publishing Co., 169 F. 386 (2d Cir. 1909); Callaghan v. Myers, 128 U.S. 617 (1888); Banks v. Manchester, 128 U.S. 244 (1888).

[52] There is some similarity here to the requirement by the Federal Communications Commission that local telephone companies provide "equal access" to all long distance carriers to the local loop.

[53] Nash v. Lathrop, 142 Mass. 29, 35 (1886).

[54] "Mead and West Publishing Co. Reach Agreement," *Business Wire,* July 22, 1988.

[55] More than half the states already claim copyright in their own statutes.

Within the ambit of intellectual property law are found many of the building blocks of governance, both political and economic, for the foreseeable future.

4.6 CHALLENGES ARISING AS NEW TECHNOLOGIES MATURE

New problems in protecting the economic value of creativity arise with each new technology of information storage, manipulation, and distribution. Lindsey Kiang, formerly general counsel for Lotus Corporation and, in late 1987, an attorney with Digital, understated the crisis in legal protection when he commented, "Copyright Laws are not entirely adequate for the software industry."[56] The present legal turmoil within the computer software industry is only a tip of the iceberg lying beneath the surface of the murky waters covering the information economy. New areas likely to create legal difficulties in the near future are artificial intelligence, dynamic databases, CD ROMs, shared computer networks, desktop publishing, computer graphics, and videodiscs, as well as computer-aided manufacturing and design, digital audio tapes, and genetic engineering.

4.6.1 Artificial Intelligence

New medical databases for the purpose of improving diagnosis could proliferate opportunities for medical malpractice suits as well as for copyright infringement. Liability for misuse will depend upon who enters the data, who uses the data, and how the data are used. The *Boston Globe*[57] reported the advent of one such database as follows:

> Beginning this week, doctors—even lay people—across the country will be able to hook up their personal computers by telephone to a big computer at Massachusetts General Hospital, punch in a number of symptoms, answer a few a questions and in a matter of moments, receive a list of possible diagnoses, ranked in order of probability.
>
> Like other technological advances, the new system, designed to aid doctors in making difficult diagnoses, is likely not only to advance the practice of medicine but also, further down the road, raise new ethical and legal questions, specialists say.
>
> Will the system, for instance, become so commonplace that a doctor

[56] Kiang, *supra,* note 7.

[57] "MGH Unveils Diagnostic Computer," *Boston Globe,* June 23, 1987, 1.

> who does not back up his diagnosis with a computer be considered negligent? On the other hand, might a doctor be held accountable for overrelying on the computer and underrelying on his own clinical skills and judgments?
>
> "There's an awful lot of uncharted legal ground here" according to Dr. Randolph Miller, associate professor of medicine at the University of Pittsburgh School of Medicine and creator of QMR (Quick Medical Reference), which he admits is not yet "safe for human use."

Artificial intelligence systems are likely to generate as much legal concern about protection from the deleterious consequences of such computerized systems as protection of the economic value contained within them. When, for example, may general practitioners in remote areas isolated from urban experts rely upon such electronic aids, and when may they be considered negligent for failure to consult more sophisticated sources of diagnostic or prescriptive aids?

4.6.2 Dynamic Databases: Computer-Aided Design and Computer-Aided Manufacturing

Online databases have been around for several decades for specialized research purposes and are only beginning to become available for widespread public use, as personal computers become more generally available. Such information searches are increasing at 9 percent per year. However, the content of such databases is constantly changing to accommodate new information. The sources are both public and proprietary, news events, facts, and creative endeavor. The boundary between what may be borrowed in "fair use" and what must be compensated for reuse is ever changing. What needs to be registered to establish ownership is cloudy, and what standards of proof are required for compensation to become available are still in a state of flux.

Perhaps the most interesting opportunity for a new look is in the area of CAD/CAM dynamic databases. Here is where the global nature of the engineering enterprise is most apparent, as design and manufacture become both separated in time and distance and interconnected by complex computerized systems. The laws of several countries may be in conflict. The interests of several companies in joint ventures may not coincide. Here is where the most creative legal solutions must be sought or havoc may reign. The forums for adjudicating transnational disputes are still in a state of infancy.

For example, it may not be possible to use centralized computerized systems if countries insist upon obtaining the encryption keys (the software to decode messages) to the databases and telecommunications transport systems. It is difficult to protect trade secrets in such an environment if the host nation has a nationalized industry that is your competitor. Consequently, nation states as well as corporations engaged in transnational computer-aided design and manufacturing (CAD/CAM operations) will need to cooperate in developing a harmonized legal environment to facilitate rather than inhibit growth of these new systems.

4.6.3 Shared Networks

Computer terminals in Western Europe alone expanded from 393,000 in 1979 to 1.6 million in 1986.[58] The rate of expansion is likely to accelerate as computers proliferate in the Pacific Basin. Shared networks mean shared creativity, so that it is not always easy to determine who is the rightful owner of the copyright in material that is computer generated in such a dynamic environment. Even if the computer could track the individual contributions and provide recompense therefor, the financial cost of monitoring as well as the complexity of the software required, might inhibit the very ease of exchange which has contributed to research and development.

4.6.4 Compact Disk Read Only Memory (CD ROM)

CD ROMs are called the new "papyrus," but they also represent a new threat to established economic interests. The storage capacity is greatly expanded over existing forms of archiving information. For example, a twenty-volume encyclopedia can be stored on less than a single disk. The information is stored in a digital form that can be reproduced on screen, can be laser printed, and can be delivered over telephone lines.

What uses of the CD ROM are permissible within the limits of current law? Can you print out the entire twenty volumes? If not, how much can you reprint before you have infringed the copyright? Can you download portions, or is this making a copy? Can you display portions in the classroom, or is this a public display, a "performance," or perhaps a "retransmission"? May you network the contents to many locations, as in a university environment to many classrooms or campuses? Isn't this making multiple copies much in the same way as on a Xerox machine? If royalties are not to be paid to the many creative

---

[58] Data from Eurodata Foundation, 1987.

and talented people who contributed to the twenty volumes, is there some other way to provide the infrastructure for intellectual productivity? How can the system detect such "uses" or copying if the record is not preserved for posterity? If the record is preserved, does this process create costs that inhibit meaningful use? Current copyright law protects the originator's value only on the "first sale" of a copy. There is no royalty on the "use" or rental thereof. However, if only a few copies are needed to provide access to masses of users, then the original charge must cover all of the development and marketing costs.

4.6.5 Desktop Publishing

The new publishers, those with personal computers and software programs that replicate the typesetting capabilities of publishing houses, will greatly increase the number of entities involved in both creating and borrowing (e.g., pirating or fair using). Thus, the problems both of compensating for use and of placing liability for misuse will multiply accordingly. More and more the users are turning to the distributors or processors of information as the culprits when something goes awry. James C. Grant, executive vice-president of the Royal Bank of Canada, recently called for telecommunications carriers to bear the liability for the ultimate damage caused by inaccurate information transmitted by the carriers.[59] Such a transfer of financial responsibility is a striking divergence from the current practice of charging the carrier only with the cost of the transmission. In addition, a recent Ninth Circuit case, *Brocklesby v. U.S. and Jeppesen & Co.*, placed the burden of compensation for a plane crash caused by an error in an aeronautical chart on a private map maker even though the maker had used U.S. government sources.[60]

4.6.6 Computer Editing of Graphics and Sound

The new technologies of cutting and pasting and reformatting images as well as sounds make the distortion of works easier to achieve. Moreover, it is more difficult to ascertain what pieces have been used for what purposes, and to determine what can be used without compensation as well as who should be compensated. The borrowing of

---

[59] Grant, James C., "Hello, Is Anyone Listening? Vital Issues for Telecommunications Users," paper presented at Telecom '87, ITU, October 21–23, 1987, Geneva, Switzerland.

[60] Brocklesby v. U.S. and Jeppesen & Co., 767 F.2d 1288 (9th cir. 1985) *cert. den.* 106 Sup. Ct. 882.

tunes in the making of music videos is rampant, as digital recording equipment permits easy mixing of sounds from several sources. A regrettable miscarriage of economic if not legal justice is found in the use without compensation of a rare Nigerian drum sequence by jazz drummer David Earle Johnson in the "Miami Vice" theme song. Johnson claims the sequence was played "for a friend" who recorded it and incorporated it into the theme song. Without a written agreement with the producer, the musicians' union was unwilling to press Johnson's case for misappropriation of an intellectual asset.

Such opportunities for borrowing or toying with the integrity of artistic and literary works are mindboggling, especially as U.S. law does not respect any "moral rights." In other countries, artists have a legal right to protect the integrity of their works in later renditions where the copyright has passed into other hands. Tom Lord-Alge, a rock music recording engineer, confirms that pandemonium reigns in his field, stating, "We're all blatantly stealing from everyone else.... That's just the way it's done in the '80s."[61]

4.6.7 Videodiscs

The new laser videodiscs are a good example of a technology that may come simultaneously under several different legal regimes. The design of the laser disc may be patented; the process by which it is manufactured may be a trade secret; the content may be copyrighted; the commercial name under which the product is marketed a be trademarked; the talent making the disc may contract for residual rights; and the work, if retransmitted by a cable system, may be subject to compulsory and statutory royalties. Handling each of these activities may require a different team of experts and will certainly consume much time and money.

4.6.8 Digital Audio Tapes (DATs)

Another new technology has been impeded from introduction into the U.S. market by doubts that copying can be prevented or controlled. Digital audio tapes (DATs) can replicate the high quality of the original musical renditions as well as the digital recording. Thus, the U.S. recording industry has been reluctant to release music to be recorded on the new DATs. Various alternatives have been considered.

---

[61] Miller, *supra,* note 2.

CBS Records (recently acquired by the Sony Corporation) has developed a technical solution calling for removal of a sliver of the recording medium; this change would be perceived by any recording device and would disable it from making the reproduction.

However, audiophiles claim this protection strategy impairs the quality of the recording. Others propose a royalty on the DAT machines and tapes. As yet no bargain has been struck that is agreeable to both manufacturers of the hardware and suppliers of the music. Nonetheless, DAT machines are creeping slowly into the U.S. market through purchases in Europe and Japan; eager consumers may not be willing to wait for a consensus solution.[62]

4.6.9 Colorization of Old Movies

A tempest in a teapot is raging over the transformation of black-and-white film to color. Famous actors, including James Stewart and Burt Lancaster, joined producers George Lucas and Steven Spielberg in lobbying Congress to enact legislation establishing "moral rights" of writers and producers to protect the integrity of their intellectual works from mutilation.[63] Ted Turner's release of films such as *Casablanca* and *It's a Wonderful Life* has precipitated such agitation for a change in the law. However, the change in the law in order to provide for "moral rights" of the originators to approve later versions would also conform U.S. law to the Berne Convention, to which it has never adhered, largely because of the lack of such rights within the United States.

In his testimony before Congress, George Lucas warned that colorization was just the tip of the iceberg concerning changes that could be easily made by engineers manipulating the new technologies:

> Tomorrow more advanced technology will be able to replace actors with "fresher faces," or alter dialogue and change the movement of the actor's lips to match. It will soon be possible to create a new "original" negative with whatever changes or alterations the copyright holder of the moment desires.[64]

---

[62] Pollack, A., "Moves to End Digital Tape Dispute," *New York Times,* January 16, 1988, sec. 2, 35. See also, Harrington, R., "CBS Records: Is It a Sony?" *Washington Post,* November 11, 1987, Style section, D7; "Not-So-Hot Sounds," *Fortune* (February 15, 1988), 8.

[63] Page, Paul, "Burt Lancaster and James Stewart Reprise Roles Before Congress," A.P., March 16, 1988.

[64] Lucas, George, "Lucas and Spielberg: In Defense of Artists' Rights," *Washington Post,* February 28, 1988, G-1.

The other side of the question was raised by Ralph Oman, U.S. Registrar of Copyrights, who decided that the colorized version of the film was sufficiently new and different to deserve its own copyright.[65] The Copyright Office, at the suggestion of Representatives Kastenmeier and Moorhead, on behalf of the House Subcommittee on Courts, Civil Liberties and the Administration of Justice, held hearings on the impact of new technologies, such as the colorization of movie classics and time compression, on the creation and exploitation of audiovisual works.[66] On this issue, Congress reached a compromise of conflicting interests by creating a National Film Board to designate some classic films to be marketed and advertised as such in original form but without prohibiting colorized versions to be offered as such.

4.6.10 Genetic Engineering

Genetic engineering is another area that is putting strains upon traditional intellectual property laws. In 1980 the Supreme Court heard a case questioning the patentability of a man-made new living organism. Despite the protests that such determination might upset the delicate balance of medical research in favor of crass commercialism, the Supreme Court confirmed the decision of the Court of Customs and Patent Appeals that the genetically engineered substance fulfilled all the requirements of the Patent Act.[67] More recently, the Patent Office has granted a patent for the first living animal, a genetically engineered mouse, intended for use in cancer research.[68]

Genetic engineering is one of the most promising areas for development in the near future. More than $2.5 billion had already been invested by 1985. Leslie Glick, president of the Genex Corporation, suggests that some $40 billion will be invested in genetic engineering by the end of the century. Along with this substantial amount of commercial interest in the field comes a complex of ethical and legal questions concerning the various components of the research process that leads to the new biological material.

A recent law journal summarizing the plethora of legal complexities arising from biotechnology suggests:

> In the field of human biologics, commercial exploitation has changed the patient's relationship with both the researcher and the research

[65] Oman, Ralph, "Black and White and Red All Over," *New York Times,* June 24, 1987, A-27. See also, 52 Fed. Reg. 2343, June 22, 1987.

[66] *Daily Report for Executives,* Bureau of National Affairs, May 27, 1988.

[67] Diamond v. Chakrabarty, 447 U.S. 303 (1980).

[68] *Boston Globe,* April 12, 1988, 9.

> institution. The introduction of pure profit motives has tainted a relationship which, idealistically, should be humanitarian in nature. Researchers may have substantial ties to corporations—they may serve as consultants or corporate directors, have stock options, and receive research support—as a result of their research on patient tissue or the commercial products resulting from this research. Universities, the most common research institutions, also stand to profit from biotechnology.[69]

How the profits are to be divided among researchers, host bodies that provide the material from which the human material is cloned or transformed, and the host institutions will provide grist for many litigators as well as legislators.

The questions go on endlessly for those who are entering new markets with untried products. The answers are not very satisfactory to the venture capitalists who fund such new enterprises.

4.6.11 Custom-Generated Musical Compositions

A computer-generated musical composer called "Jiffy Box" has made its debut in a joint effort emanating from Jerusalem and Long Beach. The brainchild of Yaakov Kirschen, "Jiffy Box" can custom generate new musical compositions in the style of any composer whose "musical genes" have been programmed into its memory. The result is "not artificial intelligence, it's artificial creativity," according to Kirschen, who expects his brainchild to revolutionize the music industry. Likewise, it will no doubt create new problems to confront the copyright lawyers and policy makers, manufacturers and users.[70]

4.7 TARGETS OF OPPORTUNITY

A number of areas offer fruitful avenues for stakeholders to pursue if they seek reform of intellectual property protection.

4.7.1 Voluntary Compliance

Public education resulting in voluntary compliance is clearly a more desirable and less onerous route than litigation for the protection of

---

[69] "Comment: Toward the Right of Commerciality: Recognizing Property Rights in the Commercial Value of Human Tissue," 34 UCLA L. Rev. 207 (October 1986).

[70] Fisher, Dan, "Like Bach or Beatles, It Writes Songs: 'Jiffy Box' Creates in Styles of Famous Composers," *Los Angeles Times*, September 1, 1988, Part 4, 1.

intellectual property. In any event, the law can only follow the consensus that certain kinds of behavior are no longer appropriate or economically viable. Consequently, the applicability of the law will remain cloudy until greater consensus is reached than exists today.

However, consensus in one society alone will not suffice. Trading partners must be brought into a more active dialogue about the desirability of improved protection within the global marketplace. There is a long and hard path to follow in the allocation of equity in the global economy.

4.7.2 Codes of Ethics

A first step in reaching global consensus may be in developing specialized codes of ethics within professional groupings. Professional associations, especially those which have international counterparts, can take the lead. Robert White, president of the National Academy of Engineering, has undertaken efforts to bring other engineering societies into a dialogue with their American colleagues about this and other areas of concern. How successful such collaborative efforts will become remains to be seen.

4.7.3 Drafting Appropriate Legislation

The Office of Technology Assessment of the U.S. Congress has provided a good foundation upon which discussions about intellectual property issues can proceed.[71] However, Congress is unlikely to draft let alone pass new legislation without much more widespread public interest than was in evidence in late 1987. Congress is more likely to act once all stakeholders have become motivated to take a more active role in the policy assessment. This includes those working with their lawyers and legislators to provide professional, commercial, and technical evaluation of what makes sense in proprietary protection of new technologies. Other stakeholders should not leave the lawyers and legislators alone as architects of public policy. Lawyers and others have their own vested interests in protecting a particular legal regime, because they have invested a professional career in understanding its intricacies. Neither should other stakeholders be intimidated by the professed expertise of such lawyers, who rarely possess the technical expertise to practice what they preach when it applies to an electronic environment.

---

[71] *OTA Report, supra,* note 18.

4.7.4 Administration of Intellectual Property Laws

Domestically, the OTA in its study found too many agencies involved in administering the various legal regimes for efficient decision making. Nineteen federal agencies are represented on the Working Group on Intellectual Property in the Office of Science and Technology. Considering this too balkanized, the OTA Report suggested that a single agency might assume responsibility for intellectual property rights within the U.S. government itself.[72] Sorting out the major institutional interests and their appropriate roles will be a major undertaking.

Internationally, the various forums engaged in some aspect of intellectual property protection include the General Agreement on Tariffs and Trade, World Intellectual Property Organization, International Telecommunication Union, United Nations Center on Transnational Corporations, and United Nations Educational Scientific and Cultural Organization. This multiplicity of interests and applications complicates consideration of reform. Merging institutional mandates in the international arena would be a major challenge. The administrators and administrative agencies governing the various legal regimes have a stake in preserving the status quo.

4.7.5 Understanding Pricing Policies

Another target area is the pricing policies employed by different entities when introducing a new product or work that embodies major intellectual components. If a major software innovation is easily copied by all, the first sale must recapture all of the research and development costs. On the other hand, if a product is leased on a basis that repays the originator through a "use" royalty, then development costs can be averaged over a long period of time. Some software firms, Freeware, for example, have found sufficient financial rewards from offering the public the right to copy diskettes freely and asking only for contributions. There exist a variety of choices for funding of development costs as well as for assuring an equitable return on investment of intellectual capital.

If deregulation is to continue to be the trend in world markets, then stakeholders in intellectual property rights must understand the economic alternatives to governmental regulation in order to preserve their financial stability.

---

[72] *OTA Report, supra,* note 18, 262–68, 282.

4.7.6 Evaluating Technological "Fixes"

Many people expect the technological geniuses who create the new problems also to create the technological solutions. In some cases this is possible or even desirable, in others not. For example, the "worms" placed in software to deter pirates have annoyed legitimate users and have eaten up valuable data. Indeed, clever entrepreneurs earned their profits by devising such "protection-busters" as Unlock. On the other hand, the encryption of satellite-delivered television signals to cable television head ends appears, at least initially, to have been successful in deterring backyard satellite antenna owners from taking the signals without compensation. However, a better assessment could be made of alternatives that may create exclusionary economic costs or create such complexity that users cannot cope with the system.

Certainly the tradeoffs between technological, legal, and pricing policies need to be better understood. A thorough evaluation of technological alternatives would provide a sound basis for exercising policy options.

4.7.7 Appraising Alternatives to Judicial Resolution of Disputes

There are substantial grounds for fear among industry leaders that litigation and judicial decision do not render sensible solutions to the complex new issues arising from the applications of new information technology. Computer literacy has not yet permeated the whole of society.

Esther Dyson, editor of *Release 1.0,* a computer industry newsletter, has expressed concern that the courts will not be able to distinguish between a clone and an improved classic when determining rights in software applications.[73] A legitimate concern, it must be considered in order to assure that creativity is compensated and encouraged while genuine improvement in technology is shared. If the lawyers and judges who usually litigate, hear, and decide such cases are not technically knowledgeable to understand the nuances of such cases, is it wise to await the maturity of a new generation of literati to reach the bench and bar? In the interim, alternative means of conflict resolution can be devised. Comparable legal arenas exist in which complex technological controversies, such as the asbestos tort liability cases, are placed into the hands of technologically competent negotiators, mediators, and/or special hearing officers before they reach the courts.

---

[73] Sanger, *supra,* note 35.

4.8 CONCLUSIONS

The problems created by new information technology cannot be swept under the rugs of current patent, copyright, trade secret, and trademark laws. As more and more creative endeavor is divorced from the manufactured products in which it has formerly been imbedded, as more and more personal computers become available around the world, as more and more of the world's economic activity is generated by information-based activities, and as more and more of the nations turn to competitive enterprise to fuel their economies and lessen the financial burdens of government-supported institutions, the demand for fair compensation for intellectual creativity and productivity will increase accordingly.

Information technology is turning our legal concepts as well as the philosophical roots of intellectual property topsy turvy, and stakeholders are going to have to learn to live with the new world that information technology is in the process of creating.

The real challenge is how to preserve an environment that encourages creativity but does not permit "rip offs" which discourage investment capital and inhibit the allocation of R&D funds. Part of the difficulty lies in the burden of the past. Outmoded laws and inadequate procedures are not coping as well as they might with the complex and fast-moving world this chapter describes. While the common law provides a steady but slow framework for filling in the interstitial spaces in legal regimes bounded by legislation, it is an unreliable vehicle for major accommodations to macroeconomic shifts. Stakeholders can work together on these difficult but technical problems.

Another part of the difficulty lies in the fact that different stakeholders stand to gain by alternative, incompatible fixes. Many prefer no fixes at all. "Working together" will happen only when interests overlap or conflict is more painful than compromise.

In the end the stakeholders themselves, working with the world's customary mechanisms for resolving disputes, must determine the outcome.

5

Publishing As a Creature of Technology*

Jerome S. Rubin and Janet Wikler

We are asked today to cast our thoughts toward the year 2000—the end of the second millennium as the Christian world reckons time. Two thousand is an awesomely round number, and that the year 2000 is less than eleven years away is an awesome notion.

Historians formerly believed that as the year 1000 approached mankind prepared for the Last Judgment, waiting in terror for the fatal dawn. In the words of Michelet:

> C'était une croyance universelle au Moyen Age, que le monde devait finir avec l'an 1000 de l'incarnation. Avant le christianisme, les Étrusques aussi avaient fixé leur terme à dix siècles, et la prédiction s'était accomplie.[1]

Given man's appalling capacities for self-destruction today—nuclear weapons and irreversible environmental damage—the end of the world seems a more likely threat as the year 2000 approaches than it

---

* This chapter is adapted from Rubin, Jerome S. and Janet Wikler, *Publishing as a Creature of Technology* (Cambridge, MA: Program on Information Resources Policy, Harvard University, 1989).

[1] "It was a universal belief in the Middle Ages that the world would end by 1000 A.D. Before Christianity, the Etruscans also had set their time span at ten centuries, and the prediction came true." Michelet, *L'Histoire de France*, Paris, 1869, Livre IV, Chapitre Premier; reprinted as Michelet, *Le Moyen Age* (Paris: Editions Robert Laffont, S.A., 1981), 229.

did as the Christian world prayed its way toward the year 1000. It is, however, an underlying assumption of ours that the world will in fact survive until the year 2000 and that the dissemination of information—publishing—will continue to be an important human activity.

5.1 HISTORY OF HUMAN COMMUNICATION

The technologies used to disseminate information have changed considerably over time and are changing with extraordinary rapidity today. To put today's and tomorrow's changes in perspective, it may help to examine their antecedents.

5.1.1 Development of Writing Systems

Since the earliest cave drawings, human beings have tried to communicate across the bounds of time by making permanent representations in symbolic form. The earliest known system of writing as a device for recording language was developed over five thousand years ago in Mesopotamia by the Sumerians, and the Egyptians, probably under Mesopotamian influence, evolved their system very shortly thereafter. More than two millennia later the Greeks created a full alphabetic system of writing, and since then the principles of writing have not undergone any fundamental change.

Writing, the greatest technology devised by man, spawned ancillary technologies—including, of course, the preparation of surfaces on which to write. As early as 3500 B.C., the Egyptians were recording their hieroglyphics on papyrus. The most important writing material of the ancient world, papyrus was made from the fibrous stem of the papyrus reed (*byblos*), which grew profusely in the Nile Delta. Not only Egypt but also Greece and Rome relied on papyrus.

Parchment, the other great ancient writing material, is the specially prepared skin of animals—mostly sheep, lambs, goats, and calves. The word *parchment* derives from Pergamum, an important center of Hellenistic culture near modern-day Izmir, which was also the center of parchment manufacture beginning in the third century B.C. Although the terms *parchment* and *vellum* are often used interchangeably, *vellum* is usually applied to the finest parchment, made from the skin of a calf. (The etymology is clear.)

The technology of making paper, the basic writing material of the modern world, was invented by an official of the Imperial court of Han China in 105 A.D., and spread westward very slowly. It reached Samarkand in 751 and Baghdad in 793, during the golden age of

Islamic culture. Although paper was extensively employed in the Arab world shortly thereafter, it was not in common use in Europe until the fourteenth century—and it came to Europe via Islam's domination of Spain. Paper, a plant-based writing material like papyrus, assumed the name of its ancient, half-forgotten predecessor.

Through most of classical antiquity, the standard form of book was the papyrus roll or scroll, consisting of papyrus sheets glued together. Taking its name from *byblos*, the papyrus plant from which it was made, it was commonly called *biblion*—which in turn gave its name to The Book, the Bible.

But the unrolling and rewinding of a long book was inconvenient and time consuming. The development of parchment made possible the codex, or book, in the form we know today. Papyrus, unlike parchment, cracks when folded; in addition, parchment could be sewn easily and scribes could write on both sides of it. The new technology, which became popular in the early days of the Christian era, involved cutting parchment into rectangular sheets, folded once into a *folio*, or twice into a *quarto*, or thrice into an *octavo*, and so on. Despite the great technological advantages of the codex, it was at first used primarily for account books; the resistance to change of both readers and booksellers permitted the literary roll to survive for centuries. The sacred Torah is still a scroll, and many legal documents continued to be written in scroll form until the twentieth century in several countries. One of those countries is Britain, where the Master of the Rolls remains the title of one of the highest judicial officers. (But the conservatism of lawyers is to be expected; the law, after all, is the second oldest profession.)

The other important writing technologies are those of inks and writing implements. The ancient inks of Egypt and China consisted of lamp-black mixed with gum or glue and formed into sticks which were mixed with water when used by the scribe. The colored juices or extracts of various plant and animal substances also served as inks in ancient times—including the black discharges of cephalopods such as octopus, squid, and cuttlefish. In later antiquity and throughout the Middle Ages, ink was also made from oak-galls steeped in a solution of vitriol (ferrous sulphate). By Gutenberg's time and until the late eighteenth century, inks were typically made by mixing varnish or boiled linseed oil with lamp-black.

The principal writing instruments of the ancient Western world were reeds. But in northern Europe, where reeds suitable for writing purposes do not grow, the quill of the feather became the principal writing instrument. A Latin word for feather, *penna,* has given us our *pen*, just as another Latin word for feather, *pluma,* gave *plume* to the French.

5.1.2 Development of Printing with Moveable Type

The technologies of writing were necessary but not sufficient; little written material was produced in the early Middle Ages, since, in the Christian world, writing and reading were skills centered in the monastery. The great majority of people relied on memory and oral tradition to spread information and preserve knowledge.

William the Conqueror was largely responsible for initiating the transition from oral tradition to written record in medieval England. His famous Domesday Book was a written survey of the conquered land. But the Domesday Book was never updated; its contents remained frozen in time and thus had little practical value.

As foreigners ruling in a tradition of conquest, William's successors bombarded the English with written demands for information and money. Land charters were put in writing, government bureaucracy flourished, and the number of documents grew. People needed to read and write to cope with government demands, and literacy became widespread. Yet it was centuries before the value of written records was fully understood. Making documents, keeping them in archives, and subsequently using them again for reference were three distinct stages of development. While the peoples of classical antiquity had developed and used indexing techniques, many medieval documents, especially government records, were not indexed. The medieval archivist seeking specific information had no way of knowing which page or roll to search.

Despite the proliferation of documents in the Middle Ages, writing was labor-intensive, and books expensive and rare. Although movable type for printing had been invented as early as the eleventh century A.D. in China, it had not spread beyond that country's borders. Gutenberg's re-invention of the technology in the mid-fifteenth century opened up for the first time in the Western world the ability to mass-produce written material, permitting man to communicate easily across space as well as time, and giving rise to the modern publishing industry.

The revolutionary technology of printing with movable type spread quickly throughout Europe. For the first time, written works could be replicated quickly and disseminated widely; among other things, the resulting standardization led to broader use of retrieval techniques such as indexing.

To "publish" a book was to print it. As the dangerous technology of printing came into general use, governments sought to control it through censorship; printers in Europe were granted exclusive rights to print and sell works, both new and old, that the official censors had approved for publication. These rights, which treated the printed book as an object and had no concern for authorship, were nonetheless the precursors of copyright. The author's right to protection was recognized for the first time in the Statute of Anne, the British copyright law of 1710. The infant French Republic provided a similar right in 1793, and other European countries followed suit during the nineteenth century. The first federal copyright act in the United States was adopted in 1790.

For many years after Gutenberg, the prices of printed materials remained artificially high despite the ease and relatively low cost with which they could be produced. In England, for example, as the feudal system declined and the mercantile middle class emerged, the upper classes sought to ensure their privileged status by preventing the masses from learning to read and keeping books expensive. In the long run, however, their efforts proved futile. Printing, binding, and papermaking techniques continued to improve; the ability to read became increasingly essential to an individual's functioning in society; more and more people became literate; and libraries, coffee-shops, and publishing "pirates" made reading matter widely available. The Industrial Revolution not only provided the new technologies of the steam-driven press and mechanically produced wood-pulp paper, but also a changed political and economic climate that imposed demands for widespread literacy. In that environment, there was no stopping the rapid dissemination of ideas and information that printing had made possible.

5.1.3 Advances in Means of Information Transmission

While print was revolutionizing society, other new technologies were being developed to speed the dissemination of information. The nineteenth century and the early part of this century brought major advances in the means of information transmission, with telegraph, telephone, and radio. Although the nineteenth century saw the development of photography and the phonograph, technologies that permitted the storage and replication of images and sound, the audiovisual era did not really begin until the 1920s, when motion pictures and radio came into widespread use. By that time, wires and radio waves were routinely used to carry coded signals, and experiments in television were underway.

The nineteenth-century British mathematician Charles Babbage hailed the printing press as the great accelerator of progress. "Until printing was very generally spread," he wrote, "civilization scarcely advanced by slow and languid steps; since that art has become cheap, its advances have been unparalleled, and its rate of progress vastly accelerated."[2] Paradoxically, in developing his "analytical engine," Babbage himself helped lay the foundation for the computer revolution that is transforming publishing—and our entire civilization—today.

The impact of the computer may be even more profound than that of the printing press. Today, text, sound, and images are stored in computer memories as combinations of on–off signals. These digital combinations, or codes, are transmitted through wires, cables, and optical fibers, and over the air and are decoded by receivers that transform them once again into images, sound, and text.

The computer and other electronic technologies have led to what the late Ithiel de Sola Pool of M.I.T. called "the convergence of modes."[3] This phenomenon, Pool pointed out, "is blurring the lines between media, even between point-to-point communications, such as the post, telephone, and telegraph, and mass communications, such as the press, radio, and television."[4] Services that in the past were provided in separate ways now share wires, cables, and radio waves. And services that once depended on a single medium, such as print, can be provided in a number of different ways.

Pool illustrated this point with examples:

> The telephone network, which was once used almost entirely for person-to-person conversation, now transmits data among computers, distributes printed matter via facsimile machines, and carries sports and weather bulletins on recorded messages. A news story that used to be distributed through newsprint and in no other way nowadays may also be broadcast on television or radio, put out on a telecommunication line for printing by a teletype or for display on the screen of a cathode ray tube (CRT), and placed in an electronic morgue for later retrieval.[5]

In an attempt to deal with all this, we have created hybrid terms. We speak of *video magazines, database publishing, electronic newsletters,* and so forth. The term *electronic publishing* typifies the confusion. By electronic publishing do we mean using electronic processes, like word processing and computerized typesetting, to make our traditional printed products? Do we mean taking information that

---

[2] Altick, Richard D., *The English Common Reader: A Social History of the Mass Reading Public, 1800–1900* (Chicago: The University of Chicago Press, 1957), 129–30; quoting from Timperley, *Encyclopaedia of Literary and Typographical Anecdote*, 808.

[3] Pool, Ithiel de Sola, *Technologies of Freedom* (Cambridge, MA: The Belknap Press of Harvard University Press, 1983), 23.

[4] Pool, *supra,* note 3.

[5] Pool, *supra,* note 3.

we have traditionally provided in printed form and delivering it on floppy disk or CD-ROM or online? Do we mean taking ideas originally presented in book form and "translating" them for videotape or videodisk? Do we mean all of this, and more?

Even the word *information* itself has become so overused that its use threatens to obscure rather than illuminate our thinking. Is a stream of digital computer code "information"? Are scholarly theories "information"? Is the text of Joyce's *Ulysses* "information"? Is a graphic representation of a molecule that can be rotated on a video screen "information"? Is a crossword puzzle "information"? Is the sound of Beethoven's Ninth Symphony "information"? Does a book that describes how the heart valves work provide the same "information" as an interactive videodisk that permits an individual to touch an image of the heart valves and see them in action? Where are the boundaries between data and information, on the one hand, and information and knowledge, on the other?

We may be able to minimize confusion by adopting the use of a neutral term like *substance* to mean the invariant substantive content of whatever we provide. Substance can be embodied in any of a number of *formats,* and the same substance can be embodied in more than one format. In the heart valve example, the substance would be the same in the book and the videodisk, but the format would vary. Similarly, a written score of Beethoven's Ninth Symphony would provide the same substance as a recording of the music, but in a different format.

Process acts on substance to produce one or more formats; process may also change substance itself. The traditional book publisher adds value to substance by applying a series of processes. First, the publisher *obtains substance*, either from an outside source, such as an author, or by using in-house researchers and writers. The substance is put through an *editorial process*, during which it is refined. Another process, usually involving a combined editorial and graphic-design effort, *specifies a format* in which the substance will be embodied. The next process, *manufacturing*, includes typesetting, platemaking, printing, and binding. Finally, the publisher puts the finished products through a *distribution process*, which includes making readers aware of the product's availability through marketing and sales, and getting the product physically into their hands, either through intermediaries like wholesalers and booksellers or by shipping to them directly.

This terminology of substance, format, and process was developed by the Harvard Program on Information Resources Policy (with some help from one of the present authors [Rubin]). As Harvard's Anthony Oettinger puts it, "Every information product or service is a bundle of substance, format, and process."[6] Oettinger points out that "infusing substance into format defines an *editorial* [function], and subjecting concrete formats, as materials, to concrete energy-consuming processes defines a formal or *operating* [function] devoid of substance"[7] (e.g., printing and distribution).

The potential of a new technology is rarely understood by the first generation of its users. It took centuries before people realized the value of updating written records, storing them in archives, and indexing them for future use. Not until television began to bring the battlefields of distant wars, the eerie landscape of the moon, and the outer reaches of the solar system into our living rooms did we begin to comprehend its power. Xerography was originally viewed as a substitute for carbon paper rather than a cheap and easy way of copying images; and the computer at its inception was seen as a calculator, replacing the slide rule and the abacus.

In the same vein, the typical publisher's initial response to computer technology was to see it as a facilitator of the traditional manufacturing processes. Next, the publisher began to suspect that the computer might provide opportunities for creating products in new formats, and the term *database publishing* came into vogue. Continuing to focus on substance as their critical asset, publishers sought opportunities to create electronic by-products of their traditional printed wares. From a single initial effort, it appeared, two revenue streams might flow. Giving little thought to the nature of differences among computer programs, publishers further tried to expand their businesses by buying the rights to publish "software" brought to them by outside "authors." If the substance was good, the publishers reasoned, the customer would value it all the more because it resided on a floppy disk.

For the most part, publishers' efforts in "electronic publishing" have been financial failures. But a handful of ventures have been successful. One that was very successful was LEXIS, a computer-assisted legal-research service that one of the present authors [Rubin] launched in 1973 with a few colleagues. It is almost certainly no accident that LEXIS was not created by a publisher. When LEXIS was developed, legal publishers saw their role as providing substance to their readers in fixed and predetermined formats. By contrast, in building LEXIS, we put process in the hands of the users, so that they could control both substance and format at will.

The LEXIS software permitted a user to search the full text of

[6] See Chapter 2 at section 2.3.3.

[7] See Chapter 2 at section 2.4.

primary-source material without the intermediation of a human indexer or editor, and to retrieve only those portions relevant to his or her needs. After employing the process provided by the software to select relevant material, the user could apply another process to specify a format in which the material would then be displayed—on the screen or in print, in full or in windows of context.

The substance that went into LEXIS was almost entirely in the public domain. Our proprietary added value was the process we provided to the user—a process that proved to be sufficiently valuable that we were able both to take significant market share from traditional publishers and to increase substantially the total number of dollars spent for legal information.

The ability to put process and format, independent of substance, into the hands of the user has spawned a new kind of "publishing" industry today. Companies like Microsoft, Lotus, Ashton-Tate, and others, in offering word processing, spreadsheet, and database-management software, provide only the minimum substance needed for users to process their own substance and put it into varied and useful formats.

Acknowledging the migration of process and format from the publisher to the user is essential to our recognizing and evaluating new business opportunities as we approach the year 2000. We perpetuate a false dichotomy when couching the debate simply in terms of whether to deliver substance in print or electronic form. We should, rather, find ways to enable our customers to engage in the processes of selecting substance at will, manipulating it in a number of ways, and specifying a variety of formats.

5.2 NEW TECHNOLOGIES: THREATS AND OPPORTUNITIES

The new technologies present serious threats as well as significant opportunities—especially to our traditional asset, the intellectual property, or substance, that has been our stock in trade. University professors take portions of our textbooks and have them photocopied, along with portions of other publishers' textbooks, to make anthologies for their students. Optical scanners digitize the text of our printed material and make it endlessly available. Video and audio cassettes are duplicated on inexpensive home equipment. Substance sent by telephone lines to remote terminals is routinely printed by users or downloaded onto floppy disks. If we add value to substance by coupling it with processing programs and provide both on floppy disks, the entire work can be copied—easily, cheaply, and quickly. Even the CD ROM, originally viewed as a nonwritable, piracy-proof medium, can now be duplicated with relative ease.

5.2.1 "Permissible Use" and Piracy

Anne Branscomb, of Harvard's Program on Information Resources Policy, highlights the difficulties of defining "permissible use" of copyrighted material in a new-technology era:

> Can you print out the entire twenty volumes [of an encyclopedia on a CD ROM]? If not, how much can you reprint before you have infringed the copyright? Can you download portions, or is this making a copy? Can you display portions in the classroom, or is this a public display, a "performance," or perhaps a "retransmission"? May you network the contents to many locations, as in a university environment to many classrooms or campuses? Isn't this making multiple copies much in the same way as on a Xerox machine? If royalties are not to be paid to the many creative and talented people who contributed to the twenty volumes, is there some other way to provide the infrastructure for intellectual productivity? How can the system detect such "uses" or copying if the record is not preserved for posterity? If the record is preserved, does it create costs that inhibit meaningful use? Current copyright law protects the originator's value only on the "first sale" of a copy. There is no royalty on the "use" or rental thereof. However, if only a few copies are needed to provide access to masses of users, then the original charge must cover all of the development and marketing costs.[8]

And the problem is deeper than defining *permissible use*. The fundamental concept of copyright as we know it is called into question by electronic technologies. Gutenberg provided a means of creating identical multiple copies. Electronic technologies, on the other hand, provide a means of creating infinite *variations* of the same material. A small subculture of computer scientists who write and edit on data networks illustrates this phenomenon, which we can expect to spread. Someone types comments on a computer terminal. Colleagues gain access to these comments on the network and modify, expand, or change them. Different versions are thus created continually, and each one can be stored on the computer. There is no one "author," nor is there any "definitive version" of the material. We are returning in spirit to Plato's Academy and the precopyright world of oral dialogue.

Pool speculated that, in the not-too-distant future,

[8] See Chapter 4 at section 4.6.4.

> Computer-based textbooks may exist in as many variants as there are teachers. All teachers on occasion desire to correct or modify the textbooks they use; if the texts are in a computer, they can and will do that. Each teacher will create a preferred version, which will be changed repeatedly over the years. Or in a literature or drama course one exercise might be to take a text and try to improve it. Reading thus becomes active and interactive. Penciled scribbles in the margin become part of the text and perhaps even part of a growing dialogue as others agree or disagree.[9]

Substance may even be generated with no human author at all. Computers can be programmed to generate indices, and by the year 2000 programs may be written that will enable the computer to generate worthwhile abstracts of text. The computer programs are copyrightable under current law. But what about the indices and abstracts that the programs generate?

As Branscomb puts it,

> Information technology is turning our legal concepts as well as the philosophical roots of intellectual property topsy turvy, and stakeholders are going to have to learn to live with the new world which information technology is in the process of creating.
>
> The real challenge is how to preserve an environment which encourages creativity but does not permit "rip offs" which discourage investment capital and inhibit the allocation of R&D funds....[10]

5.2.2 Convergence of Media

As if piracy and the other threats to copyright were not problems enough, new competitors are entering our markets as the lines blur between formerly separate industries. Cable television systems provide programs that compete with our educational and professional offerings. Television news and feature programs compete with newspapers and magazines. Online vendors provide databases with retrieval systems that may undermine the sales of printed works. Many trade books generate more income from movie and television rights than from their sales in the original printed form. In some countries, telecommunications providers compete with publishers in offering substance as well as the processes of sending, storing, organizing, and manipulating it. Even our own customers, armed with personal

[9] Pool, *supra,* note 3 at 213–14.

[10] See Chapter 4 at section 4.8.

computers, laser printers, and computer-generated mailing lists, are getting into the competitive act.

In response to the convergence of media, communications conglomerates have emerged. Our company, Times Mirror, owns book- and magazine-publishing ventures, cable television systems, and broadcast television stations as well as newspaper companies. Gulf & Western, Dow Jones, Time Inc., McGraw-Hill, International Thomson, News International, Maxwell Communications, and many others are variations on the same theme. But for the most part, the boundaries between media still exist within these conglomerates.

Paradoxically, the barriers to entry into publishing are both lower and higher than they have been. While tiny startups armed with Macintosh computers and laser printers are making serious inroads into many of our market niches, the costs of developing significant multimedia businesses can be staggeringly high. And the costs of maintaining these businesses through continued enhancement can be higher still—a point frequently overlooked. It takes considerable time and money to develop and continually enhance powerful systems that are easy to use, reliable, and fast. New, difficult-to-find skills are needed, skills at managing process as well as substance and format. Moreover, in business and professional markets, customers seek the convenience of "one-stop shopping" found in databases carried over telecommunications lines or residing on CD ROMs. Few publishers by themselves can offer the critical mass of substance that our markets are beginning to demand.

The highly leveraged nature of the new publishing businesses, and the need for critical mass in many major markets, will add fuel to the consolidation and concentration that have already begun. In addition to joining through merger and acquisition, publishers will need to unite with one another—and with companies in other industries—in joint ventures, licensing agreements, and other strategic alliances to continue to meet the needs of their markets and compete effectively. Global networks will be the norm rather than the exception.

Traditionally, the publisher has acted as intermediary between author and user, selecting and refining those portions of substance it deems most likely to be useful, and embodying that substance in fixed formats of various kinds. In the future, intermediation by the publisher may be even more critical; but increasingly it will be intermediation of a new and different kind. In a service like LEXIS, human intermediation is largely replaced by an electronic process. Yet some human intermediation is still required; someone must determine, not only what substance to include in the database, but also how the user will gain access to various portions of the substance, what processes will be provided to enable the user to select substance and format, and so forth. As artificial-intelligence techniques improve, the human effort that determines the electronic intermediating capabilities may become even more important. Knowledgeable engineers, designers, and programmers will be needed to debrief experts and create complex systems that will make substance, process, and format optimally available.

The fragmentation of markets spawned by electronic technologies creates further complexity. Today's real world is characterized by small or incompatible installed bases of hardware, formidable development costs, and users at widely varying levels of readiness to accept new technologies. Our opportunities are limited not by what technology and imagination permit us to make, but by what our customers will pay for. Nonetheless, as we move toward the year 2000, it will help to approach our businesses along the three dimensions we have discussed. In obtaining and refining substance, we must consider the multiple ways in which people may want to select, process, and retain it. Selling multiple copies of the same substance in an identical format to large numbers of users will be an increasingly difficult way to turn a profit.

It is easy to see that inherently dynamic substance, such as financial or even scientific or legal material, must be updated constantly. Perhaps less obvious is the need continually to improve the processing technologies and the formatting possibilities as well. With changing technology, a complicated "tail-chasing" relationship exists between skills and tools. People design new tools to take advantage of skills already in existence. But as people use the tools, they develop new skills, and the old tools become less satisfactory. By failing to anticipate and respond to new needs that developed as people learned to use Visicalc, a company that could have become a giant faded away. Lotus Development Corporation saw and seized the opportunity; ironically, Lotus itself is today being threatened by aggressive, innovative competitors.

We must, therefore, always be on the move—updating substance, improving process, and creating new possibilities for format. To ensure its revenue flow, even a publisher of substance that does not lend itself to updating, such as fiction, may need to provide multiple formats and processing and formatting options to the user. Today's paperback novel reader may, before the year 2000, insert a credit-card-size piece of plastic into a high-resolution, flat-screen holder the size of a mass-market paperback, select the size, face, and color of the type, and push buttons to turn the pages, or have the pages turned automatically at his or her own reading pace. It is conceivable that the reader may dispense with text altogether, electing instead to view pictures while listening as the words are read aloud. The reader may make choices that determine the outcome of the plot, may choose to receive critical reviews or descriptions of related material, and, by inserting a blank card into the machine and plugging it into a telephone, may order, pay for, and obtain additional works.

A textbook publisher might use a similar technology to even greater advantage, enabling students to rotate molecules, "see" the results of physics experiments, and so forth. The technical possibilities in all our markets are endless; the challenge will be to capitalize on these possibilities for economic advantage.

5.3 THE FUTURE OF PRINT

The era of the printed word is but a short chapter in the history of human communication. From the development of true writing it took almost five millennia for the modern publishing industry to be spawned by the technology of printing with movable type. Although for publishers print is still the dominant medium, it has been around for only about half a millennium and its era of overwhelming supremacy—before the audiovisual revolution after World War I—lasted only about three-quarters of a century. As we move toward the year 2000, text will appear increasingly in a number of other formats, and substance will be conveyed in many nontextual modes as well.

Just as the literary roll survived for centuries after the invention of the codex, literature may be the last survivor of the printed book. But, as George Steiner has pointed out, "The relationship between books and literature, as we have known it in the European-American communities, arose from an exceedingly complex and inherently unstable concatenation of technical, economic and social circumstance. It may well be that the 'age of the book' in its classical sense is now coming to a very gradual end."[11]

We believe that print is likely to withstand the avalanche of competing media for quite some time—albeit circumscribed in application and diminished in importance. But growth in publishing—and, in some cases, survival—will lie in our ability to work creatively in multiple dimensions. The successful publisher will learn to use each medium to its best advantage, providing an ever-changing variety of substance–process–format bundles.

[11] Steiner, George, "Literature Today," in *Books in the 1990s* (London: International Publishers Association and Butterworth & Co. Ltd., 1988), 41.

We may find instructive the old story about a drunkard who was looking under a street lamp for a lost key. "Is this where you dropped it?" asked a passer-by. "No," replied the drunk. "I dropped it over there, but the light is better here." As we move toward the year 2000, we must seek the key to success not in the clear, familiar light of the printed word, but on the dark and shifting landscape of substance, process, and format.

6

Electronic–Print Competition: The Critical Determinants*

Martin L. Ernst

6.1 ELECTRONIC–PRINT COMPETITION

6.1.1 The Print–Electronics Confrontation

For several decades, periodic warnings have proclaimed doom for the present role of print-on-paper as a major means for distributing information. Inspired by advances in computer technologies, visionaries have predicted that, in the near future, computer-driven electronic displays would replace paper, even for such everyday purposes as recreational reading. In addition, the very activity of reading, itself, would be changed by new electronic formats.

So far, these claims have turned out to be nonsense. At present, electronics has replaced print only in limited situations, usually those for which speed or extensive manipulation capabilities are critical to the effective use of information. Meanwhile, print has gone on its merry way, exploiting electronic techniques to lower costs and expand markets, and benefiting from the massive amounts of printed material generated by, or used to support, the marketing and operations of the supposed enemy!

Because of this history, new claims of future electronic superiority

* This chapter is adapted from Ernst, Martin L., *Electronic–Print Competition: Determinants of the Potential for Major Change* (Cambridge, MA: Program on Information Resources Policy, Harvard University, 1989).

may be underestimated, and real possibilities of change may be dismissed as just another cry of "Wolf!" Although the technologies of both presentation modes are improving, the computer-driven mode is doing so far more rapidly. As a result, some advantages of print, such as better display quality than that offered by electronics, are eroding. But are these kinds of changes enough to make a major difference in the extent to which each of the two presentation modes will be used?

One way to determine the realities is to examine in detail the tasks facing electronic contenders seeking to replace print in a broad range of activities. Accordingly, we have addressed the question: What technical, business, social, and economic barriers must new contenders overcome before electronic displays can become the dominant means to present information?

When we pursued this approach and, in the process, developed conceptual solutions and means for surmounting the barriers whenever we could, it turned out that

- As suggested by past history, the tasks facing electronic contenders are numerous and often difficult, and the solutions must be worked out in a variety of arenas.
- In spite of this challenge, most electronic weaknesses have potential cures; some are only partial cures, but many can be very effective.
- The capabilities that electronic contenders could develop during the process of overcoming current deficiencies are extremely impressive; if created, they would give electronic display systems large advantages in ways with which print, inherently, cannot compete. As a result, a change in dominance is feasible, although not rapidly.
- As usual, overcoming old problems affords an opportunity to face new ones! Major simplification and lowering of the basic user skills needed to manage the electronic equipment are essential for its success. However, to exploit the full range of new capabilities that electronics will have to develop, users will need new skills; some of these may far exceed in complexity those required to be generally competent in our current, mainly print world.

6.1.2 Relative Positions of Print and Electronics: The Key Features

6.1.2.1 Competitive status. Currently, electronic presentation modes tend to dominate in transaction activities and process operations where speed, information accessibility, capacity, and manipulation, updating, and correction capabilities are important. Print tends to dominate in the presentation of text materials, most obviously in the mass media area (newspapers, magazines, and books) and in materials where presentation quality is important, such as for art. Broad ergonomic capabilities (such as high visual quality, familiarity, comfort, and ease of handling and use) underlie this dominance, with additional support from the externality of government-provided education for use of the format and from the massive amounts of diverse materials that are available economically in print mode.

6.1.2.2 Enabling changes needed. Continuing penetration by electronics into areas now dominated by print can be anticipated. However, a prerequisite for *major* electronic advances is a high-quality, book-size, flat-panel display that would enable electronic presentation systems to approach the levels of quality, comfort, and convenience now offered by print. By making electronics far more competitive with print for reading extensive amounts of text, this change would open the possibilities for electronics to enter a number of mass markets where it currently has little or no position.

The flat-panel hardware would have to be supported by "reading" software for browsing, searching, coordinating, and filing information, as well as for manipulating a variety of visual features of reading and study materials. These capabilities can both help balance residual electronic ergonomic deficiencies and help meet some real market needs now not served well by print.

6.1.2.3 Other barriers. The enabling changes described above could help surmount a large number of the barriers now blocking electronic penetration of current print mass markets. There will remain others, however, for which only partial solutions are likely to become available, or where progress may be slowed by conflicts among stakeholder groups whose combined support is needed. These barriers include the following:

- *Operations complexity.* To achieve mass markets for electronic systems, simplification is needed in the processes used to enter materials, operate programs, and organize, manage, and back up personal files.
- *Inconsistencies and incompatibilities.* Compatibility measures, such as de facto standards, are needed to give users confidence in the security of the investments (of money, time, and effort) that they will have to make to start using electronic systems; to facilitate the simplification of system operations; and to mitigate the current rapid obsolescence of equipment and skills.

- *Vulnerability of computer records.* More rugged memory materials, with longer assured lives and lower risks of accidental loss or damage, are needed for many user purposes.
- *Property rights.* Resolution, in a broadly acceptable and enforceable manner, of a series of copyright and other intellectual property issues is required to assure that the availability and currency of electronic materials can become comparable to that now provided by print.
- *Other legal issues.* Other legal subjects need resolution if electronic systems are to be accepted for a broad range of uses. Some examples are a means for "validation" or substitutes for signatures; a clear and appropriate legal status for electronic records without paper backup; and a broadly acceptable set of privacy and security rights and obligations.
- *Training demands and costs.* Reductions in the money and individual efforts required to become effective in using electronic systems, and to stay up-to-date in their use, are important to electronic penetration of mass markets; some of the measures discussed earlier can be applicable to this need.

Many of the barriers described above derive from the dramatic rate of technical change that has characterized the computer industry in its brief history. This pace can be expected to continue during at least the decade of the nineties. A primary means to bypass or mitigate many of the barriers to electronic mass markets will involve extending and expanding on past efforts to use a portion of each technical advance to deal with the concerns of less sophisticated users, rather than simply to improve system technical power.

Projecting a rate of progress comparable to that experienced in the past, Figure 6-1 shows the potential future status of the two presentation modes in terms of a set of generic user needs derived during this work and employed throughout later sections of this chapter.

6.1.3 Eventual Relative Positions

Although the transition process is likely to be slow, inherent potential advantages of electronics should permit it eventually to achieve a dominant position relative to print. As suggested by the entries in Figure 6-2, continuing progress could make electronic presentation systems the primary means for accessing and reading all types of materials (business, professional, reference, and recreational) as well as for recording or inputting, searching, or operating on data and information. Under these conditions, print on paper would be relegated to a number of niche markets such as art works, very small or very

Figure 6-1. Toward the Future: Potential Dominance in Meeting User Needs

USER NEED	PRIMARY REASONS FOR PROSPECTIVE STATUS
PRINT REMAINS GENERALLY DOMINANT	
Convenience in Operating	Electronic advantages vastly extend user capabilities over those possible with print, but use of these advantages requires new training and skills. These new requirements constitute a major inconvenience. Doing with electronics only what can be done with print would avoid most of the inconvenience, but only at very high cost in foregone benefits.
Confidence in Format	Electronic advances are arising at a very rapid pace, opening up new options and making existing skills, hardware, and software obsolete. This already has led to the extinction of some types of equipment and skills, and to confusion over what equipment and techniques will be used widely in the future. The advances and uncertainties will continue, as will the negative impacts on Confidence in the (tools of the) Electronic Format.
PRINT REMAINS DOMINANT IN IMPORTANT SELECTED AREAS	
Cost Support	Print has a variety of traditional sources of cost "subsidies" that electronics may not be able to match. Advertising is a good example in that the very types of control that give electronics its strengths may be employable by users to defeat the purposes of advertising. This would enable print to continue its dominance in advertising-dependent media.
Substance Availability	Simple inertia will give print dominance in substance availability for a long time to come. This does not imply substance inadequacy for electronics, which may or may not be present at a given time.
Static Impact and Information Density	Advantages in static absolute visual quality and in range of practical display sizes will enable print to continue its dominance in a number of narrow areas, such as art books, posters, maps, and large diagrams.
ELECTRONICS GRADUALLY BECOMES DOMINANT ON AN OVERALL BASIS	
Physical Convenience Passive Comfort Active Comfort	In these three related areas, electronic strengths can be expected to grow while few changes are anticipated for print. Print will retain a basic quality advantage but electronic capacity, flexibility, and manipulative capabilities can be used to achieve better overall ergonomics once a full-page-size flat-panel display of adequate quality becomes available. Thereafter, residual print advantages (such as legal status, social acceptability) will begin to be outweighed by electronic advantages for this set of user needs.

Figure 6-1. (Continued)

USER NEED	PRIMARY REASONS FOR PROSPECTIVE STATUS
ELECTRONICS RETAINS CURRENT DOMINANCE	
Timeliness/Currency Confidence in Substance Control of Information Layout and Presentation Features Control of Substance Presented Operations on Substance	Continuation of very strong existing trends should keep increasing the value of electronics in all these areas.

large-size items, some forms of archival records, and, perhaps, highly advertising-dependent materials.

While in this chapter we point to the development of a suitable flat-panel display as the key to initiating major advance, progress thereafter depends on a mix of overcoming other barriers and exploiting existing and potential new electronic advantages. For a long time, electronics is likely to have residual deficiencies compared to print. Thus, the pace of change will depend strongly on using electronics' relative advantages to add features (such as zoom capability and 3-D rotation of objects) that enhance the value of electronic analogs of current print products. Also, it will be important to develop basically new formats and products. Steps in these directions will give electronics a continually broader base of products with features against which print cannot compete directly.

6.1.4 The Approach to Examining Electronic–Print Competition

The general approach used to reach the above views concerning electronic–print competition—determining barriers to be overcome and, when possible, the means for doing so—sounds quite straightforward. The actual process for carrying it out, however, is far from direct. Since some of the difficulties go to the heart of the competitive situation, the process is summarized here.

First, although much of our discussion has been in terms of electronic *barriers* to be overcome (that is, disadvantages of electronics relative to print), of at least equal importance are the *facilitators* (electronic relative advantages) that can be exploited. The effects of both barriers and facilitators show up when individual and organiza-

Figure 6-2. Future User Activities: Potential Status of Electronic and Print Presentations

ACTIVITY	ELECTRONICS POTENTIALLY SUPERIOR FOR:	PRINT SUPERIOR INDEFINITELY FOR:
TEXT ACTIVITIES		
Work-related reading	Business, professional, administrative and other	Some publications types strongly dependent on advertising support or on large display sizes
Standard reference usage	All references with large numbers of, and/or complexly interrelated, and/or frequently updated entries	Small, easily filed/found lists; some pocket-portable materials
Recreational uses	Reading; single-person games and simulations; new formats and multi-media	Multi-person (board-type) games; art books and works of many types
Recording/ inputting of all types	Almost all substantial materials—data, transactions, letters, memos, etc.	Minor materials—short notes and lists, archival records (except within well prepared organizations)
GENERAL SEARCH		
All types	All types of substantial searches; all searches of remote (electronic) sources	Very limited general searches of local sources
DATA OPERATIONS		
All types	Most aspects of use of all types of data	Portable materials of size larger than reasonable display size—such as large maps, diagrams, and plans

tional information users are faced with decisions on whether to start using electronic formats or to stay with print and paper. If both formats are available, users will base their choices on their perceptions of the net balance of relative advantages and disadvantages offered by each presentation mode. Further, they will make each evaluation in the context of their specific *user situation*—a composite of the purposes for which they are seeking or using information, the activities involved, the user environment, user skill levels, and the nature of the information itself.

This means that what users see as a major disadvantage—a large barrier—in one situation, they may view as unimportant in another. For example, the poorer visual and comfort qualities of current electronic displays, relative to print, can eliminate electronics from consideration for recreational reading. However, these same disadvantages may be ignored entirely if speed and manipulation capabilities are critical, as they are in air traffic control and financial trading operations. For the latter activities, a few of the electronic advantages are so important that they totally outweigh numerous potential weaknesses. Thus, barriers acquire significance only in terms of specific user situations.

To deal with these dynamics, we had to perform considerable preparatory work before beginning the main analysis. Our first step was to describe the battlefield—that is, determine what features could constitute an electronic "advantage" or "disadvantage." We did this by building a list of *attributes* of information (for example, speed of access and ease of manipulation) that at least some users would consider important for at least some of their activities. To provide context for this list, we associated each attribute with the *source* of its potential importance (such as criticality of time, or the need to make repeated changes or corrections). The resulting collection of sources had a second value in that, when aggregated and grouped, it provided the basis for defining a useful set of generic user needs.

The attribute list was organized by user need and then divided into those attributes for which electronics currently (that is, in the late 1980s) has an advantage, relative to print, and those for which print now has the superior position (meaning electronics is at a disadvantage). This analysis (section 6.2) gave us our list of potential barriers and facilitators, as they now exist. At the same time, it provided material to establish and compare current patterns in the relative advantages held by the two presentation modes.

To evaluate the importance or size of the barriers posed by different relative electronic disadvantages, we had to develop and characterize a test base of "user situations." In this test base, each situation was to be distinguished from the others by having a different mix in the importance of the different (sometimes conflicting) user needs. To be effective, the test base had to cover a broad range of types of situations that large populations of users frequently face. The data on sources of attribute importance collected earlier helped in developing our set of user situations (section 6.3).

With this database, we could begin to identify the relative abilities of the competing presentation modes to meet users' needs in each situation (section 6.4). We also could rank user needs in importance and estimate the sizes of the gaps left when they are not being met using electronic displays. Thereafter, we could turn to the question: How might an electronic contender make improvements to capitalize on advantages and to overcome barriers to meeting user needs? Section 6.5 looks at the opportunities for action that our resulting analysis identified. Finally, in section 6.6 we review the more significant of the material we have developed to establish some perspectives on the range of possibilities, and on the factors likely to have the greatest influence on the evolution of competition between print and electronics.

Several general points apply to all of the sections. First, in developing and analyzing user needs and the extent to which they are met by the competing technologies, we are taking a "snapshot" of the situation in the late 1980s. While we believe our list of general needs is reasonably universal and enduring, new need elements will be recognized and the relative importance of the different needs certainly will change over time. In particular, detailed user perceptions about what they need are likely to grow as computer capabilities improve and new possibilities are identified.

Second, while considerable attention is focused on factors that influence user decisions as to which presentation mode is preferable, the determinants considered are not complete. In particular, because of the continuing rapid decline in the costs of electronic equipment (noted in Chapter 3), we leave out any consideration of a primary decision factor: the relative costs of using the two modes of display. The only cost elements discussed are related to a few special print advantages.

A third characteristic of the work is the large number of estimates made concerning subjects, such as user perceptions of the importance of a need and of the extent to which electronic displays satisfy this need. These estimates are forms of rankings, where relative values are more important than absolute ones. They usually were made on a judgmental basis, derived from direct experience by the author or a close associate, in many of the example businesses or activities cited. We are aware of no satisfactory data from references that could replace these judgments. If better data can be found, we believe our approach will still provide a useful methodology for employing such material.

Throughout, this analysis goes into considerable detail, much of it perhaps obvious (once made explicit) to those experienced in the field. We believe our results show that this level of detail is important—that the competition between print and electronics is governed more by detail than by dramatic breakthroughs—and we are not aware of other analyses that have tried to treat the subject in a similarly detailed manner. An additional benefit of the detail is that it provides a check list of current status and future prospects for anyone to use, regardless of his or her stakes or perspective.

Finally, although dominance of electronic presentation over print presentation is mentioned often as if it were a goal, it *is not intended* to be a practical or even an obviously desirable one. Rather, the purpose is to use this extreme target as a means to explore the nature of the long-term competition between the two presentation methods. In the process, possibilities for shorter term, practical goals for individuals and organizations should become more evident.

6.2 USER NEEDS AND RELATIVE ADVANTAGES

6.2.1 Introduction

Where do electronic presentations of information have advantages over print? Conversely, where does print have advantages?

To begin to address these questions, we ask them in a slightly different way: What *attributes* of information use are important to users in at least some of their activities, and *why*? That is, we seek to examine simultaneously both attributes and the *sources* of importance of these attributes—the *situational features or user needs* they can help meet. When we do so, the attributes for which electronics provides better performance than print constitute advantages, or potential *facilitators* of electronic success. Further, in at least some situations, the sources of importance of these attributes can provide guidelines for altering products or services to enhance the relative position of electronics. Conversely, the attributes for which print demonstrates advantages constitute *barriers* to electronic success. These must be surmounted, or overbalanced by advantages, if electronics is to achieve a dominant position for servicing a particular user need.

By the end of this section we will have developed a small database of user needs. Building on the database, we establish the current advantages of electronics and print relative to each other in meeting user needs. We also identify general patterns in the advantages held by each mode.

6.2.2 Electronic Relative Advantages

The sources of electronics' competitive advantages—the needs behind user preferences for electronic presentations—are different from those of print. The clusters of needs outlined below, and in Figure 6-3 and Figure 6-4 (coming soon), cover areas where electronics generally is stronger than print. The clusters describing print's strengths are presented later.

6.2.2.1 Facilitators of electronic success. Figure 6-3 lists the sources (user needs or environmental conditions) that give importance to attributes in which electronics most often has an advantage relative

Figure 6-3. Electronic Presentation of Information: Sources of Advantages Relative to Print

ADVANTAGE STRENGTH DEFINITIONS

(Based on difficulty of achieving same result with paper; no consideration given to the market value of this result.)

Unique:	Effectively not possible with paper
Very Strong:	Difficult, slow, awkward, unsatisfying, and costly if done with paper
Strong:	Limited scope, slower, and more costly with paper
Moderate:	Generally more convenient, easier, and cheaper electronically, but can be done well with paper
Weak:	Little or no electronic advantage, except as part of a larger electronic package

SOURCES OF ADVANTAGE AND ATTRIBUTES	STRENGTH OF ADVANTAGE	LATE-1980s EXAMPLES
WHEN TIME IS CRITICAL FOR		
Rapid event response (in seconds)	Unique	Financial market data and transaction systems; some process control; reservation systems; air traffic control; military applications
Access speed/ convenience (in minutes, hours)	Very Strong	Electronic mail; archival and reference information; order and tracking systems
WHEN COVERAGE IS CRITICAL IN TERMS OF		
Depth/completeness	Very Strong	Precedent and background searches (such as LEXIS, NEXIS, patents and diagnostics); some types of catalogs; schedules; and very long tables (like freight tariffs)
Breadth/browsing	Weak-Mod.	Background, general purpose and "suggestive" searches; selective dissemination
Currency/updating–internal sources	Strong	Financial and market analyses; production and transport scheduling
Currency/updating–external sources	Moderate	Precedent and background searches; reference material; item availability
WHEN USERS MUST MANIPULATE SUBSTANCE		
• With structured/algorithmic techniques		
Computations	Very Strong	Financial records/analyses; scientific and other research; many others—often using commercial software packages
Ease of correction	Very Strong	Word and text processing; editing; composition; all types of review processes

Figure 6-3. (Continued)

SOURCES OF ADVANTAGE AND ATTRIBUTES	STRENGTH OF ADVANTAGE	LATE-1980s EXAMPLES
Large-scale search	Strong	Precedent and background searches; file and record management; global text changes; index development; citations
Transaction conduct	Very Strong	Reservations; order taking and inquiry; billing adjustment; funds management and transfer
Results customization	Very Strong	Market and management information systems
Commercial software packages	Very Strong	Spreadsheets; database management; investment portfolio analyses; economic analyses; statistics; simulations
• With less structured/more interactive techniques		
Fixed-constraints situations	Strong	CAD systems; composition; production and transport scheduling
Aiding/advisory systems	Very Strong	AI "assistants" (many types); AI diagnostics (equipment, processes, medical) systems; CAD AI support systems
Experience/training systems	Moderate	Education and training systems; simulators; sophisticated games
User-selected, personal information storage	Very Strong	Spin-off of selected contents to personal files
Annotation for personal storage and electronic routing	Weak	Annotation (keyboard and written) of text items, diagrams, maps and other materials
WHEN USERS MANIPULATE FORMAT FOR COMFORT/CONVENIENCE		
Comfort	Unique	Change fonts, font sizes, and colors; foreground/background reversal
Convenience	Weak-Mod.	Show multiple files on one screen; "window" tables or maps to associated text
WHEN USERS MANIPULATE FORMAT TO IMPROVE INFORMATION ABSORPTION		
Viewing 3-D features	Unique	CAD; protein chemistry; geology; geography; military
Employing magnification/zoom capability	Unique	CAD; architecture; advertising

Figure 6-3. (Continued)

SOURCES OF ADVANTAGE AND ATTRIBUTES	STRENGTH OF ADVANTAGE	LATE-1980s EXAMPLES
Using or creating motion and sound effects	Unique	Simulators; entertainment and advertising materials
Design/graphics creation	Very Strong	CAD; report graphics; professional graphics services
Color use control	Moderate	Engineering/design color coding; commercial and hobby art
WHEN CONFIDENCE IN SUBSTANCE IS CRITICAL		
Capacity to meet demand fluctuations	Very Strong	All three of these attributes (plus timeliness and currency, as covered above) are critical to numerous types of transaction systems—such as for ordering, reservations, status reports, billing, and payment—and for many scheduling, process control, and other operations activities
Very high recording accuracy	Moderate	
Great flexibility and backup capability	Very Strong	
FOR RECEIVING MATERIALS WITH HIGH IMPACT/SPECIAL BENEFITS FOR PASSIVE USERS		
• No active user control		
Color presentations	Moderate	Emphasis (including in some search systems); color coding (in some design drawings); additional "dimensionality"
Graphics presentations	Moderate	Clarity and emphasis for absorbing information
Multimedia presentations	Very Strong	No significant products yet other than simulators and some simple voice synthesis products; much experimentation

to print.[1] For each of these entries, Figure 6-3 identifies relevant attributes that make electronics superior to print and then provides estimates of the strength of each resulting advantage. These can range from providing unique capabilities that print cannot match to offering only very modest relative benefits. Finally, each of the advantages is illustrated by some examples of activities where the advantage has been, or can become, a major factor in making electronics the dominant display mode.

[1] Within a given need cluster, the order of the entries is largely arbitrary.

The electronic advantages in Figure 6-3 extend from those that already have acquired widespread application (such as for fast-response situations, a large-scale and exhaustive information search, or ease in making corrections) to others that have been proven technically practical but are not yet employed in other than very limited or experimental ways (such as artificial intelligence "assistants" and interactive multimedia presentations). The entries in the "Strength of Advantage" column, which are themselves judgmental, are concerned solely with current or near-term *capabilities*—not with current levels of use. Market positions are reviewed separately in Figure 6-4.

The example activities of the last column obviously make use of "bundles" of attributes rather than just the primary ones with which they are associated in Figure 6-3. This is no accident. Bundling is a feature of *all* uses of information, as well as all packages of information; it also is a source of methodological complications that we will discuss later in this section and in section 6.2.3.

Turning now to the contents of Figure 6-3, we can see seven clusters of attributes for which electronics has advantages over print in the presentation of information. Users tend to need electronic presentations under these circumstances:

- *When time is critical.* The relative importance of timeliness and currency provides an excellent example of the dependence of needs on the nature of the task being done. The most critical situations are those calling for fast responses based on very up-to-date information, as in financial market dealings or in the handling of industrial, civil, or military emergencies. If only very simple text is involved (such as with news wires or ticker tapes), electronics does not have a big time advantage over modern high-speed printing equipment in presenting information to users. However, the latter gear is far more costly and bulky, and it lacks the flexibility to handle multiple data streams in a format adjustable to individual users. If the information involves geometrical aspects (as with process plant schematics) or geographic features (as for air traffic control and many military purposes), electronics has even greater advantages. Finally, the ability of electronics to supply on-call alarm or decision support information (such as collision alert signals in air traffic control) cannot be matched by print. Thus, if timeliness is interpreted in the broad sense of covering not only basic information but also ability to access and use support mechanisms—such as selective back-up information, flexible formatting, and decision support tools—the advantages of electronics are unique.

  Electronics also has access speed benefits, which derive from the

Figure 6-4. Market Uses of Electronic Presentation's Relative Advantages

DEFINITIONS

TYPES OF ADVANTAGES:

P	=	Timeliness/Currency (a process variable)
S	=	Manipulation (a substance variable)
F	=	Manipulation (a format variable)
FI	=	Format Impacts/Benefits/Passive aspects (a second format variable)

EXTENT OF USE given in terms of:

POTENTIAL MARKET SIZE	**AND**	**ELECTRONIC PENETRATION**	
Negligible:	Effectively none—at most experimental uses	**Very Low:**	Only a negligible fraction of current potential market
Niches:	Very small, specialized—but often very high value-added	**Low:**	Only the advanced segment of the potential market
Small:	Small general use or large niche markets	**Medium:**	A significant fraction of the potential market
Moderate:	Considerable general use	**Large:**	The majority of the potential market
Large:	Very widespread use	**Dominant:**	The primary means employed by the market

RELATIVE ADVANTAGE	**TYPE ADV.**	**LATE-1980s EXTENT OF USE**		**COMMENTS ON MARKET CHARACTERISTICS AND TRENDS**
		Market Size	**Penetration**	
UNIQUE				
1. For event response	P	Small	Domin.	Most high value-added markets already served; current trends are to enhance current services with related products and slowly to expand into lower value-added markets.
2. To view 3-D features	F/S	Niches	Med.	Very high value-added, specialized but small markets; past growth has been slow, limited in part by high cost/performance ratio of computers. Some segments (e.g., protein chemistry) are fast growth areas; new (mainly technical information) markets may arise.

Figure 6-4. (Continued)

RELATIVE ADVANTAGE	TYPE ADV.	LATE-1980s EXTENT OF USE		COMMENTS ON MARKET CHARACTERISTICS AND TRENDS
3. To employ magnification/ zoom capability	F/S	Niches	Med.	Very limited, specialized use with very slow past growth; utilization is tied to product/ market combinations where the feature is important and there are few historical precedents to help identify these.
4. To use or create motion and sound effects	F/FI	Niches	Med.	As for 3 above. However, identifiable markets are larger and there are more historical precedents; as a result, they are better understood and unexpected new markets are less likely.
5. Manipulation for user comfort	F	Neglig.	Very Low	Technically feasible but unused; might become important if large quantities of text began to be delivered electronically.
VERY STRONG				
6. For depth/ completeness of search	S/P	Niches	Large	Well established and growing, but markets are limited by level of need for complete searches.
7. For access speed and convenience	P	Small	Large	Growing markets constrained by cost of digitizing older materials, for which relative value currently is greatest; also constrained by 22 below.
8. User correction	S/F/P	Large	Domin.	Electronics already is dominant when relevant materials are electronically available to users. This is most common for internal data and text of (or under control of) business organizations. However useful materials also are available from many business and financial services. The past trend has been for strong growth in the business work
9. User computations	S	Small	Large	
10. User results customization	S/F/P	Small	Low	
11. User transaction conduct	S/P	Large	Large	
12. User graphics creation	F/P	Mod.	Large	
13. Use of commercial software packages	S/F/P	Mod.	Large	

Figure 6-4. (Continued)

RELATIVE ADVANTAGE	TYPE ADV.	LATE-1980s EXTENT OF USE		COMMENTS ON MARKET CHARACTERISTICS AND TRENDS
				environment but limited growth elsewhere. (Note that the listed capabilities—and several others—are highly synergistic and that it is the total package of benefits that drives many decisions to adopt electronic delivery.) Home uses are still limited by many factors.
14. Manipulation with interactive aiding systems	S	Small	Low	Modest but growing markets; limited by current high production costs for software to provide the "aiding."
15. For user-selected, personal information storage	S	Neglig.	Very Low	Very small use now; significant growth probably dependent on the widespread availability of electronic versions of "fileworthy" materials.
16. Records flexibility and backup support	S/F	Mod.	Med.	A steadily growing market as more service industry companies exploit computer capabilities for competitive advantages and customers come to expect high service levels.
17. Records handling capacity	S/P	Small	Med.	A growth market as capabilities enable increased numbers and greater coordination of records and as market uses for these capabilities are created.
18. Multimedia presentation	F/FI	Neglig.	Very Low	A concept more than a reality; many proposals and target markets (entertainment, education, etc.) but no accepted products or actual markets of significance.

Figure 6-4. (Continued)

RELATIVE ADVANTAGE	TYPE ADV.	LATE-1980s EXTENT OF USE		COMMENTS ON MARKET CHARACTERISTICS AND TRENDS
STRONG				
19. Manipulation within fixed constraints	S/F/P	Niches	Med.	Limited, generally high value-added markets that are growing at a moderate pace; however, it is not clear that the total market ever will become large.
20. For currency/ updating—internal sources	P	Large	Med.	Being internal, the market is difficult to measure. Growth is constrained by standards and compatibility issues and by the costs of associated software; the market may be favored by actions of large firms (e.g., General Motors) seeking greater integration of operations with suppliers/customers. Synergies with other applications (e.g., electronic mail) may encourage growth in uses and more attention to achieving greater currency.
21. For user large-scale search	S/P	Small	Med.	Involves some small specialized markets, where capability is very valuable, and more general benefits as part of overall "package" of capabilities offered by electronic delivery; by itself, search capabilities would generate only very limited markets.
MODERATE				
22. For currency/ updating—external sources	P	Niches	Med.	Presently, markets with high external information currency tend to be narrow and specialized—catalogs, special financial data and news services, etc. A major limitation on currency in much broader markets is that most information has in

Figure 6-4. (Continued)

RELATIVE ADVANTAGE	TYPE ADV.	LATE-1980s EXTENT OF USE		COMMENTS ON MARKET CHARACTERISTICS AND TRENDS
				the past been prepared for print first; as a result, print publishers both control the process and benefit now from limiting electronic products currency.
23. Color presentation	FI	Small	Low	Growing uses for improved appearance and coding of information; however, past trends suggest that color is more effective at supporting other electronic capabilities than at opening new markets by itself.
24. Color use control	F	Niches	Med.	Important niches exhibiting steady growth. Over time, color control may gradually become a widely used technique but still will be only a moderate source of advantage for electronics.
25. Accuracy of records used	S/P	Small	Med.	This is an advantage that acquires greatest value when combined with others, such as great records currency and large system capacity.
26. Graphics presentation	FI	Mod.	Med.	As for 23 and 24 above. Electronic graphics capabilities are very important in favoring electronic production of information materials (see 12 above); they appear less important, relative to print, on the end-user delivery side.
27. Manipulation with interactive experience/ training systems	S/F	Niches	Med.	Very limited markets in high value-added simulators; systems otherwise a subject of much experimentation but few (and high production cost) marketable products.

Figure 6-4. (Continued)

RELATIVE ADVANTAGE	TYPE ADV.	LATE-1980s EXTENT OF USE		COMMENTS ON MARKET CHARACTERISTICS AND TRENDS
MODERATE–WEAK				
28. For breadth of coverage, browsing	S	Neglig.	Very Low	Very limited current usage; no market pattern yet and no major technical efforts appear to be devoted to improving present weak abilities in this area.
29. Manipulation for user convenience	F	Small	Low	Limited usage; not a product so much as a part of a total package. "Windowing" likely will become a "standard" item in the future, making electronics dominant in this attribute.
WEAK				
30. Annotation for personal storage/ electronic routing	S	Neglig.	Very Low	No significant use; again, a potential part of a total package that may be needed to be competitive with print in many situations.

ability to gain rapid access from one's desk rather than having to visit a file or a library; this also provides a great gain in convenience. In total, electronics has a very strong inherent advantage in this aspect of using information.

- *When coverage is critical.* For exhaustive searches, electronic systems offer a powerful combination of speed, thoroughness, low error rates, compactness of storage, and unmatchable cross-indexing capabilities (extending to full text indexing). An efficient search requires considerable user interaction with the files, and this would be slower and more difficult working with paper printouts than with an electronic display. Thus, even if the final format for the end user is print, the search activity is best conducted with electronic presentations.

Turning to needs for less dense but broader coverage of a subject, users have rather few formal alternatives available. Browsing, and, to some extent, well-planned use of selective dissemination systems, are probably the primary means. At present, electronic browsing is almost nonexistent, and selective dissemination systems are not strong. There are no inherent technical barriers that would stop the gradual development of much stronger electronic capabilities in both areas. Such development might permit the enormous storage capacity of electronic files to be exploited in ways that balance the current tactile and ergonomic advantages of browsing in a well-run library. However, the potential advantage is likely to be modest in early applications.

Currency of information is another element of coverage that can be of great importance, not only in the fast-response situations described in the first cluster (when time is critical) but also in many slower paced tasks. Major search operations, such as for possible patent infringements or legal precedents, furnish an example.[2] Rapid growth in electronic data collection, data entry, and word processing enable electronic files to be more current (and inherently more convenient) than any equivalent print method, given the latter's requirement for physical production and distribution of materials. There is a difference, however, between information internal to a user's organization and that for which the source is external. In the former case, the organization has control over policies and methods to make new information immediately available. In the latter, the external organization can delay availability of current information in the interest, for example, of protecting its market for current print products (as may be the case with some of the suppliers of material to databases like NEXIS). This motive can change, of course, if electronic markets grow sufficiently to compensate for loss of some or all of the related print markets.

- *When users manipulate substance.* In Figure 6-3, we split this cluster into two subgroups to highlight differences between advantages already well established in ongoing operations (*structured/algorithmic manipulations*) and those related to newer, emerging uses of computers (*less structured/more interactive manipulations*).

  Structured/algorithmic manipulations are those in which user interactions with a computer are relatively restricted, follow a limited set of well-defined procedures, and produce results whose nature is largely understood in advance. Most of the entries here are well known and obvious—they represent the primary traditional uses of computers. Although their employment is widespread, there are many possible application areas where penetration still is weak relative to long-term potential. Commercial software packages have been a key factor in speeding the penetration process as well as being the practical source of many of

[2] As a matter of convenience, in this chapter we treat timeliness and currency as though they constituted a single combined need; in fact, as this discussion shows, currency can operate as a separate individual need.

the capabilities listed in Figure 6-3. These software packages appear in the figure as a separate item, both to cover a multitude of other current and potential substance manipulation techniques and to highlight the intense entrepreneurial nature of software development. The latter characteristic suggests that software developers will rapidly meet any recognized market needs for which feasible solutions can be found.

Less structured/more interactive manipulations are those where user interactions are more intense, the range of user procedures less fully specified in advance, and the nature of the eventual results less certain. The entries in this cluster represent families of applications that in some cases are just beginning to receive effective use. At their best, they are major contributors to a process whereby computers are moving from being regarded simply as *tools* to what observers increasingly refer to as *partners*. This role calls for very close interactions between users and computers, with the users sometimes tailoring applications (or having them tailored) to meet their individual needs. The first three application areas—fixed-constraint situations, aiding/advisory systems, and experience/training systems—are somewhat arbitrary divisions of the general field. They can represent applications undertaken in different operating environments and/or for different purposes; they also turn out to relate roughly to the relative maturity of the different areas in terms of available products. The last two items (user-selected personal information storage and annotation for personal storage and electronic routing) involve more individual uses of computers; they are fairly simple in concept but embryonic in status.

- *When users manipulate format for comfort and/or convenience.* The features exemplifying manipulation for comfort (fonts, font sizes, and so on) represent unique capabilities now used in only limited ways. Manipulation for convenience is exemplified by windowing, which currently offers moderate benefits relative to print, and is rapidly becoming a standard and expected computer software feature. These entries are important because they are among the very few computer capabilities that can contribute to user comfort and convenience—areas where electronics is very weak and print is very strong.
- *When users manipulate format to improve information absorption.* The first three entries for this cluster in Figure 6-3 (3-D, magnification/ zoom, and motion and sound effects) are unique attributes of very great value to some important niche markets. Their use in these markets may suggest other applications—the capabilities are so new and so different from any previously available that some

surprise applications and new markets should be expected. The last two entries (design/graphics creation and color control) offer somewhat lesser advantages over paper. However, they are significant in many activities and, perhaps more important, they may work to change what users expect when presented with complex information.

- *When confidence in substance reliability is critical.* The items here concern substance attributes of particular importance when information must be used rapidly to take actions that may thereafter be difficult or expensive (or even impossible) to alter. The cluster is closely related to needs for timeliness and currency, but somewhat broader. Example applications include reservations and ordering systems, transportation control systems, and many military applications. Users here seek not only great information currency but also strong confidence in accuracy (in prior manipulation operations as well as in original materials) and in ability to obtain a high level of information completeness and/or back-up. In all these features, electronics has great advantages, many of which already are being utilized.
- *For receiving materials with high impacts/special benefits.* The final three items—color, graphic, and multimedia presentations—concern benefits to a passive user. Except for multimedia presentations, the capabilities also are available in print, often with better quality than in electronic formats, but not as easily or cheaply. The advantages accordingly are not now strong. This cluster is rather different from the others in character. It has been included to emphasize that the way in which material is presented can have important influences on user attitudes, as well as on both the amount of information that can be presented in a given amount of space or time and the ease with which this information can be absorbed.

6.2.2.2 Market uses of advantages. Figure 6-4 builds on the material of Figure 6-3, starting by regrouping the attributes by "Strength of Advantage."[3] For each item, the figure classifies the type of advantage, indicates current market size and penetration level, and comments on market characteristics and trends.

---

[3] Within the groups, the items again are in arbitrary order since there is no natural way to rank them. Market size, for example, probably is the best candidate for this, but it is subject to fairly rapid change as new electronic applications mature. Also, market size does not reflect either the way advantages are packaged in practical applications or the level of value added by a given advantage for a particular purpose.

Types of advantages. The *types of advantages* found in our attributes are presented in terms of the set of three basic elements—*substance, process,* and *format*—described in Chapter 2. In our case, however, these elements serve to characterize and compare the relative advantages of electronics and print.

Substance is simply the information itself—that which the author or compiler wishes to convey. Substance can be categorized in terms of its nature or purposes—as numbers, text, or images, or as news, data, advertising, or instructions, for example. The *format* is the form in which the content is perceived. Typical examples are ink on paper, images on a CRT or movie screen, or voice from a tape player or radio. At a more detailed level, format includes a variety of display features: text in different fonts or sizes; different ways of organizing material, such as in tables or outlines; and alternatives and complements to text such as graphics, drawings, or images. *Process* covers all the steps and technologies that help convert raw information into a final "product" or service made available to recipients.

Any information product can be described in terms of these three factors. And the same raw substance can end up in many different types of *bundles* (different combinations of format and process). The variety of ways that news is presented (ink on paper, text on CRT displays, voice via radio, image and voice on TV) illustrates this feature. In these terms, the basic subject of this chapter is how one format—electronics—might become able to replace another—print—in a number of major bundles where the latter is now the dominant format.

The types of advantages we use include timeliness/currency (a process variable), substance manipulation, format manipulation, and format impacts/benefits (for a passive user). The presence of two format classification types explicitly recognizes two very different types of potential users of presentations. One involves active users who need to or want to manipulate formats, which they can do electronically but not (except trivially and/or laboriously) with print on paper. The second type is concerned only with impacts and benefits for passive users who do not, or cannot, change what is presented to them.

One of our findings is that even using two format classifications does not do justice to the complexity of the relative advantages of electronic presentations: a single electronic advantage too often has features belonging to all of the basic classification types. The *substance* manipulation capability of electronics for making corrections, for example, also can involve *format* changes as part of the correction activity; and the operation will be performed faster—and thus the *process* can be more timely—than the equivalent with print on paper.[4] Further, since different applications that exploit an electronic relative advantage will do so for different reasons, or combinations of reasons, we often have to use multiple entries in Figure 6-4 to indicate the types of particular relative advantages. In a large-scale search, for example, substance is manipulated to extract only that which is expected to be relevant. If the output is also ranked and key items coded in color, then format manipulation has taken place. And in spreadsheet operations, format and substance changes can become almost inseparable.

Thus, we see again a feature of electronic technologies noted previously in this book—their tendency to blur what previously had been quite sharp divisions or categories. In the extreme, process, substance, and format variables are still both separable and useful for describing an information package. However, because of the great flexibility provided by the manipulation capabilities of electronics, we can understand better the opportunities available for electronic presentations if we are prepared to extend somewhat the basic packaging descriptors.

Market indicators. In Figure 6-4 we look at market positions in terms of estimated extent of use of the types of applications listed in Figure 6-3. The entries consider two market features: first, the size, in the late 1980s, of the potential markets for which the advantage has relevance (ranging from very small niches to widespread use); and second, the level of penetration, again in the late 1980s, into these potential markets. Here too, the fact that individual applications exploit multiple advantages leads to some multiple entries. However, the classification problem is less severe than the advantage type problem discussed earlier, and in most cases there are dominant advantages associated with particular applications.

6.2.3 Print Relative Advantages

The relative advantages of print are shown in Figure 6-5, which parallels portions of Figures 6-3 and 6-4, above. The differences between the nature of print and electronic advantages show up

[4] Note that the difficulty arises at the detailed rather than the general level. The fundamental substance and format (say, a business letter using electronic display of text) has not changed—only detailed features, such as how font and font sizes are used. Also noteworthy is that the complexity involved in classifying the types of advantages offered by electronics is not unrelated to the positioning of *computers at the center* of the Information Business Map shown in Figure 1-1 of Chapter 1.

Figure 6-5. Relative Advantages of Print Presentation of Information

ADVANTAGE STRENGTH

(Based on difficulty of achieving the same result electronically; no consideration given to the market value of this result.)

Unique:	Effectively not possible with electronics
Very Strong:	Difficult, slow, awkward, unsatisfying, and costly if done electronically
Strong:	Limited scope, slower and more costly if done electronically
Moderate:	Generally more convenient, easier and cheaper with paper

DEFINITIONS OF TYPES OF ADVANTAGES

P = Timeliness/Currency (a process variable)

SI = Substance—passive aspects, impacts, and benefits

FI = Format—passive aspects, impacts, and benefits

ADVANTAGE	STRENGTH OF ADVANTAGE	TYPE OF ADVANTAGE	COMMENTS ON VULNERABILITY OF PRINT ADVANTAGES
COMFORT			
a. Physical adaptability to user	Very Strong	FI	Significant erosion is possible if a flat-panel display of high quality and comfortable size and weight is developed.
b. Feel, familiarity, and attachment to books and the variety of forms in which they are produced	Strong	FI	Some slow erosion if/as aesthetic values change.
c. Wide range of display sizes available to meet needs	Strong	FI	Very limited erosion, in spite of electronic advances.
CONVENIENCE			
d. High portability	Strong	FI	Erosion possible if high-quality flat-panel of comfortable size/weight is developed.
e. No need for a "reading device"	Unique	FI	No erosion appears possible.
f. No need for a power source	Unique	FI	Some erosion possible if/ when computer and display

Figure 6-5. (Continued)

ADVANTAGE	STRENGTH OF ADVANTAGE	TYPE OF ADVANTAGE	COMMENTS ON VULNERABILITY OF PRINT ADVANTAGES
			power requirements are decreased. Also, less of an advantage in absence of natural light or when operating in fixed locations with electric power available.
g. No startup or "booting" is needed; neither are "device skills," such as keyboard, physical manipulation, file management, backup, and others	Very Strong	FI	Slow erosion possible if functionality of equipment increases so that it normally will be left on and ready to go, and if user is relieved of most management functions by improved interfaces and a variety of "intelligent" operating aids.
h. Browsing and annotation are easy, with comfortable page flipping and other types of manipulation	Strong	FI	Considerable erosion can arise if/as displays with fast (video speed) page "change" speeds (and other acceptable characteristics—see a, b, and d above) are developed, along with suitable "browsing" controls.
CONFIDENCE			
i. Long-life materials	Very Strong	FI	Erosion possible if/as electronic media with longer lives are developed.
j. No obsolescence of "reading device," or of associated software and information files; no in-compatibilities among major product families	Unique	FI	Some erosion possible if/as: (1) greater technical stability arises and/or (2) growth paths are established either by standards or through vendor product planning and/or (3) for businesses, widely available conversion services arise.

Figure 6-5. (Continued)

ADVANTAGE	STRENGTH OF ADVANTAGE	TYPE OF ADVANTAGE	COMMENTS ON VULNERABILITY OF PRINT ADVANTAGES
k. Training to use print is provided as an externality that is assumed not to become obsolete; thus, little or no need for retraining is anticipated	Strong	FI	Considerable erosion can arise if/as user interfaces are improved to where changes in more mass-market uses of electronic delivery are perceived as equivalent to, say, annual automobile model changes. Also, part of the externally provided basic training, concerning which cost/benefit relationships at the detailed level are poorly understood, may become increasingly out-of-date, decreasing the advantages of this training.
SUBSTANCE			
l. Massive amounts of current and older material, with much variety, are widely and easily available	Strong	SI	Slow erosion over time is possible if or when electronic markets expand and generate more electronic materials. Print also may be vulnerable to major technical advances that could facilitate changes in reading and working habits that lead to more supply of electronic materials.
m. A strong infrastructure of institutional relationships supports print products (e.g., for creation, production, marketing, and distribution); this gives print publishers a strong position of control of information sources	Strong	P	Slow erosion over time is possible if or when electronic markets expand and print publishers gradually take advantage of electronic capabilities to deliver more of their products electronically as a standard second format.

Figure 6-5. (Continued)

ADVANTAGE	STRENGTH OF ADVANTAGE	TYPE OF ADVANTAGE	COMMENTS ON VULNERABILITY OF PRINT ADVANTAGES
n. Print has a legal status for documents, notices, warnings, and other records important for both business and individuals	Very Strong	FI	Very slow erosion possible, but only if electronic terminals become widespread to where it can be assumed that all persons have easy, economical access to materials delivered through them.
QUALITY			
o. Print quality is high	Moderate	FI	Considerable erosion can arise if/as display pixel counts and other characteristics (such as presence of jitter, poor contrast, etc.) are improved—as now is happening.
COST			
p. No initial cost for a "reading device"; no direct user costs for training	Strong	FI	Some erosion possible if/as computer and display costs decrease or reading devices are subsidized.
q. Revenues provided to many important print products by advertising lead to very low user acquisition costs	Very Strong	FI/P	Some erosion possible if a marketable format for advertising in electronically delivered materials evolves; such a format has not yet been identified.

strikingly when the figures are compared. Electronic advantages are heavily concentrated on exploitation of manipulative, speed, and storage capacity capabilities, and they involve a fairly wide mix of process, substance, and format variables. Print, however, has its advantages almost entirely in the format area; its competitive strengths, not surprisingly, are concentrated on information materials that make few demands for user manipulation of substance or format.

Readers will find the entries in Figure 6-5 largely self-explanatory, because we all have great familiarity with using print materials; this, in fact, is the source of some of the strongest print advantages. Viewed as a collection, however, the print advantages have several interesting features.

First, about half of the advantages are "inherited" ones, in the sense that they have resulted from the gradual evolution of print over many years in response to market needs and technical possibilities. Physical characteristics, familiarity, widely available substance, and strong institutional infrastructure are examples. These are attributes of a maturity that electronics is still in the process of developing.

Overlapping the above, about half of the print advantages derive from its underlying technology. Some of these advantages, such as lack of any need for a reading device, can never be matched by electronics; others (for example, high portability and high display quality) could become eroded fairly rapidly by advances in electronic technology. In general, most advantages of print are potentially vulnerable to at least some erosion from various combinations of technical, economic, social and institutional changes. However, many of the advantages are embedded quite deeply in broad cultural attitudes, and this usually implies barriers to rapid change except for uses where a new technology has strong economic value.[5]

Finally, two cost advantages of print are among those listed. These derive from an inherent technical advantage of print (no requirement for a "reading device" or for special training) and from a feature of print's inherited formats and infrastructure (the frequent availability of advertising support), rather than from direct production and delivery cost factors. They, therefore, are considered appropriate for inclusion among the fundamental advantages we are reviewing.

6.2.4 Generic User Needs

At this point we can review all the attributes that have contributed to the creation of a relative advantage—whether of print or electronics—and use them to develop a list of generic user needs (Figure 6-6). These

[5] For a good discussion of the many barriers to change and the slow pace of the spread in use of first written documents and much later printed materials, see: Clanchy, M.T., *From Memory to Written Record: England 1066–1307* (Cambridge, MA: Harvard University Press, 1979); and Altick, Richard D., *The English Common Reader: A Social History of the Mass Reading Public, 1800–1900* (Chicago: Chicago University Press, 1957).

Figure 6-6. Generic User Needs Regarding Information Acquisition and Use

ATTRIBUTE NEEDED	DESCRIPTION*
1. PHYSICAL CONVENIENCE	Features such as portability, adaptability to user position and posture, freedom from use constraints (such as need for external power source), and ease of handling and mechanical operation—all derived primarily from physical attributes of the format
2. CONVENIENCE IN OPERATING	Features that contribute to easy access to desired information and functional capabilities (such as programs), and to ease in managing these resources for acquisition, absorption, use, storage, and protection of information materials
3. TIMELINESS/CURRENCY	Timeliness and currency of information adequate to the uses to which it will be put
4. PASSIVE COMFORT	Characteristics such as familiarity, social and legal status, high visual quality, and good aesthetics and tactile elements, all derived from physical features and social acceptability of the format
5. ACTIVE COMFORT	Controllable format and substance features that permit adjustments to improve the user's physical and sensory comfort when absorbing and using information
6. CONFIDENCE IN FORMAT	Sense of assurance in the viability of the format, and in both the non-obsolescence over time and the transferability across environments (home, office, equipment used, etc.) of skills, records materials, and other aspects of use of the format
7. COST SUPPORT	Measures (excluding those related to production and distribution) such as advertising and tax deductibility, that reduce user direct costs
8. SUBSTANCE AVAILABILITY	Both quantity and variety, so that adequate substance can be acquired to serve many functions and types of uses for a given situation
9. CONFIDENCE IN SUBSTANCE	Confidence in currency and in completeness and accuracy of information presented, and in operations performed, appropriate to use
10. STATIC IMPACT AND INFORMATION DENSITY	Quality and features (such as color, font variety, images, size) that increase appeal

Figure 6-6. (Continued)

ATTRIBUTE NEEDED	DESCRIPTION*
	while also increasing the absorbability of information presented in a static mode to a "passive" user
11. CONTROL OF INFORMATION LAYOUT AND PRESENTATION FEATURES	Ability to control and modify information format features to exploit fully substance features, and to meet specific needs and preferences for either personal absorption or presentation to others
12. CONTROL OF SUBSTANCE PRESENTED	Ability easily and rapidly to select and re-select specific categories, types, and items of information to be presented
13. OPERATIONS ON SUBSTANCE	Ability to alter substance by adding or deleting, performing computations, or doing any of a variety of other types of operations

*The nature of these generic user needs is further defined throughout this chapter. For example, Figures 6-14 and 6-15 clarify their importance in different user situations, and Figure 6-18 examines the extent to which they are met in these situations.

needs consolidate the "themes" of the advantage source clusters developed earlier in this section (Figure 6-3 and Figure 6-5), with some wording changes and minor reorganization. For example, comfort and convenience needs have both been split into two categories—one category is passive, in which print has major strengths, while the other covers active aspects, where electronics has some real or potential advantages. These generic needs will be used for organizing a variety of discussion topics and lists in the remainder of this section.

6.2.5 Comparison of Advantages

The major source of the advantages of electronics is the user manipulation capabilities associated with this presentation mode. As already noted, these capabilities often can be used to alter, simultaneously, both the substance and the *detailed* format of an item of information. Further, this capability almost by definition provides what amounts to a change in process, although this change may take place after the information provider has completed the information package that the user later will alter. The result is that a large fraction of electronic relative advantages must be classified as contributing to multiple elements of the detailed information-defining bundle. In Figure 6-4, some 40 percent of the entries are so classified. The remaining entries are scattered fairly evenly among the three individual definition elements.

In contrast, almost all the print relative advantages are classified as related to one element: format. The format here is a passive element, meaning that the detailed features of the element cannot be changed by a user. As a result of their very different relative advantages, electronics and print have competed in an almost indirect fashion. Each now has its own secure areas, and their current direct competition is restricted to a small portion of their individual total markets. The factors that might induce a major change in the current balance will be central to much of the material in the next three sections of this chapter.

6.3. USER SITUATIONS

6.3.1 Introduction

Our analysis of user needs for timeliness or manipulability or reliability or visual impact—to name just a few information attributes—inevitably took us to the user's *situation*. Information users operate in a wide variety of situations that determine how they perceive the importance of various needs. For example, timeliness and currency are critical to most of those engaged in transaction activities but are of far less importance among recreational readers. That information-related equipment must be simple to operate is not likely to be of major concern to computer experts or to those working in a well-supported environment, while it can be a key requirement for "amateurs" operating at home. The user situation is a critical variable.

But how exactly do user situations affect a user's choice of information presentation methods? Where could changes in electronic presentations have the greatest impact?

We begin by defining a set of four generic user situations.[6] These situations are characterized by the user activities involved, the types and formats of information commonly employed, the user operating environments, and typical user backgrounds and skill levels.

[6] User situations and the importance of different needs will change over time, as social and business requirements change and as technology makes it feasible, or simpler, to perform a given operation. For example, spreadsheets have been used for many decades, but they acquired a new importance recently because greater ease in building them has led to much wider use. This accessibility, in turn, has changed some user activities and their perceptions of needs. Our material on user situations and on the importance of needs applies only to the late 1980s.

6.3.2 Situations

The four user situations are as follow:

I. *Fast-Paced Work*: Requiring either rapid user responses to events or fast continuing operations to achieve high productivity;
II. *Moderately-Paced/Deliberate Work*: Covering a wide range of analytical, design, planning, and communications-oriented business operations;
III. *Work-Like Home*: Involving home and personal management functions, professional reading, and self-education activities; and
IV. *General Purpose/Recreational Home*: Devoted to satisfying personal relaxation interests and non-work-related, self-development activities.

This set of user situations does not cover all possibilities, but it does provide a broad range with which to probe the competition between electronics and print. Situation II applies to a large fraction of all white-collar workers in the United States as well as to increasing numbers of technicians, service industry workers, and blue-collar personnel. Situation I constitutes a smaller subset of white- and blue-collar workers involved in activities where electronic penetration has been very successful. Situation III represents another kind of subset, this time drawn from the populations of I, II, and, to a lesser extent, IV. Situation IV is faced by most of the nation's population and is a stronghold of print, relative to electronics. Basically, the situations define *roles* of individuals, rather than markets or fixed user groups, with the possibility that a given individual can and often will be involved in several situations at different times of the day.

Figures 6-7, 6-8, 6-9, and 6-10 describe for each situation

- Typical activities associated with the situation;
- The relative extent of use, by those in the situation, of different information types or formats in terms of three categories:
  1. *Data*: Numbers and/or very limited text, as in maps, situation displays, or instrument readings;
  2. *Text*: For example, letters, documents, articles, books; and
  3. *Other*: Telephone conversations, meetings, audio, video;[7]

[7] The distinction between *data* and *text* will be used later for evaluating the importance of several of the user needs. *Other* is included only to give a sense of the total information resources applied in the various situations; it will not be used further for other than background purposes.

Figure 6-7. Situation I: Fast-Paced Work

This situation includes: very fast response activities (such as in financial and commodities trading/transactions, C³I, and air traffic control); activities subject to frequent changes that may require rapid user reactions (process and factory control, and real-time transportation movement and scheduling control); and production-oriented office "factory" type operations (typing pools, data entry for all types of transactions, order taking, inquiry response).

Relative use of information types:

Data = Large
Text = Small (except typing pools = Large)
Other = Medium (except typing pools and some transaction entry jobs = Small)

Electronic environment. The electronic environment for this type of work normally involves centralized or networked computer systems, operated throughout working hours and maintained by MIS professionals. When useful, the systems are linked to external data sources. The MIS staff is responsible both for maintaining all hardware and software and for assuring that appropriate programs and data sources are available whenever needed. There is little tailoring of software to individual preferences; when tailoring is provided, it is confined to well-recognized, successful personnel in key positions.

Background and skills. Background and skills vary with occupation, ranging from good educations (for most financial/commodity traders and C³I senior operators) through middle-level backgrounds (for control operators) to lower ones (in office factories). However, in all cases, the users normally have highly honed computer skills in the narrow applications areas in which they work.

- The typical *current* electronic environment(s) in which the users in each situation operate, and
- The education and skills they *now* bring to bear in their use of information.

6.3.3 Summary Figures

Figure 6-11 summarizes the four user situations just presented. Figure 6-12 then examines them from the point of view of the component information activities involved. We will revisit these component activities when we identify areas for action in section 6.5.

6.3.4 Target Products

Users in each of the four situations currently employ (or employed in the recent past) a variety of print products, listed in Figure 6-13. For

Figure 6-8. Situation II: Moderately Paced/Deliberate Work

Users face this situation in a wide range of professional and business staff activities—for example, architectural and product design; scientific, engineering, and legal research; financial and market analyses; staff studies; and preparation of technical memoranda and reports.

Relative use of information types:
Data = Medium
Text = Medium
Other = Medium

Electronic environment. The electronic environment here includes both centralized or networked computer systems, as described for Situation I, and/or stand-alone personal computers or professional/engineering work stations. These are maintained by professional computer personnel and mostly operated throughout working hours. Although frequently not fully networked, the stations often have means of access to internal and external databases. In this environment, individual users normally are responsible for loading the programs they use (onto hard disks or with floppies), and often for selecting and/or entering their own databases. Individuals may be permitted to create or tailor software; if so, they usually will have responsibility for documentation of any programs or program modifications they create. In most cases, users have some direct responsibilities for backup of their files and output.

Background and skills. This situation represents two broad categories of user backgrounds and skills. The first level comprises well-educated professionals; the second, middle-educated support staff. The professionals usually have a fairly broad range of computer skills and employ many more applications than participants in Situation I. However, while user skills are broad, they often are rather shallow; even when users possess considerable expertise, their primary interest is in getting results, rather than in the underlying technology. Support staff have a broader range of skills than office "factory" workers, and these usually are quite well honed.

each item, we indicate the extent to which electronics already has replaced these print products and the user situations where the products (in either electronic or print form) currently are employed. The list is ranked in rough order of the timeliness that characterizes the production of the materials (thus placing ticker tapes at the top, magazines in the middle, and art books at the bottom).[8]

What might be termed the *target products*—those where print has

[8] In Figure 6-13, major uses of a product are made in those user situations *without* parentheses; those with parentheses involve more limited uses of it. Electronic penetration level estimates apply to only "eligible" user segments of the situation. For example, in transaction records, the estimate (major penetration) applies to a large fraction of Situation I users and, because of the nature of their work, a smaller fraction of Situation II users. In another case, that of ticker tapes, the penetration is major but applies to only

Figure 6-9. Situation III: Work-Like Home

Examples for this situation include managing personal, financial, household, and investment records; professional background reading; letter writing; and some forms of self-education (such as in specific business skills). For their computer work, the users frequently employ a subset or variations of the applications used in Situation II above. In many cases they also participate in that situation; but unless they perform part of their normal work at home (which we exclude from the basic definition of the situation activities), they usually have far weaker motivations for home use of electronic presentations than for office use.

Relative use of information types:
Data = Medium
Text = Medium-Large
Other = Small

Electronic environment. The home environment characteristically uses stand-alone personal computers, some with communications capabilities. Sometimes these are duplicates or compatible variants of those that users have at their offices; more often they are lower performance, less costly pieces of equipment. The computers normally are turned on only when in use. In a small fraction of cases, use is extensive; more frequently it is sporadic and averages only a few hours a week. In all cases, the user is responsible for equipment maintenance, for program and data acquisition and entry, for all aspects of file backup and protection, and for any necessary documentation (including that which might justify income tax deductions).

Background and skills. Current users in this situation include a portion of the better educated user segments of Situations I and II, others with generally good education and, increasingly, persons still going through their formal education process. Computer skills in the situation vary widely, from true experts (often hobbyists) to beginners, with the average level probably being advanced beginner/low intermediate.

maintained great strength—are in the bottom half of the list (newspapers and below). These include all the mass media, for which the main potential market—although not necessarily a realizable one—is Situation IV users.

We mentioned several of these targets in our analysis of relative advantages in section 6.2, but now they appear in identifiable user situations. Further, we now are in a position to ask why electronic delivery modes have been able to penetrate in some situations but not in others. Section 6.4 looks more closely and rigorously at the fulfillment of needs in each user situation.

---

the small fraction of Situation I participants who have a use for ticker tapes. Some broadly used products, such as catalogs, have multiple entries (e.g., industrial and consumer).

Figure 6-10. Situation IV: General Purpose/Recreational Home

Activities related to this situation are heavily oriented toward video, audio, and text (newspapers, magazines, some directories and catalogs, and books). Hobbies and games (often multi-person) also are important. Presently, the only computer applications for this situation are games (often single-person), computers as a hobby (including interest group networks), some elementary types of education activities, and very limited electronic mail and computer shopping. This situation is the one that must be penetrated strongly if electronic presentations are to replace print as the socially dominant mode for providing information.

Relative use of information types:
Data = Small
Text = Large
Other = Small (ignoring video and audio)

Electronic environment. This environment does not yet exist in meaningful form. Some recreational uses are made of stand-alone equipment, and quite a few (generally low-cost) "games"-oriented computers have been sold. Characterizing the electronic environment necessary to involve participants fully in this situation is an important part of the objective of our study.

Background and skills. Since participants in this situation comprise almost the entire population, backgrounds and skills cover a very broad range. To penetrate the full market, however, electronics must be capable of appealing to those whose backgrounds and skills are limited, and who have little willingness to learn unless clear benefits can be demonstrated.

6.4 PRESENTATION MODE DOMINANCE

With our background information on user needs and situations, we are now in a position to evaluate the practical strengths of electronics and print and to identify in considerable detail the nature of changes that could have significant impact on mode dominance. The keys to these possibilities lie in the perceptions of the users themselves in each of the user situations. In this section we first make estimates of these user perceptions concerning both the importance of each of their needs in each situation and the current performance of electronic presentations in meeting the needs. Thereafter, these perceptions lead us to the questions with which we began section 6.3: Where could changes in electronic presentations have the greatest impact?

6.4.1 Definitions: Importance of Needs and Extent Met

User perceptions of the importance of information-related needs are influenced, if not established, by the user's situation—the activities and the working and electronic environments described in section 6.3.

Figure 6.11 Summary of User Situation Characteristics: Late 1980s

	SITUATION I FAST-PACED WORK	SITUATION II MOD. PACED/ DELIB. WORK	SITUATION III WORK-LIKE HOME	SITUATION IV GEN. PURPOSE/ REC. HOME
Activities	Fast response/ reaction work; office factory work	Professional work of all types; business staff work	Household and financial management; professional reading	Recreational reading; reference/ directory search; games; hobbies
Information Sources:				
• Data	Large	Medium	Medium	Small
• Text	Small (Large for typing pools)	Medium	Medium-Large	Large
• Other	Medium (Small for office factory)	Medium	Small	Small (excluding video and audio)
Electronic Environment	Networked system; professional support of all aspects of system use	Either networked systems or stand-alone stations; professional maintenance; personal operations management	Stand-alone equipment, simpler than work machines; all support personally managed; all costs borne personally	Stand-alone, relatively simple and low cost equipment; all support and costs handled by user
Current User Skills	Very specialized; highly honed	Broad range of skills; some well honed and others fairly shallow	Broad range of skills and ability; from expert to near beginner	Limited skills and generally weak motivations
Current Electronic Penetration	Strong; electronics is the dominant mode	Moderate; growing at a moderate rate	Small; growing, but at a modest rate	Negligible (except for games); slow growth rate

In estimating the extent to which needs are met, we are concerned with how well electronic presentations perform in servicing the *totality* of a user group's *visual* information requirements, excluding only those delivered by TV/video means. In other words, we consider all materials that are now, or were in the past, provided by print or

Figure 6-12 Component Information Activities Characteristic of Different User Situations in the Late 1980s

COMPONENT ACTIVITY	SITUATION I FAST-PACED WORK	SITUATION II MODERATE PACED/DELIB. WORK	SITUATION III WORK-LIKE HOME	SITUATION IV GEN. PURPOSE/ REC. HOME
Reading	Limited business, professional and administrative document reading (internal and external sources) *and* Real-time data/ image displays* *plus*	Extensive business, professional and other document reading (both internal and external sources)	Business, professional and "hobbies" reading	Recreational and general purpose reading
Search Activities	Data and/or limited text and/or image search* *plus*	Packaged reference and on-line database search	Packaged reference and limited on-line database search	Packaged reference material look-up or search
Manipulation Activities	Conduct of transactions, operations, inquiries, etc.*	Inputs to, and operations with business/ professional/ technical computer programs, including preparations of draft texts and presentation materials	Personal financial and home management packaged program operation; Business/ professional self-education packaged program operation; Some home banking; Some interest group network operations	Personal self-education packaged program operation; Games; Some home shopping; Some "chatting"

*Users often will view the three asterisked activities as being integrated.

Figure 6-12. (Continued)

COMPONENT ACTIVITY	SITUATION I FAST-PACED WORK	SITUATION II MODERATE PACED/DELIB. WORK	SITUATION III WORK-LIKE HOME	SITUATION IV GEN. PURPOSE/ REC. HOME
System Management	None; system management provided to users	Some data, files, program and documentation management	Complete equipment and program selection and maintenance, data collection, files and documentation management	As for Situation III

print-like materials. This means that, in our estimates, where print is dominant it sets the standard of performance against which electronics must compete.

Where electronics now dominates, however, we do not automatically let it set the standard. Instead, we evaluate performance relative to what could be provided with available electronic technology. This both places emphasis on steps that could still further strengthen electronics and prevents our allowing the unique advantages of electronics to hide current weaknesses relative to what users desire. Finally, when estimating values for both the importance of needs and the extent to which they are met, we are primarily concerned with the influences of each need on *decisions* as to which of the two competing technologies to employ, rather than with ideal or absolute values.

We describe five levels of need importance:

Major	Critical to meeting a user's purposes
Significant–Major	A near necessity to meet a user's purposes
Significant	Valuable for meeting a user's purposes
Minor–Significant	Useful, but not an important determinant in user decisions
Minor	Perhaps desirable, but not a factor in user decisions

We used a scale of seven values to indicate the extent to which a user group's needs are met:

Figure 6-13 Print Products Employed in Different Situations Ranked in Rough Order of the Currency Characterizing the Products

PRODUCT	ELECTRONIC PENETRATION	USERS
Ticker tapes	Major	I
Transaction records, event records, logs	Major	I, (II)
News wires	Substantial	I, (II)
Database materials	Major	(I), II, (III, IV)
Internal business records	Some	(I), II, (III)
Internal memos	Some	(I), II, (III)
Internal reports, studies	Negligible	II, (III)
External letters, reports	Negligible	(I), II, (III)
Newsletters, special services	Some	I, II, (III)
Newspapers	None	I-IV
Sales flyers, inserts	Negligible	IV
News magazines	None	I-IV
Business, professional journals	Negligible	(I), II, III
General magazines	None	IV
Engineering drawings/records	Some	II
Schedules (commercial)	Major	I, II
Schedules (consumer)	Negligible	III, IV
Catalogs (industrial)	Some	II, (III)
Catalogs (consumer)	Negligible	IV
Directories	Negligible	II, (III, IV)
General books	None	IV
Textbooks	Negligible	II, (III, IV)
Maps, atlases	Negligible	(I, II, IV)
Art books	None	IV

Note: "Eligible" users in situations shown without parentheses make major use of products indicated; those in parentheses make at least some use.

Well	No barrier to use
Adequately–Well	No barrier to use, but improvements are possible
Adequately	No barrier to use, but improvements are important

Partly–Adequately	A minor barrier to widespread use if need is important
Partly	A substantial barrier if the need is important
Poorly–Partly	A major barrier if the need is important
Poorly	A major barrier for all except needs of minor importance

6.4.2 Status of Electronic Presentations in Meeting Needs

Figure 6-14 summarizes our evaluation of how well electronic displays meet user needs. The entries show the importance of the need and our estimate of the extent to which it is met by current electronic systems for each combination of need and user situation.

When we look at the distribution of the perceived importance of needs in each user situation (in Figure 6-15 and Figure 6-16), it appears that

- For fast-paced work, there are a few very critical needs that must be met, with all the other needs being of relatively low importance. In other words, all the other needs can be largely sacrificed if this is necessary to meet the critical ones.
- For the other situations, the needs are more widely distributed, but with only about a fifth of all needs in the lowest two importance categories. This means that a large majority of all the needs are sufficiently important to influence the decisions of members of these user situations concerning whether to use electronic presentations.
- If the needs for each situation are weighted by their importance levels (with Major = 5, Minor = 1) and then summed, Situation I has the lowest total importance "value" of needs, and Situation II has the highest. Situation I is this way because of the narrowness of the activities involved and the limited types and formats of visual information employed; these place a high premium on just a few needs. For Situation II, the wide range of activities and information types that are of interest to individual participants (and to users in the situation as a whole) put a very high fraction of all the needs into the Significant-Major category.
- All Situation I entries in the top two importance categories are needs for which electronics is very strong in meeting user needs. The top two importance categories for successively higher numbered situations keep adding more needs where print, rather than electronics, is the dominant mode, until they constitute six out of the seven listed for Situation IV.

Figure 6-14. Perceived Importance of Needs and the Extent of Their Fulfillment by Electronic Means in Different User Situations: Late 1980s

GENERIC NEED	I FAST-PACED WORK		II MOD. PACED/ DELIB. WORK		III WORK-LIKE HOME		IV GEN. PURPOSE/ REC. HOME	
	Importance	How Met	Importance	How Met	Importance	How Met	Importance	How Met
1. PHYSICAL CONVENIENCE	Minor-Signif.	Adequate	Signif.	Partly-Adequate	Signif.	Partly	Signif.-Major	Poorly-Partly
2. CONVENIENCE IN OPERATING	Minor	Well	Signif.-Major	Partly-Adequate	Signif.	Partly	Signif.-Major	Poorly
3. TIMELINESS/ CURRENCY	Major	Well	Signif.-Major	Adequate	Minor-Signif.	Partly	Minor-Signif.	Partly
4. PASSIVE COMFORT	Minor-Signif.	Partly-Adequate	Signif.-Major	Partly	Signif.-Major	Poorly-Partly	Signif.-Major	Poorly-Partly
5. ACTIVE COMFORT	Minor-Signif.	Partly-Adequate	Signif.-Major	Partly	Signif.-Major	Partly	Signif.-Major	Poorly-Partly
6. CONFIDENCE IN FORMAT	Minor	Adequate	Signif.	Partly-Adequate	Signif.-Major	Poorly-Partly	Signif.-Major	Partly
7. COST SUPPORT	Minor	Well	Minor-Signif.	Adequate	Signif.	Partly	Signif.-Major	Poorly
8. SUBSTANCE AVAILABILITY	Minor	Well	Signif.-Major	Partly-Adequate	Signif.-Major	Poorly-Partly	Major	Poorly-Partly
9. CONFIDENCE IN SUBSTANCE	Major	Adequate-Well	Signif.-Major	Adequate	Signif.	Adequate	Minor-Signif.	Adequate
10. STATIC IMPACT/INFO. DENSITY	Minor-Signif.	Partly-Adequate	Signif.-Major	Partly-Adequate	Signif.	Partly-Adequate	Signif.	Partly
11. LAYOUT/ FEATURES CONTROL	Minor-Signif.	Partly-Adequate	Signif.-Major	Partly	Signif.	Partly	Signif.	Poorly-Partly
12. SUBSTANCE PRESENTED CONTROL	Major	Adequate	Major	Partly-Adequate	Minor-Signif.	Partly	Minor-Signif.	Partly
13. OPERATIONS ON SUBSTANCE	Major	Adequate-Well	Major	Adequate-Well	Major	Adequate-Well	Minor-Signif.	Poorly-Partly

The close fit between Situation I requirements and electronic capabilities and the successively poorer fits for higher numbered situations can be illustrated better with a crude numerical analysis. We assigned each situation/need combination an importance "value," as described above (e.g., Major = 5, Minor = 1). Next, we multiplied these numbers by relative extent met "values," determined again from their rank (Well = 7, Poorly = 1), and then divided the products by 7

Figure 6-15. Distribution of Perceived Importance of User Needs: Late 1980s

	IMPORTANCE				
	MAJOR	SIGNIF.-MAJOR	SIGNIFICANT	MINOR-SIGNIF.	MINOR
SITUATION I: FAST-PACED WORK	3. Timeliness-Currency 9. Confidence in Substance 12. Substance Control 13. Substance Operations			1. Physical Convenience 4. Passive Comfort 5. Active Comfort 10. Static Impact 11. Layout/ Features	2. Convenience in Operating 6. Confidence in Format 7. Cost Support 8. Substance Availability
SITUATION II: MODERATELY-PACED/ DELIBERATE WORK	12. Substance Control 13. Substance Operations	2. Convenience in Operating 3. Timeliness-Currency 4. Passive Comfort 5. Active Comfort 8. Substance Availability 9. Confidence in Substance 10. Static Impact 11. Layout/ Features	1. Physical Convenience 6. Confidence in Format	7. Cost Support	
SITUATION III: WORK-LIKE HOME	13. Substance Operations	4. Passive Comfort 5. Active Comfort 6. Confidence in Format 8. Substance Availability	1. Physical Convenience 2. Convenience in Operating 7. Cost Support 9. Confidence in Substance 10. Static Impact 11. Layout/ Features	3. Timeliness-Currency 12. Substance Control	
SITUATION IV: GENERAL PURPOSE/ RECREATIONAL HOME	8. Substance Availability	1. Physical Convenience 2. Convenience in Operating 4. Passive Comfort 5. Active Comfort 6. Confidence in Format 7. Cost Support	10. Static Impact 11. Layout/ Features	3. Timeliness-Currency 9. Confidence in Substance 12. Substance Control 13. Substance Operations	

Figure 6-16. Distribution of Perceived Needs Importance by User Situation

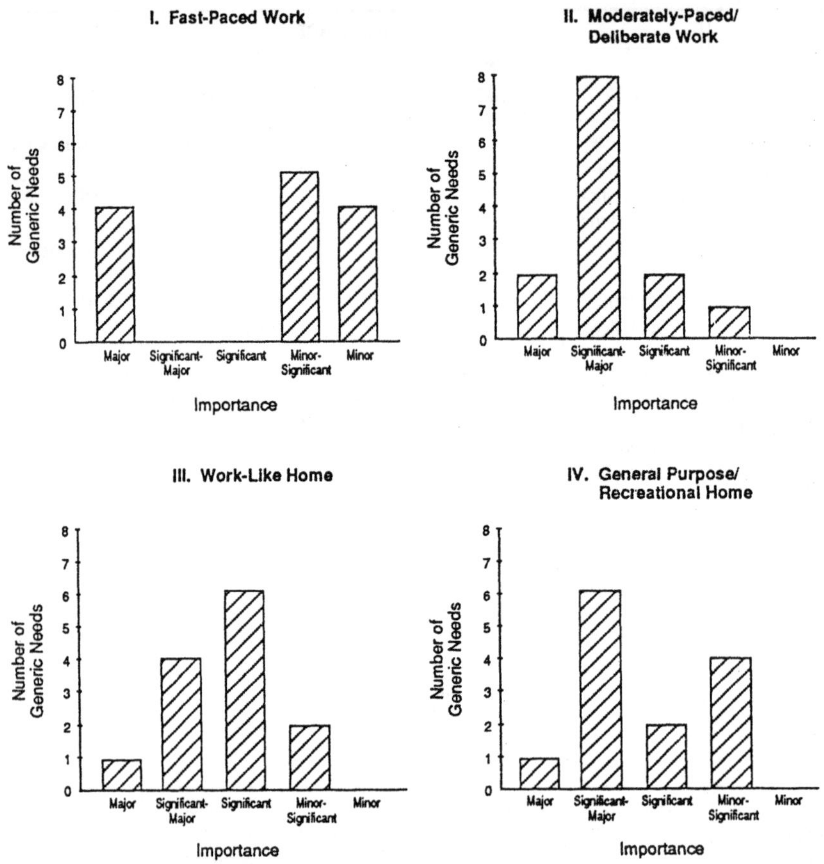

(the best possible score). The results are shown in Figure 6-17, summed (by Situation) for all the needs in each importance category.

Looking at the total for all needs in a situation, Situation I needs scored about 80 percent of being met "Well" (with the more important need categories scoring even better). The other situations had about 60 percent, 50 percent, and 30 percent of their needs met "Well," respectively, with Situation IV important needs scoring worse than the less important ones.

This is admittedly a crude procedure, but it still illustrates the magnitude of the problems faced by electronic presentations if they seek to expand into major new types of markets.

The calculations just described compared the extent that needs were met relative to the highest possible rating ("Well" met). Another way of

Figure 6-17. "Values" of Needs Importance Categories to User Situations and "Values" of Extent Met by Electronic Presentations

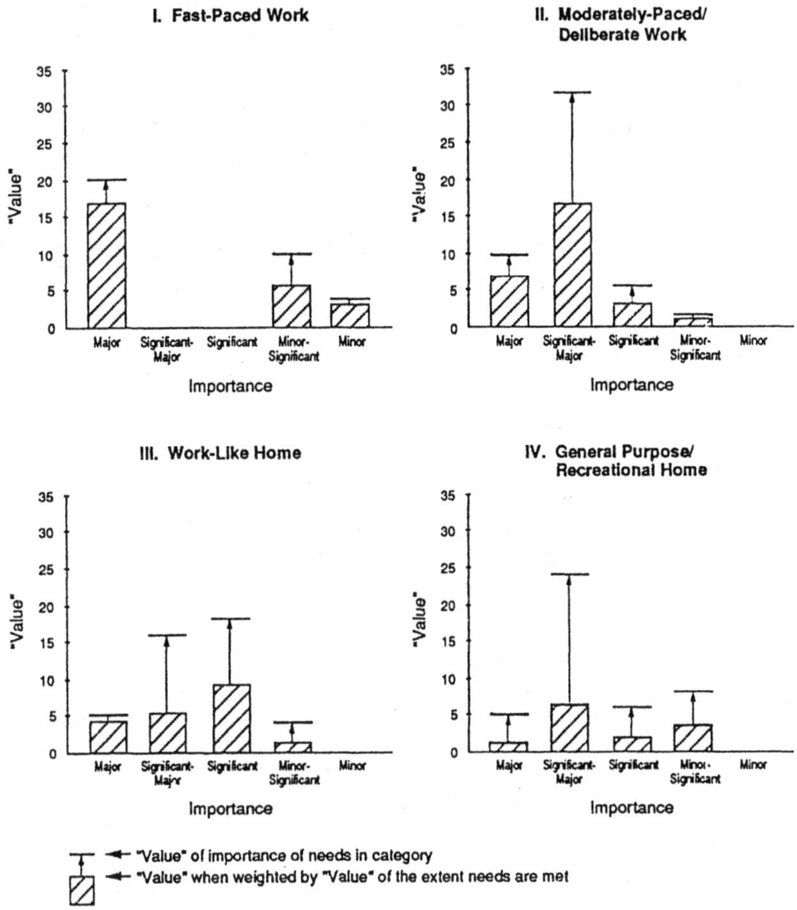

looking at the subject is to consider the "gap" in terms of adequacy, rather than the highest rating. This approach acknowledges better that failure to meet needs fully may not be disastrous; in some situations, meeting the more critical needs adequately may be all that is necessary to enable a presentation mode to maintain a position of dominance. Accordingly, we separate out, for each situation, those combinations where the importance of the need is Significant or higher, and the extent met is less than Adequate. In each of these instances, we consider that a "gap" exists, with the size of the gap dependent on a combination of need importance and the extent of less than Adequate need satisfaction. The results are shown in Figure 6-18:

- For Situation I, there are no gaps; all important needs are met at least adequately.
- For each of the other situations, there are some nine important needs where gaps exist, with the "size" of the gaps increasing as we move from Situation II to Situation IV.

A similar analysis can be performed for each need across Situations to provide a rough indication of the relative importance of the current

Figure 6-18. Perceived Need Gaps of Electronic Displays: Late 1980s

	NEED	IMPORTANCE	EXTENT MET
I FAST-PACED WORK	No perceived gaps		
II MODERATELY-PACED/ DELIBERATE WORK	12. Substance Presented Control	Major	Partly-Adeq.
	4. Passive Comfort	Signif.-Major	Partly
	5. Active Comfort	Signif.-Major	Partly
	11. Layout/Features Control	Signif.-Major	Partly
	8. Substance Availability	Signif.-Major	Partly-Adeq.
	2. Convenience in Operating	Signif.-Major	Partly-Adeq.
	10. Static Impact/ Info. Density	Signif.-Major	Partly-Adeq.
	1. Physical Convenience	Significant	Partly-Adeq.
	6. Confidence in Format	Significant	Partly-Adeq.
III WORK-LIKE HOME	4. Passive Comfort	Signif.-Major	Poorly-Partly
	6. Confidence in Format	Signif.-Major	Poorly-Partly
	8. Substance Availability	Signif.-Major	Poorly-Partly
	5. Active Comfort	Signif.-Major	Partly
	1. Physical Convenience	Significant	Partly
	2. Convenience in Operating	Significant	Partly
	7. Cost Support	Significant	Partly
	10. Static Impact/ Info. Density	Significant	Partly-Adeq.
	11. Layout/Features Control	Significant	Partly

Figure 6-18. (Continued)

	NEED	IMPORTANCE	EXTENT MET
I FAST-PACED WORK	No perceived gaps		
IV GENERAL PURPOSE/ RECREATIONAL HOME	8. Substance Availability	Major	Poorly-Partly
	2. Convenience in Operating	Signif.-Major	Poorly
	7. Cost Support	Signif.-Major	Poorly
	1. Physical Convenience	Signif.-Major	Poorly-Partly
	4. Passive Comfort	Signif.-Major	Poorly-Partly
	5. Active Comfort	Signif.-Major	Poorly-Partly
	6. Confidence in Format	Signif.-Major	Partly
	11. Layout/Features Control	Significant	Poorly-Partly
	10. Static Impact/ Info. Density	Significant	Partly

gaps faced by electronic systems in meeting a variety of families of needs. These results are as follows, ranked by the size of the gap in meeting the listed needs:

Large gaps in satisfying needs for:
Substance Availability
Passive Comfort
Active Comfort

Moderate gaps for:
Convenience in Operating
Confidence in Format
Cost Support
Physical Convenience
Layout/Features Control
Static Impact/Information Density

Negligible or no gaps for:
Control of Substance Presented
Timeliness/Currency
Confidence in Substance
Operations on Substance

6.4.3 Potential Action Areas

Print's relative advantages in meeting user needs can be viewed as barriers electronics must overcome—hence, areas where deliberate actions could be conceived and, if practical, taken. Similarly, useful opportunities for action by electronic contenders also are indicated by any current weaknesses of electronic approaches (i.e., where need components are not met "Well") even when electronics is now superior to print. Figure 6-19 lists areas where there is a potential for these types of improvements to be incorporated into electronic systems. The items are listed under the generic needs of Figure 6-6 (section 6.2) and cover separately both print advantages to overcome and electronic advantages to exploit more completely. There are duplicate entries for items that support multiple need components, but the items are identified in the same way (with a number or a letter) throughout the figure.

The following section examines these as "action areas" and postulates the steps that might (as well as those that cannot) be taken with regard to them.

6.5 ACTION AREAS

6.5.1 Introduction

In this section we explore specific possibilities for overcoming or mitigating the barriers that limit use of electronic presentations, and for taking greater advantage of electronic strengths. Here we are building on the background developed in earlier sections. We have reviewed where we are, how we got there, and why; now we want to know what might make a difference in the future. The actions described in this section start from the areas listed in Figure 6-19. The actions, themselves, are summarized in Figure 6-20 and Figure 6-21 in the same order as in Figure 6-19; Figure 6-20 looks at actions addressed to overcoming print advantages, while Figure 6-21 covers those concerned with exploiting electronic advantages. In some cases the remedial measures involve specific technical advances or changes in current practices. More often, they represent capabilities that seem likely to become available from the continuation of long-standing trends, or from the adoption of approaches that have existing precedents or analogs.

Figure 6-19. Areas in Which Improvements Are Needed If Electronics Is to Capture Major Print Markets

PRINT RELATIVE ADVANTAGE TO OVERCOME*	ELECTRONIC RELATIVE ADVANTAGE TO EXPLOIT*
NEED 1: PHYSICAL CONVENIENCE 1. Portability 2. Adaptability to user location, position, and posture 3. No equipment required 4. No external power source needed except for artificial light during darkness 5. No start-up operation—"ready to go" 6. Only simple and familiar physical manipulations needed 7. Browsing is easy and effective	a. High-density and lightweight information storage b. Less power needed for some types of electronic displays than for artificial illumination of print
NEED 2: CONVENIENCE IN OPERATIONS 5. No start-up operation 7. Easy browsing 8. Easy user annotation/underlining 9. No keyboard or other special data entry skills required 10. No elaborate program, data, or file management skills or efforts needed 11. No major investment in training needed beyond that provided during basic education 12. No special backup operations needed during normal use of format	c. Very convenient, high-speed communications with electronic mail, but with some current service weaknesses d. Very convenient, high-speed access to electronic data, independent of its storage location, but with some current complexity of use and cost disadvantages
NEED 3: CURRENCY/TIMELINESS	**A strong advantage whose full exploitation is limited by:** e. Provider fixed costs for preparing broadly useful information

*The generic needs retain the same 13 numbers as they had in Figure 6-6. However, because the items listed under the needs are different from those described earlier (in Figures 6-3 to 6-5) even though they have many similarities, they have a different number set. The earlier entries were attributes as bases of relative advantages; the new ones are attributes as potential action areas for reduction of barriers or leveraging of advantages.

Figure 6-19. (Continued)

PRINT RELATIVE ADVANTAGE TO OVERCOME	ELECTRONIC RELATIVE ADVANTAGE TO EXPLOIT
	f. Telecommunications equipment and use costs g. Current lack of a mass market over which to distribute provider and user fixed costs
NEED 4: **PASSIVE COMFORT** 13. Strong aesthetic values; familiar style and appearance 14. Established legal status in many important areas 15. Very high visual quality, even in poorer publications	
NEED 5: **ACTIVE COMFORT** 8. Easy underlining and annotation	h. Numerous means available to ease user eye strain and satisfy user preferences regarding display features i. Numerous means available to help user coordination of separated material in a document or of material from many sources
NEED 6: **CONFIDENCE IN FORMAT** 14. Established legal status in many important areas 16. Excellent records life and easy records storage; basic product is rugged (except to water or fire damage) 17. No obsolescence of records due to changes in equipment or storage media 18. No obsolescence of the skills needed to use the print format 19. No problems of compatibility, such as between different types of equipment	
NEED 7: **COST SUPPORT** 20. Large revenues from advertising support many types of print products	

Figure 6-19. (Continued)

PRINT RELATIVE ADVANTAGE TO OVERCOME	ELECTRONIC RELATIVE ADVANTAGE TO EXPLOIT
21. Availability of free (tax-supported) libraries benefits many users 22. No equipment costs before format can be used 23. No training costs, since basic training is provided as an externality	
NEED 8: SUBSTANCE AVAILABILITY 24. A very wide range and variety of materials are easily available **A well-developed infrastructure provides:** 25. A useful level of standardization 26. Effective product review mechanisms 27. Effective and reliable retailing and pricing practices 28. Accepted means for consumers to share print materials	
NEED 9: CONFIDENCE IN SUBSTANCE	**This advantage applies primarily to transaction systems, where characteristics to be exploited include:** j. Very high system capacities k. Very low error rates l. A generally high level of currency m. A high degree of flexibility, including great potential to expand system coverages into improved backup and new "adjacent" areas
NEED 10: STATIC IMPACT AND INFORMATION DENSITY 15. Very high visual quality of end products 29. Great possible variability of presentation size to match information purposes	
NEED 11: CONTROL OF INFORMATION LAYOUT AND PRESENTATION FEATURES	n. Size change/magnification/zoom capabilities

Figure 6-19. (Continued)

PRINT RELATIVE ADVANTAGE TO OVERCOME	ELECTRONIC RELATIVE ADVANTAGE TO EXPLOIT
	o. Ability to rotate solid figures in three dimensions p. Capability to create graphics, as final products or to help detect trends and patterns q. Color control for coding parts, paths or other features r. Multimedia, incorporating text, graphics, sound and video in a fixed or interactive mode (with the latter dependent on capabilities described in connection with Need 13)
NEED 12: CONTROL OF SUBSTANCE PRESENTED	s. Powerful search capabilities of many types t. Customization of tables and text to achieve useful unions of materials u. Windowing and HyperCard approaches for achieving unions of materials v. Private file development by spin-off of selected viewed material w. Aided or automatic indexing and cross-indexing
NEED 13: OPERATIONS ON SUBSTANCE	v. Private files development by selective spin-off of external and internal materials x. Correction y. Computation z. Packaging, to provide combinations of materials not practical with print aa. Interactive entries of many types ab. Artistic manipulations of many types

As presented in these two figures, the action areas and remedial steps are related only to specific print or electronic relative advantages. To better understand their significance, we will cluster them to reflect more clearly specific user activities. We believe this will offer a sounder basis for considering related market dynamics. Accordingly, we return to the component activities described for each user situation in Figure 6-12. From this figure we can define three broad functional clusters:

Reading cluster:	Concerned with relatively passive information absorption processes;
Operations cluster:	Combines search and manipulation component activities, and thereby covers active acquisition and use of information; and
Management cluster:	Devoted to assuring an effective environment for efficient conduct of the other clusters.

In addition to defining these functional clusters, we also find it useful to consider (with some overlap) two clusters that concern broader social areas: *Education and training cluster* and *Socioeconomic issues cluster*.

The remainder of this section examines these clusters. The implications of the material presented—barriers, forces acting to maintain or overcome them, and similar topics—are covered in section 6.6.

6.5.2 Reading Cluster

The reading cluster is of particular importance, since it is key to the development of mass markets for electronic displays. Thus, dominance in this cluster is *the* prerequisite for electronics to achieve dominance over print.

Extensive reading of text is an activity for which electronic displays so far have received negligible use. Changing this situation will require some specific technical advances that can lead to new hardware and software product lines. Therefore, we will review the cluster in terms of two aspects: first, the required underlying technologies, and then the market development actions that must follow. The former deals mostly with direct solutions of (or actions to mitigate) electronic weaknesses, and with measures that directly exploit existing and potential electronic strengths. The primary user needs of concern in this regard are for physical convenience, convenience in operations, and passive and active comfort. Market development here refers to actions, both direct and indirect, that are part of the process of

Figure 6-20 Summary of Possible Actions and Their Impacts: Overcoming Print Advantages

KEY TO CODES

TYPE of Action

X = No currently known practical solution
A = Specific large technical advance or innovation
T = Anticipated result of current trends
O = Currently available option; implementation dependent on perception of adequate markets
I = Market or social precedents exist but action requires multiple stakeholders agreements

IMPACTS of Action

With regard to specific need element:
S = Electronics becomes superior to print
C = Electronics becomes comparable to print
M = Electronic relative disadvantage is mitigated significantly
Z = Electronic relative disadvantage remains with, at most, minor mitigation

COMBINATION CODES (for both TYPE OF ACTIONS and IMPACT OF ACTIONS columns)

Examples: When the code is **X-T,** the values are **between X and T**
When the code is **X; T,** some have **values** = **X; others** = **T**

PRINT ADVANTAGE TO OVERCOME	MAJOR POSSIBLE ACTION ITEMS	TYPE OF ACTIONS	IMPACTS OF ACTIONS
NEED 1: PHYSICAL CONVENIENCE			
1. Portability	Exploit existing size/power/weight trends	T	C-S
2. Adaptability to user posture	High-quality, full-page flat-panel display	A	C
3. No equipment required	Exploit existing size/power/cost trends	T	M-C
4. No external power source needed	Exploit current power consumption and battery capacity trends	T	Z-M
5. No start-up operation	Available product design option	O	M
6. Only simple, familiar manipulation	Product design option plus improvements	X; T	Z-M
7. Easy browsing capability	Develop software "browsing" package	O	C-S
NEED 2: CONVENIENCE IN OPERATIONS			
5. No start-up operation	Available product design option	O	M
7. Easy browsing capability	Develop software "browsing" package	O	C-S
8. Easy annotation/underlining	Product design option plus improvements	O	C

Figure 6-20. (Continued)

PRINT ADVANTAGE TO OVERCOME	MAJOR POSSIBLE ACTIONS ITEMS	TYPE OF ACTIONS	IMPACTS OF ACTIONS
9. No keyboard/special data entry skills needed	No near-term solution; even long-term speech recognition not entirely satisfactory	X	Z
10. No elaborate program/ data/file management skills needed	No full solution; improvements by better software design and special packages	X; O-T	Z-M
11. No major training investment	Improvements through product and software design and better documentation/ diagnostics	O	Z-M
12. No special backup operations	Available product design option	O	M-C
NEED 4: PASSIVE COMFORT			
13. Aesthetic values/familiar style	Available hardware option	O	C
14. Established legal status	Many actions by multiple stakeholders	X; I-T	Z; C
15. Very high visual quality	High-quality, full-page flat-panel display	A	M-C
NEED 5: ACTIVE COMFORT			
8. Easy underlining/ annotation	Product design option plus improvements	O	C
NEED 6: CONFIDENCE IN FORMAT			
16. Excellent records life and easy storage	No near-term full solution; even current concepts for long-term erasable memory may involve too-fragile technologies	X	Z
17. No records equipment obsolescence	Upwards compatible memory hardware (but none is now in sight); records transfer services	X-O	Z-M
18. No operating skills obsolescence	Improvements through product and software design and better documentation/ diagnostics	O	Z-M

Figure 6-20. (Continued)

PRINT ADVANTAGE TO OVERCOME	MAJOR POSSIBLE ACTION ITEMS	TYPE OF ACTIONS	IMPACTS OF ACTIONS
19. No equipment compatibility problems	Product design (with cross-licensing, or equivalent, among multiple participants)	I-T	Z-M
14. Established legal status	Many actions by multiple stakeholders	X; I-T	Z; C
NEED 7: COST SUPPORT			
20. Support from advertising revenues	No specific current solution; experimentation and innovation required	X-T	Z-M
21. "Free" libraries available	Multiple stakeholders agreement; some precedents available	I	M-C
22. No equipment costs	Inherent weakness; reduced by mass production	—	—
23. No special training costs	Improvements through product and software design and better documentation/ diagnostics	O	Z-M
NEED 8: SUBSTANCE AVAILABILITY			
24. Wide range/variety of materials	Overall result if other actions successful	—	—
25. Useful level of standardization	Market dominance/ multiple stakeholders actions	I	Z; M-C
26. Effective product review system	Development of book review equivalents	O; T	M-C
27. Established retailing/ pricing practices	Normal experimentation, evolution, and maturation	T; I	M-C
28. Accepted means for consumer product sharing	Multiple stakeholders agreement; some precedents available	I	M-C
NEED 10: STATIC IMPACT AND INFORMATION DENSITY			
15. High visual quality	High-quality, full-page flat-panel display	A	M-C
29. Large variability possible in size of presentation	No known or foreseeable practical solution	X	Z

Figure 6-21. Summary of Possible Actions: Exploiting Electronic Advantages

KEY TO "TYPE OF ACTIONS" CODES
T = Anticipated result of current trends **O** = Currently available option; implementation depends on perception of adequate market **I** = Market or social precedents exist but action requires multiple stakeholders agreements
COMBINATION CODES **Examples:** When the code is **O-T,** the actions have **values between O and T** When the code is **I; O,** some actions have **value = I; others = O**

ELECTRONIC ADVANTAGE TO EXPLOIT	MAJOR POSSIBLE ACTION ITEMS	TYPE OF ACTIONS
NEED 1: PHYSICAL CONVENIENCE		
a. High density/lightweight information storage	Continuation of past trend of rapid improvement; will be helped if roles of alternative technical approaches are resolved	T
b. Less power needed than for artificial illumination of print	Continuation of past trend of improvement; aided by flat-panel developments	T
NEED 2: CONVENIENCE IN OPERATING		
c. Convenient, high-speed communications with electronic mail	Development of better software, cross-system interconnections, and on-line global directory capability	I; O-T
d. Convenient, on-line access to electronic data independent of location	Development of cross-database/systems interfaces and user aids; improved on-line catalogs of data contents	I; O-T
NEED 3: CURRENCY/TIMELINESS A strong advantage limited by:		
e. Provider fixed costs for preparing broadly useful information	Improved technical aids, such as OCR, and growth of generic coding standards	T
f. Telecommunications equipment and use costs	Improved modem cost/performance ratios; generally lower telecommunications costs	T
g. Lack of mass market/scale economies	Growth as costs drop, use becomes easier, and more widely useful materials become available	—

Figure 6-21. (Continued)

ELECTRONIC ADVANTAGE TO EXPLOIT	MAJOR POSSIBLE ACTION ITEMS	TYPE OF ACTIONS
NEED 5: ACTIVE COMFORT		
h. Capabilities to ease user eye strain and to match user display preferences	Software to enable users to change font sizes and types, reverse background/foreground, etc.	O
i. Capabilities to help user coordinate separated materials	Extension of windowing techniques; hypertext technique applications, etc.	O-T
NEED 9: CONFIDENCE IN SUBSTANCE For all types of transaction systems:		
j. Very high system capacity potential k. Very low error rates l. Very high potential currency m. Great flexibility/expandability	Growth and expansion of applications that exploit these advantages have been underway for many years; normal market factors should continue to support this trend	T
NEED 11: CONTROL OF INFORMATION LAYOUT/ FEATURES, and **NEED 12: CONTROL OF SUBSTANCE PRESENTED**, and **NEED 13: OPERATIONS ON SUBSTANCE**		
n. Size change/magnification/ zoom o. Rotation of solid figures in three dimensions p. Graphics creation, to find and portray patterns q. Color control for coding features r. Multimedia; interactive mixed media s. Powerful search capabilities t. User customization of tables and text u. Windowing to unite materials v. Spin-offs of items to private files w. Aided/automatic indexing	For applications generally, examples of desirable types of actions include: • Improved documentation, probably involving multiple layers of complexity to match user skills, needs, and experience • Improved screen aids and diagnostics; the latter might include interactive, artificial intelligence type elements to assist users • Greater use of graphics to assist users, as well as simple intuitive "linkage" programs to help unite materials from	T-O-I

Figure 6-21. (Continued)

ELECTRONIC ADVANTAGE TO EXPLOIT	MAJOR POSSIBLE ACTION ITEMS	TYPE OF ACTIONS
x. Correction/editing operations y. Computation z. Packaging combinations of materials impractical with print aa. Interactive entries of many types ab. Artistic manipulations of many types	multiple programs and more "what you see is what you get" functional capabilities • A simple way to use a single common program for saving, filing, and (computer-aided) indexing of all materials acquired or prepared	

building customer bases once the underlying technologies have become available. The main user needs addressed are for currency, substance availability, and cost support.

6.5.2.1 Reading: Underlying technologies. For the reading cluster, the required hardware and software technologies and their features are described in Figure 6-22. The figure also suggests the specific electronic weaknesses likely to be overcome or mitigated by these technologies and the strengths utilized. These are indicated in the last column where the numbers and letters shown are those of Figure 6-19.

Enabling developments. First, a full-page-size, high-quality, flat-panel display is the most fundamental requirement, since it offers the best current potential means for providing an electronic display with both quality and adaptability to user position and posture.[9] The features listed in Figure 6-22 would provide an acceptable quality level but not one equal to fairly good print. Because of this limitation, software (as described in the figure) must be utilized to give electronic displays advantages that are large enough to overcome their residual quality weakness.

Second, hardware must be developed to exploit the flat panel *as a reading display.* This implies a family of devices designed with different levels of capabilities, complexity, and cost to serve different

[9] CRTs currently can offer, and may continue to offer, better overall quality, but they have no prospect of being able to be packaged in a page-size form that is adaptable to user position.

Figure 6-22. Reading Cluster Actions: Major Technical Requirements

ELEMENT	FEATURES	WEAKNESSES OVERCOME (Number Items)* ADVANTAGES EXPLOITED (Letter Items)**
ENABLING DEVELOPMENTS		
Flat-panel display	Full page size; 1 million or more pixels; bit-mapped; contrast ratio more than 6:1; good viewing angle; back-lit	1. Portability 2. Adaptability 15. High quality (though not up to that of good print)
Hardware design emphasizing support of "reading-related" functions	As described under **Device Family** entries	As listed below
Reading software	As described below	As listed below
DEVICE FAMILY		
• **Basic Reading Device:** A stand-alone system; essentially read-only; reading controls but no keyboard (or equivalent) general input capability	Software providing: • Fast page turn • Browsing controls • Font size control • Foreground/background reversal • Index search capability	Specific to software: 7. Browsing h. Eye-strain relief Inherent to design: a. Computer memory size/density/lightweight advantages used 3. Equipment requirement (minimized) 4. Power requirements (minimized) b. Use of flat-panel power advantages over print in dark environments 5. Minimal start-up/booting process 6. Physical manipulations kept simple 9. No keyboard/data entry skills needed
• **Advanced Reading Device:** Essentially a small portable computer, with separable display, sketch pad entry capabilities, and design emphasis on "reading-related" activities; connectable (directly or with communications link) to personal (or larger) computer	Software providing above plus: • Annotation/underlining/emphasizing • Windowing • Electronic mail with added features • Database search • Selection of information to spin off to private files; spin-off when connected to personal computer	Specific to software: 8. Easy user annotation, etc. i. User capability to coordinate separated materials c. Convenient high-speed communications d. Convenient access to electronic data s. Powerful search capabilities

Figure 6-22. (Continued)

ELEMENT	FEATURES	WEAKNESSES OVERCOME (Number Items)* ADVANTAGES EXPLOITED (Letter Items)**
	• Aided/automatic indexing (when connected to personal computer)	u. Use of computer windowing capability v. Private file development by spin-off from viewed materials (Benefits from items 5, 6, and 9 of **Basic Reading Device** are largely lost except to the extent that they are made available by means described in analyses of Operations Cluster)
• **Computer Reading Display:** A display physically detachable from a computer, but still linked to it for control and data flow purposes, designed with physical features and controls to support "reading-related"	As above, but with the full capabilities of the computer split appropriately between the reading device and the computer	Exploits all manipulative capabilities of computers

*These items correspond to print relative advantages of Figure 6-19.
**These items correspond to electronic relative advantages of Figure 6-19.

market segments. A three-member example "device family" is shown,[10] with the basic reading device aimed at the mass (Situation IV user) market and the other two devices more appropriate to different segments of Situation I, II, and III users.

Third, reading software must be developed. Here again, a family with several levels of capabilities, control complexity, and cost appears desirable to match the different levels of user skills and interests.

None of the above products is yet in existence, so the device and software descriptions in Figure 6-22 are exemplary only. A Basic

[10] Other family members, such as a game-playing display, are possible. These probably will require different types of input controls and, for multiperson games, may have to be appreciably larger than reading displays. However, for mass market development, the Basic Reader may need to be designed to accept a simple set of controls to permit users to play a variety of one- or perhaps two-person games.

Reader could be viewed as a direct substitute for a book, and one that is very similar in size and shape. It would be designed to be very low cost and operable by users with no computer skills. The Advanced Reader is treated as comparable to a simple portable computer that should be easy for users with "amateur" level skills to employ. It could have a detachable, full-page display with its own controls for "pure" reading and, even when detached for easy adaptability to user posture, might be connected easily to the computer for some types of operations, such as spin-off of materials to private files. The Computer Reader provides a similar set of capabilities in the context of full-scale workstations and more highly skilled users.[11]

Reading software. The features of the reading software are divided somewhat arbitrarily among the basic and advanced reading devices, based on judgments concerning the importance of different capabilities to the target users and the skills needed to use the various capabilities. These features are reviewed briefly below:

- A "clean," fast page turn is needed to avoid the eye strain produced by display changes on most current computer equipment. The inherent change speeds of liquid crystals (the most likely candidate for the display material) should be adequate to meet this need, as evidenced by the small-size, raster scan liquid crystal screens on portable TV sets that several Japanese companies put on the U.S. market early in 1988.
- While the fast page turn may go far toward creating an electronic display browsing capability, much more could be offered to create an electronic advantage. At the simple level, place markers or page markers could be inserted (and removed). More advanced would be the ability to jump to new paragraph headings, or chapter or article titles, or to browse from table to table and figure to figure, or to successive comments, annotations, or editing corrections—or to search for specific words or phrases in a piece of text.
- Font size control and foreground–background reversal already exist in commonly used software; both capabilities offer benefits that print cannot. When color displays are used, changes in screen colors can help relieve eye strain.
- Electronic index search could be based on far more complete cross indexing (perhaps automatically or semiautomatically produced by the publisher/provider) than is practical with print. Desired pages, once located in the index, could be turned to (successively) through

[11] The timing of introduction of reading devices will influence the types of models provided. If there are long delays, decreases in electronic component costs and increases in the general level of computer skills in society could lead to bypassing the Basic Reader.

user operation of a simple control. Cross-referencing similarly could be made more complete and easier to use.

- Underlining, emphasizing, and annotation are already incorporated in a variety of software packages. Hand-written annotation is not yet easy or crisp, but this could be changed by the development of improved scratch pad technology.
- Windowing, electronic mail, and database search all exist and are being improved and, in most cases, simplified.
- Spin-off to private files could become a very valuable capability to some user segments if, or when, the current literature of interest to them becomes available in electronic form. Once started, a variety of forms of software could support the process—for example, automatic or semiautomatic referencing and indexing, improved file organizing and automatic filing systems, and improved search and retrieval. Over time, these processes could have significant impacts on work habits and skill requirements.

In summary, much of the reading software needed already exists in scattered form. Much of the remainder is well within the state of the art. If an adequate potential market arises and is recognized, the main requirement will be that of creating an effective set of integrated packages under relatively simple (and, preferably, intuitive) user control.

6.5.2.2 Reading: Market development actions. A powerful electronic display reading capability will represent a new technology. Like other new technologies, it will require a large number of supporting activities if it is to become widely used. The automobile, for example, required not only roads but also fuel and service stations, financing companies, insurance, licensing agencies, traffic laws, traffic lights, maps, tourist accommodations, and many other new activities. There is no way to predict the totality of these requirements, nor the form in which they may arise. As a result, we will concentrate only on describing the kinds of actions that now seem needed, basing these judgments on trend extrapolation and analogy.

Basic hardware and software. The starting point in the process is the availability of the flat-panel display described earlier. This initially may be offered as a "top-of-the-line" display option for standard work station equipment, or it may be used to gain competitive advantage in the portable and laptop computer markets. At some point, one or more vendors must make a deliberate effort to exploit the panel's capabilities as a reading display. The process may be a "big leap" forward, or it may arise from incremental growth—part of the continuing improvement of computer equipment. Even in the latter case, and perhaps arising when users show signs of employing their computer displays frequently for fairly extensive reading, there must be a decision to design a display with features optimized for reading purposes. To achieve mass market potential, the decision to build a Basic Reader-type display may be a necessary one.

Similar remarks apply to reading software. So many of the desired features already are available that incremental integration would be a likely initial growth pattern. However, here again, a deliberate decision to provide a well-thought-out, integrated package would mark a turning point. Also, and similar to the case of the Basic Reader hardware, basic reading software appears key to development of a mass market of individual customers. In contrast, the private file spin-off feature could have particular appeal to business and professional users.

Software standards. The vendor hardware and software decisions discussed above, and related decisions by publishers/providers, would be greatly facilitated by an environment that offered a reasonable degree of standardization, especially for features where compatibility cannot be achieved economically with software interface techniques. This does not imply a single set of standards, but a limited set of alternatives such as characterized phonograph records some decades ago and VCR cassettes and players more recently. The market can make the final decision, but this process cannot be played out rapidly from a highly fragmented starting position.[12]

The standards themselves need not be designed from scratch but can come from many possible sources. For example, a great deal of work already has been done toward establishing generic standards for publishing manuscripts. Another possible source for some purposes is facsimile standards, especially Group IV Class 3 standards (that cover both recognizing and encoding standard types of alphanumeric information and compressing noncodable information). The requirements for commonality need not be complete, but they must provide enough expectation of stability within significant functions to justify the investments that the leading stakeholders—both providers and users—will have to make.

Since effective reading software does not yet exist, some extensions of current standardization efforts to cover broadly used, reading-related functions would be valuable. On the whole, however, reading software (most likely implemented in silicon) appears to offer excellent opportunities for entrepreneurial and proprietary products.

---

[12] This remark applies most strongly to mass markets. For more specialized business types of applications, company-by-company experiments often will be undertaken even in very fragmented and uncertain conditions; these experiments can lead to identification and validation of the more desirable approaches.

Hardware standards and storage technologies. While hardware standards issues impact primarily on the operations and management areas (sections 6.5.3 and 6.5.4, below), particularly critical to the reading cluster are the roles and relationships of different optical and magnetic storage media in the provision of reading materials.

Optical ROM disks are more rugged and provide greater memory density than any other economical storage medium, and this is likely to continue. Partly because much of the same technology is used with audio disks, manufacture of both the operating equipment and the recorded disks rapidly could become quite low cost.

Optical technologies that would permit users to erase or alter records, or to make optical copies of ROM materials, are scarce and expensive. On a relative cost basis, this is likely to continue for the time scale of this study (five to ten years).

Magnetic (including, potentially, magneto-optic) media offer low-cost, easily manipulated, and reusable storage capabilities. While expected to continue to trail optical media in both capacity and effective life, they are improving steadily and should continue to do so.

These storage technology developments have a number of implications. First, because they are difficult to copy (in optical disk format), optical ROM disks likely will be attractive to publishers/providers; this attitude already has been demonstrated in the case of audio compact disks relative to digital audio tape recorders/players.

However, if sections of reading materials could not be spun off to private files (the equivalent of clipping or copying and then filing newspaper, newsletter or journal items), the potential benefits from electronic reading of business and professional literature would be hurt badly. If copying optical ROM to private files is possible (as is now the case for nonoptical disk formats) the private files are likely to remain on magnetic media for many years to come (owing to the huge installed base of magnetic equipment, the low equipment cost, and the flexibility of using magnetic disks). Once in magnetic form, the files will be simple to recopy.[13]

In the case of mass market users (both Situations III and IV, including home-based general information and recreational usage), the situation has some special features. Except for encyclopedias, some general reference materials, and, perhaps, some anthologies and

[13] It should be noted that a number of different technical advances, such as improved optical character recognition (OCR) devices and measures to provide higher speed facsimile, will also make it easier to produce unauthorized electronic versions of printed materials, independent of any movement towards electronic reading displays. The reading displays will influence the situation mainly by providing a larger potential market for such unauthorized versions.

works of favorite authors, the capacity of optical disks is so large that it can be difficult to use effectively. If the disks are fully loaded with typical reading materials, users may be put in an unacceptable position of having to buy (and pay royalties on) packages of which only a small fraction are of real interest to them.[14]

Needed here is a means to let users come closer to selecting only those materials they want. This could be done by services that selectively copy sections from a master, or by "activating" only those optical segments on a disk for which the user has paid, or an equivalent measure. A more hardware-oriented approach would be to design the disk drives to accept two sizes of disks—a full size for multiple volumes of text and a very small one for individual books, magazines, or journals.[15]

Finally, magnetic media might be used for Basic Readers. Although this would sacrifice some important benefits of the optical disk, including, perhaps, storage of large, multivolume reference texts, it would permit easy electronic downloading of material over telephone lines as well as purchase of disks with smaller increments of contents.

The matter of the roles of optical and magnetic storage media does not have to be settled once and for all (as is more apt to be the result of setting some types of software standards). As technology advances, the benefits of newer equipment and the improved price/performance ratio that can be offered make major changes practical—even if part of the cost is loss of easy access to older materials. However, an interim approach that satisfies enough of the interests of the major stakeholders is important to the market development process.

6.5.2.3 Other actions by major stakeholders.

Resolution of Copyright Issues. Although the current market is very small, a number of major publishers have demonstrated their interest in supplying materials in electronic format through conducting a variety of experiments and through entering into joint ventures with software houses and database operators. There seems little doubt that this interest would grow if electronic reading devices became available *and if* publisher and other information-provider vulnerabilities to losses of revenues from unauthorized copying, and/or excessive

---

[14] This situation already exists for materials such as newspapers, magazines, and journals. Optical disks can greatly increase the problem and extend it to books, where author royalties can become an issue. Note, however, that we do not consider here the emergence of new formats that require expanded memory, such as for graphics, video, voice, or three-dimensional viewing. These may more fully employ optical disk storage capacity.

[15] Note that the problem does not arise from the costs of disk manufacture, which may become low compared to print products. A single book or magazine on a full-size optical disk may be an economically practical, although inefficient, solution.

unauthorized sharing of electronic materials, could be constrained to an acceptable level. An initial requirement, therefore, is a resolution of copyright, royalty, and fair use issues in a manner both acceptable to the main stakeholders—publisher/providers, database operators, hardware and software vendors, retailers, *and end users*—and practical to enforce. (This issue area, and the many problems it raises, has been covered in Chapter 4; it also is discussed further in section 6.5.6, below.)

Selective marketing innovations. Given adequate resolution of copyright issues, market development could proceed by traditional measures supplemented, and eventually amplified, by selective innovations. An exemplar process, presented here to illustrate the needs and not to be considered as a prediction, is the following:

- Expansion of current efforts to package, on optical disks, reference data and texts commonly used by business, professional, and technical personnel, adding software features (such as cross-indexing, browsing, windowing, and data transfer capabilities) to provide extra value.
- Further penetration of technical and professional markets for journals, handbooks, and textbooks, especially for those market segments that can benefit from electronic manipulation capabilities (such as three-dimensional displays, packaging of data and computational programs with text, and extraction of materials to private files).

The markets for these products already are experienced with personal computers and are becoming increasingly well equipped with them. The process described would gradually convert the reading activity (where electronics now is weak) to more closely resemble a transaction process (where electronics is very strong). Several new types of actions could support such a change:

- Establishment and/or support and servicing of a wide range of interest group networks, thereby utilizing the communications capabilities of computers to improve the currency of materials.
- Development, with or by hardware vendors, of library reading systems to make heavily used materials more easily available in reading rooms.[16]

---

[16] The same approach would be even more valuable to *libraries* with regard to archival materials. However, the economics here are not likely to appear favorable to publishers, so this goal may require some combination of cooperative efforts, subsidies, or a reflection in the prices paid to publishers of the savings accruing to libraries.

Focus on Situation IV users. In general, the competitive pressures on Situation I and II users can help publishers/providers build markets in work activities. For the mass home and recreational markets, these pressures are weak and users are less prepared for electronic reception of information. As a result, the initial markets for electronic display of reading materials probably has to be that segment of Situation IV users that already are employing reading devices at work. Traditional types of actions would include:

- Establishing multiple means for user acquisition of materials, such as special subject-oriented "reading clubs," "disk of the month clubs," or popular author "complete works"; use of retail and mail- or electronic-order outlets that offer both sales and rentals; encouragement of library reading room systems (to increase exposure of potential readers); and electronic delivery of products over telephone lines.
- Increasing consumer confidence by improving software product reviews; this means that these reviews must explicitly be related to required user skill levels, and must cover carefully the quality of support materials provided, such as documentation and "help" mechanisms.
- Encouraging and supporting consistent practices that permit prospective buyers to test software and review documentation prior to purchase decisions.

More innovative actions include:

- Sponsoring and supporting publications that emphasize the graphics and image capabilities of computers (ranging from comic books to "how-to" publications and travel book–atlas combinations),
- Similarly encouraging use of simple manipulative capabilities for one-person games, and
- Expanding both of the above actions to incorporate animation and limited motion where useful.

More difficult problem areas. Electronic weaknesses in substance availability (with regard to mass market materials) and in some aspects of cost support (available to specific types of mass media print publications) may require innovative approaches. Actions may follow a pattern common in past new technology introductions—starting with near replications of applications already familiar to the potential markets, and only slowly adding radically new elements. The subjects of concern include:

- Dealing effectively with the "memory disk overcapacity" problem mentioned earlier.

- Developing formats for effective advertising vehicles, especially for publication types where print versions now rely heavily on advertising.[17]
- Developing new formats that can help electronics compete with those types of print publications that employ features electronics *will not have* in the time frame we are examining. Newspapers, for example, use page sizes far larger than those that common electronic displays will have, and they benefit from these larger sizes.
- Eventually, developing entirely new popular formats that use electronic capabilities in ways we cannot yet visualize.

Although some problems remain unsolved, most actions described in this section are extensions of what publishers/providers have been trying to do in recent years. For these efforts to be effective, other stakeholders also must be involved:

- *Retailers* must participate by providing sales and rental stores and, perhaps, user-selected disk "loading" services.
- *Libraries* can speed the process by encouraging the development of reading room systems.
- *Database and telecommunications network operators*[18] also can facilitate progress by developing consolidated electronic mail directories and cross-system interfaces; similarly developing consolidated database directories, with content descriptors better than those now available; developing improved interfaces and overlays to permit simple searching by untrained or lightly trained users across major, high-use databases; and starting to offer popular, extensive text materials
- *The government* could contribute by avoiding actions that are likely to raise the costs or lower the benefits of electronic presentations (such as the 1986 FCC proposal to apply interstate access charges to value-added service providers[19]). Government could also contribute by subsidizing acquisition of minimal reading equipment and/or access to socially important electronic information. These subsidizing actions may be highly unlikely, but they have precedents in the

[17] The severity of this competitive disadvantage is indicated by the Digital Information Group, which notes: "About 60% of information publishing revenue came from advertising sales in 1988. Less than 1% of electronic information sales come from advertising during the same period." [*Information Industry Factbook,* 1989/90 edition (Stamford, CT: Digital Information Group, 1989).]

[18] Although the actions listed are attributed to these operators, others such as publishers could also be involved.

[19] This comment is not intended to imply judgment of the FCC proposal with regard to equity or overall social/economic desirability; it simply notes the likely impact of such a move on the subject under study.

French subsidizing of Minitel and in the traditional government support of public libraries.

With the exception of the government subsidizing actions just above, the items described are for the most part already underway in at least limited form.

6.5.3 Operations Cluster

The operations cluster is concerned with a variety of measures that can extend or simplify use of the computers associated with electronic displays. Returning to the analogy with automobiles used earlier, this cluster emphasizes computer equivalents of automotive advances such as automatic starters and chokes, hydraulic brakes and steering assist, and automatic transmissions—all means for making cars both more useful and simple enough to drive that they can be handled by almost anyone.

There are, however, some important differences. From the beginning, automobiles were consumer products; the computer was, and still is, primarily a business or work environment product. Significant efforts to meet consumer and "amateur user" requirements are relatively recent. They also are weak compared to the efforts devoted to meeting business needs, and to exploiting technical advances in order to deal with more and more complex problems. As a result, present trends are split, with some operations being simplified and made more intuitive and others becoming more complicated (for the lightly trained user). In general, the mass market target set for this study requires focusing on the simplification side of the pattern, although with recognition that the path to simplicity often starts with complexity.[20]

6.5.3.1 Operations actions: electronic weaknesses. Since a relatively small number of electronic weaknesses are involved, they will be reviewed individually. Thereafter, electronic strengths to be exploited will be covered in small groups. The weaknesses include the following:

[20] Most new applications of significance start out in relatively complex form. As feedback from users clarifies their needs and interests, and as the growing power of computers makes it easier to "hide" the true complexity of operations from the users, newer versions of the applications increasingly appear simpler. This applies even to what we now consider very simple devices, as is well illustrated in Henry Petroski's *The Pencil: A History of Design and Circumstance* (New York: Alfred A. Knopf, 1990).

Portability. Portable computers have been improving rapidly in performance and shrinking slowly in size and weight. The reading cluster items can add to their utility and, because the reading hardware designs must place more emphasis on lesser bulk and weight, to their portability. Improved battery capacity could further liberate these devices by reducing the frequency with which they must be connected to external power sources.

Start-up requirements. Because heavy users of computers already often leave them on at all times, what appears to be needed (remembering that the reason start-up is viewed as a weakness is its inconvenience) are some design features to encourage this practice. These features might include improved automatic standby, with low energy consumption; safer and more user-friendly "restore activity" codes; and surge protection that is effective at all times.

Reduced requirement for keyboard. While speech recognition may relieve or eliminate this requirement in the long run, keyboards are likely to be needed for well beyond the time scale of this study. The use of keyboards can be decreased slightly by a number of software and hardware input aids, such as menus and icons, cursors, and mouse and (improved) joystick controls. For annotation purposes, a vastly improved sketch pad entry system could be useful. For example, a pressure-sensitive overlay on the display screen could be turned off when not in use, or a separate sketch pad with ability to move entries to desired positions on the display could be useful. However, keyboard skills still will be needed, except for very simple operations.

Operating systems. Operating systems have tended to get more complicated over time, in part owing to the need to manage more types of resources and configurations (floppy and hard disks, single- and multiple-user and networked systems, a wider variety of classes and types of peripheral equipment) and in part to efforts to expand system performance capabilities. Most of these configurations and many of the newer capabilities are of little interest to the relatively unskilled—individual users who will have to form the major market if electronics is to become the dominant display medium.

So far, the only approach that appears to be comfortable to the least skilled users is that offered by the Macintosh. Although this approach may be too limited to satisfy all the interests of a wide spectrum of users, it suggests the type of requirement that may arise in the future.

What may be needed, for all types of equipment aimed at the personal computer market, is a family of operating systems. These would range from a simple, limited, highly intuitive (and probably largely image-oriented) system through several more advanced levels, up to the professional computer scientist level. Individuals could then select the level appropriate to their needs and abilities, advancing up the scale if/as their needs and abilities increased. This schema *does not* imply a need for *multiple* operating systems, but rather a need for multiple subsets of a single system, with multiple sets of documentation. The simpler levels could benefit by being supplemented with improved help/diagnostic screens and simple cancel–return–recover capabilities (for easy recovery from an amateur mistake or accident), and, perhaps, by having some functions disabled by removable instructions.

File management. The file management problem also is multilayered, but it is more complex. At the lowest level, where limited records and documents are to be filed and stored, the Macintosh approach (including HyperCard-type features) probably offers a reasonable, simple, and easily understood path to be followed. At higher levels, at least two problems are encountered:

- **Problem 1**: For the types of private information files that reading devices will enable (through downloading from reading materials), there exist no fully satisfactory organizing principles. The primary file structures now in use—hierarchical, relational, and object oriented—are inadequate except for narrow subject areas. An object-oriented approach, which appears most suitable for extension to handle more general knowledge, is extremely complex to establish and maintain.
- **Problem 2**: Except for specialists, few existing or potential users have ever received training in file or information or knowledge organization during their general education. We appear to assume that skills in these areas are "natural" ones. This situation applies as much to the organization of print materials as it does to that of electronic materials. However, the problem is more obvious and will become more critical with electronics, if only because its use can vastly expand the amount of (potentially) useful material that individuals can access and store. With print materials, it is also far easier *now* to "tag" items of personal interest by remembering noncontent features (such as appearance or related events) than it is with electronic information.

The first problem, lack of organizing principles, applies mainly to advanced users and information service organizations. This problem appears to have no satisfactory answer at the present time. The second problem at least can be alleviated through a variety of events and measures. For the most simple types of use, the Macintosh approach seems likely to provide an adequate mechanism. For more complex situations, growth in computer power and in disk capacity will enable utilization of more advanced filing techniques. All application programs and files can reside in the same memory, permitting consistent filing practices and easier construction of master indices and file search databases.

In addition, movement to change filing, for user-selected materials, from a simple filepath/filename (or equivalent) operation toward a largely menu-driven, form-filling process might help. The entries could cover both formal items (type of material, source or destination, general subject, date, filing date-time stamp) that the computer would enter automatically to the extent practical, and user-generated "association" tags presented in menu or HyperCard-type form. Also helpful would be incorporation, as practical, of simple automatic or aided indexing by key words or concepts and automatic computer construction of master indices.

While it cannot fully substitute for improved filing and file identification techniques, a fairly powerful second approach is available—computer full-text indexing accompanied by simple but effective search procedures. This is essentially a transfer, to the personal computer level, of methods already in widespread use in large databases, such as LEXIS/NEXIS© and DIALOG©. Effective examples already existed in the late 1980s, one of them being LOTUS's MAGELLAN® program.

Our review of electronic weaknesses related to operations continues:

Training. Training is a major aspect of operations, but discussion will be deferred to the training cluster, below.

Backup. For most users, backup is at least an inconvenience and in some cases a fairly complicated, time-consuming activity. Ideally, backup should be automatic, with the computer requesting it whenever an application is exited and/or at timed intervals—and always before equipment can be turned off. It should be initiated by a single instruction and should require no further user action other than, on instruction, inserting any independent backup storage device being used. While automatic backup should be a user option, it should be so easy that it seldom is declined.

6.5.3.2 Operations actions: electronic strengths. The electronic strengths that might be exploited cover the full range of computer manipulation capabilities. A useful way to look at them is to build clusters in terms of user interests. For our purposes, this means relating them to the types of user activities in which they are likely to be most valuable. This is done in Figure 6-23.

The electronic advantages noted in Figure 6-23 are rarely employed

Figure 6-23. Electronic Manipulative Advantages Grouped by User Types

(The letters labelling electronic advantages are from Figure 6-21)

POTENTIAL INTEREST TO ALL TYPES OF USERS*

p. Graphics capabilities
s. Search capabilities
u. Windowing to unite information display
x. Correction
y. Computation
ab. Artistic manipulation

POTENTIAL INTEREST TO ALL WORK-ENVIRONMENT USERS

l. High level of currency
q. Color control for coding information
t. Customization of tables and text
v. Spin-off of selected materials to private files
w. Aided/automatic indexing
aa. Interactive entries of many types

PRIMARILY OF INTEREST TO PROFESSIONAL, SCIENTIFIC, AND TECHNICAL USERS

n. Size change/magnification/zoom capability**
o. Solid figure rotation in three dimensions**
z. Custom packaging of combinations of materials

PRIMARILY OF INTEREST TO BUSINESS AND COMMERCIAL USERS

j. High system capacities
k. Very low error rates
m. High degree of flexibility to expand system coverages

*Advantages for work purposes in work environments may apply mainly to recreation in Situation IV, the home general information/recreational environment.
**Potentially of interest in home recreation markets.

singly but are packaged in the form of applications packages. Excluding highly specialized and customized programs, we can note two historical trends:

- Among more mature application types, such as word processing and spreadsheets, the main trend has been toward simplification of the essentials, but without loss of extra benefits to experienced users. Even when they incorporate new capabilities, the more recent versions of these programs are more intuitive, easer to understand, and simpler to use than the older ones. At the same time, many of these programs provide more skilled users with greater flexibility and personalization capabilities, such as through the use of macros.
- Newer types of applications, and especially those that integrate rather different application areas (such as early systems for desktop publishing) tend to be far more difficult to employ without considerable training.

This pattern is fairly common with new technologies; one might anticipate the continual emergence of new, complex "leading edge" applications that gradually are simplified as experience is gained and penetration of new market segments is sought. For the purposes of our study, the actions required to exploit electronic manipulative advantages would focus on speeding the simplification process if, as, or when the capabilities of the reading cluster become available.

The required actions resemble those needed for the operating and file management systems cluster:

- Greater use of multilevel documentation, even early in the life cycle of new types of applications, to ease the process of self-training. For example, most word processing programs are targeted at professional secretaries. The documentation tends not to recognize adequately that a growing number of users are not interested, at least initially, in many of the capabilities of the programs.
- Improved "help" screens and means to diagnose and recover easily from mistakes.
- Improved, simple, and intuitive "linkage" programs that allow users to combine and organize materials from a variety of simple, independent programs rather than the typically more complex integrated programs for this purpose. Also useful for some applications, and already quite widely available, is the opposite approach: designing simple, special purpose overlays that operate by using the capabilities of more complex, more general purpose programs.
- Greater commonality in the terms and symbols used for common operations to ease transitions from one program to another. This may be extremely difficult to achieve in the short term because of vendor interests in maintaining exclusive software applications and/or user interface features.
- A means for easily accessing and employing a single, common program or technique for saving and filing all materials acquired or produced, to mitigate some of the file management problem discussed earlier.

Some aspects of these action areas are discussed further in the training cluster (section 6.5.5, below).

6.5.4 Management Cluster

Management-related electronic weaknesses fall primarily under the need for Confidence in Format. They also include concerns about legal status and liabilities and the establishment and maintenance of good work practices. The importance of these subjects is greatest in the work environments of Situations II and III. They include the following:

File and program management and backup. There are two concerns here. First, personal files should be well organized, backed up, and indexed so that materials won't be lost, and that appropriate[21] ones can be accessed during the absence, or after the departure of, the individual involved. Second, personally generated application programs should be well checked and documented, so that quality control can be exercised and the programs (to the extent appropriate) can be employed effectively by others.[22]

Training. (See discussion in the training cluster, section 6.5.5, below.)

Legal status. (See socioeconomic cluster, section 6.5.6, below.)

Records life and storage. Although not yet life-tested in use, optical ROM appears likely to be the first computer memory medium that will compete with print in terms of general ruggedness and useful life. However, ROM has limited applications; and the technologies that now seem most likely to be used for write-once and for erasable optical disks appear to be more "tender" (especially the erasable disk technologies). Also, as noted earlier, the equipment involved will almost certainly be quite expensive for the period of interest to us. Accordingly, although the weakness may be alleviated somewhat, there presently is no known means for overcoming it.

Records equipment obsolescence. Processing equipment traditionally has been partly protected from obsolescence by upwards compatibility and software emulation techniques. This has been possible because the rapid growth in processing capabilities has allowed part of the added resources to be devoted to this protective activity, and the market has demanded such action. There has been no equivalent in the area of memory, where the technologies, the media, and the equipment have all changed over time and seem likely to continue to do so. As a result, a lot of existing records are becoming difficult—or even impossible—to access and use efficiently.

In these circumstances, the only mitigating measures involve

---

[21] The term *appropriate* refers to files and programs that properly belong to an organization or, say, to a surviving spouse. As with paper items, there may be personal materials that others should not be able to access and/or use.

[22] The file management and backup areas were discussed earlier in section 6.5.3. Given advances of the type discussed (or equivalents), both these and the program checking problem are matters of applying good management practices. The same is partly true of program documentation, where the problem is eased by the decline in personal programming (among most users of concern) as packaged programs are used increasingly. However, there still is a need for improved documentation aids to encourage more consistent and better quality documentation. All of these are old problems and a great amount of relevant experience is available.

providing means to transfer old records to new media. Here the hardware vendors can assist (as IBM made plans to do in connection with its introduction of smaller floppy disks). Special service organizations may also help. The latter are apt (but not certain) to arise if a significant market develops. This has not happened to date, so the present situation leaves the weakness largely unsolved. (Note that, even if these measures do arise, there will be considerable expense involved in replacing files that may represent years of work. Also, considerable management and organizing skills may be needed to decide which of the older files should be copied to the new format.)

Obsolescence of skills. (See the training cluster, section 6.5.5, below.)

Compatibility of equipment. Compatibility between both equipment models produced by a single vendor and equipment produced by different vendors has been a subject of intense interest in recent years. Largely because of market demands, a great deal of progress has been made, using both hardware and software approaches. At present, it seems that this problem will be adequately solved within the next five years for the types of equipment of interest to us.[23] However, the current trend toward greater compatibility could be stalled to at least some extent if a successful manufacturer should happen to gain a technical edge and decide not to cooperate in the process.

For the management cluster, in general, electronics' manipulative capabilities can make many of the needed actions feasible, especially as aided by continuing progress in computer technology.

6.5.5 Education and Training Cluster

This cluster targets three action areas: the need for considerable investment of time and personal effort in training before enough skills are acquired to make a computer useful; the rapid obsolescence of skills on the heels of rapid technical advances, making extension of skills and retraining almost a continuing requirement; and the financial costs of the two training requirements.

These action areas are characteristic of a period when new technology is being introduced on a broad front. Most of our primary educational institutions are public and reactive in nature, and tend to be slow to recognize and act on what is happening. At least part of this lag is caused by the problems they face in financing a new activity and training their own staffs. As a result, alternative ways to meet the

---

[23] This statement does not apply to potential new types of equipment, such as reading devices; here, based on historical experience, initial incompatibility among types seems more likely.

need arise, but these often involve costs beyond the means of many potential users.

Based on past experience and current trends, the general pattern one can anticipate is as follows:

1. Public school systems *gradually* will incorporate at least some elementary computer and keyboard training at most schools and for all students.
2. Private and public universities, colleges, and trade schools will include fairly general advanced computer training as part of their professional education curricula, and more specialized computer training in subprofessional areas, such as for secretaries and medical technicians.
3. Government and other sponsored retraining activities will add increasing amounts of computer-related materials to their programs.
4. Individual companies, especially larger ones, will continue to provide or sponsor a wide variety of work-related computer training.
5. A tremendous amount of training, particularly in moderately advanced application areas, will be made available through special short courses, seminars, workshops, and similar types of activities offered by a wide range of types of organizations.
6. Hardware vendors will continue to simplify the operation of their equipment as part of their efforts to expand their markets; this will be most visible at the lower end of their product lines.
7. With similar goals, software vendors will simplify the routine use of their products as they gain experience in specific application areas. Whether they simultaneously and consistently will improve their documentation and tutorials is less certain.
8. Self-education and peer education will continue to be major sources of training at all levels of experience.

6.5.5.1 Education and training: user situation impacts. Users in all the situations we have been considering will benefit from the increased computer training public school systems will offer (1), and/or from participation in those formal retraining programs (3) that include computer experience.

Situation I users, who have strong motivations and operate in a favorable economic environment, will rely on specialized training by private and public education institutions (2), company programs (4), and, to a lesser extent, seminars (5) and self-/peer education (8).

Situation II users, also with strong motivations but more diffuse needs, will rely on experience gained during their professional education (2) supplemented with company programs (4), short courses and seminars (5), and self-/peer education (8). If, for any reason (such as age cohort or disadvantaged background), users have not been trained in computers, they will depend on their companies for support, or they may have to make a large (and not entirely discretionary) investment in personal training.

Situation III users often will have gained basic training in their education and/or work. For home work types of applications, they will be dependent on software vendors (7) and self-/peer education supplemented by seminars and short courses (perhaps sponsored by a local computer club or society). If not previously trained, they will be even more dependent on hardware and software vendors (6 and 7) to get started.

Situation IV users have the minimum resources available and the weakest motivations. Unless trained at school or work, the only source that most users will have for developing the skill level needed is self-/peer education (8); this will be made easier if hardware and software vendors (6 and 7) have done a good job at simplification and explanation.

6.5.5.2 Education and training: actions. Examples of the types of actions that could speed growth in the use of electronic displays are as follow:

Government actions: These include (1) direct or indirect subsidization of equipment and software for public schools and/or students, (2) subsidization of minimal equipment for, and limited access to, socially important information sources by individual users (as discussed earlier), and (3) support of the development of improved self-education techniques, using the computer, itself, as the primary training tool.

Hardware/software vendor actions: These cover (1) equipment and operating/files management system designs, especially for the low-price end of product lines, that are simpler to use and more intuitive (as discussed earlier), (2) improved, multilevel applications documentation and tutorials, and better screen aids and diagnostics (also described earlier), and (3) improved self-training techniques (as mentioned under government actions).

These items have concentrated on increasing the accessibility of computer experience and facilitating easier and more effective self-training. Limited examples of all the measures already exist in the United States or elsewhere.

6.5.6 Socioeconomic Cluster

The most critical element of this cluster is the selection of appropriate measures for the protection of intellectual property (e.g., the copyright–patent issue area), but the cluster is also concerned with the legal status of electronic records and with achieving widespread availability of desired materials in the face of some competitive economic advantages that print versions currently have.

6.5.6.1 Intellectual property protection. Since this subject is discussed extensively in Chapter 4, it is only summarized briefly here. A number of means are available for the protection of intellectual property within the United States, and these already are being applied to software and computer delivery of information. Within the U.S. fair use practices, payment of royalties through database operators or organizations such as the Copyright Clearance Center, and licensing of software seem to be respected increasingly in the educational, library, and business markets. Extension of the mechanisms may be all that is needed for satisfactory resolution of fair use, copyright, and royalty issues in these markets.

The at-home mass market seems likely to pose greater problems. Unless purchase prices are quite low, individuals have strong incentives to make copies of materials that they expect to use frequently. Analogs for this are audio tapes and computer programs, where unauthorized copying has been endemic. For mostly "one-time" use materials, such as electronic recreational "books," incentives for copying will be weaker. However, electronics can be placed at a great market disadvantage if a number of present legitimate print practices are not preserved in the electronic format. These include personal loaning and borrowing of materials, and their availability at public and/or lending (rental) libraries. With regard to the last of these, an example is furnished by videocassettes, for which low rental costs have discouraged widespread unauthorized user copying. However, this may be more difficult with electronic books, where longer typical rental periods may make it difficult to keep prices sufficiently low to inhibit copying. For some types of home materials, publishers may try to incorporate hardware/software copy-protect mechanisms; this practice would be similar to what software program publishers have done in the past and what audio publishers have been trying to do with regard to audio digital tape equipment. In general, such efforts have not been very successful; publishers, therefore, face some difficult pricing and policy questions in dealing with mass home market electronic presentation products.

The dominant actor in this area is government, acting through legislation and court decisions. This is a slow process and a difficult one to hasten until a subject has become widely recognized as being critical. Being reactive rather than proactive, government action will tend to be most rapid when complaints and difficulties between stakeholders are not too critical or vociferous. This suggests that the steps most likely to be effective for increasing the pace of electronic penetration are a form of "self-help." This self-help would be aimed at resolving issues without government intervention and/or developing support to bring an issue area before government with a relatively unified position on how it should be handled.

While this process is limited by both antitrust and competitive considerations, a wide variety of industry and interindustry agreements are practical, sometimes facilitated by government sponsorship. The most common application is in the development of standards, but here the word "standards" should be viewed in the broad sense of including a range of business practices. In general terms, if industry can deal with its own issues through a process that provides for participation by all stakeholders (including, when appropriate, consumer as well as business representatives), then progress often will be both sounder and more rapid than relying primarily on government action.

6.5.6.2 Legal status. Many additional legal subjects also are of concern, such as the following:

- The validity and acceptability, in different situations, of electronics records without paper backup which, in turn, can involve (1) means to assure records have not been altered in any way, and (2) an adequate readable life of electronic materials (including assurance of the availability of equipment to do the reading);
- The applicability, again in different situations, of other legal paper-analogs such as slander, verification techniques (including equivalents of signatures and witnesses), and illegal file entry or use;
- Transnational data flow regulation or restriction; and
- Many others.

The agenda will continue to grow as electronic materials are used in previously unforeseen ways.

6.5.6.3 Economic issues. We have discussed a number of economic factors: the importance of developing a successful format for electronic advertising if electronics is to compete with print magazines and newspapers; the competitive need to have electronic equivalents of the current "free" library services available for printed materials; and training costs. The major remaining items concern equipment and materials costs.

The general requirements in this area are as follow:

Materials costs. For recreational and general information reading materials, the user costs probably will have to be comparable to or less than current equivalents. Even if the electronic versions have some advantages from the start, it will take time for the market to recognize and employ these advantages effectively. However, for successful new formats that extend (or have no) current equivalents, higher user costs should be acceptable.

For business materials, and especially those that meet user needs that are difficult or impossible to meet with print, higher user costs are not likely to constitute major barriers.

Popular references, such as encyclopedias, also potentially can justify at least somewhat higher user costs than print equivalents because of their greater ease of updating, convenience, and use effectiveness (arising from better indexing, cross-indexing, and other features). Similar remarks apply to many home work publications.

Materials currency. For some types of publications, such as newspapers, publication speed is critical. For electronics to compete *directly*, it may have to be possible to manufacture large numbers of reproductions both cheaply and within a period of hours.

Equipment cost. The user cost for a Basic Reader must be very low. Eventually, one or more Readers per household member will be needed since, if the reading device is to compete with easily shared print publications (such as newspapers), conflicts over use of equipment by several people at the same time must be avoided. However, this very low-cost requirement applies only to serving extremely large markets, which implies very large scale, mass production of the Basic Reader equipment. Earlier in the penetration process, when both demand and production levels are smaller, the majority of users of reading devices are likely to be in work situations where cost sensitivity is apt to be lower and benefits more obvious.

Meeting the user cost criteria will, at a minimum, involve mass production of both equipment and many types of information materials. This level of production, in turn, suggests that a reasonable degree of standardization of reading device designs, disk media, and disk-loading processes will have to arise if electronics is to be successful. If either the cost or production speed requirements for competing with particular types of current print products (for example, newspapers) cannot be met, then alternative electronic formats will be needed that will enable effective indirect competition.

The actions discussed here cover a wide range with regard to how likely, how fast, and in what form they (or equivalents in terms of impacts) may become accomplished. In section 6.6 we look at the implications of some of these differences and seek to derive an overall sense of the status, potential, and most critical elements influencing the future of electronic displays.

6.6 THE CRITICAL ACTION AREAS

Are current improvements in electronics enough to erode print dominance in the presentation of information in our society? In some areas, perhaps. Many steps already being taken as part of the normal electronics growth pattern address the barriers and exploit the advantages we have identified; further changes are likely to arise from the continuation of current trends, or from adoption of existing print precedents and other analogs. On the negative side, however, some action areas are relatively intractable, in the sense that conceivable or possible steps are weak, or provide incomplete solutions, or face difficult implementation environments. Finally, some possible actions are particularly critical because they are prerequisites of yet other important steps.

In this final section, we first consider the potential of electronics relative to print in terms of several perspectives. Can electronics dominate in meeting the major user needs? Can it become superior in supporting a wider range of different user activities? In addition, what is the potential for closing the various user group need gaps described in section 6.4? Thereafter, we look at the more difficult (that is, more intractable or critical) action areas mentioned above. We conclude with a brief summation of the competitive situation between electronics and print.

6.6.1 Toward the Future

Assuming a reasonable level of progress in implementation of the actions we have reviewed (or equivalents) and successful development of an economical, high-quality, flat-panel display,[24] Figure 6-24 and

[24] There already has been some progress in developing such displays. As of early 1988, miniature Japanese TV sets were available with good quality, 5.6 square inch, liquid crystal color displays having 85,000 color pixels (equivalent to 256,000 black-and-white pixels). Past experience suggests approximately a three-year size-doubling period if advances are pursued vigorously. This would lead in about six years to a 1 million pixel black-and-white display with a text area equal to that of a typical paperback book.

Figure 6-24. Toward the Future: Potential Dominance in Meeting Generic User Needs

USER NEED	PRIMARY REASONS FOR PROSPECTIVE STATUS
PRINT REMAINS GENERALLY DOMINANT	
2. Convenience in Operating	Electronic advantages vastly extend user capabilities over those possible with print, but use of these advantages requires new training and skills. These new requirements constitute a major inconvenience. Doing with electronics only what can be done with print would avoid most of the inconvenience, but only at very high cost in foregone benefits.
6. Confidence in Format	Electronic advances are arising at a very rapid pace, opening up new options and making existing skills, hardware, and software obsolete. This already has led to the extinction of some types of equipment and skills, and to confusion over what equipment and techniques will be used widely in the future. The advances and uncertainties will continue, as will the negative impacts on Confidence in the (tools of the) Electronic Format.
PRINT REMAINS DOMINANT IN IMPORTANT SELECTED AREAS	
7. Cost Support	Print has a variety of traditional sources of cost "subsidies" that electronics may not be able to match. Advertising is a good example in that the very types of control that give electronics its strengths may be employable by users to defeat the purposes of advertising. This would enable print to continue its dominance in advertising-dependent media.
8. Substance Availability	Simple inertia will give print dominance in substance availability for a long time to come. This does not imply substance inadequacy for electronics, which may or may not be present at a given time.
10. Static Impact and Information Density	Advantages in static absolute visual quality and in range of practical display sizes will enable print to continue its dominance in a number of narrow areas, such as art books, posters, maps, and large diagrams.
ELECTRONICS GRADUALLY BECOMES DOMINANT ON AN OVERALL BASIS	
1. Physical Convenience 4. Passive Comfort 5. Active Comfort	In these three related areas, electronic strengths can be expected to grow while few changes are anticipated for print. Print will retain a basic quality advantage but electronic capacity, flexibility, and manipulative capabilities can be used to achieve better overall ergonomics once

Figure 6-24. (Continued)

USER NEED	PRIMARY REASONS FOR PROSPECTIVE STATUS
	a full-page-size flat-panel display of adequate quality becomes available. Thereafter, residual print advantages (such as legal status, social acceptability) will begin to be outweighed by electronic advantages for this set of user needs.
ELECTRONICS RETAINS CURRENT DOMINANCE	
3. Timeliness/Currency 9. Confidence in Substance 11. Control of Information Layout and Presentation Features 12. Control of Substance Presented 13. Operations on Substance	Continuation of very strong existing trends should keep increasing the value of electronics in all these areas.

Figure 6-25 look, respectively, at potential future dominance patterns of electronics and print for meeting generic user needs and for supporting different user activities.

Figure 6-24 (which is similar to Figure 6-1 in section 6.1) suggests that, although electronics has some inherent long-term disadvantages relative to print (such as a need for display equipment, poorer absolute display quality, and a more limited range of practical display sizes), these are in many respects less important than some current electronics deficiencies that are at least partly transient. In particular, training and skill requirements (to benefit from electronic strengths) and uncertainties introduced by the speed of electronic hardware advances (that are critical to the future strength of electronics) currently act to weaken electronics' position in some key need attributes.

Unless or until alleviated, these weaknesses can, at a minimum, act as a brake on electronics' speed of penetration into new, prospective, mass-oriented information activities. Penetration speed also will be limited by other sources of inertia, such as the lack of widespread availability of different types of substance in electronic format, the need for more completely defined legal doctrine, and a variety of marketing factors.

Thus, even under the most favorable of circumstances for electronics, print will maintain dominance in attributes critical to success in some important media. Despite these problems, however, electronics could, within a moderate timeframe, become the "rationally

Figure 6-25. Future User Activities: Potential Status of Electronic and Print Presentations

ACTIVITY	ELECTRONICS POTENTIALLY SUPERIOR FOR:	PRINT SUPERIOR INDEFINITELY FOR:
TEXT ACTIVITIES		
Work-related reading	Business, professional, administrative and other	Some publications types strongly dependent on advertising support or on large display sizes
Standard reference usage	All references with large numbers of, and/or complexly interrelated, and/or frequently updated entries	Small, easily filed/found lists; some pocket-portable materials
Recreational uses	Reading; single-person games and simulations; new formats and multi-media	Multi-person (board-type) games; art books and works of many types
Recording/ inputting of all types	Almost all substantial materials—data, transactions, letters, memos, etc.	Minor materials—short notes and lists, archival records (except within well-prepared organizations)
GENERAL SEARCH		
All types	All types of substantial searches; all searches of remote (electronic) sources	Very limited general searches of local sources
DATA OPERATIONS		
All types	Most aspects of use of all types of data	Portable materials of size larger than reasonable display size—such as large maps, diagrams, and plans

superior"—but not necessarily the "market superior"—means for viewing and using information in a very large majority of information-related activities.[25]

Figure 6-25 illustrates some of these points in more detail. This figure (seen previously as Figure 6-2) considers only the operational aspects of the two formats and the various user activities, ignoring many of the partly transient and inertial weaknesses for the sake of concentrating on the longer-term future. The figure, therefore, focuses on the "rationally superior but not necessarily market superior" potential.

[25] Clanchy, *supra*, note 5, provides an excellent description of how slow the pace of transition was in moving from an oral tradition for maintaining records to a written tradition—a move we now certainly would regard as a very rational one!

A third way to review the impacts of possible actions is in terms of their influences on the perceived need gaps described in Figure 6-18 (section 6.4). Using a judgmental analysis and weighing changes in "extent met" by "importance," we can estimate roughly that the set of actions described can reduce the gaps perceived by each of the user groups by an average of 50 to 60 percent. The size of the current perceived gap increases with user situation number, roughly doubling between Situations II (Moderately-Paced/Deliberate Work) and IV (General Purpose/Recreational Home). Accordingly, users in Situation IV, constituting the main market for mass media, still are not likely to view themselves as being truly well served. To a considerable extent, the residual gaps are the result of continuing electronic weaknesses in the action areas that we described earlier as the more intractable ones; we now turn to these areas.

6.6.2 Critical Action Areas

The more critical action areas listed in Figure 6-26 reiterate electronics' key weaknesses with regard to future competition with print. In all other action areas, there is strong support from existing trends and/or well-established precedents or analogs for effective actions favorable to electronics. The areas of difficulty can be grouped into a few general categories, which follow.

6.6.2.1 Technological uncertainties.* Technological uncertainties have arisen primarily from the high speed with which technical advances have been and are continuing to be made. These uncertainties are expressed in many ways; some important ones are lack of standards in many technical/operational areas, rapid obsolescence and displacement of different technical approaches to designing and building equipment, rapid changes in software concepts and implementations, obsolescence of specific personal skills, and quite different technologies competing for the same future functional roles. These uncertainties threaten to inflict direct future costs on users and, thereby, inhibit some forms of more aggressive planning.

Cumulative nature of computer operations. Over time, both institutions and individual users build or acquire, learn, modify and extend programs, and store increasing amounts of data of value—that is, these processes are cumulative ones. Also, these processes involve dollar costs and require, from the individuals involved, personal effort

* See Figure 6-26, items 1.2, 3.3, 4.2, and 4.3.

Figure 6-26. Status of More Critical Action Areas

1. NO ANTICIPATED PRACTICAL SOLUTION WITHIN TIME FRAME for:
- 1.1 Long-term basis for organizing files/knowledge
- 1.2 Long-life, erasable-memory materials with low-cost entry/reading devices
- 1.3 Low-cost, practical electronic displays in wide range of sizes
- 1.4 Elimination of need for keyboard skills

2. CRITICAL TECHNOLOGY ADVANCE REQUIRED:
- 2.1 Full-page, high-quality, lightweight flat-panel display

3. ONLY LIMITED OR PARTIAL SOLUTION AVAILABLE regarding:
- 3.1 Reduction of high investment (time, effort, money) in training; slower skills obsolescence
- 3.2 Electronic equivalent of print advertising
- 3.3 Improved electronic records life; slower records entry/reading equipment obsolescence
- 3.4 Improved computer-aided program, file and records indexing, organization and management support
- 3.5 Fewer uncertainties about legal status of electronic records
- 3.6 More effective copyright protection (or equivalent) for some materials
- 3.7 Equipment costs low enough to not limit mass markets

4. PRECEDENTS EXIST BUT STAKEHOLDER CONTENTION LIKELY during:
- 4.1 Development of accepted use practices ("fair use" copying; library and user "sharing")
- 4.2 Establishment of hardware and software standards; access and compatibility across equipment systems, databases
- 4.3 Evolution of accepted "interim" market pattern for use of alternative types of memory materials
- 4.4 Directories production for electronic mail and public databases

costs. Because of the cumulative nature of computer operations, over time

- Users have found themselves with (often massive) investments in old programs that are still actively being employed. At some point this situation leads to a need for (often large) new investments in rewriting the old programs, and/or use of slow and inefficient processing techniques (such as using an emulation mode), and/or the maintenance of otherwise unneeded equipment. The process also has led to deskilling or special training requirements (such as when a language stops being used).[26]
- Users similarly have developed or acquired large amounts of data

[26] In the extreme, some organizations have faced a "backwards" training requirement—teaching new staff an old technology—just to survive. This obviously creates a poor environment for attracting and keeping good staff.

> that may have long-term value. If these data were not to be effectively lost as they aged, they have required conversion to non-electronic form, or repeated "rewriting" and/or conversion to new electronic storage media and memory processing equipment.

Other problems also derive from the cumulative nature of computer activity. Manufacturers face restrictions in their technical choices in new equipment design if they are to provide the "forward" compatibility that the market increasingly demands. At least some additional equipment and software complexity is needed to protect customer past investments. And, especially since many important technical standards are still lacking (and in some cases are being established de facto in the marketplace), users and using organizations face difficult re-equipping decisions that inevitably inhibit growth in user activities.

While these types of problems have been recognized intellectually for quite a while, it has taken time for the mass of applications and records to grow, the variety of types and interests of users to increase, and the extent of technical change to become sufficiently large that the impacts are either causing pain or inhibiting the rate of expansion of usage. Meanwhile, the "new challenges" facing electronics involve many potential uses (such as building personal files from electronically presented reading materials) that are sensitive to assurances of long-term future access to such records. The possible inhibiting effects of inadequacies in this regard (which we have identified as lack of Confidence in the Format) are obvious.

Software role. It is not unusual for a rapidly advancing area of technology to be characterized by fast obsolescence of products; radio and automobiles during their key growth periods furnish good examples. What is different about computers is not only the faster pace of change but also the unusual role played by software. In addition to the cumulative effects discussed earlier, software has acted almost as an equivalent of physical infrastructure.

Consider the difficulty of trading in an old computer as part of the process of buying a new one. In contrast, during the peak period of change in automobile technology, it was standard for original owners of automobiles to trade them in after one or two years of use. These owners accordingly kept having the most technically up-to-date cars, and a series of later owners were able to obtain fairly new cars at prices they could afford. Even though many original owners of computers might like to have such strong trade-in and second-hand markets available, they have never arisen. Staying up-to-date has required either frequent purchases of new computers (normally without trade-ins to the vendor) or gradual owner upgrading of equipment.

In the case of the automobile, the second-hand cars could be driven (although perhaps more slowly and less comfortably) on any existing roads and bridges. With second-hand computers, in contrast, there are whole areas of applications, and often the more desirable ones, for which the older equipment simply is inadequate. The equivalent automobile situation would have been one where all second-hand cars were banned from being driven on most first-class highways!

6.6.2.2 Organization of information/knowledge.* A second family of weaknesses is related to the problems of organizing, indexing, and managing personal and business files in a period of rapidly growing availability of more and more information. To the extent that a well-touted information overload is real, it can be greatly magnified as electronic databases expand. In the logical extreme, the expansion can make most of the Library of Congress accessible to any modem-equipped user. From the mass of such materials, users in theory will be able to extract data, text, analytical, and software techniques, and visual and other information to build their own professional and business files. In fact, if information is as valuable as claimed, there should be enormous benefits to skillful use of the wide range of information resources that can be made easily available sometime in the future.

Skill and filing requirements. Given the prevailing level of skills in finding information within library-type collections, and in the reverse process of structuring, filing, and indexing selected materials, the future situation probably should be viewed as much with horror as with anticipation. Most in-depth searches of significance currently require the services of a capable librarian; further, the development of an information structure for a filing system that will be useful for more than a few years requires at least as much skill and even more effort. The future seems likely to bring us far more theoretical capabilities than we will be able to manage in any practical way.

In viewing this problem area, it is important to remember that we are suffering from indigestion, not starvation. Electronics can make easily available to individuals far more potentially useful information than print ever could; it is this capability that increases the difficulties of search/selection and drives us beyond the capabilities of traditional information/file management systems. It also is important to recognize that the computer, itself, can go a long way to ease the problems through software and system processes that are just beginning to receive attention. Even though we have no complete philosoph-

* See Figure 6-26, items 1.1 and 3.4.

ical basis for organizing and indexing information/knowledge, much improvement is possible.

Historical precedent. Finally, it is worth noting that the difficulties we face in organizing electronics materials so as to use them better has its historical precedents. Each technology that has impacted strongly on the quantity and form of the information used by society has had to create new management techniques. When the oral tradition in England gave way to written records, it took about one hundred years before records began to be stored in a consistent fashion—and about another one hundred years before effective efforts to record, inventory, and index these records were started![27] Similarly, the development of modern library cataloging systems started well after, and largely in response to, the development of book collections that had grown to the point at which loss of control had become a major concern of those responsible for the collections.

6.6.2.3 Training and skills retention.* Users of electronic systems who want to be relatively up to date face a third intractable barrier: the need for continual training. For some limited purposes, such as simple recreational reading, systems can be designed so that little or no training is needed. For a higher level of use, however, considerable training over time probably must be treated as the "price of admission" to the current electronic age—much as reading, writing, and basic arithmetic were the price for a chance to become an effective participant in the latter part of the "heat engine" age. This should not be confused with any simplistic concepts of "computer literacy"; analysts are at best only beginning to discern the nature of the training that will be important in the future.

A range of considerations is likely to impact future training needs:

- For most uses, keyboard skills will be needed. Macintosh-type approaches and a variety of special input devices can ease but not eliminate this requirement. In theory, speech recognition could do so sometime in the future. However, learning how to use speech control effectively may take more training than learning how to type; the former may eventually become a skill associated with a "higher" level of future literacy (much as skillful dictation was a part of the higher literacy of the Middle Ages).
- The magnitude of the training needed will vary with many factors: equipment and software obsolescence rates (including the effects of

[27] Clanchy, *supra,* note 5.

* See Figure 6-26, items 1.4 and 3.1.

basic changes in computer architecture over time), the extent to which some impacts of obsolescence may be slowed by the adoption of standards, and the degree of attention that vendors pay to developing effective self-training programs for their products are just a few examples.

- While training requirements could be simplified and standardized if the pace of change in electronics were slowed, this seems highly unlikely. In fact, with the intense interest being shown in ever-more-complex computer architectures (such as parallel processors and neural networks), and given the historical speed with which hardware advances have moved into the general marketplace, the opposite seems more apt to be the case.
- There are strong market incentives to broaden the range of computer usage, expanding at the top to application areas not practical with current architectures and, at the bottom, to users having at most limited skills. This raises several key questions:
  1. *How will the market be stratified?* In particular, will (or can) relatively stable practices and procedures be adopted for the lower end of the hardware/software spectrum, as a means to simplify training and skill requirements and thereby ease expansion into mass markets?
  2. *Will there be broadly applicable "learning" skills that can help meet the continuing needs for new training by moderately advanced but nonspecialized users?* For example, will training that makes it easier to understand, as they arise, the implications and uses of future architecture options, and/or training in information/ knowledge structuring, become both practical and valuable?

And finally,

3. *Will the dream of vastly improved training through computer interactive techniques be realized?* Given the likely costs for developing high-quality interactive training modules, will individuals be able to afford them, or only institutions?

6.6.2.4 Social-legal issues.* The items in this group all concern social management of intellectual property rights. The key problem is the balancing of creator/vendor and acquirer/user rights in a way that is socially constructive. To a considerable extent, this balancing implies that the patterns and traditions that have evolved for use of print property would not change abruptly when electronics is serving as an alternative to print. However, for many purposes the two formats

* See Figure 6-26, items 3.5, 3.6, and 4.1.

are not realistic alternatives. From the user's point of view, there is no good print analog to a widely used computer program in terms of its function, its role as an infrastructure/communications element, and the extent to which users can become dependent on having rights to use it. From the producer's side, there is no good print parallel to the program's vulnerability to easy and economical illegal copying.

Establishing an appropriate set of laws and practices for electronic publications will take time. "Errors" made in the process (such as either overly restricting user rights or inadequately protecting producers) can slow the penetration of electronics and act to increase illegal activities. Again, the nature of the problem is not new; intellectual property as a concept hardly existed before printing was invented, and copyright has had a long history of changes. For electronic products and services that closely parallel current print versions, existing laws and practices may be transferable; for the many quite different types of products, they at best offer only a starting point.

6.6.2.5 Other items.

Flat-panel display. We already have emphasized item 2.1, the requirement for a flat panel of adequate size and quality, as a critical enabling advance.

Electronic advertising. Item 3.2 is concerned with the development of an electronic form of advertising that can provide benefits equivalent to those that print obtains; this may be a key factor for electronic success in competing in a number of mass media markets.

In many respects, the flat-panel display marks the real starting point of a potential electronic movement toward a position of general dominance in the presentation of information, while electronic advertising deals with a major barrier that electronics encounters thereafter.

6.6.3 Summary

For two decades, visionaries have prophesied the inevitability of electronics becoming the only significant medium for the presentation of information. During the same period, commentators have pointed out a growing danger of our "drowning" in paper while on our way to this electronic future. Our own review suggests a middle path:

- There is no single breakthrough that can swiftly alter the competitive positions of print and electronics—although a breakthrough of sorts in the flat-panel area is needed to enable a longer term transition.

- The spread of electronics is constrained by a large number of "messy" details and minibarriers, rather than by a few well-defined problems; many of its enemies are inertial in nature.
- Rapid progress is hindered by the stakeholder incentives involved in the situation. These potentially are very strong but, in the near term, they also are quite diffuse, often in conflict, and all too likely to make difficult the types of integration and partial standardization that eventually will be needed.
- There appear to be many possible intermediate products and services that should be economically self-sustaining. However, success in such ventures is likely to depend on absorption and understanding of much detail during product and/or service selection, definition, and engineering.

As with other forms of technological progress, there will be problems, issues, and losses associated with the benefits that future electronic presentations can bring. At present, we probably understand the potential benefits better than we do the possible problems and issues. Even now, however, it seems clear that both the conditions necessary for electronics to achieve dominance and the results of this dominance are likely to have very widespread political, social, and economic consequences. Based on the history of past transitions of similar magnitude in the technologies of information, we must anticipate that at least some of the associated problems and issues will be big and difficult ones.

BIBLIOGRAPHY

Abramson, Jeffrey B., F. Christopher Arterton, and Gary R. Orren. 1988. *The Electronic Commonwealth: The Impact of New Media Technologies on Democratic Politics*. New York: Basic Books.

A'Hearn, Francis W. 1984. *The Information Arsenal: A C³I Profile*. Cambridge, MA: Program on Information Resources Policy, Harvard University, P-84-2.

———. 1983. *Northeast Power Failure and Lyndon B. Johnson: An Interview with Donald F. Hornig, June 30, 1983*. Cambridge, MA: Program on Information Resources Policy, Harvard University, I-83-3.

Alchian, A.E., and W. Allen. 1977. *Exchange and Production: Competition, Coordination & Control*, 2d ed. Belmont, CA: Wadsworth Publishing Company.

Altick, Richard D. 1957. *The English Common Reader: A Social History of the Mass Reading Public, 1800–1900*. Chicago: Chicago University Press.

Antonoff, M. 1987. "Can We End Software Piracy?" *Personal Computing* (May 1987).

Arrow, Kenneth J. 1974. *The Limits of Organization*. New York: W.W. Norton.

Baker, Thomas E. 1983. *Computers and Political Campaigns: A Look at Technology and Social Change*. Cambridge, MA: Program on Information Resources Policy, Harvard University, P-83-4.

Barnouw, Erik. 1975. *Tube of Plenty*. New York: Oxford University Press.

Barthelme, Donald. 1967. *Snow White*. New York: Atheneum.

Benda, Charles G. 1978. *State Organization and Policy Formation: The Reorganization of the Post Office Department*. Cambridge, MA: Program on Information Resources Policy, Harvard University, I-78-11.

Beniger, James R. 1986. *The Control Revolution: Technological and Economic Origins of the Information Society*. Cambridge, MA: Harvard University Press.

Betts, Mitch. 1988. "High-tech Pirates Said to Reap Billions." *Computerworld* (March 14, 1988).

Blair, Homer. 1987. Statement given at conference on Counterfeiting of Trademarks, Copyrights, and Patents: What Lawyers Should Know, March 20, 1987, at Franklin Pierce Law Center, Concord, NH.

Boorstin, Daniel J. 1973. *The Democratic Experience*. Vol. 2 of *The Americans*. New York: Random House.

Borchardt, Kurt. 1976. *Towards a Theory of Legislative Compromise*. Cambridge, MA: Program on Information Resources Policy, Harvard University, P-76-4.

———. 1970. *Structure and Performance of the U.S. Communications Industry: Government Regulation and Company Planning*. Boston: Harvard Business School, Division of Research.

Branscomb, Anne W. 1988. *Nurturing Creativity in a Competitive Global Economy: Intellectual Property and New Technologies*. Cambridge, MA: Program on Information Resources Policy, Harvard University, P-88-4.

Brillouin, Leon. 1956. *Science and Information Theory.* New York: Academic Press.

Brozen, Y. 1974. "Entry Barriers: Advertising and Production Differentiations." In *Industrial Concentration: The New Learning*, eds. H.J. Goldschmid, H.M. Mann, and J.F. Weston. Boston: Little, Brown.

Chamberlin, E. 1956. *The Theory of Monopolistic Competition.* Cambridge, MA: Harvard University Press.

Clanchy, M.T. 1979. *From Memory to Written Record: England 1066–1307.* Cambridge, MA: Harvard University Press.

Cline, Ray. 1976. *Secrets, Spies and Scholars.* Washington, DC: Acropolis Books.

Commission of the European Community. 1988. "Green Paper on Copyright and the Challenge of Technology: Copyright Issues Requiring Immediate Action," Com (88) 172 final, June 7, 1988.

Compaine, Benjamin M. 1988. *Issues in New Information Technology.* Norwood, NJ: Ablex Publishing Corp.

____. 1986. *Size and Growth Trends of the Information Industry, 1970–1983.* Cambridge, MA: Program on Information Resources Policy, Harvard University, I-86-2.

____. 1985. *New Competition and New Media.* Cambridge, MA: Program on Information Resources Policy, Harvard University, I-85-1.

____. 1984a. *Information Technology and Cultural Change: Toward a New Literacy?* Cambridge, MA: Program on Information Resources Policy, Harvard University, P-84-5.

____. 1984b. *Understanding New Media.* Cambridge, MA: Ballinger Publishing Company.

____. 1980. *A New Framework for the Media Arena: Content, Process and Format.* Cambridge, MA: Program on Information Resources Policy, Harvard University.

Compaine, Benjamin M., and Robert F. Litro. 1984. *Instructor's Manual for Business: An Introduction.* Chicago: The Dryden Press.

____. 1980. *The Newspaper Industry in the 1980s.* White Plains, NY: Knowledge Industry Publications.

Compaine, Benjamin M., and John F. McLaughlin. 1986. *Management Information: Back to Basics.* Cambridge, MA: Program on Information Resources Policy, Harvard University, P-86-6.

Crawford, Morris H. 1988. *EC'92: The Making of a Common Market in Telecommunications.* Cambridge, MA: Program on Information Resources Policy, Harvard University, I-88-2.

____. 1986. *Programming the Invisible Hand: The Computerization of Korea and Taiwan.* Cambridge, MA: Program on Information Resources Policy, Harvard University, P-86-7.

Cushman, John H. 1986. *Command and Control of Theater Forces: The Korea Command and Other Cases.* Cambridge, MA: Program on Information Resources Policy, Harvard University, P-86-2.

____. 1985. *Command and Control of Theater Forces: Adequacy.* Washington, DC: AFCEA International Press.

Dewey, Godfrey. 1923. *Relative Frequency of English Speech Sounds.* Cambridge, MA: Harvard University Press.

Digital. 1989/90. *Information Industry Factbook,* 1989/90 edition. Stamford, CT: Digital Information Group.

Dow Jones. 1983. *1983 Annual Report.*

Ernst, Martin L. 1989. *Electronic–Print Competition: Determinants of the Potential for Major Change.* Cambridge, MA: Program on Information Resources Policy, Harvard University, P-89-4.

Federal Technology Transfer Act of 1986, Public Law No. 99-502.

Finkelstein, Sidney. 1968. *Sense and Nonsense of McLuhan.* New York: International Publications.

Fleishman, Joel L. 1982. *Postal Policy and Public Accountability: Is the 1970 Bargain Coming Unglued?* Cambridge, MA: Program on Information Resources Policy, Harvard University, P-82-12.

Fortune. 1988. "Not-So-Hot Sounds." *Fortune* (February 15, 1988).

Fourier, Joseph. 1878. *Analytical Theory of Heat.* Cambridge, UK: The University Press.

Ganley, Gladys D., and Oswald H. Ganley. 1987. *Global Political Fallout: The VCR's First Decade.* Norwood, NJ: Ablex Publishing Corp.

____. 1984. *Unexpected War in the Information Age: Communications and Information in the Falklands Conflict.* Cambridge, MA: Program on Information Resources Policy, Harvard University, P-84-3.

Ganley, Oswald H. 1988. *International Communications and Information in the 1990s: Forces and Trends.* Cambridge, MA: Program on Information Resources Policy, Harvard University, I-88-3.

____. 1982. *U.S. Trade in Communications and Information vs. General Trade: Is There Really a Difference?* Cambridge, MA: Program on Information Resources Policy, Harvard University, P-82-11.

Ganley, Oswald H., and Gladys D. Ganley. 1989. *To Inform or To Control? The New Communications Networks.* 2d ed. Norwood, NJ: Ablex Publishing Corp.

Gervaise, Davis G. 1986. "Fair use of Software and Databases with an Emphasis on Education." Paper prepared for the Computer Law Association conference on "Update on Computer Software," November 3–4, 1986, Washington, DC.

Godbey, Robert C. 1981. *A Distance-Insensitive Uniform National Telephone Rate Structure: A Speculative Exercise in Federalism.* Cambridge, MA: Program on Information Resources Policy, Harvard University, P-81-4.

____. 1979. *Revenue and Cost Allocations: Policy Means and Ends in the Railroad and Telecommunications Industries.* Cambridge, MA: Program on Information Resources Policy, Harvard University, P-79-2.

Graham, Daniel O. 1983. "Quality in U.S. Intelligence." In *Intelligence Requirements for the 1980's: Elements of Intelligence,* ed. Roy Godson. Washington, DC: National Strategic Information Center.

Grant, James C. 1987. "Hello, Is Anyone Listening? Vital Issues for Telecommunications Users." Paper presented at Telecom '87, ITU, October 21–23, 1987, Geneva.

Green, Anthony T. 1986. *U.S.–Japan Technology Transfer: Accommodating Different Interests*. Cambridge, MA: Program on Information Resources Policy, Harvard University, P-86-1.

Gumpert, Gary. 1987. *Talking Tombstones and Other Tales of the Media Age*. New York: Oxford University Press.

Hamming, Richard. 1950. "Error Detecting and Error Correcting Codes." *The Bell System Technical Journal* 26, no. 2 (April 1950).

Hapgood, John. 1984. "The Connection." *Science* 5, no. 8 (October 1984).

Hooper, Richard. 1984. *Prestel, Escher, Bach: Changes Within Changes*. Cambridge, MA: Program on Information Resources Policy, Harvard University, I-84-1.

Huffman, David. 1952. "Method for Construction of Minimum Redundancy Codes." *Institute of Radio Engineers—Proceedings* 40, no. 9 (September 1952).

IEEE Spectrum. 1990. "Innovations." *IEEE Spectrum* (July 1990).

Jakobson, Roman, and Morris Halle. 1971. *Fundamentals of Language*. The Hague: Mouton and Company.

Jelen, George F. 1985. *Information Security: An Elusive Goal*. Cambridge, MA: Program on Information Resources Policy, Harvard University, P-85-8.

Kiang, Lindsey. 1987. Presentation at conference on "Counterfeiting of Trademarks, Copyrights, and Patents: What Lawyers Should Know," March 20, 1987, at Franklin Pierce Law Center, Concord, NH.

Kidder, Tracy. 1981. *The Soul of a New Machine*. Boston: Little, Brown and Company.

Kira, Masao. 1987. *Where to Put the Smarts: Network or CPE?* Cambridge, MA: Program on Information Resources Policy, Harvard University, P-87-5.

Koff, James B. 1987. Presentation at conference on "Counterfeiting of Trademarks, Copyrights, and Patents: What Lawyers Should Know," March 20, 1987, at Franklin Pierce Law Center, Concord, NH.

Krasnow, Erwin G., and Jill Abeshouse Stern. 1985. *The New Video Marketplace: A Regulatory Identity Crisis*. Cambridge, MA: Program on Information Resources Policy, Harvard University, P-85-9.

Kreps, Robert P. 1988. *Buying Hens Not Eggs: The Acquisition of Information Technology by the People's Republic of China*. Cambridge, MA: Program on Information Resources Policy, Harvard University, P-88-3.

Kuhn, Thomas. 1970. "The Structure of Scientific Revolutions." In *International Encyclopedia of Unified Science*. Chicago: The University of Chicago Press.

Landes, David S. 1983. *Revolution in Time: Clocks and the Making of the Modern World*. Cambridge, MA: Harvard University Press.

Lebow, Irwin. 1991. *The Digital Connection*. New York: Computer Science Press.

LeGates, John C., and John F. McLaughlin. 1989. *Forces, Trends, and Glitches in the World of Compunications*. Cambridge, MA: Program on Information Resources Policy, Harvard University, P-89-2.

Levitt, Theodore. 1975. "Marketing Myopia." In *Harvard Business Review* (September-October 1975). Reprint.

McCarthy, J. Thomas. 1984. *Trademarks and Unfair Competition.* 2d ed. San Francisco: Bancroft-Whitney.

McEliece, Robert J. 1977. *The Theory of Information and Coding.* Reading, MA: Addison-Wesley.

McLaughlin, John F. 1989. "Marketing Megalomania: The Lure of the Information Business." *PIRP Perspectives.* Cambridge, MA: Program on Information Resources Policy, Harvard University.

McLaughlin, John F., with Anne Louise Antonoff. 1986. *Mapping the Information Business.* Cambridge, MA: Program on Information Resources Policy, Harvard University, P-86-9.

McLuhan, Marshall. 1964. *Understanding Media.* New York: McGraw-Hill Book Company.

Michelet. 1869. *L'Histoire de France.* Paris. Livre IV, Chapitre Premier. Reprint. *Le Moyen Age.* Paris, 1981. Editions Robert Laffont.

National Technology Innovation Act of 1979, Public Law No. 96-480 (October 21, 1980).

Nora, Simon, and Alain Minc. 1980. *The Computerization of Society.* A report to the President of France. Cambridge, MA: The MIT Press.

Odum, Howard T. 1988. "Self-Organization, Transformity, and Information." *Science* 242, no. 4882 (November 25, 1988).

Oettinger, Anthony G. 1990. *Whence and Whither Intelligence, Command and Control: The Certainty of Uncertainty.* Cambridge, MA: Program on Information Resources Policy, Harvard University, P-90-1.

——. 1989. *The Information Evolution: Building Blocks and Bursting Bundles.* Cambridge, MA: Program on Information Resources Policy, Harvard University, P-89-5.

——. 1988a. *The Formula is Everything: Costing and Pricing in the Telecommunications Industry.* Cambridge, MA: Program on Information Resources Policy, Harvard University, P-88-2.

——. 1988b. "Political, Scientific and Other Truths in the Information World." The Samuel Lazerow Memorial Lecture, November 10, 1988. Pittsburg: University of Pittsburgh School of Library and Information Science.

——. 1985. *The Abundant and Versatile Digital Way.* Cambridge, MA: Program on Information Resources Policy, Harvard University.

——. 1980. *Information Resources: Knowledge and Power in the 21st Century.* Cambridge, MA: Program on Information Resources Policy, Harvard University, I-80-4.

——. 1975. *Elements of Information Resources Policy: Library and Other Information Services.* Cambridge, MA: Program on Information Resources Policy.

——. 1971. "Compunications in the National Decision-Making Process." In *Computers, Communications, and the Public Interest.* Baltimore: The Johns Hopkins University Press.

——. 1964. "A Bull's Eye View of Management and Engineering Information Systems." *Proceedings of the 19th National ACM Conference.* ACM Publication P 64. New York, 1964. Reprinted in *Information Technology in a Democracy,* by Alan F. Westin. Cambridge, MA: Harvard University Press, 1971.

Ongstad, Per. 1981. *Information Resources Viewed by an Outskirter*. Cambridge, MA: Program on Information Resources Policy, Harvard University, I-81-5.

Paepke, C. Owen. 1987. "An Economic Interpretation of the Misappropriation Doctrine: Common Law Protection for Investments in Innovation." *High Technology Law Journal*. 2, no. 1 (Spring 1987).

Pepper, Robert. 1983. *Competition in Local Distribution: The Cable Television Industry*. Cambridge, MA: Program on Information Resources Policy, Harvard University, P-83-5.

Perry, William G. 1963. "Examsmanship in the Liberal Arts: A Study in Educational Epistemology," Harvard College, 1963. Reprinted in *Persuasive Writing: A College Reader*, Karl Zeender, and Linda Morris, eds. New York: Harcourt Brace Jovanovich, 1981.

Peterson, Wesley, and Edward Weldon. 1972. *Error-Correcting Codes*. Cambridge, MA: The MIT Press.

Petroski, Henry. 1990. *The Pencil: A History of Design and Circumstance*. New York: Alfred A. Knopf.

Phister, Jr., Montgomery. 1979. *Data Processing Technology and Economics*. Bedford, MA: Digital Press.

Pierce, John R., and A. Michael Noll. 1990. *Signals: The Science of Telecommunications*. New York: Scientific American Library Books.

Pool, Ithiel de Sola. 1983a. *Forecasting the Telephone: A Retrospective Technology Assessment*. Norwood, NJ: Ablex Publishing Corp.

____. 1983b. *Technologies of Freedom*. Cambridge, MA: The Belknap Press of Harvard University Press.

Program on Information Resources Policy. 1990. *Seminar on Command, Control, Communications and Intelligence: Guest Presentations, Spring 1989*. Cambridge, MA: Program on Information Resources Policy, Harvard University, I-90-3.

____. 1980a. *Seminar on Command, Control, Communications and Intelligence: Guest Presentations, Spring 1980*. Cambridge, MA: Program on Information Resources Policy, Harvard University, I-80-6.

____. 1980b. *Seminar on Command, Control, Communications and Intelligence: Student Papers, Spring 1980*. Cambridge, MA: Program on Information Resources Policy, Harvard University, I-81-1.

____. 1981. *Seminar on Command, Control, Communications and Intelligence: Guest Presentations, Spring 1981*. Cambridge, MA: Program on Information Resources Policy, Harvard University, I-81-9.

____. 1982. *Seminar on Command, Control, Communications and Intelligence: Guest Presentations, Spring 1982*. Cambridge, MA: Program on Information Resources Policy, Harvard University, I-82-3.

____. 1985. *Seminar on Command, Control, Communications and Intelligence: Guest Presentations, Spring 1984*. Cambridge, MA: Program on Information Resources Policy, Harvard University, I-85-2.

____. 1986. *Seminar on Command, Control, Communications and Intelligence: Guest Presentations, Spring 1985*. Cambridge, MA: Program on Information Resources Policy, Harvard University, I-86-I.

———. 1987. *Seminar on Command, Control, Communications and Intelligence: Guest Presentations, Spring 1986*. Cambridge, MA: Program on Information Resources Policy, Harvard University, I-87-1.

———. 1988. *Seminar on Command, Control, Communications and Intelligence: Guest Presentations, Spring 1987*. Cambridge, MA: Program on Information Resources Policy, Harvard University, I-88-1.

———. 1989. *Seminar on Command, Control, Communications and Intelligence: Guest Presentations, Spring 1988*. Cambridge, MA: Program on Information Resources Policy, Harvard University, I-89-1.

Quine, Willard Van Orman. 1953. *From a Logical Point of View: Nine Logico-Philosophical Essays*. Cambridge, MA: Harvard University Press.

Research News Science. 1984. "Natural Language Understanding." *Research News Science* 224, no. 4647 (April 1984).

Robinson, J. 1938. *Economics of Imperfect Competition*. London: Macmillan.

Rosenberg, Robert. 1980. "The Influence of Policy Making on C^3I." In *Seminar on Command, Control, Communications and Intelligence, Spring 1980*. Cambridge, MA: Program on Information Resources Policy, Harvard University.

Rosenbloom, Richard S. 1981. *The Continuing Revolution in Communications Technology: Implications for the Broadcasting Business*. Cambridge, MA: Program on Information Resources Policy, Harvard University, I-81-4.

Rozynski, Edward. 1987. Statement given at Counterfeiting of Trademarks, Copyrights, and Patents: What Lawyers Should Know, March 20, 1987, at Franklin Pierce Law Center, Concord, NH.

Rubin, Jerome S., and Janet Wikler. 1989. *Publishing as a Creature of Technology*. Cambridge, MA: Program on Information Resources Policy, Harvard University, I-89-2.

Shannon, Claude E., and Warren Weaver. 1949. *The Mathematical Theory of Communication*. Urbana, IL: The University of Illinois Press.

Sichter, James W. 1987. *Profits, Politics, and Capital Formation: The Economics of the Traditional Telephone Industry*. Cambridge, MA: Program on Information Resources Policy, Harvard University, P-87-7.

———. 1977. *Separations Procedures in the Telephone Industry: The Historical Origins of a Public Policy*. Cambridge, MA: Program on Information Resources Policy, Harvard University, P-77-2.

Simon, Herbert A. 1971. "Designing Organizations for an Information-Rich World." In *Computers, Communications, and the Public Interest*, ed. Martin Greenberger. Baltimore, MD: Johns Hopkins Press.

Smith, Anthony. 1980. *Goodbye Gutenberg*. New York: Oxford University Press.

Snyder, Frank M. 1989. *Command and Control: Readings and Commentary*. Cambridge, MA: Program on Information Resources Policy, Harvard University, P-89-1.

Steiner, George. 1988. "Literature Today." In *Books in the 1990s*. London: International Publishers Association and Butterworth and Company.

Theall, Donald. 1971. *The Medium Is the Rear View Mirror.* Montreal: McGill-Queens University Press.

Szuprowicz, Bohdan O. 1984. "Battle Lines Being Drawn for Global Technology Markets." *High Technology* (October 1984).

Toffler, Alvin. 1970. *Future Shock.* New York: Random House.

Trademark Counterfeiting Act of 1984, Title 18 U.S.C Chapter 113 1502(a) as amended by 2320.

Tymshare Inc. 1981. *1981 Annual Report.*

UCLA Law Review. 1986. "Comment: Toward the Right of Commerciality: Recognizing Property Rights in the Commercial Value of Human Tissue," 34 UCLA L. Rev. 207 (October 1986).

Urban, Christine. 1984. "Factors Influencing Media Consumption." In *Understanding New Media,* ed. Benjamin M. Compaine. Cambridge, MA: Ballinger Publishing Company.

U.S. Bureau of National Affairs. 1988. "Senate Subcommittee Hears Views on Berne Adherence Legislation." *Daily Report for Executives* (March 4, 1988).

U.S. Congress. House. Committee on Government Operations. 1980. *Electronic Collection and Dissemination of Information by Federal Agencies: A Policy Overview.* H.R. No. 560, 99th Cong., 2d Sess. Washington, DC: Government Printing Office.

U.S. Congress. House. 1989. Consumer Telecommunications Services Act of 1989. H.R. 2140, 101st Cong., 1st Sess. Washington, DC: Government Printing Office.

U.S. Congress. Office of Technology Assessment. 1988a. *Informing the Nation: Federal Information Dissemination in an Electronic Age.* OTA-CIT-396. Washington, DC: Government Printing Office (October 1988). GPO#: 052-003-01130-1.

———. 1982. *Medlars and Health Information Policy: A Technical Memorandum.* OTA-TM-H-11. Washington, DC: GPO (September 1982).

———. 1985. *Federal Government Information Technology: Electronic Surveillance and Civil Liberties.* OTA-CIT-293. Washington, DC: GPO (October 1985). GPO#: 052-003-01015-1.

———. 1986a. *Federal Government Information Technology: Management, Security and Congressional Oversight.* OTA-CIT-297. Washington, DC: GPO.

———. 1986b. *Intellectual Property in an Age of Electronics and Information.* Washington, DC: GPO (April 1986).

———. 1987a. *Defending Secrets, Sharing Data: New Locks and Keys for Electronic Information.* OTA-CIT-310. Washington, DC: GPO (October 1987). GPO#: 052-003-01083-6.

———. 1987b. *The Electronic Supervisor: New Technology, New Tensions.* OTA-CIT-333. Washington, DC: GPO (September 1987).

———. 1988b. *Power On!: New Tools for Teaching and Learning.* OTA-SET-379. Washington, DC: GPO (September 1988). GPO#: 052-003-01125-5.

U.S. Congress. Senate. Committee on Banking, Housing and Urban Affairs. 1975. *Electronic Funds Transfer Moratorium Act of 1975: Hearings Before the Subcommittee on Financial Institutions*. 94th Cong., 1st Sess. Washington, DC: Government Printing Office.

von Auw, Alvin. 1983. *Heritage and Destiny: Reflections on the Bell System in Transition*. New York: Praeger Publications.

von Clausewitz, Carl. 1950. *On War*. Washington: Infantry Journal Press.

Ware, Donald R. 1985. "Trade Secret Protection of Computer Software: The Common Law Encounters High Technology." *Boston Bar Journal* (November–December 1985).

Weinhaus, Carol L., and Anthony G. Oettinger. 1988. *Behind the Telephone Debates*. Norwood, NJ: Ablex Publishing Corp.

White, Thomas, and Gladys D. Ganley. 1983. *The "Death of a Princess" Controversy*. Cambridge, MA: Program on Information Resources Policy, Harvard University, P-83-9.

Wohlstetter, Roberta. 1962. *Pearl Harbor: Warning and Decision*. Stanford, CA: Stanford University Press.

CONTRIBUTORS

Anne W. Branscomb is a research affiliate of the Program on Information Resources Policy. She is a communications lawyer with practical experience representing broadcasters, cable television companies, database providers, semiconductor chip manufacturers, publishers of newsletters, newspapers, and books. Currently, she is a trustee of the Rensselaer Polytechnic Institute and the Pacific Telecommunications Council, and a contributing editor of the *Information Society* and the *Journal of Communication*. She is an honor graduate of the George Washington University Law School, holds degrees in political science from Harvard University and the University of North Carolina, and studied international relations at the London School of Economics as a Rotary Foundation Fellow. In 1985 she became one of three Inaugural Fellows of the Gannet Center for Study of the Media at Columbia University.

Martin L. Ernst is a research affiliate of the Program on Information Resources Policy. He guides the Program's research in electronic publishing and in establishing the impacts of computer-related advances on the skills that future business and workforce members will require. He joined the Program after 27 years at Arthur D. Little, Inc., where his last position was vice-president of Advanced Information Technologies. Prior to that position, he had responsibility for the company's management sciences activities, which included operations research, information systems, information technologies, and social systems. Before joining Arthur D. Little, he worked in the operations research groups of the U.S. Air Force and the U.S. Navy. He is a past president of the Operations Research Society of America.

Anthony G. Oettinger is chairman of the Program on Information Resources Policy and chairman of the Center for Information Policy Research. He is Gordon McKay Professor of Applied Mathematics, Professor of Information Resources Policy, and a member of the Faculty of Government at Harvard University. He is a member of the Board of Visitors of the Defense Intelligence College. He was chairman of the CATV Commission of the Commonwealth of Massachusetts (1975–79) and a member of that commission from its creation in 1972. He has served as a consultant to the President's Foreign Intelligence Advisory Board (1981–90), the National Security Council (1975–81), and to the Office of Science and Technology (1961–73). He has also been a member of the Scientific Advisory Group of the Defense Communications Agency (1978–82), a member of the Command, Control, Communications and Intelligence Panel of the Naval Research Advisory Committee (1978–82), a member of the Research Advisory Board of The Committee for Economic Development (1975–79), and a consultant to Arthur D. Little, Inc. (1956–80). He is a member of the Council on Foreign Relations and a Fellow of the American Academy of Arts and Sciences, the American Association for the Advancement of Science, and the Institute of Electrical and Electronic Engineers. He was president of the Association for Computing Machinery (1966–68) and chairman of the Computer Science and Engineering Board of the National Academy of Sciences (1967–73).

Jerome S. Rubin is chairman of the Professional Information and Book Publishing Group of Times Mirror, Inc., having served as vice-president of this group since joining the company in January 1983. Before joining Times Mirror, he was president and CEO of Mead Data Central, where he pioneered the LEXIS and NEXIS online information retrieval systems. Prior to this position, he practiced international business law in New York City. He is chairman of the Association of American Publishers and is a member of the International Committee of the International Publishers Association. A 1944 honors graduate of Harvard College with a Bachelor of Science degree in physics, he received a Bachelor of Laws degree from the Harvard Law School in 1949.

Janet Wikler is senior vice president and director of Strategic Planning for Simon & Schuster. She previously served as vice president of Business Development and as director of Media Development for U.K.-based Pearson, Inc. She has worked in the publishing business since 1968 and has been involved in applying new technologies to publishing since 1977, when she successfully launched three computer-based construction cost-estimating services at McGraw-Hill. In 1981, she joined Mead Data Central (MDC) as director of Communications. When MDC moved to Ohio, she joined CBS as director of Electronic Publishing Development. She played a similar role at Times Mirror, Inc., which she joined in 1983. She holds a B.A. in English and an M.S. in education from the University of Pennsylvania and an M.B.A. from the Wharton School.

August 1992

APPENDIX A
PROGRAM ON INFORMATION RESOURCES POLICY

Harvard University **Center for Information Policy Research**

Affiliates

ABRH Consulting, Inc.
Advertising Mail Marketing Association
American Telephone & Telegraph Co.
Ameritech Corporation
Apple Computer, Inc.
Arthur D. Little, Inc.
Auerbach Publishers Inc.
Australian & Overseas Telecommunications Corp.
Bell Atlantic
Bell Canada
BellSouth Corporation
Bull, S.A. (France)
Centel Corporation
CMC Limited (India)
Commission of the European Communities
Communications Workers of America
Computer & Communications Industry Assoc.
Cox Enterprises, Inc.
Dialog Information Services, Inc.
DRI/McGraw Hill
European Parliament
France Telecom
Gartner Group, Inc.
GTE Corporation
Hitachi Research Institute (Japan)
IBM Corp.
IQ, Inc.
Information Gatekeepers, Inc.
Information Industry Association
International Data Corp.
International Monetary Fund
International Resource Development, Inc.
Invoco AB Gunnar Bergvall (Sweden)
I.T. Direction Ltd. (UK)
Japan Telecom Company
Kapor Family Foundation
Knowledge Industry Publications, Inc.
Korea Telecom
Lee Enterprises, Inc.
John and Mary R. Markle Foundation
Martin Marietta
McCaw Cellular Communications, Inc.
Mead Data Central
MITRE Corp.
National Telephone Cooperative Assoc.
The New York Times Co.
NEC Corp. (Japan)
Newspaper Association of America
Nippon Telegraph & Telephone Corp. (Japan)
Northeast Consulting Resources, Inc.
Northern Telecom
Nova Systems Inc.
NYNEX
Pacific Telesis Group
Philips Kommunikations (Netherlands)
Public Agenda Foundation
Puerto Rico Telephone Co.
Research Institute of Telecommunications and Economics (Japan)
RESEAU (Italy)
Revista Nacional de Telematica (Brazil)
Rhode Island Public Utilities Commission

Scaife Family Charitable Trusts
SEAT S.P.A. (Italy)
Siemens Corp.
Southam Inc. (Canada)
Southern New England Telecommunications Corp.
Southwestern Bell
Sprint Communications Company L.P.
State of California Public Utilities Commission
TEKNIBANK S.p.A. (Italy)
The College Board
Times Mirror Co.
Tribune Company
United States Government:
Department of Commerce
National Telecommunications and Information Administration
Department of Defense
National Defense University
Department of Health and Human Services
National Library of Medicine
Department of State
Office of Communications
Federal Communications Commission
General Services Administration
National Aeronautics and Space Administration
National Security Agency
U.S. General Accounting Office
United States Postal Rate Commission
U S West

August 1992

AUTHOR INDEX

Subject Index

D

Q

R

Printed by Libri Plureos GmbH in Hamburg,
Germany

9 780893 918767